The Art of Invective
Selected Non-Fiction
1953–94

The Art of Invective
Selected Non-Fiction
1953–94

Dennis Potter

edited by
Ian Greaves
David Rolinson
John Williams

First published in paperback in 2015 by Oberon Books Ltd
521 Caledonian Road, London N7 9RH
Tel: +44 (0) 20 7607 3637 / Fax: +44 (0) 20 7607 3629
e-mail: info@oberonbooks.com
www.oberonbooks.com

PB ISBN: 978-1-78319-203-8
E ISBN: 978-1-78319-702-6

eBook conversion by CPI Group.

Visit www.oberonbooks.com to read more about all our books and to buy them. You will also find features, author interviews and news of any author events, and you can sign up for e-newsletters so that you're always first to hear about our new releases.

CONTENTS

Part One

The Confidence Course

Part Two

Telling Stories

Part Three

Ticket to Ride

Dennis Potter and Me
A foreword by Peter Bowker

Like many a 1970s hysteric, I can lay claim to having been titillated by the work of Dennis Potter long before I had actually seen any of it. Our family didn't get BBC2 till the mid-Seventies so, for some time, my only acquaintance with his work was the BBC1 announcer intoning, 'And now over on BBC2, *Casanova*' for six weeks. In fairness, that was probably all the TV filth a 13-year-old in 1970s Stockport could handle without imploding.

But the real beginning – the real meeting with his work – was the moment in *Pennies from Heaven* when Bob Hoskins' Arthur first turned to camera and opened his mouth and Elsie Carlisle's voice came out. I can remember sitting there and thinking, 'Are they allowed to do that?' It was so audacious but yet it made perfect sense. It was experimental but it was impossible to imagine the story being told in a better way. And like all great ideas, you were left wondering why nobody had thought to do it before.

As the years went by and I took in *Blue Remembered Hills*, *The Singing Detective* and *Cream in My Coffee*, I used to fantasize that me and Dennis Potter could be mates. Reading this collection does make me think that he would have been a tough mate to have.

The cruel and witheringly precise humour that we see Philip Marlow exercise in *The Singing Detective* is very much present in both his views on television and his views on himself. Reading this collection it is clear that critically, he didn't appear to have a safety catch. He seemed not to recognize that simultaneously being a practising dramatist and a drama critic was problematic in any way, or, being Potter, relished the fact.

Just as his best drama simultaneously provided a critical and often musical analysis of the drama as it unfolded, so his non-fiction often reads as a dramatic monologue disguised as analysis. The musical rhythm of his dialogue and the savage put downs are all present and correct in his prose style.

Here he is reviewing a 1972 adaptation of *War and Peace* and taking on his familiar anti-realist position. Noting how much the director lingers on the soup plates, he goes on, 'Naturalism might well demand that life be turned into one damned dish after another, but the insights of a great novelist are rather more interesting than the eye-line of the head waiter.'

And here again, in a review of *Till Death Us Do Part* in which he worries that the character Alf Garnett has become a hero to the very racists he was invented to parody. He opens with an anecdote about a recent stay in hospital in which he found himself sharing a ward with

> assembled Alfs addressing themselves to the unpalatable fact subdued Pakistanis had somehow managed to infiltrate into the ward under the pretence of chronic sickness. We all knew as a matter of course that these cunning brown bastards were only there to draw social security payments, an argument which temporarily wavered when one of them so miscalculated his ruse that he actually went so far as to die. "There's yer bleed'n curry for you," observed my nearest Alf, not entirely without compassion.

As a piece of satire, I can't think of a finer or wittier skewering of the myth of 'health tourism' and 'benefits cheats' in the space of one paragraph.

As a piece of prose it has elegance and playfulness, that final 'not entirely without compassion' reading almost like a stage direction and, like a perfectly weighted pass, allowing the reader to take it in their stride.

Most rewarding of all for the Potter geek, it is recognisably the blueprint for a moment in *The Singing Detective* where Ali – the Pakistani in the next bed to Philip Marlow – turns the expectation of racist abuse into a moment of shared hilarity between Marlow and himself at the expense of a liberal young houseman.

With his eye for absurdity and precision of language, how I would have loved to have read Dennis Potter on the likes of Iain Duncan Smith or Nigel Farage. Indeed, Farage, with his strained combination of fake bonhomie and victimized suburban bluster, could almost be a character invented by Potter – and played by Denholm Elliott. Cameron, you suspect, would be too easy a target, although I would like to see what he would have made of Nick Clegg's avowed love of Samuel Beckett.

There's a tone in Potter's prose and in his voice in interviews that reflects the masochism at the heart of his greatest work. He endlessly tortures himself with the notion that TV isn't worthy of the same intellectual interrogation as literature or art but then makes it clear that he intends to ignore his misgivings and give the same forensic attention to an episode of *Steptoe and Son* or *Coronation Street* as he would, indeed does to *War and Peace*.

Naturalism, as Dennis was keen to remind us throughout his career, was just one way (and a flawed way at that) of writing television drama, but it had, partly through soaps and long running series like *Z Cars*, become the most familiar and dominant form by the time *Pennies from Heaven* burst on to our screen. Watching it now it reads as a largely naturalistic drama with music. The only time it really steps out of its realist framework is during the song sequences and during the encounters with the mystical Accordion Man. *The Singing Detective* then used the *Pennies from Heaven* template as its starting point to gloriously and triumphantly deconstruct the whole way in which we tell stories.

The towering achievement of *The Singing Detective* was to be simultaneously formally adventurous (A man in bed with a skin disease is writing or rewriting a detective novel, reminiscing about a traumatic childhood, peopling the film adaptation of his detective novel with characters that may or may not be characters from that troubled childhood. He is simultaneously being ripped off by his agent or wife or both for the film rights to the story he is writing. He is being psychoanalyzed. These multiple worlds bleed into each other from the beginning, and the musical sequences emphasize and restage his fears of illness, of betrayal, of loss of mind, of loss of conscience) and yet still to create a character who we cared about, who we believed and with whom we emotionally engaged. When Philip Marlow raises his still misshapen hands in triumph as he leaves the ward for the last time, I cry every time. He has won. He has beaten his sickness. He has taken up his bed and walked. He has become the triumphant hero of his own story – his own stories even.

You can catch the rhythm and technique of Potter's drama in nearly every review, essay and interview in this collection. Potter's sense of humour too, his relentless search for the right phrase, his restless pursuit of the metaphor – rewriting as a habit of mind. Hard to resist those sickness metaphors but his self-consciousness infects his prose style every bit as much as it does his drama. As with *The Singing Detective*, so he is often writing a review of himself reviewing in more critical terms than the work he is criticising.

After he delivered the "Realism and Non-naturalism" lecture at the Edinburgh International Television Festival in 1977, Potter wrote an article that November that started with a reference to him having delivered that very lecture and being harangued in the pub afterwards by an aggressive David Hare. This in itself develops into a list of writers who were rumoured to wish him physical harm...and this anecdotage is, in his words, a 'nervous and self-conscious preamble' to a review of *Abigail's Party* which he then proceeds to savage as a play that 'sank under its own immense condescension.'

As he says of the non-naturalist scriptwriter, who may or may not be called Dennis Potter: 'He wants to look at our way of looking even as he is looking.'

His public self-examination and exposure of form is an expression of the same creative instinct which has him publicly expose and examine those areas where shame resides, and fear, and lack of control. He is a writer who writes about the open wound – physical and metaphorical. Whether it be Marlow's fear of an unwanted ejaculation when he is at his most vulnerable in *The Singing Detective* or whether it be Arthur Parker's unrequited lust in *Pennies From Heaven*.

The glorious failure of language in Arthur symbolizes his greater tragedy – his inability to communicate ultimately leads him to the scaffold. His cry of 'Blimey Joan, love a duck!' when his young wife has rouged her nipples in a desperate bid to keep him from leaving her is both hilarious and tragically inadequate and foreshadows his final words before he is hanged. 'Hang on a bit – I got an itchy conk! I said, hang on will you? Or scratch me nose for me bloody hell.'

A man can't reach his nose for a final scratch because he is hooded up, handcuffed, being led to the scaffold. Impotence again. Bondage. Lack of relief. Even Arthur's tragic dying words are a sexual metaphor, although Arthur himself doesn't know it.

Potter is a writer who, like most working-class writers, has a morbid fear of being seen to 'show off' while simultaneously finding it impossible to resist displaying his scholarship. His contradictions are what makes him great. A snob and a democrat, a Labour supporter with no truck with populism, a writer of immense generosity who could be enthusiastically mean in print. A humane misanthrope. All of these contradictions are on display in this collection – and they remain exhilarating.

He writes television criticism because he knows at its best television can be art and at its worst a piece of talking furniture in the corner of the room. And it was this very challenge which I feel drove him to make television that could not be ignored, that demanded your attention.

Potter was and remains a great influence on my own writing. *Blackpool* is the most obvious descendant of Potter, not just the lip-synched songs, but Ripley Holden as a latter day Arthur Parker, frustrated by the smallness of his life, the fact that Blackpool is not Vegas, and also the evangelical David Bradley as a distant relative of the Accordion Man.

But I would argue that the inspiration I continue to draw from Potter runs deeper than the stylistic trappings and would hope his lasting influence on me and my generation of television writers was in terms of ambition – ambition of form, of structure, of characterisation and of language. No writer appreciated more that the gap between what a character needs to express and is capable of expressing is where the drama lies. No writer conveyed the complexity and shifting nature of character with greater panache than Dennis Potter. No writer looked as forensically at the pain in our hearts and the darkness in our souls until he found some light in there.

Best of all, as this collection testifies, Dennis Potter is a writer who likes to start an argument. And it is a tribute to his qualities as a screenwriter and critic that we continue to argue with him still…

PETER BOWKER
March 2015

Preface

Dennis Potter's non-fiction output was extensive. He was a journalist for most of his life, either as a reporter, columnist, or reviewer, and this was supplemented by regular appearances on television and radio. Overall he wrote around 750,000 words of journalism, and generated many thousands more from his interviews, broadcasts and speeches. This large and varied body of work has been selectively drawn upon by biographers, critics and academics to help pursue their arguments and theories about Potter's life and work, but this has inevitably undervalued the richness of his 'extra-curricular' writing, which deserves more than to be treated as mere supplementary material to the dramatic works. We contend that it is half the story, and a vital part of the playwright's ongoing dialogue with his audience.

Potter had a varied journalistic career, ranging from his early days as jobbing reporter during the slow demise of the *Daily Herald*, to his position as the high-profile television critic of the *Sunday Times*. Over the intervening years he was a literary critic with the *Times*, *Guardian* and *New Society*, and had a long association with the *New Statesman*, again as a television critic.

These different platforms gave him the opportunity to air his views on politics, sport, faith, community and, of course, television and the people who make it. He engaged full-bloodedly with contemporary events, and across his journalism, whatever the subject, he combined thoughtfulness with gut reaction, and was not afraid to identify and analyse his own prejudices.

Potter explored topics and preoccupations that are still resonant today, such as the future of public service broadcasting, the failure of party politics, the commodification of society, the commercialisation of sport, and the fracturing of working-class communities. As part of this exploration, he also wrote about *Doctor Who*, *Coronation Street*, *Fawlty*

Towers, Bruce Forsyth and Emu. Potter's distinctive voice spoke loudly, scurrilously and hilariously to all of these subjects and more, but until now his journalism, talks and interviews have only been discoverable in archives or rarely seen television documentaries.

The purpose of this volume is to bring together for the first time a representative selection of the best of Potter's non-fiction writing. The pieces, with one exception, are presented chronologically from his early articles for the student magazine *Isis*, to the posthumously published introduction to his final works of drama. There are three overall sections, each headed by an essay setting Potter's non-fictional work in its historic context, and explanatory endnotes are included where the passage of time has given rise to possible obscurities. Otherwise we have tried to leave Potter to speak for himself, as he would surely have wished.

Acknowledgements

First of all we must thank Dennis Potter for decades of inspiration. Biographers often moan about their subject after prolonged exposure, yet many months of deep research and the difficult process of reading, selecting and debating pieces did nothing to dent our enthusiasm.

Judy Daish made this project possible. As Potter's friend and agent, her blessing on behalf of the Estate was essential. The trust placed in us to present his words and to investigate rights issues on her behalf was greatly appreciated.

We have been blessed with an endlessly accommodating publisher in Oberon Books. All of its staff were supportive along the way but particular thanks must go to our patient editor George Spender and designer James Illman.

For permitting the use of two sketches written by Potter in collaboration with David Nathan, we would like to thank John Nathan. Trinity Mirror allowed the use of articles from the *Daily Herald*. The book as a reflection of Potter's full range would have been far poorer without them.

We follow in the footsteps of many Potter scholars. Dave Evans was the first to see the value in republishing Potter's non-fiction, as part of the *Clenched Fists* website, and his initiative gave us early inspiration. Our introductions and endnotes to the present volume owe a debt to others who went before: Humphrey Carpenter, John R. Cook, Glen Creeber, Graham Fuller, Adam Ganz, Joanne Garde-Hansen, W. Stephen Gilbert, Vernon Gras, Hannah Grist, Philip Purser, Peter Stead and John Wyver. We are particularly grateful to Cook, Creeber, Garde-Hansen, Gilbert and Wyver for their collegiate support along the way.

Several institutions provided vital support to the gathering of material for *The Art of Invective*. The British Library St Pancras was virtually a second home, and in the final weeks of research we were delighted to be reunited with their newspaper collections, which had been held in deep storage for much of our production period owing to a protracted relocation project. The Newsroom, Rare Books & Music and the National Sound Archive at BL each boast a great team, but we would particularly like to thank Steven Dryden for going beyond the call of duty in tracking down key Potter recordings. Diligent is also the middle name of Louise North at the BBC Written Archives Centre, who took our long lists of demands with typical grace and enabled us to mine the Corporation's Potter holdings in the hunt for 'new' material. We would also like to thank the BFI National Archive (Kathleen Dickson), BFI Reuben Library (Sarah Currant and Nina Bishop), the Dean Heritage Centre in the Forest of Dean (Phillippa Turner), The Mary Evans Picture Library, John Frost Newspapers for helping us out of a *Herald*-shaped hole, the National Library of Scotland, and the University of Bournemouth, keepers of the IBA Archive. David Rolinson would like to thank the University of Stirling for research leave and support that helped with the early stages of research. John Williams would like to thank Newcastle University Library, particularly Chris Stevens and Stacey Whittle who helped with access to Potter material back in the days when the book was being planned.

For advice, assistance, discussion and friendship: Alan Andres, Jamie Andrews, Claire Armspach, Steve Arnold, Louis Barfe, Ian Beard, John Belcher, Shaun Brennan, Mark Cairns, Cheryl Campbell, Lez Cooke, Nick Cooper, Simon Coward, Caroline Cowie, Gareth Davies, Laura Earley, Robert Fairclough, Simon Farquhar, Dick Fiddy, Gavin Stewart Gaughan, Darren Giddings, Jonathon Green, Jason Griffiths, Mark Griffiths, Simon Harries, Alan Hayes, Alys Hayes, Jason Hazeley, Iain Hepburn, John Hill, Veronica Hitchcock, Gary Hope, Emily Jane Jenkins, Paul Kobasa, Stephen Lacey, James Leggott, Phil Lepherd, Justin Lewis, Mark Lewisohn, Richard Marson, Andrew Martin, Tom May, Adam McLean, Jonny Mohun, Joel Morris, Daniel Norcross, Jonathan Norton, Leah Panos, Andrew Pixley, Ian Potter, Marcus Prince, Paul Putner, John Roberts, John Robinson, Robert Ross, Tim Scullion, Catherine Shrimpton, Neil Sinyard, Billy Smart, Richard Stilgoe, Vicky Thomas, Keith Topping, Kenith Trodd, Simon Usher, Anthony Wall, Christian Wentzell, Keith Wickham, Zoe Wilcox, Mike Winstanley, Andrew Wright and the Northern Television Research Group. Many are owed apologies for apparently ceaseless, seemingly irrelevant Potter chatter during the book's gestation, but the most patient were surely Simon Scott, Marina Dekavalla and Shirley Tindle for sharing the worst of it and at such close range. Shirley also has our thanks for proofreading the manuscript. Any remaining errors are the responsibility of the editors.

A Note on the Text

The text has been gathered from a large number of sources, with newspapers, magazines, broadcast interviews and programme transcripts making up the bulk of the material. The sources also ranged across many decades which have seen numerous changes in newspaper style guides and common usage. In newspaper articles printed before 1970, hyphenated words proliferated, block capitals were frequently used for emphasis, and initial capital letters abounded. These have been silently amended: most hyphens have been dropped, italics have been used for emphasis, and capitalization has been minimised. Although this diminishes the period effect of the pieces, it was considered worth sacrificing for a more consistently readable text.

Many pieces from the *Daily Herald* and the *Sun* offered a particular challenge due to the textual variations between the editions produced in England and Scotland. Titles differed, as did paragraphing; words, sentences and whole sections came and went. Wherever this occurred, an optimal version has been created in order to present something closer to what Potter would have originally submitted before the constraints of space and the editor's blade intervened. Of course, there remains the possibility that a 1960s sub-editor's hand has crept in to our new text from time to time. We have also chosen to reduce the generous paragraphing endemic to tabloids, with readability our overriding goal.

A similar challenge presented itself with BBC material. Where scripts were available they were used as a master text, and compared with transmission versions if they too existed. In the case of the sketch from *That Was the Week That Was*, there was a further variant first published by W.H. Allen. As always, a true reflection of the unexpurgated Potter was our aim.

All interviews were transcribed by the editors directly from complete recordings, and in the case of *Tonight* making use of untransmitted material. The broken sentences and hesitations of spoken English have been smoothed on occasion, but we believe that nothing important has been lost in the process.

Of the broadcast talks, we were able to compare the script and recording of "And with no language but a cry". Sadly, due to archive retention policies at the BBC, recordings of "The Establishment" and "The other side of the dark" no longer survive, so we were forced to rely on scripts.

Chronology

1935 Dennis Christopher George Potter (DP) is born on 17 May in Berry Hill, Forest of Dean, Gloucestershire.

1940–53 DP attends Christchurch School, Berry Hill (1940–45), then Bell's Grammar School, Coleford (1946–49). He moves to Hammersmith for a period of seven months in 1945 and then more permanently four years later, when he attends St Clement Dane's Grammar School (1949–53).

Journalism: *The Dane* (school magazine).

1953–55 National Service, with postings at the International Corps Centre, Maresfield Park (where DP meets Kenneth Trodd), the Joint Services School for Linguistics, Bodmin (where DP learns Russian) and finally at MI3 in the War Office, London, where DP serves as a language clerk.

1956–59 DP arrives with state scholarship at New College, Oxford. Editor of *Isis*, *Clarion* and chair of Oxford University Labour Club. Marries Margaret Morgan in January 1959. On graduating, DP joins BBC in July 1959 as a trainee and moves to London.

Journalism: *Dean Forest Guardian*, *Oxford Clarion*, *Isis*, *Granta*, *Clarion* and *New Statesman*.

_TV_: *Does Class Matter?* (BBC, 1958) and *Panorama* (BBC, 1959).

1960 Birth of first daughter, Jane.

Books: *The Glittering Coffin* (Gollancz).

_TV_: *Between Two Rivers* (BBC) and *Bookstand* (BBC).

Journalism: *Tribune*, *Daily Herald*, *Punch* and *Twentieth Century*.

1961   Birth of second daughter, Sarah.

_TV_: _Bookstand_ (BBC).

Journalism: _Daily Herald_ and _New Left Review_.

1962   Diagnosed with psoriatic arthropathy. Writes first television review.

Journalism: _Daily Herald_ and _Sunday Times_.

Books: _The Changing Forest_ (Secker and Warburg).

1963

Journalism: _Daily Herald_.

_TV_: _That Was the Week That Was_ (BBC).

Stage: Sketches for _Dear Sir, Stroke Madam_ and _Is It True What They Say About...?_

1964   Runs as a Labour candidate in East Hertfordshire during the General Election. DP's first two plays are commissioned for BBC Television.

Journalism: _Daily Herald_, _Views_ and _What's On In London_.

_TV_: _Tonight_ (BBC), _A Last Word on the Election_ (BBC) and _Not So Much a Programme More a Way of Life_ (BBC).

Stage: Sketches for _Excuse Fingers_.

1965   Birth of DP's third child, Robert.

_TV_: _Not So Much a Programme More a Way of Life_ (BBC) and four plays – _The Confidence Course_, _Alice_, _Stand Up, Nigel Barton_ and _Vote, Vote, Vote for Nigel Barton_ (all BBC).

Journalism: _New Society_.

1966   The Potters, having lived for a time in Norfolk, move to Lydney, Forest of Dean.

_TV_: _Emergency – Ward 9_ (BBC) and _Where the Buffalo Roam_ (BBC).

Journalism: _New Society_.

1967   The Potters move to Morecambe Lodge, Duxmere, Ross-on-Wye.

_TV_: _Message for Posterity_ (BBC) and _Bravo and Ballyhoo_ (BBC).

Journalism: _New Society_, _New Statesman_, _Sunday Times_ and _Times_.

1968

_TV_: The Bone-grinder (Rediffusion), _Shaggy Dog_ (London Weekend Television) and _A Beast with Two Backs_ (BBC).

Journalism: Sun, _New Society_ and _Times_.

Stage: Vote, Vote, Vote for Nigel Barton (Bristol).

1969

_TV_: Moonlight on the Highway (LWT/Kestrel) and _Son of Man_ (BBC).

Journalism: Punch and _Times_.

Stage: Son of Man (Leicester; Camden).

1970

_TV_: Lay Down Your Arms (LWT/Kestrel) and _Angels are so Few_ (BBC).

Journalism: Times.

1971

_TV_: Paper Roses (Granada), _Traitor_ (BBC) and _Casanova_ (BBC).

Journalism: Times and _Plays and Players_.

1972 A severe and prolonged attack of psoriatic arthropathy permanently damages DP's hands.

_TV_: Follow the Yellow Brick Road (BBC).

Journalism: Times and _New Statesman_.

1973

_TV_: Only Make Believe (BBC) and _A Tragedy of Two Ambitions_ (BBC).

Books: Hide and Seek (Andre Deutsch/Quartet).

Journalism: Times.

1974

_TV_: Joe's Ark (BBC) and _Schmoedipus_ (BBC).

Journalism: New Statesman and _Guardian_.

Stage: Only Make Believe (Oxford).

1975	Death of Walter Potter, father of DP.
_TV_:	_Late Call_ (BBC).
Journalism:	_New Statesman, New Society, Guardian_ and _Observer Magazine_.
1976	_Brimstone & Treacle_, commissioned and produced by the BBC, is banned before transmission.
_TV_:	_Double Dare_ (BBC) and _Where Adam Stood_ (BBC).
Journalism:	_New Statesman, Sunday Times, Evening Standard_ and _Guardian_.
Talks:	_With Great Pleasure_ (BBC) and "And with no language but a cry" (BBC).
1977	DP begins treatment with 'miracle drug' razoxane, which provides him with greater mobility.
Journalism:	_Sunday Times, Guardian_ and _New Statesman_.
Talks:	"Realism and non-naturalism" (Edinburgh), "Tell it not in Gath" (Cheltenham) and "A Christmas Forest" (BBC).
1978	Forms Pennies from Heaven Limited with Kenith Trodd. DP ceases to write regular journalism following his departure from the _Sunday Times_ in November.
_TV_:	_The Mayor of Casterbridge_ (BBC) and _Pennies from Heaven_ (BBC).
Talks:	_Serendipity_ (BBC) and "The other side of the dark" (BBC).
Stage:	_Brimstone & Treacle_ (Sheffield).
Journalism:	_Sunday Times, Sunday Times Magazine_ and _New Statesman_.
1979	
_TV_:	_Blue Remembered Hills_ (BBC)
Journalism:	_Daily Mail_ and _Tatler_.
Stage:	_Brimstone & Treacle_ (Camden).
1980	
_TV_:	_Blade on the Feather_ (LWT/PfH), _Rain on the Roof_ (LWT/PfH) and _Cream in My Coffee_ (LWT/PfH).
Journalism:	_Tatler, Over 21, Daily Mail_ and _TV Times_.

1981

Cinema: _Pennies from Heaven_ (MGM).

Books: _Pennies from Heaven_ (Quartet).

1982

Cinema: _Brimstone & Treacle_ (PfH).

Talks: DP addresses the Eighth International James Joyce Symposium (Dublin).

1983   DP ends his use of razoxane.

Cinema: _Gorky Park_ (Orion).

Stage: _Sufficient Carbohydrate_ (Hampstead).

Talks: "Cymbeline" (BBC).

Journalism: _Sunday Times Magazine_ and _Guardian_.

1984

Stage: _Sufficient Carbohydrate_ (West End).

Journalism: _Guardian_.

1985

_TV_: _Tender is the Night_ (BBC).

Cinema: _Dreamchild_ (Thorn EMI).

Journalism: _Guardian_.

1986

_TV_: _The Singing Detective_ (BBC).

Books: _Ticket to Ride_ (Faber and Faber).

1987

_TV_: _Visitors_ (BBC) and _Brimstone & Treacle_ (BBC; recorded 1976).

Books: _Blackeyes_ (Faber and Faber).

1988   US transmission of _The Singing Detective_ prompts renewed interest in DP abroad.

TV:	*Christabel* (BBC).
Cinema:	*Track 29* (Handmade).

1989 Forms Whistling Gypsy Productions.
TV: *Blackeyes* (BBC).
Journalism: *Sunday Telegraph*.

1990

Journalism: *Independent Magazine* and *New York Times*.

1992 Margaret Potter diagnosed with breast cancer.

First US retrospective of DP's television work, at the Museum of Television and Radio, New York.

Cinema: *Secret Friends* (Film Four).

1993

TV: *Lipstick on Your Collar* (Channel 4).
Cinema: *Midnight Movie* (BBC).
Talks: *Opinions* (Channel 4) and "Occupying Powers" (Edinburgh).

1994 DP diagnosed with pancreatic cancer in February. Death of Margaret Potter on 28 May. Death of DP at Morecambe Lodge on 7 June.

TV: *Without Walls Special: An Interview with Dennis Potter* (Channel 4).
Cinema: *Mesmer* (Mayfair).

1996

TV: *Karaoke* (BBC/Channel 4) and *Cold Lazarus* (Channel 4/BBC).

2003

Cinema: *The Singing Detective* (Icon).

2014–15 *Messages for Posterity: The Complete Dennis Potter* – season at BFI Southbank, London, the first to comprise DP's entire surviving television and film canon.

Part One
The Confidence Course

Dennis Potter once commented that 'any writer really has a very small field to keep ploughing, and eventually you turn up the coins or the treasure or whatever it is you want.'[1] He was born on 17 May 1935 in Berry Hill, in the Forest of Dean, and his lifelong contemplation and reinvention of this childhood 'land of lost content'[2] fuelled some of his greatest drama, such as *The Singing Detective* (1986), *Stand Up, Nigel Barton* (1965) and *Blue Remembered Hills* (1979). Potter always denied that these were truly autobiographical works, but they often reflected a version of his early life as a coalminer's son that he told not only through his plays but also in his non-fiction and even in the personal history he portrayed to friends and colleagues.

Potter's 'authorized version' of his early life was often simplified to a progression from Christchurch School, Berry Hill, to New College, Oxford, 'giving the impression that he had gone directly from the village school to Oxford.'[3] In fact, once Potter passed his Eleven Plus[4] in 1946, he started at Bell's Grammar School in Coleford, local to the Forest of Dean, and then moved on to St Clement Danes Grammar School when his family moved to Hammersmith[5] in 1949. The latter had a profound influence on Potter: 'None of the almost suffocatingly close Forest of Dean atmosphere persisted at all. That turned me very much to academic work. They said you must try for Oxford – and that seemed to me the way out.'[6]

St Clement Danes not only pointed Potter in the direction of Oxford, but it also gave him the opportunity to act, to become a star in the debating society, and to write for the school magazine. Potter's first piece for *The Dane*, an account of a sixth-form trip, appeared in July 1952,[7] and he subsequently became a regular contributor, culminating in his editorship of a literary supplement to the July 1953 issue.[8] By then, Potter had already accepted a place at New College, Oxford reading Politics, Philosophy and Economics, although his arrival would be delayed by another three years owing to his failure to pass his Latin Responsions[9] and the requirement to take up his National Service.

Potter's National Service made a lasting impact on him. As well as providing rich material for his play *Lay Down Your Arms* (1970) and his serial *Lipstick on Your Collar* (1993), the posting to the Intelligence Corps Centre, Maresfield Park brought him into contact with Kenneth (later Kenith) Trodd, his future producer, collaborator and sparring partner.[10] Potter and Trodd were transferred to the Joint Services School for Linguistics in Bodmin in order to learn Russian, after which they were posted to MI3 in the War Office. The work was stultifying, and even after Potter was discharged in October 1955, he still had another year to kill before going up to Oxford, and so passed the time working at the Meredith & Drew biscuit factory in Cinderford. By the time he finally arrived at Oxford in 1956, he was formidably well read, and anxious to make his mark.

Potter's time at Oxford was both exhilarating and fraught as he battled his way to most of the influential positions available to him: editor of *Isis*,[11] editor of *Clarion*[12] and Chair of the University Labour Club. Only the position of President of the Oxford Union eluded him, but he created more controversy and garnered more national press than any of his contemporaries. Whether accusing his rival Brian Walden of electoral malpractice,[13] confronting the owners of *Isis*,[14] or taking on Special Branch,[15] Potter was rarely out of the newspapers. This success deepened his preoccupation with class, and his thoughts on the issue were given shape by Richard Hoggart's influential 1957 book *The Uses of Literacy*.[16]

Hoggart's work inevitably struck a chord with Potter, as it described the vibrant working-class culture of the recent past and its transformation into a spiritless, commodified and commercialized existence. The book also made specific reference to the difficulties faced by scholarship boys as they traversed the class divide. Another influence on Potter was the concept of Admass, a word coined by J.B. Priestley and Jacquetta Hawkes to describe 'the whole system of an increasing productivity, plus inflation, plus a rising standard of material living, plus high-pressure advertising and salesmanship, plus mass communication, plus cultural democracy and the creation of the mass mind, the mass man.'[17] It is hard to overstate the importance of this idea to Potter, and he returned to it regularly in his non-fiction throughout his life. In the short term however, these influences drove Potter in a way that gained him even greater student fame, and some measure of notoriety.

In May 1958, the *New Statesman* published Potter's article "Base Ingratitude?",[18] which revisited concerns about class that he had addressed on a number of occasions in his earlier pieces for *Isis*, and which were further honed by the influence of Hoggart. The article drew the attention of Jack Ashley, a producer at the BBC who invited Potter to contribute to a series that would eventually become *Does Class Matter?*[19] Potter's interview for the programme focused on his difficulties negotiating the differences between his new life in Oxford and family life back in the Forest of Dean, and he later came to regret some of his comments such as 'my father is forced to communicate with me almost, as it were, with a kind of contempt.'

The *Reynolds News* pre-empted the transmission with a lurid headline – "Miner's son at Oxford felt ashamed of home" – and Potter considered a libel action such was his anger at the accompanying article. However, he subsequently used a similar scenario in his play *Stand Up, Nigel Barton* and later admitted that he'd betrayed his parents and 'been a shit, and *mea culpa*.'[20] The interview also caused controversy in the pages of his local newspaper the *Dean Forest Guardian*, for which Potter had previously written, and so he once again took to the pages with a strongly argued defence of his conduct.[21] These trials and tribulations were grist to the mill of his many enemies in Oxford, who reported gleefully that the 'natives had been enraged.'[22] However, Potter learned at this point that attention from the press is a double-edged sword, as despite the heartache at home, the high profile that resulted from various Oxford altercations and his television appearance had brought him a book commission,[23] and an informal offer of a job at the BBC once he had taken his degree.[24] His subsequent career reflected this early pattern – various controversies boosted his profile and gave him great opportunities, but often at a cost.

Potter joined the BBC as a general trainee in July 1959, and although accounts vary as to his initial postings,[25] he was eventually transferred to *Panorama* (BBC, 1953–) on attachment to Robin Day. Despite seemingly following a typical path into the Establishment, from Oxford to the BBC, Potter was no ordinary trainee. His book *The Glittering Coffin*[26] – a strident summation of his views on class and Admass culture – had marked him out as an 'Angry Young Man,' despite his protestations to the contrary,[27] and its serialization in the *Daily Sketch* as "What's eating Dennis Potter?"[28] again showed his willingness to seize upon the popular press as a vehicle to get his ideas across to the widest range of people. He quickly, and perhaps unwisely, persuaded the *Panorama* team to run a feature on the state of mining in the Forest of Dean,[29] and after he was sent on attachment to documentary maker Denis Mitchell,[30] he and producer Anthony de Lotbiniere set to work on *Between Two Rivers* (1960),[31] a half-hour documentary about the Forest of Dean which caused yet more controversy in the pages of the *Dean Forest Guardian*.[32]

Only a couple of months after the transmission of *Between Two Rivers*, Potter tendered his resignation to the BBC,[33] ostensibly because he had been commissioned to write *The Changing Forest*,[34] but also because he feared that his political work would continue to bring him into conflict with the Corporation. His resignation also gave him the opportunity for freelance work as a writer on a planned BBC book series that eventually reached the screen in October 1960 under the title *Bookstand*.[35] The series attempted to make 'difficult' novels accessible, and Potter was responsible for dramatizing sequences from the featured novels. The Director-General Hugh Carleton Greene disapproved of these extracts and frowned upon the series,[36] but the *Bookstand* staff 'were trying to make [the programme] speak to non-book-readers'[37] as well as the usual literary audiences.

The desire to communicate beyond a narrow cultural elite had preoccupied Potter during this period, and he returned to the work of Raymond Williams, another writer, like Hoggart, who was one of his major influences at University. Potter was particularly interested in Williams's concept of a 'common culture' that could reach across the class divide.[38] When Potter later reviewed Williams's novel *Border Country* for the *New Left Review*, the book, which featured a London-based university lecturer returning to his working-class home in Wales, had obvious resonances for him, particularly in light of the furore around *Between Two Rivers*. This caused him to reflect that 'when I think back to the arguments at home, the genuinely desperate attempts to force comprehension of at least some part of the things I felt after going up to Oxford [...] I do not feel very happy. But, writing this now in the Forest, I do not want to go on and on in this fashion, and [...] I know that it has made me take stock of my own position...'[39]

Although *Bookstand* continued, the dramatized sequences were dropped, which left Potter out of a job. He had married while still at Oxford, and now also had a family to support, so he accepted with alacrity when offered a job at the *Daily Herald*,[40] a Labour-leaning newspaper. Initially he was a reporter-at-large, but his work became hampered when he first displayed symptoms of what was to become a lifelong condition: psoriatic arthropathy.[41] He was first hospitalized in June 1962, and shortly afterwards he took over the role of television critic for the *Daily Herald*.[42]

It was during this period that Potter became immersed in what Raymond Williams would later call the 'flow' of television.[43] His *Herald* column covers every kind of programme, from light entertainment to *Panorama* by way of *Compact*,[44] *Emergency – Ward 10*,[45] *Sportsview*,[46] and the antics of Hughie Green.[47]

Potter's daily column was 'phoned in' the previous night meaning that only peak-time programmes were reviewed, although he rapidly picked up an additional, more expansive column on Saturdays where he had the opportunity to revisit a show at greater length. Although his time at the *Herald* generally produced rather slight pieces, it was a formative period. Potter had seen the potential of television as a teenager: 'Here was a medium of great power, of potentially wondrous delights, that could slice through all the tedious hierarchies of the printed word and help to emancipate us from many of the stifling tyrannies of class and status and gutter-press ignorance'[48] and during his years as a television critic, with Raymond Williams's 'common culture' in mind, it seems that Potter became convinced of television's potential as a democratic medium.

The *Herald* years also helped Potter's career in more practical ways. He favourably reviewed[49] the BBC's new satire show *That Was the Week That Was* (1962–63), popularly known as *TW3*, and David Nathan, his colleague at the *Herald*, managed to sell producer Ned Sherrin a gag during an interview. Nathan and Potter subsequently teamed up, and wrote a number of sketches for *TW3* and its successor *Not So Much a Programme More a Way of Life* (BBC1, 1964–65), as well as contributing to various shows at The Poor Millionaire satire club.[50]

By this time, Potter had been selected as a Labour candidate for East Hertfordshire, and was actively seeking a career in politics. Also of concern during this period was his health: the psoriatic arthropathy became more severe, leading to spells of hospitalisation and a growing realisation that his choice of career might be limited by his lack of mobility.

1964 was a crucial year for Potter. The *Daily Herald* closed down and was reborn as the *Sun*[51] shortly before Potter unsuccessfully stood as a candidate in the October General Election.[52] Although he briefly worked as leader writer for the *Sun* around the time of the election, he resigned shortly afterwards, and left payroll journalism for good. However, he already had the makings of another career. Earlier in the year, Potter had been commissioned to write his first television play *The Confidence Course* (1965)[53] and also a play based on his experiences during the General Election, which would become *Vote, Vote, Vote for Nigel Barton* (1965). These two commissions at least gave Potter the reassurance that there might be a viable way of continuing to support his family, and one that could also accommodate his increasingly fragile health.

Potter was convinced that the potential of television drama had not yet been realised. When reviewing Granada's recent production of *War and Peace* (1963), his praise contained heavy criticism of the status quo: 'this superb production showed convincingly that the simple, naturalistic, tediously "authentic" drama is not the only way of liberating the TV play.'[54] This conviction was strengthened by writer Troy Kennedy Martin's celebrated essay "nats go home",[55] a rallying cry for the use of non-naturalism in television drama, duly followed by his experimental series *Diary of a Young Man*.[56]

It was in this febrile atmosphere that Potter wrote his first two plays, with *Vote, Vote, Vote for Nigel Barton* showing its formal experimentation with the inclusion of newsreel elements more commonly used in documentaries. This was a step too far for BBC management. Although the play should have been broadcast on 23 June 1965 as part of *The Wednesday Play* (BBC1, 1964–70) strand, it was pulled from the schedules a mere seven hours ahead of transmission, amid fears that the programme looked too much like a documentary, and was politically biased.[57] Potter was hauled up in front of the Head of Drama Sydney Newman, who, amongst other things, asked why Potter wanted to 'shit on the Queen.'[58] The controversy raged in the media, partly engineered by Potter himself, and eventually it was agreed that he would rewrite some scenes, which would then be reshot, and the play was finally screened in December 1965.[59] Despite the hoo-hah about *Vote, Vote, Vote for Nigel Barton*, Potter was still in demand, and in a short space of time he was commissioned for several more plays, including *Alice* (1965),[60] *Message for Posterity* (1967, much delayed)[61] and *Stand Up, Nigel Barton* (1965).[62] Partly from financial necessity, but also due to temperament, Potter thrived on his demanding schedule, and seemed to relish the controversy that was steadily becoming his constant companion.

Despite the blizzard of television commissions – to which *Where the Buffalo Roam* (1966)[63] and *Emergency – Ward 9* (1966)[64] were soon added – Potter took the opportunity of his raised profile to return to journalism. His work for *New Society*[65] was wide ranging, and featured a standout piece of reportage as an eye-witness to the aftermath of the Aberfan tragedy.[66] He was employed as the television critic of *New Statesman*,[67] which was then followed by a long stint as book reviewer for the *Times*.[68] These platforms gave Potter the opportunity to build his reputation as a literary critic alongside his more obvious role as a controversial playwright.

Potter's television career continued on its turbulent way. He won a Writers' Guild award[69] for the Nigel Barton plays, but he had run into another row with his proposed play *Cinderella*.[70] Although the script was initially accepted by the BBC, the Head of Plays Gerald Savory later decided this adult fairy tale was not suitable for production.[71] Potter's reaction was to leak the story to Hunter Davies of the *Times*,[72] something that did not escape Savory's attention: 'My personal view is that Potter feels that the only way his two Barton plays got on to the screen was by yelling to the Press, and that it might work again.'[73] In this case it didn't 'work again' and *Cinderella* was cancelled.

Perhaps because of his discontent with the BBC over *Cinderella*, Potter subsequently accepted commissions from Rediffusion (*The Bone-grinder* (1968)[74]), London Weekend Television (*Shaggy Dog* (1968)[75]) and the National Theatre.[76] Despite this hectic schedule, he also briefly stood in for Nancy Banks-Smith as television critic for the *Sun*, before taking up a role as 'columnist-at-large'[77] from March 1968. His column was frequently confessional, most notably in the way he exposed his illness, and his painful vulnerability as he waited for his plays to be transmitted: 'In my own case I have long since learned to digest the terrible proposition that I am either going to be a shrivelled, laughable nut, or a good writer… Why be so extreme? Why insist on being so perpetually at risk…?'[78] Potter was already making himself his own subject, and he understandably turned inward after spending a long period in hospital.[79] Although he had hoped to return, his final column for the *Sun* appeared in October 1968, and he was also forced to leave the *Times* a few months later.

His career in journalism had faltered, but Potter continued writing plays despite the desperate nature of his condition. He completed for the BBC what would become *Son of Man* (1969)[80] – an account of the last days of Christ – while in Birmingham Skin Hospital, and it would appear that he also salvaged his stalled National Theatre commission in the form of ITV's *Moonlight on the Highway* (1969).[81] By a fluke of scheduling, the plays were transmitted in the same week, and in retrospect they show a significant departure for Potter, bringing together as they do a more explicit engagement with religion, but also with repression and fantasy as embodied in his use of popular music. At the time though, it appeared to some that Potter had yet again proved adept at generating another controversy,[82] and that this detracted from his work.

Potter seemed to have found a route in to the Establishment – he left the Forest of Dean to become an undergraduate star at Oxford, and had subsequently gained a much-prized traineeship at the BBC and was on course for a career in politics – but he had now withdrawn. As a result of both illness and choice, he'd instead turned his attention to television which he saw as a democratic medium that might break down some of the class distinctions that so vexed him as a younger man. He had developed a reputation as a dramatist, but perhaps one who was seen as being more controversial than distinguished, and as his health problems worsened, his future as any kind of writer was in the balance.

A hint of that future could be discerned in his play *A Beast with Two Backs* (1968),[83] which was set in the Forest of Dean. Potter had returned to 'the same old ploughed field' of his youth. The play received mixed reviews, but one, by Maurice Wiggin, was particularly perceptive: 'What distinguishes Mr Potter from the run of writers […] is a radical wrath, Swiftian in its ferocity. […] He is but human; his fire can fizzle out in petulant squibs […] but by and large his control and eloquence are increasing; one day he will touch off the big explosion.'[84]

JOHN WILLIAMS

Changes at the top
Isis, 22 May 1957

At twenty-five past three in the afternoon the morning shift would crunch down the road that dropped through the village, their work over for the day. 'Evenings' came back at half-past eleven at night, and the others at six in the mornings, so this was the only returning shift you could see properly, and it was accordingly always something of an event in the day. The ponderous and out-of-step clamp, clamp, clamp of steel-toed pit boots could be heard minutes before the men came by, and I was able to rush to the wall, eager to see the coal-black faces, the corduroy trousers hitched and string-tied just below the padded knees, and the helmets shaped rather like those worn by the Nazi soldiers in my weekly copy of the *Champion* (the comic everyone seemed to take to supplement the *Daily Herald* or the *Daily Mirror*). For me, and, I suspect, for the adults as well, those returning, grimy men up from the bowels of the earth had a peculiar glamour that inevitably disappeared when the pale, scrubbed faces and collars and ties came out later in the evening; anyway, most people came to the door when this shift passed, including the miserable-looking whippets, tails curved to a taper under their trembling tube-thin bodies.

My grandfather had silicosis after more than fifty years working at the coal face, yet he would always try and come to the wall, breathing so heavily that I was never quite sure whether he was laughing to himself, or humming some old tune. He could neither read nor write, nor remember the time before he went down the pit, so all his conversations were on this one theme, and he constructed elaborate pieces of invective about some event that had happened years before. He would invariably greet the first man by with a set question, and a little formalized dialogue would take place:

'And how's him been, butty?' ('Him' was the pit manager. This was occasionally rephrased as 'the bastard,' but without any particularly violent connotation, being used merely as an accepted and perfectly natural description.)

'Not too bad today, ol' un.' Pause. 'And how's your chest?'

'Middlin', middlin', butty.'

Only something as exciting as a severe accident at pit-bottom or a sudden change in the weather would upset the pattern of this conversation. The men were never very eager to stop and talk, since in their homes the tin baths had already been unhooked from the back-kitchen walls, and kettles would be boiling, ready for the scrub.

It is only when remembering the normal events of the past that even I fully realize the incredible changes that have taken place in the coal industry during and since the war. Judging by the frequency of its use 'Britain's peaceful social revolution' appears to be one of those convenient phrases that has been elevated to the statesmanlike level of the politely platitudinous, along with 'democracy' and 'the free world.' When the museum-piece correspondence columns of the *Daily Telegraph* and the inanities of 'Peter Simple'[85] lay claim to the phrase, the coinage is certainly in danger of being debased. But 'revolution' is the one word that can be legitimately used in any discussion on coalmining and the people that live by it, a revolution made by the combined effects of the war, the Labour Government and the National Coal Board[86] and most immediately felt by the fortunate people of my generation.

Ten years ago this New Year the NCB flag was hoisted with celebrations and joyful demonstrations at every pit-head in the country. This anniversary has been politely greeted by even those sections of the press that had most consistently opposed the idea of nationalization. The articles have been almost solely concerned with the economics of the industry, and, if fair, have shown that the Coal Board is engaged in a heavy investment programme, sinking new shafts and modernizing equipment in even the smallest mines. Any comprehensive review of the industry will also show that, with less men, the NCB has raised production from 178 million to 210 million tons a year, that our coal is cheaper than any other in Western Europe, and the British miner (whose 'absenteeism' is, I gather often made much of in discussions on their work) has gained a lead in efficiency and effort over his European counterparts.

It might also be remembered that the Board has achieved this despite a statutory obligation to avoid a financial loss over a period of years (in an industry that was badly in need of heavy capital investment), continual difficulties in recruiting sufficient manpower, and a dangerous shortage of top-flight managers and administrators.

All of which is very commendable – but to me, and to everyone who is at all intimate with the mining communities, the 10-year anniversary of the NCB should emphasize not only the economic difficulties and achievements, but also the amazing and sweeping changes in morale, habits and outlook that has at long last been achieved. *The Road to Wigan Pier* is now, thank God, a book for the shilling-all-this-shelf, one of the many invaluable social protests held in the floppy mustard covers of the Left Book Club,[87] a piece of *history*.

The miners were undoubtedly the most militant and closely-knit section of the working classes, people who seemed to have the lessons of the past stamped irremovably into their very minds. It is difficult to convey just how this was so without exciting the incredulity of those who do not know the mining areas. I was brought up to regard 'tory' as the dirtiest of all oaths, and the Royal Family as useless, miserable wasters. Sir Winston Churchill is remembered today more as the man who once ordered the troops to South Wales than the great war leader intoning about the beaches. (This is merely reported as a fact, not as a provocative remark. I once made a similar, factual observation in the Union, and was surprised to be accused of undue bitterness! It may perhaps be some consolation to know that the day Mr Attlee received his title he joined the legions in the Party who were 'in it for what they could get.')

The NCB inherited a tremendous capital of initial goodwill, but also a vast heritage of hatred and suspicion, two emotions that had often grown into sheer unreasonableness and were certainly not those most conducive to successful labour relations. There was inevitably much disappointment when the Board had, from necessity, to retain many of the old, discredited administrative personnel and the old system of 'incentives,' so great was the national need for coal. Neither would it be truthful to maintain that the relations between the NUM and the NCB were always ideal, or that many resentments were not still being aired: 'The NCB, the servant of the Tory Government and big business, intend to get the last ounce of work out of the miners...the plans are for more production, with greater speed and fewer men. At Bedwas[88] we have 17 men on the list for redundancy at the present moment. Don't forget the Fleck Committee's findings[89] – drive and discipline for the miners. We should stop them *now*.' Thus finishes a letter in a NUM magazine, an attitude which is certainly not widespread, but indicative of the sort of suspicion the NCB has had to overcome. Significantly, the same issue of this magazine contained a list of scholarships for degree courses, post-graduate courses, travel scholarships, etc, available for miners and their dependents, and offered by the NCB.

The nationalized industries often appear merely to have changed their ownership, and made little effort to enter into the life of the community. The National Coal Board is to be congratulated on making a genuine effort to get to terms with the mining communities, and the full scope of its achievement is not often realized or praised. Drive and initiative are all too commonly assumed to be an attribute only of 'capitalism,' but the NCB has increased production, carried through tremendous changes and yet kept to a very substantial degree the goodwill of the miners.

The morning shift still comes home at twenty-five past three, but not with black faces and steel-tipped boots. Pigeons and whippets are now rare pets; television aerials finger from the roofs; there has been only one fatal accident this year in my father's pit. Admass, of course, has seen to it that some of the changes have actually been for the worse, and I prefer the old whippet to Elvis Presley's "Hound Dog". But it is a strange thought that the NCB of all organizations is mostly responsible for the thinly attended and faintly apologetic shuffle still called the May Day Demonstration, an unrecognisably anaemic descendent of the long, hungry marches of the Thirties.

Stubbornyuddedness
Dean Forest Guardian, 4 October 1957

'The world is as round…as round as as…as a…hosses yud!'

The visiting Sunday School preacher had arrived at such a revelation with understandable throat-clearing hesitancy, then, realising what he had said, glared truculently round the half-empty chapel benches, daring anyone to challenge his profundity.

The momentary and embarrassed silence that followed was shattered suddenly by a small boy blushing furiously with genuine indignation.

'But Sir,' came his protesting but tremulous voice, 'but Sir, a hosses yud yunt *really* round, sir!'

Eyebrows went up; there was the kind of chapel tension that allowed you to hear the branches brushing against the far windows; and the very amateur preacher wrestled with this difficulty like a very professional politician: 'Come come come, my lad,' he boomed, fruity voiced. 'What doost thou know about hosses? There yunt a cleaner animal. And cleanliness, my boy, is next to Godliness.' This remarkable comeback seemed to settle the issue, and everyone was later able to accept as perfectly obvious that since 'blessed is the land between the two rivers' was a fact, then we were indeed lucky to have been born in the Forest of Dean, heaving up green and lonely between the Severn and the Wye.

Such local pride is entirely natural. The story occurred to me while wondering why this wooded and hilly part of Gloucestershire has kept its identity to such a remarkable extent, when in most parts of the land the onslaught of mass communications, slick jazzy entertainments, jukeboxes, jeans and Teddy Boys is flattening out England's rich regional diversity into something uglier, glossier and less real.

But Foresters still allow sheep (as well as the occasional lion, we are told) to roam their highways. Bad pedestrians, they still walk stubbornly down the middle of the road, even when a pavement exists (a habit continued on the club or pub outings to Barry and Porthcawl, to the hooting exasperation of the less civilised). These lingering, somehow graceful attitudes can perhaps be best described by a homegrown word – 'Stubbornyuddedness.' A virtue? I think so!

It is a pride that must not be beaten, an infuriating weapon in argument, but endearing in many ways. Last winter, for instance, I saw a Forest rugby forward in a neat and quiet little Welsh teashop noisily demanding with an alcoholic insistence that he be served with fish and chips. '*And* with vinegar.' It took all of five minutes before the perspiring proprietor was able to make him understand that this particular shop, strangely enough, did *not* sell chips. Defeated, the Forester stood ruminatively still while he thought out the situation. 'Well kip 'um then' he announced at the top of his voice, strode to the door, paused and turned for the parting shot, '*and* the vinegar!' The bewildered proprietor probably became a Welsh Nationalist from that day.

When such stubbornness is allied to the occasional and perhaps inevitable narrow-mindedness of village life you find the disconcerting phenomenon known as 'talking stroite,' which usually means holding tenaciously to something you know to be wrong, but daren't admit. Narrow-mindedness is perhaps the wrong word, for it is only an excessive parochialism, which has more virtues than vices, although anyone deviating from the norm (from neon-bright socks to a top hat) is likely to be greeted with the scornful 'look at thick!'

Similarly, each village is of course superior to the others. At Berry Hill it is permissible to make the most outrageous story appear perfectly credible by prefacing the tale with 'this happened Yarkley woy,' where, it goes without saying, *anything* can happen. I know, too, of a Colefordian who prayed for it to rain one Cinderford carnival day because it had rained at Coleford, a delicious parochialism sometimes seen in the well-read Forest newspapers, which for example, treat Mr Harvey's delightful little poem "Ducks" as the ultimate statement of transcendent, theological truth,[90] certainly greater than the scribblings of Shakespeare, Milton, Blake and other non-Foresters.

Yet a solid sense of humour rarely deserts us, whether of the perverse kind, like the very old inhabitant of Joyford, steadily and gravely misdirecting Symonds Yat traffic through Bicknor with the air of a dignified patrician, or the more blunt and to outsiders, frightening variety – as exampled by the miner who on his dart club's day trip had somehow reached the floor of a London nightclub, only to be approached by a slinky 'hostess' who purred 'Would you like to buy me a drink?' no doubt mistaking his cloth cap for the eccentric garb of a millionaire. She retreated with speed after he had looked her over and announced: 'Thou go back to thee old mon, ol' but. This is a big round and I byunt buyin' nern of them baby-champs for thee!' She probably thought that he was speaking in one of the smaller Scandinavian dialects.

The humour, the habits and the independence are all cemented into coherence by the possession of a valuable passport, a Forest accent. School in London, a hectic Russian course in the Intelligence Corps and a year so far spent at Oxford University has not removed mine, even though I have to tread carefully at first in my desire for acceptance. Pride of region, of custom and tradition are not out of place in this telly-ridden, soporific England of today. But even here the pseudo-American asides now stud the local speech, the one thing that had seemed the safest of all. Can we keep the 'old Forest'?

Well, I found a heartening answer at Cinderford the other week. Sheltering from the rain in a jukebox equipped café, having grown tired of the hilly town which really is best seen in the wet, when the peculiar, dull glint of rain on old slate stones into the narrow streets and ugly houses in a pattern of determined misery, I watched fascinated at the exchange between the glittering jukebox and a teenage girl:

The mechanical arm slid over, the record clicked, slipped and turned, and the shop throbbed suddenly with the insistent neurotic wah-wah-wah beat of rock 'n' roll. Wide-eyed, the girl's head revolved hypnotically from side to side, her limbs moving restlessly, almost desperately under the tight, shiny black skirt. I watched in silent misery, but then came 'the vocal,' and what sounded like an American delinquent sobbed to the world that he was 'all shook up!' This was the moment of truth; I eyed the girl hopefully as she shook to the music. And then she showed that all was not lost, that the Brave New World had not yet won. An expression of incredulity flitted on to her face.

'Hark at thick!' she said.

Base ingratitude?
New Statesman, 3 May 1958[91]

'So you're another of these self-appointed experts on the working classes, with your boot firmly planted on the proletariat's pulse?' This was a deliberate provocation designed to revive a flagging Oxford party conversation, but despite the friendly and conventionally flippant manner, behind the banter lurked a vague irritation, probably reflecting that same specifically middle class social discomfort that finds temporary relief in shy smiles at the dustman or window cleaner.

'No. Not an expert.' Fractional, but calculated, pause – decorated with a deprecating smile, too much like an actor with a throwaway curtain line. 'Just one of them.' And then I felt a pang of guilt, for this was a typical example of how class is dramatized in welfare state Oxford. The brevity and manner of delivery was an attempt to sound sincere, hard and effective, foreshadowing yet another highly coloured but profitless conversation in which I forced myself into dramatizing the not-so-unusual circumstance of being a coal miner's son, whippet-fancying and bitter by descent as it were, set down among the dreaming spires.

The justifiably irritating public school voice spluttered into a justifiably irritated objection, shifting the exchange into the more prosaic plane of reality. 'Now look,' initial finger eagerly jabbing, 'simply by being a member of New College you cannot possibly be a member of the working classes, whoever *they* may be. You don't belong to any class.' Holding a waiting-to-be-filled glass that had contained sherry ('Do you prefer sweet or dry?' and I had answered with conscious assurance) there was nothing to do but agree.

'Well, in a way, yes, but…' and so on, making the carefully qualified withdrawal.

Perhaps I hunt it out, but there always seems to be a kind of tension, quiet and slow developing, that ripples beneath the surface of such conversations. Here at Oxford the social changes of the last decade have given us continual confrontations of the reality of division by class, in speech, habit and outlook. This worries many people. You can sense this at many of the dismally similar Oxford parties, where, before the room patterns into a peopled unity, you will find separate groups whirring round seemingly distinct poles, occasionally throwing off the single person or two, who, whether from shyness or exceptional confidence, spins from one cluster to another. Public conversations at Oxford almost always dwindle into the perpetual game of appearing as a person of some significance, the only solace for the creeping and endemic loneliness of the place. And class aggravates things: a whole generation is making claims, but it is not so easy to shout when muffled by what still appears to be a medieval establishment, even if it is garnished with cavalry twill and cut-glass accents. Shared education stops the place being the battleground of Teddy Boys and British Warms,[92] for only one of these poles of social irresponsibility finds a home here, but you can still stumble upon tremendous differences of background and attitude, emphasized by the quivering sensibilities of the young.

Paradoxically enough, these differences erupt in the most apparent and uncomfortable fashion in the University Labour Club,[93] where a few observations might lead one to startling conclusions about the purpose and nature of the middle-class socialism characteristic of the Labour Party leadership. The resultant small, but definite measure of personal torment regarding class has, for me and others, added urgency and formulation to latent political or journalistic ambitions.

For me, at least, the vices of a hierarchical society such as the present one impinge in two distinct and contrasting ways. At home, my parents grew away as I grew up; not their fault or mine. The atmosphere and cohesion disintegrates only gradually, but inevitably. Fish and chips with vinegar, and public-bar benches, furnished with round tables that squat on warped-outwards iron legs erupting into moulded lions' heads, all now seen and sensed not, perhaps, as an outsider, but certainly as a visitor. By now, my father is forced to communicate with me, much of the time, with an edgy kind of shyness, possibly tinged with contempt as well as admiration, rarely flashing into the real stuff except when one of us is angry or inebriated. Again, the allocation of radio time is a subject for negotiation, and the very fairness of the rest of the family on this is apt to make me feel unreasonable in switching from *Life with the Lyons*. Sometimes I wish I had left school at 15.

But at Oxford, too, events sometimes appear as unreal and take control. My closest friends at New College seem to take the undergraduate/scout relationship for granted, which is perhaps natural in the products of Eton, Rugby and Winchester. With the best will in the world, they have to quote from *The Uses of Literacy*[94] in assessing communication with the working classes as such, and even on occasion irritate me, declassed as I am, without realizing it (and no doubt vice-versa). What else could they do? Wearing a dirty shirt would be no answer. They are in a much worse position than I am: intelligent middle-class people must feel the evils of class more than the newly emancipated.

Both these environments have seemed to me to be quite manageable, so long as the occasional and inevitable discomforts are accepted and I did not brood over accumulated irritations or imaginary insults. A perhaps arrogant belief in my own abilities has been sufficient consolation for the necessary rootlessness. Life was just a series of distinct circles, revolving in their own field, and never quite touching except in the person of the social traveller, plodding across the muddy reaches of the English class system. So long as I kept the circles apart, the dimensions of any problem were that much lessened.

Impossible, thank God. When I leave Oxford, I am going to get married to a girl from home,[95] with exactly the same background as myself, the daughter of a man invalided out of the pit at which my father works, although she had her life determined differently at the age of 11, thanks to a criminally stupid education system. It is difficult to try to convey the new parameters of the problem without being misunderstood. When my girl first came up to Oxford to meet some of my friends, it was something of a strain for both, and almost with guilt only I could see how or why fully. She must have felt like I once felt as a private in the officers' mess. Personal kindness from them, and her own natural intelligence and vitality were sufficient to make me more comfortable than I had half-anticipated.

What is wrong about all this is that it should not be possible. A working-class undergraduate can accept the glint of subdued silver and mumbled Latin prayer in Hall, or conversation about the relative merits of two obscure European cities, and get to know the trappings of middle-class society. But he cannot stomach the two languages that sharply divide up the year, the torn loyalties and perpetual adjustments, the huge chasm between the classes. It has become trite to say that, once upon a long time ago, the worker had some access to the cultural life of the land, even if cramped by poverty. Now that he is materially much more prosperous he has no access to the valuable things in life except by removing himself from his own class – the gap has become wider in absolute terms. And at Oxford, people like myself have to listen to middle-class socialists maintaining despondently that the workers *choose* Radio Luxembourg.

This is rubbish. It is equal rubbish to look at the problem of social democracy as the provision of a greater range of choice for all citizens, unless one also regards most decisions as being conditioned by the pseudo-scientists of the new Admass society – to widen the area of choice without narrowing the types of choice is a typical vice for a social democratic party led by the middle classes. To us, the Labour Party is concerned only, as always, with bread when there is plenty of bread, and thinking that that is enough – a crude heresy all in a mood with the comfortable shuffle towards a new hierarchy, a new kind of right-wing society, where the people at the bottom will no longer have the consolation of knowing that they are there by accident rather than examination.

Naturally, I am a socialist, and believe with all my heart and mind in the possibilities of socialism – this has always been taken for granted. But as one from a working-class background, I also now believe, with others like me in the universities, that the first necessity for the Labour Party must be contempt for much that is labelled 'working class.' Socialists who talk to excess about the virtues of the proletariat often appear to be liberals escaping the full implications of the class system, or fundamentalists whose spectacles steam over with emotion at the thought of their noble working-class backgrounds. The most important political and industrial battle that the workers have ever had is that of moving towards a proper 'use of literacy,' and it is a struggle that becomes of unusual importance to the young socialist – of what used to be described as 'humble origins.'

Small wonder we were miserable about Brighton, and are unhappy with the pin-striped Executive of the Labour Party, stinking as it does with the air of neat suburban houses and well-mannered conversation over garden fences. When are we going to get people who care whether the welfare state by itself creates opportunities for an extension rather than a diminution of capitalist values? When are we going to get the practical attacks upon the whole glittering structure of Admass? Why the depressing diffidence towards the arts? Dignity means more than washing machines and jukeboxes. It seems to us that the party we have been taught to venerate has turned into a new and powerful kind of Establishment, a little proud of its old snapshots, a little patronizing about its beginnings, happy with its own orthodoxy and traditions, watching the cost-of-living index and imagining that in the process it is furthering the interests of the workers.

Petty, that's the word. Except that the very act of saying it seems to be the ingratitude of a miner's son at Oxford, and represents, somehow, some kind of betrayal. Or does it?

Just gimmicks
Isis, 4 June 1958

Eight great thoughts, and all of them local ones. And there, maybe, lie the limits of undergraduate weekly editorials. But although accepting much of the spirit of this, sometimes one just has to be pompous or portentous, and occasionally we can take ourselves seriously. But with caution, since looking back to the *Isis* of the 1930s is apt to be a painful experience, for there on the pages like our own are strewn clear and bold and vulnerable the passion and argument that was subsequently so cruelly rewarded. Was it all misplaced, are the young and articulate doomed to be foolish? Hitler is only a film comedian, claims one editor, and another assures the outside world that come what may young Oxford will not stoop to fighting to save the shabby and unjust capitalists. Yes, yes, you would want to shout back across the years, across the gulf of world war that has made us so different, yes, you had all the noble thoughts, the integrity, the courage – must it always be so horribly warped? Does it always dissipate when events become too hard to bear? There are plenty of people, of course, who want to draw fine parallels between the two situations, ours and theirs, but this is only to satisfy a nostalgia or give edge to a contempt, for we must reject these parallels, even if only out of the strutting pride of a generation's sense of identity. The collapse of all the great political myths sent up a cloud of dust that still obscures the sharpness of optimism or confidence. 'Why are you all so *angry?*' asked an American friend, genuinely bewildered by the attitudes of young Englishmen, and the question was difficult to answer. And yet not so long ago this country seemed to breathe with the same lungs; there was a sense of identity. All the revolt, the contempt for our institutions and leaders had merged incredibly into a genuine kind of national unity – see it, for example, in Orwell. 1945 seemed to carry on this happy rapprochement just a little further – turn back to the old *Horizon*, for example, and gape at the different atmosphere, share the strange mystique of participation.

But that's all gone now. Thanks to the stupid philistinism of the Labour Party, in part, and the resilience of the old, rotten traditions they were trying to attack. Now, and inevitably, the anger, the revolt has seeped back into the younger generation, incomprehensible though it may be to some. Reviewing 'The Angry Decade,' following on from the journalist's label-sticking, the *Sunday Express* asked if you wanted to sparkle at 'intellectual parties.' Well, do you? Then it's easy as pie – mug up your Osborne, Tynan, Anderson, Wilson and crowd, and there you are, you too can be 'angry.'

No thought about why, though. Hostility or blank incomprehension or fashionable amusement. 'Are you going all angry this term?' someone asked. 'All these attacks, the bomb, the monarchy, the Establishment, and so forth, bit of a gimmick, isn't it?' *No!* Maybe the great big emotional orgies have disappeared, as Jimmy Porter raves, but a great greyness has blanketed all the rest – Admass, a diluted welfare state, a sense of shame and disillusion, contempt for authority, a widespread desire to emigrate or cheat or compromise, a feeling of the flatness and bleakness of everyday England. Look at the American servicemen in Oxford, and you can almost argue that they in their confidence and vigour have more right to be here than we. 'Inhibition is more deadly than sincerity,' and how true. 'Undergraduates addressed by Teddy Boys' is the startling headline in the *Oxford Mail*. And there among the jukeboxes is an affinity of spirit, a revolt. They have the courage to express it in a trouser length, that's all, but how much do we share? Is it just the stupidity of being young?

No, it mustn't be. We have seen people a little older than ourselves shed many of their ideals, and make too many concessions. Happy little copywriters. But, pom-pom, 'do not commit against the confused and universal that which you do not wish it to do to you.' Personal commitment has degenerated into yet another of the okay worlds, garnishing the intellectual's reading list, but don't let us grow tired of it, *please*. Maybe it is easy to shine with the gloss of idealism amongst the gowns and coffee cups and chiming clock-towers, but surely it is possible to extend it beyond the stage of dark suits and sickly, manly smiles? In all the ranting and the anger typical of some of this generation (and characteristic even of this term's *Isis*) there is a core of dedication. Why, then, should we be so ashamed of our commitment? Rather our immaturity than Guy Mollet[96] or even Hugh Gaitskell, rather a contempt for the monarchy and many of our institutions than acquiescence in Suez, Cyprus, South and Central Africa, rather 'a certain vulgar rudeness' than the sterility of our elders and betters. Maybe, anyway. Warden Sparrow and Vice Chancellor Masterman[97] and the rest can bring out their brigades of 'honour,' but it was much, much better to have taken out those whitewash brushes by night. Don't let us forget those emotions; Selwyn Lloyd is still there, Macmillan renews acquaintance with de Gaulle, the Queen watches her horses and Brize Norton H-bombers fly over the dreaming spires and the new Woolworths, and the Conservative women dedicate themselves to restoring full capital punishment, or even the cat. Doesn't it all make you sick? Or does it make you certain of the need to be awake and articulate, pompous perhaps, but *alive*?

I am proud of my home and family...no obsession
Dean Forest Guardian, 5 September 1958

Sir,

Under the heading "Class" in your last issue was an item (unsigned, I might add) about my attitude to this subject, based, presumably upon an article I wrote for the *New Statesman* four months ago (not 'a few weeks ago' as was reported – I trust the writer *read* the article), and the unscripted TV interview of last week.[98] If this was meant as a news item it should not have contained pure *opinion*; and if it was meant as a comment upon a local person, then the writer should have been polite enough to sign it.[99] Anyway, the piece said that I was 'obsessed with class' (in what manner?) and continued, 'I very much doubt whether he (Dennis Potter) is typical of Foresters from working class homes who have secured admission to our older universities.'

To say that I am 'obsessed' with class is so curt an explanation of my attitudes, and so obviously capable of the worst possible meaning (snobs are obsessed with class), that I feel I must object. Presumably the writer considers class to be less important than I do, and that's just *his* opinion. Or perhaps he is being downright uncharitable, as was a Sunday newspaper some weeks ago,[100] whose opinion I am contesting through solicitor and counsel. I don't know, since the item is so badly written that it is capable of a hundred different meanings.

I admit without shame that I am very concerned (not 'obsessed') that class differences should exist in this country, concerned because I believe with all my heart that it is wrong and harmful that such barriers should exist. It is wrong that the worker should have to use a different lavatory or eat in a different part of the canteen to the 'staff,' wrong that the conditions of work should be so different, wrong that people should be able to purchase a superior education, wrong that men who work with their muscles should be regarded as in some way inferior to characters with gold-plated Daimlers and enough unearned money to paper every house in Coleford, wrong that accent should matter so much or that people should forget some of the happenings of the recent past.

My grandfather died of silicosis after years of thankless labour in the pits of South Wales and the Forest, unable to read or write. My father has worked in the pit for over 30 years, a time which includes unemployment and the 1926 strike. But I am very comfortable, thank you, at Oxford, and will probably enjoy quite a high standard of living. 'So what?' people may say – and this is where my 'obsession' creeps in. Yes, I *hate* class. I dislike the different languages, the different accents, the grossly different incomes, the different meal-times, the snobberies and the petty, strutting pride that divides up England. Shall I then, go on to Oxford without remembering all these things?

Shall I change my Forest accent, play for a different rugby team, use a different pub, change my habits, condescend to my friends, yap about how 'civilized' Oxford is, marry a girl from a different class? Shall I join the miserable Young Conservatives and try to convince the worker that this wretched, deceitful government is looking after his interests? Shall I change my meal-times, hold my head in the air and assume myself 'better' than the stock I am proud to have come from? Shall I cease to feel guilty about having things so easy while my father is at the coalface? Shall I shrug my shoulders and trumpet that class doesn't matter, and that the workers can be left to stew in their own juice?

No! A thousand times no! And yet so many so-called working class undergraduates, or working class people who have 'got on' do just that. I despise those who forget the class they came from, who say the workers are too class-conscious, too crude, etc, earn too much and so on: let those well-dressed creatures who criticize the miners, for instance, go and work in the pit for a month, then they might change their tune. Whether in the Army (where, incidentally, I refused the chance of a commission for this very reason), at University, in the factory, the mine or the home, class matters. Deny it, and you are blind. Look at the Royal Enclosure, Lady Docker, the debs and an average Officer's Mess, then turn to the cloth-caps, the poverty-stricken old age pensioner and an income spread of 20:1. Are Teddy Boys treated the same way as rowdy, braying fools at a smart Mayfair party? Does the 'old school tie' not help people get jobs – local factories included? Everyone knows the answers.

The only way to approach such a delicate and intricate subject as class is in personal and frank terms. This I have tried to do. Obviously some will be offended or will misunderstand. I had not thought it would include our local paper (did "Up Berry Hill" or "Stubbornyuddedness" and my various other contributions to your columns give the impression of snobbery, or of genuine regard for the people of the Forest?) I write about class only where I have seen its evils – at Oxford, still a place of champagne, debs' escorts and coloured waistcoats. What is happening to me there emphasises the gap between the working and middle classes, a gap I do not wish for and cannot help. Thus, I was deeply upset to have a servant, and so very concerned at being waited upon by a man with a son older than myself that, shamefully, for a moment on that first day I wanted him to think that I was middle class like the others. Is it an 'obsession' not to want to be waited upon by another human being? I got over the problem, and made a friend. Similarly, and with equal candour, I described tensions that are bound to be created now and then at home, and here it is the most delicate of all: I so love my father and mother that I dislike the world that makes them and hard-working people like them so justly suspicious of 'education' and Oxford. An ability to quote Latin has so often gone hand-in-hand with an ability to talk down to one's fellow men.

I am proud of my home and family – I challenge anyone to dispute this. It is this very pride that makes me class-conscious, a member of the Labour Party and concerned with the problems of identity when crossing class frontiers. Cannot you see that? Don't you realise that a class 'obsession,' as you unkindly describe my feelings, comes from a desire not to leave the working classes, and not to desert them as so many, many others have done in the past. Turn your attention to them.

Dennis Potter
Spion Kop
Joyford Hill
Coleford

Potter: 1
Isis, 21 January 1959

The Peter Simples and Strix-slops[101] have often pointed out to presumptuous young critics of the tight little isle that 'if you know a better 'ole, go to it.' And I suppose it is true that a good proportion of this post-war generation is beginning to ask the same question: to emigrate, or stay. The former course is attractive not simply because we could get out to much better material conditions, and, like Mikoyan, enjoy our fin-tailed motorcars and deep-freeze boxes, but because, from this distance, there seems to be less smugness, less suffocation and more purpose in the ethos of the younger nations. But it would be dishonest of me to pretend that I could live elsewhere. Love of place is something so fundamental that it must be divorced from the claims of jingoistic nationalism or sophisticated insularity, just as there are certain human truths and dignities that need have little or nothing to do with a Christian religion that points to them as evidence of its social worth. I could not attempt to give a full and rational justification for this emotion, least of all for the benefit of *Isis* advertisers, but it can be recognised in the merest greeting, or an overwhelming sense of place and a valid, if obscure, sense of community. The rather jaded nationalism of the old European countries is far less attractive, much less dynamic, than that of the old colonial territories, but regard for one's own culture and language, the vague identity of landscape, climate, a shared past, a necessary sense of continuity and, at the lowest level, the strength of habit and conditioned response to the familiar, can make love of place a real political and social force. Why is it, then, that socialists – and particularly young socialists – have to lower their eyes with something approaching shame when they admit to a regard for the country, and the region, of their birth?

In part, of course, the answer is obvious: all 'patriotism,' however liberally defined, is in some sense an abdication of individual responsibility; a muttering, sheep-like incantation to irrational gods. Allegiances are demanded that no socialist, and, indeed, no rational person, could possibly give, for authentic and individual existence is denied by the flag and the idea of the nation. But everyone recognises the dangers of this kind of *Daily Mail* bleat, with its savage thematic 'British Lion roars again' headlines. The more likely explanation for our juvenile mockery of established institutions and 'respectable' emotions can be discovered in the gap that exists between the England of popular legend and schoolroom maps, the England of our parents, and the facts of our quite pronounced and irreversible international decline.

Again, the past of this nation, patterned as it is into a huge and dubiously wealthy canvas of traditions, institutions and all that makes for hushed voices from BBC commentators, has come to belong to only one side in the political arena. Lord Hailsham is continually seeking to underline this point in his usual distressing way: 'The British,' he claimed, just before the Loyalists were removed in a thunder of blood and upturned benches, 'are a highly civilized and sophisticated people, and we (the Conservatives) are a very British party.' The past is thus presented by these highly civilised and sophisticated inheritors as a kind of packaged totality, where the struggles and emotions that made it are smoothed over with awesome talk of 'our heritage.' The burning, passionate radicalism of one age comes by degrees to be the dearly regarded, faintly stuffy convention of the next, and is used to blanket further reform or question the legitimacy of continual radicalism. 'We are all workers now,' claims a Tory cabinet minister and company director, and that bizarre organization Operation Britain[102] generates further euphoria in its self-appointed task of telling the British of British achievements by means of gigantic poster hoardings – we hold the speed record in this, or the largest in that. We are first in something else. We pioneered television, the peaceful uses of atomic energy, radar, and even invented the water closet. There are no bounds to British genius, from the lavatory upwards.

Indiscriminately, but passionately, every triumph, every success, no matter how small, how marginal or how short-lived is pressed into this tub-thumping service – be it in the ballet, theatre, cinema, sport or industry. The constitution itself is well-nigh perfect, the monarchy is magical, the Duke of Edinburgh can be guaranteed to ask intelligent questions at the slightest provocation, and even our unemployment figures are 'the envy of the western world,' according to Miss Olive Lloyd-Baker, a prospective Tory candidate in a mining constituency. A sickening, smug euphoria envelopes every activity, a great clucking of all the suburban hens takes the edge off any genuine achievement, and the young feel bound to qualify any real pride of success until even that appears hardly worth talking about. Many of the so-called angries mock as savagely as they do because they cannot share involvement in this xenophobia – they know only too well that their own 'revolt,' their own indignation, is likely to be woven into this fabric of self-congratulation. Criticising Britain from within is like beating with puny fists against a thick wall of sponge. Criticising her from without is only to provide examples of the ingratitude or understandable envy of foreigners. John Bull is like the classic villain of the silent screen – scream, my dear, for no one will hear you!

It's time to get out of the rut
Daily Mirror, 3 October 1959

Sir,

Labour remains the only possible instrument for carving a better society out of the smug, hypocritical espresso-bar froth of present-day England.

But why, oh why, is Labour so apologetic for its suggestion of radicalism?

Are we, who grew up in an atmosphere of comparative prosperity, to be denied the genuine vision of a really just and yet dynamic society?

Are we to be boxed up in the stale framework of 'Great Power' idiocies – H-bombs and all – we, who have heard talk of 'total destruction' or 'brinkmanship' since we first shaved?

Or will Mr Gaitskell learn to identify his future with the yearnings of a generation stifled by the mistrust of the prime glory of youth – generous radicalism?

Dennis Potter (24)
Dunheved-road North
Thornton Heath
Surrey

Mr Potter wins 10 guineas for today's STAR LETTER.

Paradise Gained: Dennis Potter on Television
Isis, 27 January 1960

This is the second of a series 'From Another Ladder' by ex-Editors of Isis.

Oxford was a nice place in which to live, but a better place to leave. My last memories are of sour and amusingly pedantic Professor Austin at a time-wasting *viva*, ridiculous to the extreme point of his rigorously banal linguistics.[103] At least I am free of all those parchment-backsided academic types, good at crosswords and even better at SCR intrigue[104] – free, too, of the frantic, desperately gay purposelessness of so much undergraduate life, with its inevitable and perpetual sense of frustration. I care not now that the Proctors remain as earnestly stupid, wrapped in their funny garb, or the Labour Club as reactionary or the Union as pompous. No, I am a citizen of the Great Outside – or, as the Editor of *Isis* puts it in his usual squalidly ambitious fashion, my feet are on Another Ladder.

I work for the BBC, a huge and strange organization facing at the moment its own confusion, its own uncertain pride and an honest ignorance of where it is supposed to be going. Unlike commercial television or the popular press, the public Corporation is unsure of itself. This comforting uncertainty I take to be, in part at least, the sign of bewildered integrity, a sight more wholesome than brash, cash-register certainty.

Indeed, I now think, with some important qualifications, that the BBC, despite its history of sycophantic, high-toned conformity, remains the *last*, positively the last, place where one can attempt to come to terms with this society of ours, where one can grapple with seemingly unquestionable cultural hierarchies, and translate feeling or any sort of creative ability into wider channels than can be reached, say, on the *New Statesman*, the *Guardian* or in an Oxford SCR. People As Well As Top People Tune To The BBC (how's that for a bright new slogan?) But, for these and the following remarks not to sound ludicrous, I must make it clear that I am talking about television rather than radio, and discussing potentialities rather than the past. Unless we think that the potential, the possible, is the more exciting, we would all do well to emigrate, leaving behind the present for the Bullingdon Club, S.P.B. Mais,[105] and those who deserve it.

On sound radio, the current assumption seems to be that people walk around with little buttons on their foreheads indicating 'Home' ('the broad middle section'), 'Light' and 'Third' (Wage Differentials in the Dominican Republic). Even the comedy shows are divided into two categories – 'fairly sophisticated' and 'less sophisticated,' although these are perhaps posh euphemisms for 'fairly funny' and 'less funny.' Television is a completely different world, however, with a smaller output, younger personnel and, above all, a rich competitor. I'll admit that the concept of public corporation television excites me more than I had anticipated: given the existence of television and the shimmery Admass society of which it is a part, then the remnant of an older and more ambiguous 'public service' ideal (whatever it may have meant to the prim and rather snooty culture-vultures of the past) has become a blessed, a valuable anachronism. Our cultural situation has changed so rapidly that the BBC, once the despair of so many, has become a crucial sector in the fight against slap-happy commerce and the social power of the canned food tycoons. Its traditional 'balance' and 'impartiality' are both capable of much more flexibility than one at first assumes, and at least imply that optimistic 'admystification' is only one side of the question. These things can be woven into a personal response and a personal view without the kind of sordid concessions expected – and demanded – elsewhere. They need not *necessarily* lead to dead-weight quietism or relentless exploration of the platitudinous and the uninteresting – if I thought they did, I would look for another job.

No, the irritations are of a different and more manageable order. Television, for all its youth, has quickly made for itself a series of myths, dogmas and fears which can only upset bumptious newcomers like myself. The camera too often appears a thing to be feared, and 'ideas' are part of this general flatness: hence the dull, predictable discussions across low coffee-bar type tables, the quick, pointless 'entertaining' man-in-the-street montage interviews, and the relentlessly ironed out appearance of so much interesting and lively material.

Yet these are technical objections, and not final condemnations. In little more than a year my training to be a television producer will be coming to an end. And, emphatically, I feel confident that I can both be happy and constructive in the job – especially when I think of certain scenes and movements, of the visual expression and clarification of ideas and emotions important to me, of people's faces, old people's faces, Teddy Boy swagger, upturned faces, of long-fingered hands, nervously expressive hands, of town streets and ugly factories, of someone walking without going anywhere, of a pop singer coiled around a microphone, children leaping across a hop-scotch square, a slag heap steaming with its own inner combustion and grey streets pushing up their shapes to the rain – and hundreds of moments and impressions sidling, leaping or lying exhausted before the mind and eye of the camera. Television has to come to terms, in its own distinctive fashion, with problems around us more subtle, more confusing and yet somehow more urgent than in the past. I think, too, that television can do this more completely, more excitingly, than any other medium, thanks to its immediacy and its audiences. But television is still in its weaning stage, and to work within it gives one opportunities never dreamed of before – opportunities and dreadful warnings. The misuse of television will be the most important crime to add to existing misuse of literacy – and I like to think that at Oxford we were perhaps training for something like this: I cannot convey what a relief it has become to *do* things and not just talk about or evade them in lazy undergraduate terminology. In short the opportunities given (and often encouraged) at the BBC far outweigh the numerous reservations one must have, and must keep, about so large an organisation. The Admass society is full of real pockets of resistance.

The Establishment
Ten O'Clock, BBC Home Service, 6 October 1961

The Establishment[106] is a mock name for a night club devoted to satire against all the established powers that be, from God Almighty to Macmillan and the bomb almighty. It is, in other words, a place for sticking out tongues, for the irreverent, the blasphemous and the politically disenchanted. A place that London needed.

But satire or even the mildest form of literary rebellion in this country is soon absorbed by those who are its targets. The sleek hands of fashion, of applause in Beaverbrook newspapers and acclaim in the glossy magazines reach out to strangle it; every revolt is made painless, marginal, *cute* even.

Perhaps this is why I left The Establishment last night feeling pretty fed up. All around me was the sweet smell of success. Middle class voices tinkled with all the gentleness of a hammer on broken glass; a sweating waiter pushed a way through the milling horde with scallops-in-wine-sauce-with-mushroom, and outside, in the sleazy wet Soho street, a few anxious proles pressed their noses against the windows as though this really were the Establishment itself, or, at least, a fashionable gathering place for Top People.

The whole affair, indeed, went with a bang. And since the only truly valid kind of success for a place like this is *failure* so far as fashion is concerned, I am not sure that the establishment of The Establishment are feeling wholly satisfied this morning. If, however, they *are* happy about it all, then they might as well resign themselves to becoming 'smart' rather than poisonously clever.

Last night the only obviously non-Establishment type accents came from a small group of the more weary and cynical of the many journalists. They gathered round one of the deb-type girls employed by the Club to help publicity, and were baiting her pretty successfully. 'I'm not saying any more,' she flounced eventually, 'you're just jealous of success.'

'I've been working *damned* hard all vac,' a distant voice brayed, and a nearby face as well-bred as that of a racing greyhound murmured loftily to a girl with a flower on her back: 'Isn't it all gorgeously funny?'

Later, a small number of the assembled hundreds from Oxford, Cambridge, Hampstead and Chelsea managed to see some of the satirical turns.

I can't give an honest impression of the cabaret itself, unfortunately, because I was part of a milling crowd jostling uncomfortably on the fringe, trampling eagerly upon each other. What little I did see, I'm sorry to say, was too mild, and a lot too cosy, as much a part of the real Establishment in its way as a republican joke cracked in the Royal Enclosure. A row of masked Macmillans struck me as less funny than the real thing. The audience was conspiratorially in an 'aren't we clever' sort of mood. Someone gave a passable imitation of a working class accent. There was much generous applause, no heckling, nothing to get alarmed about. I've heard more entertainingly vicious remarks in a working-men's club, but places like that don't charge £2 a year membership fee.

As I turned to go, elbowing one of the mercifully few dinner jackets in the midriff, I was comforted by a Fellow of All Souls, the alleged headquarters of the *real* Establishment. 'Never mind,' he said. 'It's the best satirical night club we've got.'

And the best remark of all greeted me from a character with a cigarette holder, languidly draped over the bar. 'Jolly good idea, this,' he burbled, 'we *ought* to be able to laugh at *ourselves*.'

Flyover in my eyes
Daily Herald, 18 November 1961

The blue ribbon has been cut, and the Hammersmith flyover declared open.

It is, I admit, a beautiful thing, a cross between a Roman aqueduct and a Hollywood epic, soaring above earth-bound streets in an ecstasy of concrete, cable and sheer bravado.

But I *hate* it.

You see, I live on the top floor of a block of flats on a bloodshot-eye level with the thing. Only a few yards of exhaust-laden air separates us from The Start Of A New Age, as Transport Minister Marples threateningly called the flyover.

The only other intimate link I have with the future, apart from my pension payments, is the fact that my silver wedding anniversary falls, very nicely thank you, in 1984, Orwell's year of prophetic doom.

But this flyover is here and now. Zoom…zooOOOM!… Cars, trucks, coaches hurtle in front of our windows like chariots in the air. At night, headlamps and huge concrete standards, pouring out their orange lights, penetrate our heavy curtains with contemptuous ease. We can see to read without turning on the light.

And when I do get off to sleep, the flyover, like some telepathic monster from some other planet, infiltrates between my eyelids and creeps into the deepest reaches of sleep. Zoom…zooOOOM!

The opening ceremony was, for us, merely the final twist of the knife. For months and months they have been building The Start Of a New Age…pneumatic drills, monstrous, creaking cranes, shouting foremen, acetylene burners, bulldozers, portable radios, and all the other things which more than justify a tea-break.

I spent a little time leaning out of the window, in a vain attempt to foment a strike, when our second baby was born one warm night in July,[107] but she came into the world while a grotesque new machine was dropping concrete girders into position with all the gentility of a front-row rugby forward bearing down on a tiny full-back.

But we have had to come to terms with the New Age. The light, after all, saves us electricity, and if we confuse the coming of the posse on *Wagon Train* with the passing of a lorry loaded with barrels of beer, such mingling of sound-effects all adds to the fun.

'That clean, clear, country feeling…' the voice on the commercial began. Zoom, ZooOOOM…went the flyover.

'And what do you say to this?' asks the television interviewer of some pompous ass. As the fellow opens his mouth to say something, a motor-coach with rusty nails in the engine censors what he has to burble.

That, at least, gives us one excuse for not shifting into the back rooms, as in the best science-fiction, we are coming to love as well as hate our new monster. Besides, the back rooms overlook an all-night bus garage.

Zoom!…if you know what I mean. ZooOOOM!

Pre-packed childhood
Sunday Times, 20 May 1962

Green Wood by Leonard Clark (Parrish)

A book about childhood, unbruised and idyllic, with pretty little drawings at the end of the decorative chapters…that, to me, is a dead formula (if a frequent one) where the illusion of movement is created by delicious spasms of sentimentality. 'Stay at peace in your shades, until I am able to call you forth, and place you in the foreground of memory,' writes Leonard Clark of his boyhood friends in the long ago, neatly combining the illusion of objectivity with the pre-packaged idea of childhood, to which you have to add only the flow of adult memory.

But if you lop off childhood and hold it up like a precious vase, your adult hands will tremble thus, and what is in reality a mere sequence of summer days without rain will come to sound as a faint, sweet sadness, carefully evocative, dewily 'poetic.'

Mr Clark writes of an Edwardian childhood in the Forest of Dean, mostly set in the steep little mining town of Cinderford, ugly but 'surrounded by trees, hills and fields.' He is excellent on the scenery of the Forest, humping up in a Gothic tangle between the Severn and the Wye. No one can write of this little island between the two rivers without catching some of its complex oddity, and Mr Clark can do it better than most.

But the years in between have acted as a filter, so that even if there is no flavour-blur, the harsh irritants have been trapped and thrown away. The place shimmers in memory, yet not in time. We are given a childhood which is that of recollection rather than creation, censored of childhood's dirty jokes, of hasty alliances and arbitrarily assigned victims.

Ultimately, even the Forest itself submerges under the weight of a 'past' seen so gently: in *Green Wood* the ugly power of the pit has gone, the defensive rituals of a closed, tight community do not bounce back into the 'foreground of memory.' This is an enjoyable book, but an artificial one. Childhood does not lie at peace in the shadows for any of us, and needs more than a rich satisfaction of prose to make us say 'Yes, that's how it must have been.'

At last – free speech is creeping into TV
Daily Herald, 29 September 1962

Let's begin this week with a story. It happened at the Lime Grove TV studios a few years ago, but I promise that it isn't fiction. A television producer who was entertaining a few prospective contributors to his documentary programme, noticed that someone had left the key in a small bureau next to the whisky and gin bottles.

When his last guest had gulped the last free drink, the producer (an inquisitive type) opened the drawer. Inside he found what can only be called an appallingly illiberal 'blacklist.'

On it was a list of names sent by a top administrator to a lesser administrator. Producers were not to be given permission to employ any of the people named. The legion of the forbidden included Communists, anti-Monarchists, militant atheists and other offensive types.

Our peeping producer put the list back carefully, locked the bureau, dropped the key behind the soda syphon – and told everyone he met.

And I tell the same tale because it shows how dangerous timidity of the BBC kind can be.

Politics cannot be regulated like a card game at a hotel in the Home Counties – even if we have weathered a decade of quietism in this country, where ideas were less important than levels of purchase tax and doctrinal differences mere expressions of personal animosity.

TV offered us lifeless, predictable 'discussions' between two official antagonists, further deluding people that the guts of politics were simply a matter of sloganising wrangling between pensionable tub-thumpers.

But the weary tempo of public life is changing. Dramatically so. And I am glad to say that the cautious, sanctimonious blacklist mentality of our TV controllers is being brushed aside by the bolder and more proficient presentation of *genuine* argument on our screens.

Almost unbelievably, the BBC have allowed four weekly journals to thunder out their own opinions in their own programmes. *Tribune* tore up a poster of Macmillan before the cameras, an action which would have given the blacklist compiler a heart attack.

ITV's *Questions in the House* and the BBC's *Gallery* have broken away from the tired old 'discussion' format; the first to show the doubts and the concrete substance behind the probing of our MPs in the Commons, the second to take cameras out into the streets and interlace the pompous or platitudinous language of statesmen with the halting voice of the people they represent.

Granada is pioneering the live showing of political conferences, and we had some splendidly uninhibited table talk from Boothby's dinner guests on ITV last Monday.

And next Monday *Panorama* comes back, with the promise of new style profiles of leading politicians that could be as sharp as cider apples.

Watching TV regularly, I can at last sense that our TV authorities are dropping the blacklist mentality, becoming bolder and technically more proficient in the difficult task of presenting genuine argument.

So my Once Upon a Time might end happily after all.

Greed in the corn
Daily Herald, 6 October 1962

Money, I agree, is nice. I like it. If someone offered me a lot of cash for doing nothing particularly useful on TV (like being Minister of Transport, say) I'd probably take it like a shot.

Most of us could be greedy if given the chance, but that is no reason why ITV should make greed the basis of one of their family entertainments. Which one? Well, I agree that there is an awful lot of rubbish to choose from, so here are two clues:

ONE: It decks out greed as jolly, rollicking fun, with a heap of back-slapping condescension and a cluster of corn-store jokes thrown in for good measure.

TWO: The star of the show, flapping the glad hand like a furniture salesman in a slum, is that figure for the age, the one and only Mr Hughie Green.

Yes, yes (give him a round of applause, folks) it's *Double Your Money*, the ITV quiz show which is still dribbling out its distasteful philosophy on Thursday nights.

Hughie has a lot of talent for lighthearted entertainment, but here the material forces him to be painfully, energetically 'sincere' ('now isn't that wonderful?'), with his great big helpless grin plastered across the screen.

An organ begins to play – a sure sign that somebody is ashamed of something – and a few hopefuls hop on stage in the same trance-like state in which people choose between two piles of washing in the commercials.

Then the questions start. But these, of course, are merely an excuse: tossing a coin would do just as well.

Telling hardworking Hughie whether or not a tom cat can have kittens is a little ritual designed to show what little effort is needed to win such a lot of nice crinkly banknotes.

If the prizes were book tokens or luncheon vouchers, this programme would deceive nobody with its syrupy mateyness. In other words, *Double Your Money* has no intrinsic entertainment value beyond the cheap thrill of watching someone grab all he can get.

I cannot see one good reason why the ITA should not sweep this banal quiz game back into the dustbin where it belongs, and release Mr Green for the kind of happy-go-lucky entertainment he can provide so well. For he – as we realize when the last desperate smile has faded from the screen – is the biggest victim of the lot. It takes more than organ music to compensate for this pitiful waste of his talent.

TV *can* make religion dramatic
Daily Herald, 17 November 1962

Nowadays most of us are only nominally interested in organized religion, and come Epilogue time we switch off a TV priest a great deal faster than we would a cowboy.

And that, I think, is how it should be. For the obligation is on the religious departments of both channels to appeal to us in ways more exciting and more instantly relevant than they have done in the past.

Television may have a duty to interest us in religion, but it has no mandate to bore us to tears with it. Religion, like politics, can of course be meaningful and dynamic on television. There is certainly nothing intrinsically ludicrous in using the mass media to challenge our bloated and callous materialism.

But religion – again like politics – can be thrown at us simply because some prestige-conscious tycoon or nervous administrator thinks it *ought* to be slotted in somewhere on a dull Sunday afternoon. When this happens what we see on our screens is often a mish-mash of tatty and condescending humbug.

While now and then there are speakers with conviction and presence, frequently the spokesmen – of all sects – we see are like parodies of bumbling clergymen in a malicious and badly written atheistic novel. One divine, I swear, had to look down at his notes when halfway through the Lord's Prayer. Another prominent cleric, swathed in purple vestments like an elderly Kewpie doll, so insulted his eager teenage questioners that I was avidly waiting for some sort of punch-up to follow.

Granada TV is currently showing us that it is possible to discard the little tricks and stale language of religious broadcasting. In the series *I Believe*, on Monday nights, the viewer is presumed to be intelligent yet not passionately interested in the claims of religion. A valid assumption.

Last Monday the subject of the programme was the Chief Rabbi, Dr Israel Brodie. There was none of the tedious flog-you-salvation grinning which some telepriests mistake for 'sincerity.' Dr Brodie sat quite still. He spoke very slowly…at almost dictation speed. At first sight, a dreary programme. But Dr Brodie's face was full of mobility, the dynamic mobility of passion and belief. There are few things more thrilling on TV than the considered expression of a body of ideas by someone with the conviction and dignity to make them dramatic.

I hope all the Epilogue mongers were watching. Television, they should know, is more and more a market place for conflicting ideas, slogans and attitudes. Those who presume too much upon our goodwill will deserve the indifference, even hostility, they will reap.

This TV newcomer smiles as she bites
Daily Herald, 26 November 1962

Satire – or how to laugh when something is gripping your throat and trying to shake you to death – is getting a foothold in the most unlikely places nowadays. And now even Auntie BBC, nervously prepared to forget its obligations to the old ladies and retired colonels of Cheltenham, is having a go.

This morning the Corporation officials (who didn't sleep very well over the weekend) are surprised to learn that the public are delighted, rather than offended, with the new satirical tele-revue, *That Was the Week That Was.*

On Saturday night the lollipops were put away, the carving knives whetted. *That Was the Week That Was* gave us an hour-long mixture of cabaret, punch-up comedy and heartless assassination worthy of a gang of articulate Teds in the Athenæum.

One or two items fell flat, as is inevitable in an opening programme, but more than enough blows thudded home for the purple bruises to be counted.

There was, for instance, an outrageous onslaught on that renowned angel-maker pop-music man Norrie Paramor who 'takes all the messy unpredictability and excitement out of music.' Poor (figuratively speaking) Norrie's candyfloss orchestrations were cruelly used to illustrate the justice of this and other more brutal claims. We will probably never be able to listen to that gooey syncopation in quite the same helpless fashion again.

Then Bernard Levin – who exults in the label of odious – grandly but calmly insulted a panel of public relations consultants. He called their trade both corrupt and (what probably upsets them even more) incompetent.

Best of all, perhaps, was the electronic insanity of a Party Political Broadcast on behalf of Independent ex-Service candidates who flooded the recent by-election scene. This was flung at us with barrack-room aplomb by a damp lance-corporal in the Cape and Gas Mask Store, catching both blanco-choked rhythms of Army speech and the political claptrap more usual on these occasions. The brave corporal referred predictably to those living East of Suez as 'wogs' and 'nig-nogs.' He proposed in trenchant style 'to clear the nancy boys out of the security jobs.' I suspect that if this scabrous little exercise in denim politics had been shown before polling day last week, an ex-Service candidate might have saved his deposit.[108]

That Was the Week That Was was written by a variety of people with chips, rather than pips, on their shoulders. And its importance lies not so much in the witty asides ('Harwich for the Continent, Paris for the inContinent') or in the zestful performances of Millicent Martin and David Frost as the two 'stars,' but in the fact that it ever got on to the television screen.

'We put this on because we have a feeling there is a large audience late on Saturday night prepared to listen to comment which is funny and impudent,' says the producer, Ned Sherrin.

But a year or two ago such a programme would not have been considered, let alone produced. Somewhere in the long, drab corridors of the Lime Grove studios, a burp of irreverence, a raspberry of impudence has not been hidden behind the hand. Instead, wildly funny, dubiously improper, it has been allowed to burst on to our screens.

And the reaction? Only two people bothered to telephone Auntie with allegations of 'bad taste.' Three more (who may be public relations consultants) objected to Mr Bernard Levin. And – most astounding of all – 83 people telephoned their congratulations.

Maybe after all, staid, cautious, cunning old Auntie knew what she was doing all along.

Secret of *Coronation Street*
Daily Herald, 12 January 1963

In a week which included the French mime artists on BBC, a workmanlike ATV documentary on the Russian-Chinese quarrel, a *Panorama* portrait of Harold Macmillan, and Steptoe senior actually taking a bath, it may seem perverse to turn to that old familiar, *Coronation Street*.

But, sooner or later, every TV critic has to steel his nerves to grapple with this astonishingly popular serial.

Twice a week this backstreet drama trundles on to our screens, completely unaffected by savage criticism or lyrical praise.

I first watched this programme with a certain affected disdain, my critical faculties crippled by some of the sniffy, coffee-bar comments I had heard about it. But now I switch on almost eagerly. *Coronation Street* has become for me one of the most consistently *enjoyable* half-hours on TV.

Yet no one could pretend that this apparently drab little serial is either great drama or accurate documentary. The virtually unavoidable necessity of introducing tension and surprise (stock ingredients of any episodic yarn) frequently burdens the programme beyond all hope of credibility.

Nevertheless, I keep returning to it, caught by the lively surges of dialogue and closely-coiled strands of warm intimacy. The characters are now so familiar that the scriptwriters can begin to shed the husks of caricature and dig deeper into motive, mood and aspiration.

I think that the writers could afford to be bolder than they are. But we can still be jolted by vividly-composed passages which crash out of the humdrum plotting as excitingly and unpredictably as a six-hit in a dull cricket match.

Inevitably, perhaps, a cartload of corny sentimentality and shamelessly contrived humour bumps noisily along in the background. This is part of the high price to be paid for overexposure and excessive concern with the TAM ratings.[109]

Even so, *Coronation Street* has managed to steer clear of its most obvious temptation – the mannered degradation of stage-charlady speech.

It used to be assumed in the lower reaches of TV drama that the inarticulate lacked feelings and that regional accents were merely an excuse for condescending comedy. After all, the basic fallacy propagated by our class-choked educational system is that people who work with their hands are somehow incapable of either deep feelings or finely pointed sensitivity.

I like to think that *Coronation Street* holds its popularity because of the brash but heartening manner in which it has kicked aside such a squalid heresy.

Stop nagging at us!
Daily Herald, 9 February 1963

There was once a Hollywood film, harmless and mediocre, called *None But the Lonely Heart*. In America's dark days of doubt it was hauled before the Senate Committee on Un-American Activities.

During the Goon-like testimony, a Mrs Leila Rogers solemnly and ludicrously declared that 'the movie is un-American because it is gloomy.'

Everyone knew what she was talking about. The film had no sugared pill, no cheerful moral, no little package of orthodox opinions to foist on our unwilling heads. For there is an unwritten law that the organs of mass culture – cinema and now, even more so, television – should keep our noses clean. Better still, they should keep on nagging at us to smile, darn ya, smile.

Gangsters are never allowed to win, pessimists are seen not to prosper, allied soldiers are never defeated, nice men never fail to get their girl, cowboys always gun down the outlaws. The great bulk of drama on TV ends like advertisements on the escalators, with a distinct note of uplift.

Yet this is a far from cheerful prospect. The little screen bullies us all the time. We are lectured at, sniped at and slapped on the back by large, fatherly hands.

This week, for instance, ATV began an ambitious new series, *The Plane Makers*. Each hour-long episode is set in an imaginary but very convincing aircraft factory and purports to show us the rhythms of industrial life from workbench to panelled boardroom. A laudable aim, certainly.

But propaganda had to sidle on to the scene. The one dramatic sequence in the hour showed a rather dim-witted apprentice disobeying safety regulations. Predictably, he was punished by getting his arms crushed in a power press.

Immediately we discerned the bleak outlines of yet another lecture. I was waiting to see the words OBEY SAFETY REGULATIONS AT ALL TIMES come up with the credit titles at the end.

Bad scripts and unimaginative plots are made worse, not better, by introducing little snippets of sanctimonious advice.

When PC Dixon pads forward to tell us to look out for old ladies on pedestrian crossings, we are seeing what is basically a half-hearted attempt to introduce realism into a phoney programme.

And when Dr Kildare gazes mistily into the white tiles to deliver some pitiful little aphorism about Social Responsibility, the only decent reaction is to switch the rubbish off.

I appeal to script editors and producers to slice out all these dreary cant phrases and stale passages of second-hand indoctrination. We don't take any notice of them anyway.

Entitled to Know: Nationalization Pamphlet
Co-written with David Nathan
That Was the Week That Was, BBC-TV, 2 March 1963

Originally performed by Willie Rushton, David Frost, Kenneth Cope, Lance Percival, David Kernan and Millicent Martin.

WILLIE: *(Holds pamphlet 'Entitled to Know'.)* Here it is, then, the first clod of pure mud in the next General Election campaign. This is the new Conservative pamphlet based on sentences and half-sentences torn out of Labour Party policy documents and speeches *proving* that *hundreds* of firms are going to be nationalized if – or should it be when – Labour gets into power. And since nationalization is going to be the rude word of the campaign, Labour itself can use the same techniques to Tory speeches and pamphlets. Every quote is guaranteed. The people are *entitled to know*.

DAVID F: Really, you know, these meddling, doctrinaire Tories have a dismal record of nationalizing everything in sight. In 1887 they first gave *compulsory* powers for the *public* purchase of land. They provided public baths and public post-offices. In 1926 they set up the public Central Electricity Board; in 1933, the London Passenger Transport Act. And then, gorging themselves with a great private industry they *nationalized civil aviation* in 1939 by purchasing Imperial Airways and British Airways to make BOAC. *Why?* The Tory pamphlets explain.

WILLIE: *(Reading.)* 'The development of farsighted, long-range policy in British aircraft production cannot be attained by private companies. A public corporation can raise capital more cheaply.'

SLIDE: 'Threatened Firms: Handley Page, Gloster Aircraft Co., Saunders-Roe, Rolls-Royce.'

DAVID F: In 1945, the Conservative Party committed itself to a Water Act with *public boards* – and an extension of the Forestry Commission! 10 years later the Tory Government opened Calder Hall and *deliberately extended nationalization to the field of atomic power stations*. Oh, yes. For, as they said:

WILLIE: *(Reading.)* 'Conservatives realise that there is no clear-cut division between nationalization and other forms of industrial organisation.'

SLIDE: 'Threatened Firms: Woolworths, Boots, Unilever, ICI.'

DAVID F: In 1955 the Tories also set up a new public authority in Scotland. Oh, yes. They called it the South of Scotland Electricity Board.

KEN: 'These arrangements have considerably improved and strengthened the administration of Scottish affairs.'

DAVID F: Worse by far, the Tories in their hated National Parks legislation have taken over the Cambridgeshire coast, the Pembrokeshire coast, the North Yorkshire Moors, Exmoor and *large parts* of the Yorkshire Dales. As Sir Anthony Eden put it in October 1954:

LANCE: 'The use of property must be conditioned by the need to preserve the countryside or to secure development for *sound public purposes*.'

SLIDE: 'Threatened Areas: Lake District, Bodmin Moor, New Forest, BOW.'

DAVID F: It is, unfortunately, true, that the Labour Party nationalized a few firms…but only the dead-beat ones, the failures. The Tories, on the other hand, see these industries as a platform for *yet further advance*. In 1951, for instance, Tory MPs Ted Leather and Harold Watkinson issued a pamphlet full of praise for public ownership.

DAVID K: 'Conservatives believe that in the nationalized industries is to be found an *ideal proving ground*, where the Government should pioneer advances in labour relations and management techniques as an *example* and a *spur* to *(Sneers.)* private enterprise.'

DAVID F: Oh, yes. Labour policy offers every man a house and a car. But the Tories built more *public houses* and then made hissing noises at the *private car*. In February 1962, a Tory document ominously called *Change and Challenge* declared:

MILLY: 'The private car *cannot supersede* public transport. Experience has proved that *free movement* within a town or city is only possible by *public transport.*'

DAVID F: And if big companies like Ford think they can wriggle out of that one, let them ponder on this savage Tory remark in a Conservative Political Centre pamphlet of 1950!

WILLIE: 'Large undertakings tend by their nature to be bureaucratic... when the form of control is out of date and unadaptable, complete nationalization might represent a freeing of endeavour.

SLIDE: 'Threatened Firms: Ford (again), Woolworths (again), Rolls-Royce (three times).'

WILLIE: 'Unlike the Labour Party, the Conservative Party would not have a slogan of nationalization for 30 years and discover, when in office, that there was great difficulty in giving effect to it.'

DAVID F: And that is no idle boast. The Labour Party had been content to nationalize only the medical profession, but the *One Nation* Tory pamphlet of 1950 went further.

LANCE: 'The present scheme is not really comprehensive. Many services have yet to take their full part...chiropody is an obvious example!'

SLIDE: 'Threatened services: Chiropody, plastic surgery, faith healing.'

DAVID F: And then, in 1954, the Tories set up *public slaughterhouses*.

KEN: 'The general policy, which will take some years to work out, is to work towards a moderate concentration of *slaughterhouses throughout the country.*'

SLIDE: 'Threatened Animals: Cows, sheep, pigs, poultry.'

DAVID F: Yes, the Tories were getting bloodthirsty all right. Not content with the *public* slaughter of your meat, the Tory policy document *The Right Road for Britain* demanded a *determined public policy* for the fishing industry.

DAVID K: 'It is of the greatest *public* importance to preserve the fertility of the fishing grounds. We shall enact legislation to set up a White Fish Marketing Board.'

DAVID F: Mac Fisheries – please note! Bird's Eye Fish Fingers – beware! You have been warned! Tory meddling with private enterprise has a long and sad heritage. Winston Churchill first advocated nationalization of railways in 1919.

WILLIE: 'There is a broadening field for state ownership and enterprise, especially in relation to monopolies of all kinds.'

DAVID F: But this wretched faith is not confined to the past. Lord Hailsham is the voice of Toryism rampant, and in his Penguin Special *The Case for Conservatism* – written when he was a Hogg – he makes even more threats.

WILLIE: 'The Conservatives have instituted or helped to institute a variety of different forms of public ownership and control which they see no reason to repent of doing. The collection of the variety of forms of public ownership *cannot yet be regarded as complete.*'

DAVID F: What a prospect, ladies and gentlemen! We can, thanks to the Tories, cook our publicly-bred fish or publicly-slaughtered meat with publicly-owned electricity and drive to our publicly-owned offices in our publicly-owned transport which may soon run on publicly-owned atomic power. Or we can walk the publicly-owned pavements until our private feet need the attentions of a publicly-owned chiropodist or soaking in a bowl of publicly-owned water drawn from a publicly-owned reservoir in a publicly-owned mountain district patrolled by a publicly-owned aircraft. (*He has read this at the fastest possible speed, and now gasps for breath.*) Set (*gasp*) the people (*gasp*) free! Labour freedom works! Hands off private industry!

WILLIE: (*Tapping DAVID F on shoulder.*) Would you kindly control yourself, sir? You are, after all, speaking on the publicly-owned British Broadcasting Corporation. And the Tories did that, too.

CHORD

Culture leaps out of its cage
Daily Herald, 9 March 1963

Smells of chalk and sounds of creaking chairs! The idea of an illustrated lecture is not, to say the least, immediately palatable.

I recall a boring little man with bald head and gravel voice, who once made me shrivel with anguish as he droned on and on and on about a Greek temple. His magic lantern threw cocoa-coloured pictures on the classroom wall.

Surely then, it would be unthinkable, in this age of candy-bright commerce, to put an hour-long lecture about classical music on our television screens at a peak hour?

But that's just what Granada did on Wednesday night.

'What is a melody?' asked Leonard Bernstein, facing an audience of some 2,000 children in Manchester's Free Trade Hall. I thought I caught a spasm of misery on the faces of the orchestra behind him, and I reached for the switch with venomous alacrity.

But wait a moment.

'The melody,' said Mr. Bernstein, 'is the real meat and potatoes of music.' This was decidely *not* magic lantern language, and I decided to listen for a while.

Leonard Bernstein, versatile conductor of the New York Philharmonic, is no ordinary mortal. Some Americans, indeed, think him a reasonable approximation to the Almighty – and Mr B himself looks as though he considers the comparison to be just.

Soberly handsome in his dark suit and gleaming triangle of pocket handkerchief, he stood at the rostrum like a Liberace with brains – and spoke with the prowling persuasiveness of a Perry Mason.

'Don't you *ever* be scared of counterpoint,' he smiled, taking us firmly by the hand as we tripped gaily through the melodic complexities of the Masters. 'There, you see how *simple* it is?'

Humming "Mack the Knife", alluding to Cliff Richard, talking of countdown and three-stage ballistic missiles, Bernstein is prepared to use almost any old image to get his lesson across. 'Now let's listen to the whole sandwich,' he cajoles, matily referring to a fragment of Mozart, 'top slice, bottom slice, and clarinet filling.'

These methods worked spectacularly. Their jumping-bean urgency showed again that TV is too willing to draw a sharp boundary between so-called 'education' and so-called 'entertainment.' Adult education and arts programmes are carefully and clinically segregated from the main category of TV fare, like virus bags trapped in a sterile bottle.

Bernstein proved that, given enthusiasm, energy and uninhibited language free of the pretentious verbiage of professional culture-vultures, TV can break free of the cosy minority-cult atmosphere, still clinging to arts programmes.

Must we leave this advance to the Americans, too?

This was a glorious wallop
Daily Herald, 30 March 1963

The gaudy banners unfurled, drums rolled, distant guns thundered and the short, dread rhythm of marching feet broke from the screen.

Granada's marathon production of *War and Peace*[110] on Tuesday seemed about to choke on the rainbow Errol Flynnery of Hollywood costume drama.

Time after time, I have seen the little screen rupture itself by contriving an ill-advised flamboyancy or tarted-up grandeur. But here, before the shrill trumpets had died away, a figure in a neat lounge suit stepped out of the chaos and blandly announced that he was going to tell us a story.

Any narrator who leads us through the massive complexities of such a great novel is bound to irritate at first. He cannot help sounding like a cross between Huw Wheldon and Ernest Marples.

This one was more than the chain yoking the fragments together. He was also a war correspondent, liberator of ideas, God-like observer and a brisk spokesman for other characters. He made sense out of it all.

Even more important, the part of the narrator in this superb production showed convincingly that the simple, naturalistic, tediously 'authentic' drama is not the only way of liberating the TV play.

Granada used a slightly shortened version of the brilliant Piscator-Neumann-Prüfer adaptation of *War and Peace* – a work that has a long overdue message for drama departments. The message (perhaps wisely left out of Tuesday's production) packs a glorious wallop: 'For us,' the adaptors say, 'the theatre is not a place for anaemic, cautious, art-for-art's-sake, but the last surviving platform of prophecy, a place in which to proclaim, to judge, to confess, to shock.'

Assess the bulk of TV drama by these belligerent standards and you are left with the putrid froth of decaying candy floss. Recently we have sickened over a sticky pile of plays[111] caked together by tape recorder observation. Everything is so damned 'authentic' that we can hear something just as good, or bad, in the chatter at the bus stop.

Tomorrow night at nine, however, the BBC promises us the first nugget from 'a new season of TV plays on contemporary themes.' Let's hope that the people responsible have realized that the time has come to cry halt to all the repetitive and purposeless ventriloquism we have suffered of late.

Granada's telemarathon was more than just a thrilling experience. It must also be the launching pad for a great deal more thought about the uses and possibilities of good television drama.

Don't be so T–Victorian
Daily Herald, 3 August 1963

An ancient libel claims that the British act more kindly towards their dogs than to their children. So far as our offspring are concerned, we still faithfully follow the heavy-handed dictum of our starch-collared forefathers – that children should be seen and not heard.

Even more depressing than this betrayal of the toddler's right to be a noisy and grubby nuisance is the equally rigid Victorian attitude about children's entertainment. This week, for instance, the Independent Television Authority's annual report promises yet another of those woolly-minded, sanctimonious 'codes for producers' concerning children's television.

I agree wholeheartedly with the demand that TV producers should be responsible people fully aware of the social consequences of their trade. This is a far more urgent topic than the mere turnip-counting of so-called audience ratings. Such responsibility applies to every type of programme.

Yet instead of a purposeful survey of the role and influence of the most potent means of communication ever invented, we get these little dribbles of humbug about children's viewing.

I may be in a minority of one, but I do not believe that it is disastrous if children enjoy a violent piece of fiction. Indeed, if we accept any other assumption, then the Brothers Grimm and Hans Christian Andersen must be the biggest corruptors of children in history. Beheaded giants, abandoned waifs, cackling ogres and the long-fanged cannibalism of the evil gingerbread witch are part of all our childhoods. Don't let cosy adult nostalgia blur the fact that we responded to these lurid fantasies with white hot imagination and nailbiting apprehension.

Children are not the innocent little sunbeams of Sunday school mythology. If they were, the later onslaught of the wicked grown-up world would tear gaping holes in their flimsy sensibilities. The issue is less that of violence and far more that of the social values implicit in *all* television. I personally would be much more upset if my children grew to accept the values paraded in *Double Your Money* than if they saw a pirate with a cutlass driven into his heart.

Maybe this argument is intolerable to some parents. But I wish there was more debate before these proliferating 'codes' were drafted. Otherwise, we may foist antiseptic cotton-wool programmes upon our children. And then, instead of protecting the young, we shall merely blunt their fertile imaginations.

And everyone seemed slightly ashamed
Daily Herald, 26 August 1963

First rehearsals are painful: chalk marks, stutters and rustling scripts. Even such a tried and trusted team as the Dock Green constabulary[112] splutter back into life like an elderly car on a frosty morning.

All except Old George, of course. For Jack Warner slips into PC Dixon's well-worn uniform as easily and as comfortably as a foot into a familiar bed sock. After all, he's been doing it now for eight years.

'I treat it like a business,' he told me yesterday, taking a breather from the camera and the plaster prison of the sets. 'I've had a good holiday and I'm ready for our 10th series.'

An anxious looking make-up girl in blue overalls scurried forward to examine his hair line. 'Could you pencil a little farther in?' she pleaded.

Actors dressed as policemen prowled round the studio floor, a civilian slouch hat still betraying their pretence.

'Right!' snapped the floor manager, ears encased in awkward headphones. 'The fight scene, please!' Dock Green was slowly coming to life for the new series.

First, a frozen silence, an artificial immobility. Then the sudden eruption of violence, collapsing almost immediately into embarrassed throat clearing.

Punch-up and Dock Green, one feels, do not mix easily. Everyone seemed slightly shamefaced. Old George himself looked momentarily peeved.

'Isn't this more like *Z Cars?*' I asked maliciously.

'I must be careful what I say,' Dixon replied, immediately defensive. 'The only difference is that they're on wheels and I'm on my feet.'

But consider the two worlds of Dock Green and *Z Cars*. They are poles apart, like the slang of two generations. It is the difference between Gracie Fields and The Beatles, or front-room pictures of Highland cattle and the restless sploshes of an action painter.

Dock Green is the stewed tea of television. As English as a fly-blown transport caff. Superbly fashioned by its own standards, each series gives a great deal of harmless pleasure to a great many people. Fourteen million of us, in fact.

Yesterday, at the BBC TV Centre, I immediately got the feel of this famous show, despite the chalk mark, the confused pauses and the bad-tempered shouts for silence. Everything was safe, warm, predictable – and as full of uplift as a Hollywood starlet. Not that Old George ever would think of such a dubious image. To him, a woman is someone you help across the road. Even the Dock Green tarts have golden hearts. Dixon is virtue in uniform. We like him because he's not too clever, because he smiles, and because he's so very, very polite to his many betters.

His stories have a beginning, a middle and an end. We know exactly where we are, and where we are going. We know, too, that Old George will plod forward when the tale is over to give us some kindly advice about locking the front door at night.

'People look forward to it,' he said yesterday. 'And I know for a fact that my advice does a lot of good. My letters show that.'

Jack Warner is proud of Dixon. The part has become so built in to his own personality that he even refers to himself as 'an old copper.' And he walks like a policeman, too.

'The plain truth is that I enjoy it,' he smiled. The make-up girl began hovering around us again.

Afterwards, emerging in the shuttered and sleazy calm of a Shepherd's Bush Sunday, I hesitantly stopped a ponderous but kindly-looking policeman who had just been refusing to show a schoolboy the way to the nearest cigarette machine.

'Excuse me,' I said, 'but – speaking professionally – do you prefer George Dixon or the *Z Cars* men?'

'I haven't,' he replied, in the icy tone undoubtedly kept for making old lags move on, 'got any opinion on the matter at all.'

But, truth to tell, he *did* look a bit like Old George.

The sweet screams of success
Daily Herald, 14 October 1963

Amplified guitars throb-throb-throb into the thick, ear-cracking Mersey Beat. Open-mouthed fans scream with a strangely joyless, almost desperate abandon.

The Beatles once again vibrate the stage with the crude, electric surge of raucous sound.

Certainly this mop-headed outfit from Liverpool jerked last night's ITV Palladium show out of its tired and anaemic despondency. In collarless suits and tight trousers, with cocky grins flickering on their faces, the Beatles were undeniably entertaining in the furiously yobbish style now all the rave.

I thought their showmanship was extremely accomplished. Drummer Ringo Starr held himself momentarily poised – deliberately condensing the excitement in a half-second of alarming, scream-filled torment. Then came the shattering, driving plunge into the familiar thump-thump-thump that has made the Beatles such a fantastically popular foursome.

And like it or not, no one can deny that the group do not provoke a scalding, immediate response. Mine went the full circle from disdain to gleeful pleasure – and all the while the audience screamed and screamed, eventually unnerving even the performers themselves.

I won't say no to *Doctor Who*
Daily Herald, 30 November 1963

Huge, hairy spiders and giant psychopathic crabs. Web-footed monsters crawling painfully out of the slimy deep. Hideous, gurgling creatures wailing like wounded bagpipes, with single, blood-shot eyes swivelling menacingly in their jelly-like foreheads.

Say what you will about science fiction: its villains are utterly enchanting. For SF, as wide-eyed addicts have it, can be great fun. Even if it keeps you awake at night, such bilious fantasy is also a very potent means of throwing up vivid ideas about our more humdrum human predicaments.[113]

Disappointingly, TV has never really gone overboard for this type of adventure. True, the BBC almost paralysed social life years ago with three brilliant *Quatermass* serials, each as stunning as a kick in the forehead from a New Zealand rugby forward. But they followed Nigel Kneale's masterpieces with a windy and wordy weirdy named *Andromeda*.[114] Last year, too, Boris Karloff's terror-haunted features introduced an otherwise forgettable SF series on ITV.[115]

After that, almost nothing of note. The plastic monsters and foam-rubber spiders gather cobwebs in the props room along with the dust-choked theatre organ used in the far-off days of the nine-inch screen.

A crackerjack peak-hour SF serial launched this winter would soon zoom up the popularity charts – especially as British SF writers, both in output and quality, are undoubtedly among the best of a gloriously gruesome bunch.

Meanwhile, I shall watch with sympathetic interest the progress of the BBC's new Saturday afternoon serial, *Doctor Who*. This cliffhanger is about a distinctly Marples-free machine which transports four characters through space *and* time.

The programme is 'designed to bridge the family viewing gap between afternoon and evening audiences.' Fair enough. We need an escape from grunting all-in wrestlers and tongue-tied *Grandstand* commentators. Yet this official BBC description implies more action than ideas, something rather less-than-sophisticated in content. Kids' stuff, in fact.

However, today's episode sees us firmly, if unsafely, planted in Paleolithic times – or the Stone Age, if you don't read SF. And that will certainly make a diverting change of scene.

Mind you, it should come as no great surprise to find weekend TV plunging back amongst pterodactyls and cavemen. Those withered Hollywood repeats, for instance, have long since had the authentic odour of the Stone Age clinging to their celluloid.

Treasures of the past
Daily Herald, 14 December 1963

Every Monday on most ITV channels we are able to saturate ourselves in moody nostalgia by turning the clock back exactly 25 years. Back, if you can bear it, to a Europe sick to its very spine.

Next Monday, for example, as the cold comfort Christmas of 1938 approaches, there are silly pictures of Englishmen playing polo on bicycles and sickening ones of Germans launching a huge aircraft carrier.

Granada's weekly scrapbook, *All Our Yesterdays*, feeds on these old cinema newsreels with the slightly indecent relish of an old man recalling a youthful flirtation. Cemented together by the impassive, cool-headed comments of Brian Inglis, the dossier is certainly one of the most intriguing half hours in the weekly fare.

Every time television plunders the film libraries it finds so many nuggets of purest gold that I wish it would go back more often.

True, there has recently been a torrent of material unleashed from the past. The icily relentless French film record of World War I, for instance, or this week's boisterous compilation from Television Reporters International, *The Face of Fraud* (ITV).

The BBC have shown us a few scratchy, flittering feet of film of a gesticulating Lenin leaping to life against the backdrop of a gigantic red banner billowing in a bitter Moscow breeze. Truly the wind of change.

These figures from the past, preserved on film, are the flesh and bones of history. As exciting as almost anything we are likely to see on the little screen.

Unfortunately, cinema and television have been in conflict for so long, for so many harsh economic reasons, that programme makers too readily shut their minds off from the archives of the older art.

Yet who knows what glistening treasures lie mouldering in scattered libraries? Sad to say, a systematic search is rarely carried out. There is no single unit of either ITV or BBC solely responsible for such an undoubtedly tedious but potentially enriching job of research.

BBC2, however, are going to launch a gigantic series on World War I.[116] We may be sure that for this at least the records have been combed as earnestly as a police search for stolen loot.

Chronic shortage of material and the current poverty of ideas are forcing the television companies to dredge the past for fresh programmes. This is all to the good. *All Our Yesterdays*, in its quiet, unsung fashion, may have started a revolution.

And television is discovering, thank heavens, that there is *another* way to beat the clock.[117]

Steptoe pushes out the television junk
Daily Herald, 18 January 1964

The face is as sour and withered as a crab apple left in the damp grass. A mildewy muffler hangs in greasy folds about the scraggy neck. The voice, squeezed through long brown teeth, is tired and plaintive.

No prizes for identifying Albert Steptoe, the shuffling senior partner in the ramshackle rag-and-bone business in Shepherd's Bush. There he sits, knee deep in debris: a broken grandfather clock, a pile of old books and a cracked chamber pot on an ancient chest of drawers. Sometimes the pathos becomes almost too cruel, for Wilfrid Brambell can pluck at our heart strings as easily as he makes us shudder.

'I shall never enjoy the Steptoes again!' declared a grief-stricken viewer to the BBC after poor, cringing Albert had been packed off to an old folks' home by treacherous, dark-eyed Harold.

Writers Simpson and Galton are taking appalling risks with the crabbed conventions of TV comedy. Like the old movie comics, they seem determined to tempt the tear-ducts as well as tickle the larynx. TV comedy, in fact, is grabbing many of the stock preserves of drama

– which, considering the present miserable plight of the electronic theatre, is perhaps just as well.

Steptoe and Son has swung TV humour into a brilliant new dimension. How distant it all seems from the days of Mr Pastry and the lingering red-nosed humour of television's equivalents of *Workers' Playtime*. Instead of pumping out mere buffoonery or joke-a-minute patter, the little screen now thrives on adult comedy, tailored to the mood of the times.

The Arthur Haynes Show on ITV, for instance, has an anarchical, bitter note of protest rippling through even its wilder moments. Perhaps it is no accident that scriptwriter Johnny Speight's two straight plays[118] have dealt with mental illness. Echoes of them thud through his workaday comedies like footsteps in the dark.

I'm in favour of this new trend. It breaks down yet another compartment, yet another phoney distinction between 'popular' and 'intellectual.' Some of it may be sick. But the TV we see *must* respond to the drift of the time.

Writers are kings without riches
Daily Herald, 25 January 1964

Television drama executives tend to chain-smoke and drink strong black coffee in the small hours. Sharp-tongued rumour has it that one of these nerve-racked impresarios has even taken to rummaging in old dustbins in search of new material.

The current shortage of writing talent has reached crisis point. BBC drama boss Sydney Newman[119] confesses that he would 'go down on his knees' before a fresh new writer.

And yet TV organisations still exploit their writers abominably – the ultimate in short-sighted lunacy. Underpayment is the first and most crucial sin. Even a *Coronation Street* script fetches only about £125, or about 1d for every 700 viewers.

Rehearsal time is inadequate. Many writers are not invited to the rehearsals anyway. The talented John Arden, for example, wrote a play called *Wet Fish* for BBC-TV, deliberately leaving many points obscure until he could see the problems on the studio floor. But he was not asked to attend rehearsals. 'I found out afterwards from meeting the cast that they were rather bewildered by this because they did not quite understand the play,' he complained later.

Graham Greene withdrew his *The Complaisant Lover* from ITV because of the way they wanted to mangle it. Less famous writers are not so fortunate, and have to put up with arbitrary cuts and additions to their original dialogue – without consultation.

'Television is a tragedy,' snaps the brilliant young American writer Clancy Sigal, who lives in Britain.

And who can blame the writers for being bitter? For the various TV stations have to churn out between them some 400 plays a year.

'Everything begins and ends with the script,' says Howard Thomas, chief of ABC TV. 'And it is upon the skill and selectivity of a script department that a company has to stake its reputation.'

All praise, then, to a long, long overdue experiment from ATV. It has brought a group of directors and writers together to create six plays from blank paper right through to transmission. *Studio 64*, as the series is called, began on Sunday with Nigel Kneale's nuclear nightmare, *The Crunch*. A very appetising fruit of a very sensible policy.

Clearly, a collective, honest effort at genuine creation in TV drama is now being attempted. The writer takes his place as the kingpin rather than the lackey. And that's even better than giving him a life peerage.

Did I hear the poodle growl?
Daily Herald, 15 February 1964

Audiences at live television shows have always been as tame as shampooed poodles. No matter how appalling the performances, the applause could be absolutely guaranteed. After all, the seats are free.

Yet suddenly, amazingly, there is a whiff of rebellion in the air. Even poodles are occasionally prepared to snap and snarl.

Take that mildewed institution, *Sunday Night at the London Palladium*. I usually sit and stare glassy-eyed at the long-limbed lovelies, the muscle-bound acrobats, the popsters, as unprepared for surprise as a night-watchman nodding over a coke brazier.

However, the last two Palladium shows have been *different*. The acts have been much the same, but the audience have changed. The free seats are beginning to get restless. They are starting to mutter and mumble. And even to shout out objections. In short, the unthinkable has happened.

This week, for instance, a belligerent voice from the gods advised talented compere Bruce Forsyth to 'Get on with it!' as he dragged himself through one of those interminably twee introductions. An even less friendly customer advised the compere to 'Get off!' when he brought himself into one of the more popular acts. And when poor Bruce tried to push a plug for the *Golden Hour* to follow, the tide of abuse made him quickly change his leisurely condescension. 'All right. All right. I'll say no more,' he conceded, as visibly put out as Canute must have been when he got his feet wet.

At the moment, the catcalls are isolated and half-hearted. But these things catch on fast and a new note of tension has crept into the Palladium show. Someone is wondering anxiously how long it will be before the audience *really* rise in wrath.

Far be it from me to encourage such anarchy. Val Parnell can sleep soundly so far as I am concerned. But I must admit that one of my recurrent fantasies, like the hope of seeing a hostess clobbering a quizmaster with a heavy bag of bullion, is that of a Palladium audience hissing *Beat the Clock* off the stage.

Such miracles do not happen. It would be like catching a perceptive comment on *Juke Box Jury*, where the illiteracy is as calculated as the camera angles. But I shall not be the only one watching tomorrow's Palladium show with a flutter of wondrous apprehension.

Z Cars comes to the end of the alley
Daily Herald, 14 March 1964

Car headlights slither along the wet street. A drunk staggers by. Liverpool windows darken. Cats screech in the alleys – and back at the copshop bully-boy Barlow stabs out a podgy finger. There's another case to solve.

Z Cars clicks into place easily now. Last week the BBC stored away the 100th episode and on Wednesday the long haul towards the second hundred got under way.

One thousand actors, 14 scriptwriters, 30 directors, 5,000 minutes of live drama – the statistics measure out one of television's biggest success stories since Baird said, 'Hey! Look what I've found!'

Big television series often start with a bang and end in a whimper. Boredom grabs them by the throat. Success corrupts, and invention hardens into mere habit. I fear that it's happening even to *Z Cars*.

'Enjoy your trip, did you?' says one copper to another.

'Eh?'

'London.'

'Oh.'

And so on. Dialogue full of grunts and snorts and hums and hahs; realism gone phoney.

Z Cars is still entertaining but once it was brilliant. The programme no longer writhes with life, no longer submerges itself in the moods and manners of Britain's Beat City.

When Troy Kennedy Martin began the thing 26 months ago he was eager to create a new style of TV police drama. Lord Ted Dixon was giving him the bellyache. Me too.

Kennedy Martin went to Liverpool and used his eyes. He stored up detail, plotted a mood, analysed attitudes, and then created the shock which had every top cop talking angrily into the telephone.

But now the police *like* it. The plots edge out observation, the hums and hahs and oohs and ohs pick away at the accuracy.

Perhaps this is inevitable. Invention never did come on a conveyor belt. A flexible formula rapidly stiffens into Holy Writ. It is the old story of cheese in plastic film, the supermarket culture. This week's programme might have been imprinted on the screen with a rubber stamp.

But television's insatiable and monstrous gluttony will ensure that the Z Cars grind on till they fall foul of the 10-year test.

Meanwhile Fancy Smith belches, Watt slams his pork pie hat on his puzzled nut and the headlights slide along Newtown.

Perhaps the death of PC Sweet,[120] sucked under the dark and dirty Mersey, makes a neat enough symbol for the whole series. He has left the others to a slower, more grudging death. For 100 is enough, whackers, 100 will *do*.

Out goes pomposity
Daily Herald, 22 April 1964

Baptized by apologies on Black Monday, luckless BBC2 finally launched itself into history with Humpty Dumpty and the sight of a grown man on his hands and knees grunting like a pig.

No, this was not a distraught BBC executive with a hangover, but a pleasant young man jollying up the under-fives in yesterday morning's programme for toddlers, *Play School*.

It was in a similar position – if with less rude noises – that I anxiously adjusted the fine tuner to capture the first bright new pictures of the evening premiere postponed by the previous night's power blackout.

But the first thing we saw was a single, flickering candle in the modish setting of an apparently deserted studio.

'Good evening. This is BBC2,' said soft-voiced newcomer Denis Tuohy – then he blew out the candle. *Line Up* was under way. The great adventure had begun with a bad joke.

Dreadful jokes abounded, too, in the first comedy show, *The Alberts' Channel Too*,[121] which in madcap fashion traced the growth of broadcasting from prehistoric days to BBC2. But here, at least, there was such exuberance and such anarchical audacity that we got the first welcome clues about the kind of channel to expect.

BBC2 is not going to be pompous. The ancient BBC Auntie image is going to be fractured good – and I rejoice that Britain's third TV channel can begin with a bad joke instead of, say, Richard Dimbleby, champagne and a telegram from Buckingham Palace.

The maniacal irreverence of The Alberts – jeering at many hallowed British obsessions – was supplemented later by the import of no less an oddity than Kruschev's favourite comedian. Compared with the stiff bow-tied propriety which (so I'm told) marked the opening of BBC1, this was certainly more pleasing. But the Russian Arkady Raikin could not crash the language barrier, and his mobile, podgy Slav face was unable to rescue some of the drearily sentimental routines.

In between, the big show of the night, *Kiss Me, Kate*, soothed any offended nerves. Howard Keel was in sparkling form, and it was good to see gander-voiced Millicent Martin staking her claims on the new channel. But surely Cole Porter's now well-worn musical – however dazzlingly performed – was a tedious bending of the knee to the dying Gods of Broadway.

A pomp-free BBC2, yes – but a middle-aged one, too. Even with beautiful, wind-blown fireworks and (thank goodness) jazz giant Duke Ellington.

Sport is too good to leave with the experts
Daily Herald, 25 July 1964

World-class boxer Benny Paret signed his contracts with his thumb print and was beaten to death in the ring.

'I'm sorry what happened to Benny, really,' said Emile Griffith, the champ who chopped him so hard. Benny left a pile of debts, a widow, a child who reads *Ring* magazine, and a nasty taste in the mouth for all those who insist on calling boxing a sport.

Two summers ago *Panorama* shocked the British public when it showed the murderous spectacle from the ringside in America.[122] Poor Benny, as his wealthy manager called him, was propped helplessly against the ropes, his head lolling on his damp chest like a broken doll. Griffith hit him again and again. The spectators howled for blood. The referee hovered impotently in the background. The bright lights beat down, concentrating the scene like something in a Hitchcock film.

This week's NBC documentary on ITV, *Boxing's Last Round*, recalled that incredible scene with still photographs, and amassed more evidence of pugilistic chicanery and brutality than even Baroness Summerskill dreamt existed.

But the significance of this television documentary lay in the manner in which fact, imagination, impassioned argument and superb technical resources were used to analyse a major American 'sport.'

Boxing, by its very nature, is brutish and melodramatic. It can make exciting television. But other sports can also stand treatment which uses the probing camera eye rather than the commentator's cliché.

Sport, in other words, is sometimes too serious, too terrible and too beautiful to be left to the sports departments. Intensely dramatic, deliberately sensational, often quite appallingly moving, I regard big-time sport as one of the major pleasures of life.

But I am also curious about its background, intrigued by dressing-room pep talk, interested by the finance and organization of what is a major industry.

Whenever writers and directors, normally working in other sectors, are brought into sports television, the result is unusually diverting and informative. Stephen Hearst, for example, made a film for BBC Television about a British footballer in Italy that not only rippled with physical excitement, but also thrummed with sociological symbolism.

I would like to see a Denis Mitchell film about football, a *Monitor* study of Rugby League, a poet's celebration of cricket, that Englishman's concept of eternity.

It is the kind of initiative that poor old BBC2 might well consider. Anything to jerk it out of an overplanned rut.

School Sketch
Co-written with David Nathan
Not So Much a Programme More a Way of Life, BBC1, 9 January 1965

Performed by Willie Rushton, John Bird and Doug Fisher.

WILLIE: A new book out this week suggests that it's time that we should begin to apply to popular arts, the standards of criticism that are still only generally applied to serious music, drama and books. Of course as soon as those subjects are taken seriously, they'll have to be taught seriously and children can look forward to the day – not far off – when the last inspiring address before they face their O-levels will sound like this.

JOHN: Well chaps, your exams start tomorrow but I'm sure you've got nothing to worry about, particularly in the first paper, 'Looking at Media' – or as they used to call it in the old days, 'Literary Criticism.' We've covered all the syllabus from Barbara Cartland to Hank Janson, and there's no reason to believe that the questions will be very different this year from previous years. Indeed, last year there was a question about Cartland and Janson…ah, here it is. 'Compare and contrast the use of (a) Cartland's abrupt chapter endings at a moment when copulation seems imminent with (b) Hank's lingering detail.' I don't think that sort of thing should give you any trouble, do you?

Or this, on Burt Bacharach's verse structure as interpreted by (a) Cilla Black and (b) Dionne Warwick. You'll get a choice of questions on Adam Faith and this year there'll almost certainly be something on the social impact of his South African trip. I know a lot of you like that sort of question, and if you've cribbed a few smart phrases from the *Observer* then good luck to you. Personally, though, that's what I call biography criticism, not real criticism at all; I may be old fashioned but I like to stick to the text. For example, it's very interesting and sometimes very helpful to know what sort of clothes Georgie Fame wears or what kind of car he drives, but in the last analysis there can be no substitute for a close study of what Georgie actually *sings*. It's quite likely that you'll be asked to compare the rhythmic and tonal differences between Georgie's "Yeh Yeh" and The Beatles' "Yeah, Yeah, Yeah", and to do that you've *got* to know your texts.

Now then, well, you can bank on a question about films. That's for the highbrows among you. (*Ha, ha.*) Although the examiners are being more realistic now in avoiding things on the work of directors and actors and concentrating on producers. The set films this year are Joseph E. Levine's early works, which I hope you've all seen. Another word of warning here. Please, please, *please* read the questions carefully. I had an unfortunate pupil last year who wrote two pages comparing the subtleties of two French nude films when he'd been asked to compare their subtitles. So, remember that. Now, my last word of advice to you. I know exactly how you feel. You'll go into that examination room worrying about *Maigret* and *Z Cars*; you may feel you haven't mugged up enough on Hughie Green and Michael Miles. The point I want you to remember is this. You are studying this subject for a purpose, and that purpose is to make each one of you a fuller, richer human being. Not richer merely in the intellectual or spiritual sense but in the materialistic sense. Most of you will be earning a living soon. You will find the world outside a tough competitive place where the successful product is often the shoddiest product. What you have been studying here with me are shoddy bits of pop culture and perhaps through your studies some of it has rubbed off on you and you will be as a result shoddier, more successful people. I hope so.

Pull back to show back of DOUG at school desk. He holds up hand to ask question.

JOHN: Yes what is it?

DOUG: Can I ask a question sir?

JOHN: Yes. What is it?

DOUG: Was that live, Sir – or were you miming?

CHORD

Letter to the *Stage*
Stage, 29 July 1965

Sir,

I have just been trying to imagine the conversation between the astonishing Mrs Mary Whitehouse and the 14-year-old girl who 'offered herself to a boy of the same age because of what she saw in a television play.' Let us hope that the startled boy refused the offer because of what he had seen on *Blue Peter*.

What does Mrs Mary Whitehouse do as a result of watching television plays? Unfortunately we know the answer to that one, too. This boring woman and the 14-year-old girl appear to have such different reactions to what was perhaps the same work that I am left in considerable awe about the potency of the television play.

But Mrs Whitehouse may care to know that when I was 14 I offered myself to a girl of the same age because of what I had read in a Shakespeare play. Unfortunately the girl was not so literate.

Yours faithfully,
Dennis Potter
Old Club House
Northrepps
Cromer
Norfolk

Drama with no safety curtain
New Society, 30 December 1965

The Complete Plays of D.H. Lawrence (Heinemann)

Reading a play dead on the page is often an exceedingly frustrating exercise, not unlike watching a football match when one thickly rusted girder of the stand obscures the crucial penalty area. You can easily enough follow the dramatic sequence, be gripped by the gradual accumulation of emotion or the pungency of the design and then, at the critical moment, be denied the ultimate satisfaction of full-blooded excitement.

D.H. Lawrence the dramatist certainly makes sure the girders are well in place and properly rusted. A tremendously vivid passage of dialogue will abruptly degenerate into the kind of literary horsehair which would tempt an ambitious actor to orate through his nose. Yet one cannot be sure. The alleged degeneration may work in performance, the heightened speech may only be noticed by a sudden constriction of the throat and a delighted submission to the potency of 'good theatre.' All of these plays are well worth reading, even if only as semantic footnotes to the novels (and the attractive way this hefty book has been produced adds to the pleasure). More importantly, some of them cry out for production.

Lawrence is particularly fascinating when showing coal miners. Violent men, as he sees them: boorish, ignorant, drink-sodden, superstitious tyrants. And yet, almost in spite of the glinting spitefulness of their creator, they are left in full, dark, dramatic possession of an awful and indestructible sort of dignity.

Melodrama flutters across these pages like too familiar tunes in a Bart musical. At critical moments one often wants to giggle with reluctant embarrassment; and I suspect that Lawrence had a sneaking admiration for a line like 'Dead! ...and never called me Mother!'[123] Yet in the disturbing *The Widowing of Mrs Holroyd*, for example, what seems like melodrama turns with menacing precision upon the narrow circle of coal-mining superstition. A young, abused wife wishes her miner husband dead. The inevitable pit accident therefore – and the 'therefore' is very real – makes her a murderer. A gruesome final scene brings the body of the hulking victim back into the tiny kitchen where wife and mother must pull off the big boots and wash the blood and raw flesh off their man's finger nails.

'Eh – and he's fair as a lily,' moans the mother as she cleans the corpse. 'Did you ever see a man with whiter skin – and flesh as fine as the driven snow. He's beautiful he is, the lamb. Many's the time I've looked at him, and I've felt proud of him I have. And now he lies here. And such arms on him! Look at the vaccination marks, Lizzie. When I took him to be vaccinated, he had a little pink bonnet with a feather. Don't cry, my girl, don't. Sit up and wash him a' that side or wes'll never have him done.'

The women grieve and the women have the poetry. So often, too, it is marvellous language, perfectly rooted in poisoned soil and as yet not 'naturalistic' in any dreary drama-documentary fashion. Short, laconic jabs of dialogue, as in *The Daughter-in-Law*, can explode into a fitful, uncomfortable but awesomely compelling rhetoric: extremely powerful, barely controlled passages which would surely be even more successful on the stage.

Lawrence wrote eight plays and left two more dramatic fragments. All are collected here in a definitive edition. It is full of the Laurentian qualities, heavy with fine language, glowering emotion and brutality. There are dud passages by the square yard; but even these are consumed by the energy and eloquence of the man. Pull up the safety curtain, please.

The art of true invective
New Society, 27 January 1966

H.G. Wells: Journalism and Prophecy 1893–1946 edited by W. Warren Wagar (Bodley Head)

H.G. Wells churned out words by the million, columns by the yard and books by the hundred. What a shame that such a promiscuous opinionator should have flaked out before the bright, bright era of late night telly-talk. Like his own Mr Britling, he could 'no more help having ideas about everything than a dog can resist smelling at your heels.' A podgy, bouncy little mongrel with needle-sharp teeth, crystal balls and a tendency to pant through pulling too eagerly at the leash.

'I am a journalist,' he piped in his high voice, 'I refuse to play the "artist."' It is left to posterity to say 'Down boy,' or throw the odd bone of rather condescending praise.

Journalism, however, does not often keep. The syncopated passions of the moment are all too likely to turn into quaint nostalgia-artefacts, like odd dance tunes heard through floating chains of coloured balloons on long-gone summer nights.

But Wells comes through very well indeed: some of the invective is mercilessly skin-ripping and the zestful proliferation of subjects, moods, opinions and prophesies would even keep one good-tempered on a winter tram journey with a querulous bishop.

The portraits of the great are by far the most fascinating segments of this fat but over-pruned collection. 'Lloyd George has with him the affectionate distrust of a great multitude of his countrymen.' And the whole piece helps one put Harold Wilson into perspective. Here, as in many such articles, Wells shows a fleet, cheeky, deceptively incisive approach that can still smack back through all the vagaries of time and fashion. An honest, forceful, quirky style which manages to preserve even this ephemera.

Genuine invective is an almost lost art in our wild satirical age. Certainly, there is more and more electronic abuse, and tongues of all sorts have been poked out for so long that they have become quite withered. But the motives have usually been so diffuse and targets so rotted and irrelevant that all we gain is some small increment in public entertainment. What, precisely, is the point of attacking a redundant institution if your only reward – and perhaps, even, your only *purpose* – is to gain a seat next to Harvey Orkin? Admittedly, this is a depressingly circular argument.

No, on second thoughts, Wells would not have gone down too well at Wood Lane. He could put out a tongue and hold up two fingers with the best of them – but Wells also had the disconcerting habit of refusing to bend the knee. His conviction and vigorous sense of purpose overruled the rudeness and bumptiousness. He wrote a lot because there was a lot to say and not because it was a profitable habit.

Consider him on Winston Churchill, the great embalmed: 'His ideology, picked up in the garrison life of India, on the reefs of South Africa, the maternal home and the conversation of wealthy conservative households, is a pitiful jumble of incoherent nonsense. A boy scout is better equipped.' And that, please note, was written in 1944. Exactly the right thing to say at the right time, the sharp honesty which draws blood when eyes are shut and knees are creaking.

As editor, W. Warren Wagar has put together a very enjoyable and surprisingly instructive anthology. It is enough to make one yearn for good journalism and thinner newspapers.

A Boswell in the bicarbonate
New Society, 26 May 1966

Churchill: The Struggle for Survival by Lord Moran (Constable)

'We must get the waiters away first; he can't walk.'

The faithful Christopher Soames had noticed that the Prime Minister could not heave himself up from the table. Less perceptive guests at the dinner for Italy's de Gasperi presumed merely that Churchill had had too much to drink. Lord Moran, with history bumping about inside his head like a cobblestone, went off stage to jot down every wry little comment, every slobbering lurch towards the grave. The comedy, though black, is distinctly cumulative: at this point we are only on page 408 and there are almost as many more to go.

The good doctor has come up with an astonishingly frank and gruesomely enthralling casebook. We are not, for once, pushed out of sight with the waiters and the washing up; the wine glasses, medicine bottles and dirty linen are rinsed in public. We have found a Boswell in the bicarbonate.

And Moran, who is certainly no slouch as a writer, shades in detail with the callous brilliance of a dramatist clutching at the huge figures which plod up and down in his own dark dreams. Almost every diary entry is like a little sketch, neatly fitted out with curtain line and continuing reverberation. But – I cannot put my finger on it – there is something almost unbalanced in the cold, meticulous precision of it all: it is rather like the oblique enactment of a vague, obscurely uncomfortable sense of revenge.

The doctor lays out the red pills and the green pills and the balms and sprays on the bedside table, gossips with amiable deference about the doubtful future of mankind, listens to the ailing flutter of the heart, watches a testy giant insult a manservant and then scurries away to write it down and perhaps cleanse himself.

'I am bewildered by the world,' mutters the Grand Old Man while still clinging to office, 'the confusion is terrible.' The second half of the book is wormeaten with Churchill's unconnected sentences, egotistic meanderings and tearful pauses. On the level of a personal drama these are the expected quaverings of a selfish and rather gluttonous old man with tottery legs and an empty head.

But, of course, the clinical description of approaching senility turns inevitably into a diagnosis of a whole ideology gone addled. Lord Moran is not himself aware of this; but, then he doesn't have to be. Let us remember, though, a Free World led by ancient carcases with antique prejudices and the time-locked imaginations of Omdurman lancers. Spread out before us, so well that you can almost smell it, is the bleak world of Churchill, Adenauer and Eisenhower. A political nightmare tangled with the coils of an oxygen mask.

'There might be a crisis. There might be war. Mendès-France is only thinking of keeping in office. All my sympathies are with the Germans. Adenauer has sent a big silver goblet for my birthday...' Few novelists would dare to put those last two sentences together in such fashion. Immediately afterwards Lord Moran began to check the heap of medicines beside the bed. Hysteria might have been a more adequate response.

Yet this is not to deny that, even in his decrepitude, there was a grandeur about Churchill which will still protect the legend for those who need legends. He battled hard with old age and shored up his pride with more than pills and walking sticks. And every now and again the all but extinct volcano would erupt in the old style to send the hangers-on running for the cover of the nearest museum.

But whether Churchill should have been allowed to carry on this struggle while Prime Minister is quite another matter. Moran's portrait shows with unanswerable brutality how ill-led we were at an extremely critical time. When bedpans become interchangeable with despatch boxes and cabinet meetings with blood counts then the personal drama – powerful though it is – becomes a sentimental irrelevance. The culpability, cowardice and duplicity of the people around the sick goliath seems then to be of greater importance. A culpability which Lord Moran himself must share up to the eyeballs.

It is the glimpse we get of those around Churchill, in fact, which helps make this sensational book so damaging to the Old Order. They are, for the most part, a wretched lot, steeped in prejudice and stupidity.

Montgomery, it seems, cannot help but make as big a fool of himself on the croquet lawn as he does in the Lords. But this is endearing, to say the least, when compared to, say, Sir Gerald Templer. 'Are we going soft as a nation?' this barbarian burbles. 'But I feel it can be put right. The death penalty is necessary.' And he went on to recount how he tried to get 20 soldiers executed for refusing to carry ammunition up a slope raked by fire.

But, as I say, the book is quite funny in parts. Some sort of choking sensation can be guaranteed.

Aberfan
New Society, 27 October 1966

A man-made mountain of lumpy black treacle collapsed into itself last Friday[124] and slid down upon the school at Aberfan 'just after morning prayers.' The phrase is not, as I had first assumed, a distasteful journalistic device for somehow mixing inappropriate irony with an even more cruel piety. The phrase was also used in my presence by some of the stricken people of Aberfan, and with just enough frequency to force one to look for the bleak significance that seems to lurk behind the words.

For here, among this hideous litter of squat, white-painted stone chapels, it is not only the insurance companies who refer to an Act of God. And it is surely to be expected that whatever deity is worshipped – or propitiated – in these scarred valleys should be a harsh and pitiless creature. Faith can move mountains, boyo, but it bloody well won't *stop* them. Mothers and fathers queue outside Bethania Welsh Congregational to identify and weep over the soiled bodies of their children. Nothing nor nobody, curse nor prayer, God nor Coal Board, can now assuage the awful grief and anguish of this pitiful place.

Huddled beneath terrible headlines in a desecrated, bracken-browned hollow of the hills, Aberfan is awash with mud, slime and strangers. The police have sealed it off, just as they do a building where a violent crime has been committed: but the criminal is still there, still shifting and slithering, still quite capable of yet more bestiality.

The collapsed slag heap looks weirdly, wickedly voluptuous as you see it from a distance, for it sprawls into the village like a reclining female monster, a wanton negress shifting awkwardly on smelly hams. The sense of outrage and impotent disgust seems to coil itself into the very walk of those who approach the defilement, their gumboots slip-slap-slopping on the slime.

Everywhere, too, is the stench – something like a mixture of mouldering bread and wet coal. Newcomers lift their heads, like gundogs, to sniff momentarily at the foul air. The cringing brown houses are splattered with mud up to the tiny top windows, where curtains are drawn to keep in the grief. Filth is everywhere, sucking at your feet and working into the corners of your eyes. It is the dirtiest, nastiest and most evil conglomeration that I ever wish to see, an affront which would make even prayers seem like sacrilege. Certainly, the prayers were not answered. Aberfan was totally abandoned to tragedy.

When people are faced with a disaster so complete and so terrible, they cluster in small, hapless groups and begin to manufacture their own sort of optimism as though to try and keep at bay the resignation and despair they know will have to come. At Aberfan, before and after daybreak on Saturday, 'hope' was created among some of the bruised bands of people standing ankle-deep in slime. It was an unbearable thing to witness, a collective self-deception that was as inevitable as it was tormenting.

'Hey. Hey,' cried an old man in a tight muffler to a young woman standing with splashed stockings in the queue outside a telephone box. 'I've just heard that some little boy dug himself out and wandered off on his own without telling anybody!'

'Do they know *who?*' her voice lifted itself beyond the normal upward inflexion of the Welsh lilt.

The old man's head seemed to shrink back into his shoulders. 'No,' he said, very quietly, probably realising at that very moment that what he had almost shouted was completely untrue and unforgivably cruel. He stood still awhile, then mumbled again and shuffled off towards the growling yellow machinery at the top of the rubble. The woman stared after him.

'It's what a boy might do,' she said, either laughing or crying, 'wander off like that. He might think he'd done something wrong, see.' The others in the queue moved their heads or twitched their hands in a tiny conspiracy of guilt.

The wild rumours were about as helpful, and fell into exactly the same category, as the redundant prayers. As the chill morning dragged on into first light the incredible, almost cretinous tales and miracles ebbed away, leaving only a miniscule and hardly discernible residue of hope to temper reality. 'That stuff's like roof insulation,' someone said. 'It don't leave any gaps.' Pause. 'You never know, though.' The bereaved either waited on the steps of their grim Bethania or retreated back into the splattered rows of shrivelled, rust-coloured houses. White smoke from their chimneys climbed up in a dead straight line towards the surrounding hills where a few sheep grazed. A man said that this was a sure sign of rain. Everyone looked up at the invading slag once more.

A newspaper reporter in a curly felt hat lost his shoe to the suction of the ubiquitous and still thickening mud. He swivelled perilously, comically, on one leg, arms splaying out wildly, but nobody dared to laugh. The reporter grinned with a toothy embarrassment, then consciously straightened his face. Everyone not immediately involved thought it only right and proper to take on the caricatured as well as the genuine lineaments of gloom: the difference between the two was instantly obvious, if impossible to put into words. I saw, for instance, a middle-aged man approaching the contaminated streets carrying a pair of wellington boots under his arm. The expression on his face was one of such naked misery and exhaustion that I lit a cigarette with cupped hands in order to hide my stranger's face. Even without the collapsed slag, Aberfan is a place that can and should make you feel guilty. And when the anger of the tragedy has left the front pages, there is more and still more and yet more to be angry about for a place and a people like this.

Scratched on the whitened window of an abandoned pub down in Station Square are the crudely lettered names of some of the children of the village. 'Pam loves Terry.' Margaret, Elaine, Janis, Maureen, Heather and Pamela are scrawled in a sloping list by the side of the bulbous heart: children's scribble, the usual marks left by kids at play. I saw an old woman put her stubby finger to the glass, make a sort of hissing noise under her breath, and then turn to ask an AA man, very angrily, whether or not the bus to Merthyr was going to run as usual. It was an exact verbal equivalent of the careful, angry precision with which the housewives of Aberfan began to clean the muck off their windows.

A demand for the normal routine and the ordinary rhythms of the ordinary day was perfectly understandable, for it does not do to stand still and think, think, think about that lost generation.

What had they had, those children?

Love, certainly. The tightly-knit confines of such a traditionally working-class community are so total that those who are heartless and gutless and witless enough to send their offspring away to school could never even begin to comprehend it. Those slaughtered children will be mourned, dear God, with a passion that is almost strong enough to destroy, and I grieve now for their poor, wrecked and heartbroken parents. You cannot possibly walk away from the misery of Aberfan without aching throat muscles and a fury that is all the worse for being so impotent.

And that mangled generation also had – *what*?

A horizon ringed with towering slag. Generations of filth thrust at them as soon as they opened their doors, decades of dirt and more dirt pressing in like an avalanche upon the tiny, baked-brown, bathroom-less houses of a stinking valley. An old, defensive culture withering on their scrubbed doorsteps. Posters advertising bingo four nights a week. Examine, too, the lists of the dead, classroom by classroom: between 30 and 40 children per class in an ugly old school at the foot of a gigantic heap of industrial shit. O Great Social Revolution, O Wondrous Welfare State. And thank you, Lord, for the kindly editorials.

On Saturday morning the paper boys stopped every now and then on the slimy pavements with a stupefied wonder to read about the sudden fame which had come upon their nondescript village like a visitation from hell. But hours later, when the dank ground-mist had floated back up to the hilltops, the folded *Daily Mirror*s had still not been dragged in from the narrow letterboxes. All the unclaimed papers seemed to have been folded in an identical manner, so that the incomplete caption, "SWEPT DOWN ON ABERFAN", was repeated from front door to front door along the row. These houses were uncannily quiet. No music from radios, no raised voices, no cooking smells, no young children shrieking at their play. The postman came with a slow tread and a big bundle, but no messages of joy.

A black and white mongrel with a bad limp and mud on its back went down the street, so obviously bewildered by the heavy trucks and scurrying hordes of men that it walked with a peculiar sideways gait, feet dippling a tiny pattern in the slime. Most poignant of all, to me, was the sight of a child's bicycle splattered with filth. Most perverse, the singing of a fat blackbird with a wagging tail, perched high and trilling on a sagging electric cable: it was an affront that notes so clean and clear should claim attention at such a time and in such a place as this. More in character, surely, was the BP Visco-Static oil can swirling with a hollow clank in the narrow Taff, and the half-eaten cheese sandwich resting on the bonnet of a parked car.

Very tired miners tramped back to the Merthyr Vale colliery down the road after a day and a night shovelling at the murderous rubble. There was none of the usual quick lilt, the shouted camaraderie of their kind. They had worked with a patient, back-breaking diligence, soft-voiced and without anger, a marvel to all who saw it. But now their bodies were touched with fatigue and some of these men must surely have been on the point of collapse. One of them leaned over the small stone bridge crossing the Taff and stared down at the water, his head sinking forward on to his chest like a man nodding off in a railway carriage. A heavy-jowled woman with a camera round her neck went by, talking too loudly in French to her companion. The miner lifted his head and stared after her, and his thoughts seemed to spit out in a sudden and perhaps unjust venom.

Later in the day we had the Duke of Edinburgh and his carload of attendants from the Welsh Office, but the less I say about that the better. Aberfan undoubtedly wanted its grief to be recognized and its tragedy to be measured. The condolences of the mighty and the messages of sympathy from all round the globe inevitably shrink and narrow and curdle to the proportions of something dangerously near irony as you stand in these violated streets. But it is only right, of course, that the boys of Winchester and Eton and other places should offer up their cut-glass prayers with the rest. Aberfan can probably be relied upon to be grateful.

As the rain came again, thickening and darkening the sky above the surrounding mounds of black, brown and grey-green, anxious eyes turned once more to the gigantic conical slag still towering so malignantly above the village. All hope had done by now, but the tip might still slide further into the beleaguered houses, might yet scatter the busy yellow machines and shovelling men. It was then, especially, that one felt the enormity of the dead slag's power, and the disgust that such gargantuan waste should have been piled at people's backyards. Why should it be? Why is it thought necessary to be so loathsomely uncivilized?

The past is piled all around one here, and the bad, mean-minded, short-sighted methods of the past have not yet been discarded. Hence the fatalistic language and the half-formulated idea that some God has cheated. 'If only…' people kept saying at Aberfan. 'If only' it had collapsed earlier in the morning. 'If only' it had fallen after midday, when the children would have dispersed in noisily happy throngs for their half-term holiday. 'If only' it had stopped raining a day earlier. 'If only' someone had rung the Coal Board the night before. 'If only' the powers that be had taken the slightest notice of all the earlier fears and warnings about the tip. If only… If only… If only…the inevitable, tragic punctuation of any disaster.

But there are much more resounding, much more accusing, much more fundamental If Onlys.

If only the National Coal Board took seriously the conception of a publicly owned industry designed to serve the whole community, not least that section upon which it depends for all its wealth.

If only the so-called socialists who run this ugly country would yap less about their glorious heritage and do a damned sight more to remove the inglorious legacy which is still rammed down so many people's throats every time they open their mouths to breathe.

And not even then, especially not then, will it be possible to say that Aberfan 'was not in vain.' Do not dare to say that. Aberfan *was* in vain. Those children *were* murdered. This was no senseless Act of God, but a crime committed by senseless man.

Young Ibsen: towards the southbound steamer
Times, 9 December 1967

Henrik Ibsen: The Making of a Dramatist 1828–1864 by Michael Meyer (Hart-Davis)

There have been some studies of famous writers and artists which read a little like out-patient dossiers – lending support to the mechanistic but degenerate thesis that 'creativity' itself is but kindred to, say, a raw psoriatic rash which itches deep into infancy, bits of the bleeding flesh of childhood caught under hard adult fingernails. In such dreary circumstances biography can become a gargoyled extension to the path-lab rather than the last legitimate sanctuary for 'great men' or even (antique concept) heroes.

Henrik Ibsen, the withdrawn and properly melancholic Northerner, has for perilously long been kept on ice as an obvious candidate for such dubious treatment. Why, comes the expected voice, do bankruptcy and bastardy haunt his plays like wilful old dreams that lie coiled and throbbing in the corners of a wakeful mind? Perhaps it is almost enough to know that he was acquainted since schooldays with local crab-apple-faced rumours of his own illegitimacy, and that his father (real or nominal) subsided weakly into humiliating penury when the great dramatist-to-be was only seven years old. How dangerously tempting it is to solder the two facts and thereby achieve in one operation the two most definitive characteristics of so much contemporary criticism: glibness and philistinism.

Forty years have gone by since Halvdan Koht's massive but understandably rather nationalistic attempt at a two-volume life of Ibsen, and tempers as well as flagpoles have changed a lot since then. We nowadays sensibly include impertinence as one of the virtues of a critical intelligence, and the great dramatist can so easily be portrayed as an ugly little depressive with a peculiarly tight expression gripping like a perpetual pain at his mouth.

The pinched and hairy face described by a lighthearted fellow student at Christiania glowers menacingly back from the jacket of Michael Meyer's first volume of biography. Ibsen, one feels, looks as if he knows that he has covered his tracks too well to be badly damaged by subsequent life-mongers, and the long delay since Koht would seem to bear him out. But – and it should be recorded with delight or even astonishment – there emerges from behind *this* immense coal-black beard the man as a playwright rather than as the expected victim of facile amateur psychiatry. Mr Meyer, in short, has stoutly resisted all the standard temptations, insisting on putting first things well and truly first. He will, of course, be accused of 'dullness.'

This opening volume is a restrained, extremely informative, exhaustively researched, critically acute and hence continually rewarding exercise, in many vital ways the model of what a biography of a great writer should be. Mr Meyer is, of course, rightly celebrated as the translator of Ibsen into our English now, and that long, impeccably fulfilled task has obviously equipped him to relate the life to the craft and the craft to the conditions of the theatre at that time and place. He is, for example, able to hold the balance between the aspirations and the failures of the often confused young Ibsen, allowing apprentice ambitions and tedious, mind-rotting practical difficulties to mingle together (as they must) in convincing and strangely encouraging authenticity. The blurb's statutory claim that 'this new biography will be an indispensable addition to the study of modern European drama' is, in the event, wholly justified.

For if Mr Meyer steadfastly avoids the conventional temptations of 'explaining' a writer's work simply in terms of personal experiences and traumas, if he refuses to inflate what is possible into what is certain, he nevertheless does not tumble back into a soft ooze of uncritical reverence. Although the book is permeated throughout by a sort of background warmth of proper but cautious admiration it is also, on occasion, quite sharp and on all important details admirably objective. Ibsen is not here cast in the stone of statues or laid upon the couch: instead we have a detailed picture of a young dramatist feeling his way through 'the unholy trade' as writer, director, instructor, wardrobe manager and jack-of-all-business in the small, inefficient and impoverished theatres of Bergen and Christiania.

The provincialism of the culture out of which Ibsen grew into a giant must have been as soddenly all-pervasive as the wind and rain which smacked down upon the wooden houses. Virtually without a real literature of her own, Norway at the time of Ibsen's birth was politically yoked to Sweden while culturally still a province of Denmark. The written Norwegian language, or *riksmaal*, was all but indistinguishable from written Danish. Inland, the cattle wintered in stalls built without standing-room or light (so giving maximum warmth) and they were lifted out as living skeletons when spring came – an image which somehow seems almost a symbol of the way in which Ibsen himself was lifted out of the narrow, suffocating provincialism which so afflicted him.

The book ends with just such a cracking of the ice, a thawing of the spirit. In April 1864, Ibsen left his homeland on the first southbound steamer of the year, and it was to be 17 years before he returned to live in Norway. He made his way southward across the Alps, the tallow-candled years of failure, frustration and poverty slipping away. Then, the first sight of Italy, and Ibsen describes his emotion as 'a feeling of being released from the darkness into light, emerging from mists through a tunnel into the sunshine.'

A splendid moment to conclude this first volume; the warmth of it refracts back through the grey chapters, and the huge achievements lie shimmering on the horizon. I look forward to the second volume.

George Orwell
New Society, 1 February 1968

With a characteristic precision tempered by an equally typical distaste for the infinite nuances of English hypocrisy, George Orwell once described himself as a member of the 'lower upper-middle class.' And as befitted a man born if not called to such social eminence he stood – or due to the subsequent subtleties of conscience, stooped – all of six feet two and a half inches above the gutters. But to use a graphic working-class insult he might have documented as well as appreciated, his nose was too near his mouth for his own good. Orwell too easily, and ultimately too completely, recognized the putrescence seeping slowly out of the pores of the time and was unwilling to lift his nostrils clear. It was almost as if he sniffed and wrote and choked in the same quivering reflex: his very ideas seem macrosmatic, a wilfully extended attribute of the ground-snuffer. He was able to locate a distant whiff of gangrene in the dustily genteel parlours of the 'aspirin chewing outer suburbs' and to bury a face contorted with disgust deep into the foul armpits of malodorous ideology; moods, emotions, premonitions, obscure prejudices and even the lightest of random speculations could be mutated into a lingering smell on the landing or the grubby sheets on the bed in the attic.

By the same token Orwell was dangerously willing to reduce almost all abstract doctrines, however huge and liberating, into 'smelly little orthodoxies' and even to diminish past grandeurs down to the uncomfortable proportions of a domestic stench. 'Columbus sailed the Atlantic, the first steam engines tottered into motion, the British squares stood firm under French guns at Waterloo, the one-eyed scoundrels of the nineteenth century praised God and filled their pockets; and this is where it all led – to labyrinthine slums and dark back kitchens with sickly, ageing people creeping round and round them like black beetles. It is a kind of duty to see and smell such places now and again, especially smell them, lest you should forget that they exist.' Biologists and police-dogs share the knowledge that smell is species-specific, but it must be an almost unique characteristic to be able, as Orwell was, to recognise vegetarianism or priggishness by their smell and to identify the British working-classes by their distinct odour as well as their stunted configurations.

Louis XI, according to a delectable passage in Burton's *Anatomy of Melancholy*, had a conceit that 'everything did stink about him, all the odoriferous perfumes they could get would not ease him, but still he smelled a filthy stink.' The unlikely parallel cannot be pursued, for Orwell, who sometimes gave the impression that he felt the slime sticking to his skin in a sort of disfiguring or even disabling anguish, never looked for the familiar deodorants of self-deception or sought escape in the soothing literary balms of elegant evasion. The man who wistfully confessed that 'in a peaceful age I might have written ornate or merely descriptive books' instead finished his days in exhausted pessimism, a tubercular wreck sniffing at the future as though it were the stink from a medieval torture chamber.

'The essence of being human,' he wrote in his essay "Reflections on Gandhi", 'is that…one is prepared in the end to be defeated and broken up by life, which is the inevitable price of fastening one's love upon other human individuals.' And in the disused farmhouse on the chilled and appropriately bleak island off the west coast of Scotland where he struggled to complete *Nineteen Eighty-Four* Orwell perhaps reached that final stage of desperation. He spat the book out with his lungs, giving verbal expression to his own disease and loss of political faith by imagining a world where it was a punishable offence to dare to 'fasten one's love upon other human individuals.' This last novel, despite or perhaps even because of its many serious flaws, can still make the reader recoil from a political pessimism so complete, so intransigent that it can only but seem pathological.

> Power is in inflicting pain and humiliation. Power is in tearing human minds to pieces and putting them together again in new shapes of your own choosing. Do you begin to see, then, what kind of world we are creating? [...] A world of fear and treachery and torment, a world of trampling and being trampled upon, a world which will grow not less but *more* merciless as it refines itself. Progress in our world will be towards more pain. [...] A world of victory after victory, triumph after triumph after triumph: an endless pressing, pressing, pressing upon the nerve of power.

Fear, hatred and unrelieved cruelty are here built into the very structure of society and the book would have provoked nightmares whenever it first appeared. But *Nineteen Eighty-Four* came at a time – the end of the Forties – when even the most complacent could smell sulphur in the hedgerows. The elderly ruffians of the west glowered back across the still uncleared minefields at the awful paranoiac domineering in the Kremlin.

It was the right moment for inducing fear, rejecting charity, coining geno-suicidal slogans and striking terroristic political attitudes. Almost all overtly political writing and 'higher journalism' had by then become more or less tinged with these poisons and hysteria seemed to be the most prevalent mood. *Nineteen Eighty-Four* dropped into place with a fearful inevitability, an appropriate parable for the times or a prophecy that everyone seemed bent upon fulfilling. The slabs of bad writing in the book, the ugly repetition of phrase upon phrase upon phrase (like this), the obvious weariness of the characterization and the almost total misanthropy which permeates the story, all came together at the right moment and with the right amount of bludgeoning cruelty to buffet and badly bruise the consciousness of what was coming to be known without any element of irony as 'the free world.'

Orwell himself was scarcely capable of deliberately seeking to nourish this atavism, but by the end of his career his name had grown into almost a synonym for despair as well as honesty – two concepts which have in our day increasingly threatened to merge. Orwell 'the man' constantly gave evidence of an unsanctimonious and tough-minded moral rectitude, apparently as resolutely honest about himself as he was to the world which pressed around his nostrils.

It is not surprising, therefore, that in the hysterical atmosphere of the early Fifties – and when he was no longer around to argue – there should have been plenty of critics who could make the ugly hopelessness of *Nineteen Eighty-Four* seem the logical culmination of the spare but somehow always zestful and even joyous lucidity of Orwell's earlier essays, tracts and novels. Here, the argument went, was the 'socialist' who had been compelled to recoil from the disastrous consequences of his own creed, the 'honest man' who had finally peeled off the scales from his own eyes. Ironically enough, there has been a lot of tendentious or downright dishonest quacking about Orwell's famous honesty.

Party political verbiage has by now made us properly suspicious of those who use the language and the poses of so-called 'straight talking.' As soon as the words drop like drivel from the big face on the television screen we instinctively recoil; at one level the terminology of the 'frank' man is simply yet one more aspect of deviousness; and at another, even deeper level the existence of plain-speaking, morally upright commentators can only seem a comic anachronism, or (even worse) a satirical device by which we infiltrate into the muddy turmoil. But Orwell was the genuine article, perhaps even the last of this particular breed. He was not, for instance, in the slightest degree interested in modern psychology and hence was always able to enjoy the advantages of what he took to be his own objectivity.

Those derided aspirin chewers in the privet belt might almost have been persuaded to feel that here was a man who could at least be trusted, however offensive the things he appeared to be saying. Reassuringly free from political extremism, recognizably philistine in a comfortingly English way, and quite likely to use pleasant words like 'duty,' Orwell nevertheless put himself at the eye of the storm.

He was a witness incapable of yapping from the sidelines about the 'necessary murder' (a phrase which always sounds to me as though it was delivered through a mouthful of cucumber sandwich), a soldier literally unable to shoot a fascist enemy who had been caught with his pants down, and, above all, a man observant enough to notice the tiniest of stains (real and metaphorical) while remaining fastidious enough to shudder in doing so.

Poor put-upon Dorothy, the patient and upright and very Orwellian heroine of his second novel *A Clergyman's Daughter*, manages to persuade herself to take the chalice at the altar rail immediately after it has passed the mouth of another communicant with yellow teeth and a fringe of dark, dewy moustache above her moistly pendulous lips. Dorothy's dutiful 'act of self-abasement' is so like Orwell's own, where the shudder of revulsion became almost sacred (the confirmation of good faith), the wet imprint a mark of commitment and the conscious degradation a necessity – whether as tramp, dishwasher, rifleman or reluctant, sharp-eyed lodger in a despicable Lancashire tripe-shop. Smells, stains, thumb-prints, blackbeetles, dirty false teeth, bowls of filthy washing-up water, gummed-up marmalade pots, dead bluebottles: these become the early punctuation marks or preparatory tribulations in the career of a writer who would rather have been 'a happy vicar' bumbling through harmlessly amiable sermons on damp English Sunday mornings.

Orwell's wistful dream floats up out of his weirdly conservative romanticism, his self-induced but inevitably equivocal nostalgia for other (and better) days, his shuddery distaste for most manifestations of modern industrialism, and his angry longing for order, stability and discipline. It is these things – and not the legendary honesty – which brought him to *Nineteen Eighty-Four*.

The tendentious critics are in a sense right to claim the final horror-fable as the logical culmination of his previous works, but only because *Nineteen Eighty-Four* is much more the last, exhausted expression of the hatred he felt for the modern world. Whether by accident or design, its hero is given the name of Winston: the good old days are raised up in order to discover the real horrors of totalitarianism, and humanity is celebrated by Smith's struggle to recall to his mind an old tune.

Nostalgia becomes a political weapon – the angry, remorseful, mocking nostalgia which is so often the identifying wound of the genuine conservative. 'My novel *Nineteen Eighty-Four* is *not* intended as an attack on socialism, or on the British Labour Party,' Orwell wrote shortly before he died, 'but as a show-up of the perversions to which a centralized economy is liable...'

Even if we dismiss the contented cleric we must still accept the brave truth that the conditions of the time compelled Orwell to become what he over-modestly called 'a sort of political pamphleteer,' unwilling to turn aside from those ubiquitous smells and screams. Instead of behaving like an ornate essayist embellishing delicious middles while eating peaches in a southern sun, Orwell spent his time amongst the rejects and cripples of that 'centralised economy.' Failures were, for him, expressions of the only possible sort of success, and he nosed around in the back-street newsagent's shop for signs of an opposition culture.

'Every suspicion of self-advancement even to "succeed" in life to the extent of earning a few hundred a year, seemed to me spiritually ugly, a species of bullying,' went the attitude he held at the age of 24 when returning from his tormenting stint as a colonial policeman in Burma. He went straight to the Paris kitchens almost as a complicated (and yet also very basic, very simple) act of atonement for being one of the colonial oppressors himself. The shame and disaffection he felt as a public schoolboy curdled within after his experiences in the Empire. In Burma he saw the white rulers as bilious and hysterical frauds, but absorbed enough of their orthodoxy to portray the Burmese themselves as a corrupt and childish people. Orwell's victims collude with the exploiters: and this, too, is but one aspect of conservatism.

His first novel, *Burmese Days* (1934) is in many ways the best, a prolonged and brilliant outburst where the disgust does not quite overwhelm the situation or the characters. But even then, with the exception of the Indian doctor Veraswami (victim of both the Burmese and their snobbery-ridden English masters) the characters are little more than caricatures. We can indeed accept that the prejudiced Memsahib is 'a scraggy old boiling fowl' but hardly that she is a real human being.

But all Orwell's novels can be criticised – or praised – for a relentlessness towards human beings which tightens at times to the extreme point of misanthropy. In between *Burmese Days* and *Nineteen Eighty-Four* there is remarkably little variation in tone or feel, the grey gradually thickening into the black, the grunt of disgust swelling to the howl of anguish, the snobbery and racialism of the white rulers in the first novel growing into the awful cruelty of the totalitarian bosses in the last one. The author of both shows himself to be deficient in the easier forms of human sympathy and yet unable to compensate for this with the elegance of a frivolous literary 'style.'

Orwell had no time for delicacy of composition simply because he had something hard and angry and urgent to get down on the page in slabs of remorseless earnestness. His nausea was perpetually at war with his antique nostalgia, his real pity for the oppressed tangling always with his guilty identification with the oppressors.

It is this tension, in his life and in his prose, that made Orwell such a disturbing and influential writer: we draw out of him our own guilts and nightmares and hypocrisies.

'I don't think I ever once saw his hands clean.'

The line can be blown up like a bomb into a general accusation, fragments scattering to the right and to the left, a remark Orwell could direct at his supposed allies as well as the more predictable enemies. It was in fact written about the wretched Mr Brooker, owner of the fly-blown tripeshop and Orwell's landlord (if that is not too grand a term) in *The Road to Wigan Pier*. Orwell showed here that he undoubtedly felt a sense of community with the struggling and the unemployed, just as he was later to find a sense of comradeship amongst the betrayed militiamen in Spain.

But even then, even when the loneliness of his fight against a hostile world seemed at last to be extinguished in the companionship of battle or social struggle, he looked around for the dirty hands, the full chamberpot under the newly spread table and the grubby deceptions of political 'extremists.' In *Animal Farm* the revolution is betrayed by the dirtiest and yet the most intelligent of the animals.

Orwell could not dare to hope too much, and would not take that huge step forward into political opportunism. The world was getting worse not better, dirtier rather than cleaner. When the hero of *Coming Up for Air* eats a sausage in a milk bar he 'bites into the modern world and discovers what it is really made of.' And that about sums it up, in lumps of fat and gristle masquerading as something else, or in deeply ingrained conservatism expressed as a form of socialism.

There are conservatives who have no eyes – the dangerous, conventional kind – and there are conservatives who have sensitive noses. Orwell deserved to survive because of his sense of smell. He is the only English writer who has managed to suggest that even guilt has its own peculiar yet productive stench.

DENNIS POTTER

I really must tell you I'm so very happy[125]
Sun, 13 May 1968

Will you be watching the play on ITV tonight? Millions of people will, many millions.

But when I think now of all those glazed eyeballs, all those multiplied ears, all those duplicated smiles or snarls or yawns I can feel the adrenalin flopping about inside like I was a Tory candidate looking at a polling booth.

That's because I wrote the play, you see.

The title is very appetising: *The Bone-grinder*. But tonight between 8.30 and 10 o'clock it will be my limbs on the rack. And when (no, if) you irritably jab the button to change channels the bonegrinding will really start to get personal.

Come what may, though, I shall stay with the play until the bitter end. Watch the bright little box with the same avaricious attention as a beady-eyed crow contemplating a miserable little worm.

It takes courage to look at your own work on TV. Sheer, animal courage!

I know one writer of some repute who plays Bo-Peep with his own stuff on the box from behind a fat and high-winged armchair. Every now and then he pokes his head round the upholstery to peep at the screen. And then quickly averts his eyes again in shocked distaste, for all the world like a dear old lady inadvertently confronted with a pair of amorous dogs on her doorstep.

Another playwright approaches his moment of crisis by throwing a cork-popping party at which he addresses everyone in sight with maniac exuberance. And then he slowly, painfully, very comically subsides into total face-twitching gloom while his giggling, champagne-soaked guests are left too tipsy to enjoy anything but the giggling, champagne-soaked commercials.

But I am much, much more rational. I simply chain-smoke and tremble at the back of the kneecaps, listening to the dialogue and pretending not to know what is going to happen next.

'Oh, this is good,' I hiss through my lying teeth. 'This is very good. Very, very good.'

86

'Yes,' says my wife. With a heavy sigh.

Meanwhile on the other channel…no, there's no need to think about that, is there?

Millions of viewers, yes. But I can't see them or touch them, hidden away under their aerials. A colossal audience fragmented into hundreds of thousands of private rooms. A huge throng broken down into small family units, swamping the set in a tide of domestic chatter or a cataract of boiling kettles, and flushing cisterns.

Many, many more people will see my play tonight than have seen *The Mousetrap* in its entire 16-year run at the Ambassadors Theatre, London.

But tonight, alas, there will be no sense of occasion. No applause. No curtain calls. No clatter of uptipped seats. No reverberating murmurs from the slowly departing audience.

The TV set is as domesticated as the washing machine or the cooker.

And as the final credits zip up on the electronic tube the sense of anticlimax is paralysingly complete. The pictures flow on as easy as tap water. One programme after another, every night of the week, every week of the year.

A play which has taken months to write, characters who have leapt up gibbering in your mind when you are trying to sleep, ideas which have simmered feverishly in your blood like a virus – all used up, all at once, all gone.

All wasted? I don't know. But at one minute past 10 tonight I know very well that I shall be feeling rather dejected. For the anti-climax – which is a sort of exhaustion – inevitably breeds self-doubt and pessimism. Were those *really* my lines? Those banal, boring, weary little exchanges flopping out of the hired set squatting so malignantly in the corner of the room?

The real irony, the genuine comedy, is that as a dramatist I am afflicted with the ambitions of a ravening wolf.

So six years of sometimes intense physical pain, through plaster casts and plastic occlusive dressings and injections and hospital beds and mouthfuls of steroids. I have literally been sustained by one overriding, overwhelming and no doubt intrinsically ludicrous idea: the conviction that one day I will write a masterpiece.

No, not tonight's play, though.

I have another TV play in rehearsal in London this week.[126] An anguished sort of comedy which was in large part written with my ballpen strapped on to my right hand. That play – for London Weekend Television – is not a masterpiece either. I suspect that the stress will spill out on the page, insufficiently controlled.

But I can write about this now because suddenly, gloriously, incredibly and (to others) quite incomprehensibly I have been given back my health. On Thursday a specialist in Birmingham acknowledged that something peculiar had happened. Something psychogenic, as he put it. Or mind over body, joy over pain, defiance over despair.

All at once I stopped taking such a heavy daily dose of steroids that I might have, should have, collapsed. It was stupid and arrogant. But worked!

And now the National Theatre has commissioned me to write a play. And now I have my first film script all lined up. And now the BBC have agreed that I should write a life of Christ as a TV play…

All the perspectives shift. I no longer get a hot stab of pain when I turn my head. I am filled with big, bright bubbles of exuberance and gratitude.

Happiness is a terrible thing to try to communicate in a newspaper column. You aren't used to it, are you? But sorry, I cannot hold it back. Why, I might even enjoy that play on ITV tonight. But don't ask me at one minute past 10. Any time but that.

Dennis Potter exposed
Sun, 20 May 1968

Sour. Malicious. Full of hatred. Bilious. Venomous. Crude. Spiteful…

That's me, apparently. Forget the blue eyes and golden hair, dear reader. And look at the festering mess deep in the marrow of my stunted bones.

The TV critics savaged my play on ITV last week almost to a man. Their scornful unanimity was so appalling that I hardly dare to look in the shaving mirror in case some gibbering monster spits back at its own hideous reflection.

One of the happy scribes went so far as to claim that I hate everyone and everything *except coal miners*! Ah, now – there's a ray of light, a gleam of hope shaped like a black diamond. Love makes the world go round, even when you are trapped underground. And as long as I love someone there is yet hope for me and mine.

But I was so badly shaken by the reviews that I examined my conscience and scraped fearfully at what is left of my soul. Could it be, oh, could it be that I hate coal miners, too? The terrible question kept hammering in my skull like a pickaxe on a dwindling seam in an uneconomic pit.

No. Be reassured. The right answer bobbed up through the bile. Coal miners are lovable, coal miners are. But then, despite myself, I thought of Lord Robens, the Alf in charge of the NCB. Cupid in a safety helmet?

Dear, dear…perhaps I need psychiatric help after all. Expert advice to help me breach this wall of hatred.

Sour, malicious, bilious, venomous, crude: after all, when critics use words like that about a writer they know what they are talking about. You bet your sweet life they do!

Wait, though. Last week I wrote that I was *happy*. The alien word leapt up in a blaze of euphoria when I discovered that I had been given my health and strength.

Yes. It's still true. I can open jars again. And hold a pen in a proper grip. And on Thursday I wriggled all my toes in the bath. A month ago they were stiff, purple-looking, useless slabs of meat stuck on the end of my foot. On Friday I ran again. Friday was also my thirty-third birthday – and I hadn't run since I was 27.

So the critics didn't hurt one little bit. How could they? No, that's not quite true. Peter Black in the *Daily Mail* and Stanley Reynolds in the *Guardian* squeezed a few tears of humiliation through all those big bright bubbles of joy. Both of them always write without spite, and both of them can write like angels when the mood takes them. And like all gifted critics, they have that ability to halt you in mid-stride and make you reassess what you have done. Reluctantly, I have to acknowledge complete and utter failure. I was deeply ashamed of the play and therefore ashamed of myself.

The sense of failure is one of those emotions which can cripple a human being, be he a carpenter, or a cobbler or a writer.

In my own case I have long since learned to digest the terrible proposition that I am either going to be a shrivelled, laughable nut, or a good writer. No – not a proposition: an ultimatum. Surely – you say – there must be some in-between way? Why be so extreme? Why insist on being perpetually at risk, like a psychotic acrobat condemned forever to walk along a thin, twanging wire high above a tiny circle of smelly sawdust?

I cannot easily answer those so sensible, so reasonable, so moderate questions.

Even this column is willy-nilly turning into a weekly exercise in self-exposure. I find that in my writing I can only use myself, use up myself. So when I die I want to be completely emptied and completely exhausted.

Which means, of course, that I am still rejoicing. Only a happy human being can write a sentence like that!

Oh. God – I have just read Philip Purser in yesterday's *Sunday Telegraph*. 'I wonder if a case couldn't be brought against Dennis Potter and Rediffusion under the Race Relations Act – for discrimination against the human race,' he wrote about that pitiful little play. 'On any level it was unbelievably vulgar and spiteful,' adds Mr Purser, who undoubtedly finds both these disfiguring emotions alien to himself.

I hope he enjoyed the ads in between the acts. The commercials were happy enough for anybody. Contentment can be bought at the corner store. Joy is simply a question of fitted carpets and the right brand of instant coffee.

This jingle-jangle message ought to invade the pictures on either side of the commercial break. And then we could all collapse on top of each other in a mindless, giggling, giggling heap.

Why not lock up those who think it would be a meaningful sacrament if people occasionally gathered in the streets in order to be sick?[127]

Now, now, be careful… Sour, malicious, full of hatred. Bilious. Venomous. Crude and spiteful. Those labels might stick if I don't watch it.

Smile, darn you, smile! But pardon me if I cannot eat my Sunday lunch. Mr Purser is there in the mustard pot.

Come, come. Pick up that knife and fork. Slice into that bit of dead cow on the plate. Think about coal miners, eh?

Armchair revolution
New Society, 20 June 1968

In the last month I have started coming up to London more frequently, seeing people I have not seen for a year or so, catching up on busy metropolitan chatter. Ross-on-Wye, where I live, continues to feel the same as it ever did, a prosperous, placid little market town quietly festering amidst acres of greenery and full of angry little Minis with Wilson Must Go stickers doing their little bit to increase the number of road accidents. But London – which is defined for you by the people you visit – seems much more like a huge studio where one set has just been struck and a new one hurriedly built out of plaster, plywood, red paint and make-believe.

Most of the flats or houses into which I ventured had Vietcong flags stuck in pots, vases or candlesticks. And posters of Che Guevara on the walls, with a little text beneath which is undoubtedly moving and heroic but tends to become blurred or even ironic when the record players get going. 'If I only had time…,' as the late chart-climber had it, many times amplified.[128]

And almost all of them had copies of the first full issue of the *Black Dwarf* fluttering about the place, the new left-wing fortnightly which has high hopes of not degenerating into yet another *Tribune*. 'Anybody can read the *Black Dwarf*. Age, sex, education, income group – these things don't matter to us. All of you are permitted to read the *Black Dwarf* if you can get hold of a copy. You might find some news you wouldn't get elsewhere.' Age, sex, education, income group: by revealing that these marginalia do not matter to them, the editorial group are already showing an admirable determination to cut out trivial side-issues and get down to real, raw essentials.

The small dark stranger – as it was coyly dubbed in the May Day pre-issue – is the inheritor of a great name and an agitator in a great cause. Continuity with its rumbustious nineteenth century predecessor (the first *Black Dwarf* closed down 130 years ago) is indicated by putting 'Est. 1817. Volume 13, Number One' below the banner. A splendidly romantic gesture, not entirely out of keeping with the poorly proofed, badly written, purposefully strident and yet curiously nostalgic contents.

The first *Black Dwarf*, edited by Tom Wooler,[129] was worn by working men in their caps. The second *Black Dwarf* has already achieved a readership amongst those who wield typewriters, frequent the Tratoo[130] or the newest boutique and who are more likely to think of a cap as a by now rather old-fashioned form of contraception. This is viciously unfair, of course, but also happens to fit in with my immediate if scattered observations. I will apologize later, and joyously, but a protesting correspondence might help to define the sort of arena in which the *Black Dwarf* wants to operate and the kind of people it hopes to reach.

A fund-raising, ideology-defining inaugural meeting to launch the magnificent idea of a resurrected *Black Dwarf* took place in a Cromwell Road flat last autumn. It was an odd, uninspiring occasion, relieved by lethal sniping of a sort worse even than this, a great deal of tragi-comic bickering and the sensible late arrival as well as early departure of Kenneth Tynan.[131] I wouldn't have missed airing some of my class prejudices for a lifetime's subscription.

The editor-to-be, D.A.N. Jones, understandably and endearingly dry-mouthed and slogan-ridden in the face of such a posturing horde, identified both himself and his audience as 'the arty left,' talked reverently of the London dockers, fenced with some savage questions and appeared to indicate that the paper would not only be willing to be educated by your actual working man, but would be read by him as well. Many of us in the room were well off, but not all of us nodded too eagerly. One scriptwriter (money is tied up in the Bahamas) nobly assented to these unusual propositions.

Jones, the theatre critic, also had sufficient sense of the dramatic to claim that the *Black Dwarf* would not pick quarrels with other left-wing factions but only with the principal enemy, capitalism. Naturally, this immediately provoked entirely necessary quarrels between the left-wing factions and a restless, even agitated, shifting of hams on a luxurious settee which must have cost well over a hundred capitalist pounds.

It was, in short, one of those occasions that the workers are seldom privileged to witness, a function as savagely revealing as any ICI boardroom meeting or *Daily Express* editorial conference. If the TV cameras had been present...?

By the end of the meeting, or social gathering, or happening, few things had been adequately defined. The editor-to-be was adamant, however, about the need to fully report and support any strike action, once more mentioning the dockers – who have since stopped work only in order to cheer Enoch Powell and jeer at a coloured chauffeur outside the big White Mother Cow of Parliaments.

Gloomily we forked out our money (with cheque books, of course), sipped our pretty drinks, talked about Harold and dispersed without fervour into the damp chill of the huge, complacent city. And I tried a little too hard not to write this sort of hatchet job, swallowing an ill-timed crack about that imported, canned sweetcorn brand named The Green Giant. But bad jokes, like bad blood, will out – a personal defect which Tom Wooler, at least, might well have understood.

But months later, soon after May Day,[132] a single sheet pre-issue taster came out with a battery of pugnacious promises about the kind of newspaper we scarcely had the right to expect. 'We will write about real politics: the things done to this country by oil magnates, bankers, sterling and property speculators, insurance companies, strike breakers and press lords.' If only we could at last have such a journal!

In between the properly fiery sheet and the first full issue, D.A.N. Jones was sacked from the editorship, not for avoiding quarrels with other left wing factions but apparently because of a lack of revolutionary zeal, an attitude which might have been predicted of one who tenaciously retains membership of the Labour Party. Resolution or insurrections had suddenly leapt too vibrantly into the mind. This was no longer a time for half-measures or caution or literary style or persuasive argument or infiltration among those who warbled "Bye, Bye, Blackbird" with such cheerful venom.

So Volume 13, Number One, has a stirring front page, tagged as a 'slogan heard outside the French Embassy, London, Sunday – 25 May': 'WE SHALL FIGHT, WE WILL WIN, PARIS LONDON ROME BERLIN.' If the list had been compiled out of, say, Oldham and Cardiff and Rochdale and Glasgow, the contents might have had more scalpel-like relevance and the muscularity of a more genuine urgency. But no. The familiar old, tired old phrases pile up like cobblestones, except that you cannot even throw them. Volume 13 begins with a mechanical 'flamboyance,' full of totally humourless attacks on prosperous respectable men by other prosperous if determinedly unrespectable men.

Exhortation is no substitute for analysis, and hard facts are considerably more potent than antique, unpersuasive rhetoric. Why start a new newspaper if you are only going to fill it with old ghosts for the entertainment of a small and privileged intellectual or pseudo-intellectual elite?

I am not being entirely sour, insular and destructive in this piece. We need a paper like the *Black Dwarf*, arrowing in on specific targets with specific facts for its weapons. But it needs, too, an aggressive gaiety, a cool irony, a cynicism tempered by bold optimism, a rumbustious vulgarity, a sense of the surrounding hypocrisy and the wit to draw on the real experiences of its contributors and supporters.

These guilt-laden experiences come out of the mass media and the politically odious communications industries, out of hilarious television script conferences, the dollar-backed film industry, the theatre and newspapers – the so-called 'leisure' sectors (chuckle) which so consistently put themselves in the service of the established powers and degradingly add their own peculiar corruptions to the political process. Here, indeed, would be a meaningful exercise in communication, in exposing our own hypocrisies, amongst many other forms of desirable revelation or agitation. My own literary agent[133] is a member of the editorial group and although I still expect him to know on which side his and my bread are buttered we both ought to keep the ivory-handled knife in our hands a bit longer.

But when I unwisely put some of these premature gripes to an enthusiastic revolutionary in a ludicrously expensive restaurant he angrily concluded that I was, 'An Enemy. Yes. An Enemy!' We both swallowed our coffee and then sipped at our brandies, contemplating each other coldly, without a tremor of amusement or a saving flicker of irony. Terrible things happen between respectable men during the time their non-readers are at their lathes.

The face at the window
Times, 3 August 1968

'Brow-hanging, shoe-contemplative, *strange*.' Coleridge's famous description of William Hazlitt (1778–1830)[134] has the swift neatness of a stage direction introducing a character weird enough to commit a murder or deliver an uninvited sermon. The hyphen-hung words flap out like admonitory fingers, all pointing a praise so ambiguous that it becomes an uneasy accusation. A hundred or so years later the vivid immediacy of personal acquaintance hardens into a more headmasterly sort of disapproval within the solidified slabs of the *Oxford Companion to English Literature*. By now the brow-hanging essayist has curdled into 'a quarrelsome and unamiable man, of a curiously divided nature.'

Hazlitt disturbed people – and can still do so, very effectively. It was his intellectual distinction and social misfortune to have no time to spare for those 'who think by proxy and talk by rote.' The unamiable fellow was blessed with a mind at least as tough, grainy and waterproof as the walking shoes he was alleged to contemplate during one of those sudden silences which so agitated his acquaintances. And he could use invective with such viperish skill that his victims might well have examined themselves in a hand-mirror to see if the venomous prose had erupted into discoloured flesh or broken skin. A quirky, pungent, obsessive, honest and extremely forceful writer who alienated most of his friends, he exposed himself without mercy, and yet 'never gave the lie to his own soul'.

The personality of this born dissenter lies across his voluminous prose like a too quickly uncoiling adder encountered in the middle of a woodland path. You cannot see the wood for the sting. And as a result, through what is almost an accumulation of nervous gossip or those constant depositions of a too genteel distaste, Hazlitt has been relegated to the unhappy status of a 'character' in literature, a crab apple in a rich orchard. He is a man honoured by refraction through other and greater writers, a footnote in other biographies, but who is now little enough read except, dismembered, in books of quotations or pinned down in those dusty butterfly cases called Anthologies of English Prose or even (incredibly) at the head of idyllic, grocery-shop calendars.

'The art of pleasing consists in being pleased'
– Wm. Hazlitt, essayist, 1778–1830.

I have seen these splendidly ironic words above the picture for the month of May and the lower case but equally misleading promise of 'fresh farm produce our speciality.' Embroidered quotations can be almost as effective as marriage or a mortgage in domesticating a writer, and little bits of Hazlitt constantly turn up in calendars or delicious middles or similarly unlikely places. But in spite of the curious enthusiasms of motto-mongers and the occasional leader-writer, and in the yellowing teeth of the general if rather automatic acknowledgment that Hazlitt was an essayist of genius, the alternative image persists of an ill-tempered dabbler pressing his scowling face against the windows of a warm and well-lit room. We feel a sudden chill and pull the curtains. We shut the book and turn to a more comforting blaze or some warmer slop. Hazlitt can stay outside, rubbing his hands and hard words together in that cheerless damp which descends with the dusk of unjust neglect.

Perhaps it would be better, in a way, if we knew less about Hazlitt as a person and came uninitiated upon those 21 volumes of collected works. The 'quarrelsome and unamiable man' has too often been dismissed in contemptuous terms which have more to do with the alleged defects of his personality rather than any actual flaws in his prose – and as Hazlitt himself acknowledged, in motto-mood, 'a nickname is the heaviest stone that the devil can throw at a man.' Confrontation with the actual text can still be, in such instances, as salutary an experience as going direct to the subject rather than just the source of a poisonous rumour: the parameters shift a little, a few dried-up presumptions flake off like psoriatic scales, and we may even find ourselves shamed or surprised into an unexpected sympathy. Hazlitt has been hidden for too long in the glass case in the darker corner of the library, slowly losing all colour and vibrancy in the steady dust of other men's prejudices and other ages' fashions.

But the prejudices or even enmity of his acquaintances, and the very English distaste of some of his subsequent critics are still there to press against the eyeball when approaching Hazlitt as an essayist. It is an academic delusion to maintain that a writer can be so easily separated from his writing. That strange but tenacious matrix of extraneous expectations, curiosity, hope, fear and magic-hunger which readers so often insist upon bringing to a writer of genius cannot sensibly be denied. We want to know, needs must know, what sort of person in what sort of circumstance put together those words we are reading. The author, after all, can be powerful enough to scrape at our insides with an awful diligence – or he may just be a comforting raconteur babbling away in the opposite armchair. It is as if a work of art cannot have a complete autonomy of its own.

Thus it is that, as though in deliberate compensation for the suffocating discipline of close textual analysis which characterises modern literary criticism, modern lit-biographies seize greedily upon the most trivial events or quirks of character or accidents of inheritance which make the man as opposed to the works. And in Hazlitt's case it is exceptionally difficult to separate the two: he used himself, used up himself, in so unique a fashion that it would even be perverse to attempt the exercise. The adder on the path has to be stepped on, or stepped over. Hazlitt virtually demands that we judge him as a person as well as a master of prose.

'Well, I've had a happy life,' he croaked just before he died in a bleak little room in Soho, after months of penury and great physical pain and the contemplation of hopes broken or abandoned. Last words, like first acquaintances or maiden speeches, are more likely to deceive than to enlighten, and in any case are often the timely inventions of those gathered around the bedside, eager to add some pious epitaph or malicious valediction to give a suitably retrospective flavour to the life of the dear departing. But Hazlitt's reputed farewell is not without credibility, despite the poverty, the accumulated humiliation, and the cancer of the stomach.

He used up his days with sufficient intensity to wring out of them more than enough genuine delight, more than a usual amount of personal revelation, a fine anger and a fearless, ennobling consistency. The torments and depressions and sometimes feverish sensuality could not in the end outbalance the vigorousness or even joy of his talk, his writing and his blazing enthusiasms. He was the type of manic depressive who was able to use even the black moments to reach deep down into himself and find an extremity of meaning or experience which could be communicated to others.

Hazlitt was also one of those prickly, introspective radicals who have conservative tastes and a longing for the past which is too lyrical or too melancholic to be dismissed as mere nostalgia, that second-hand emotion which second-rate writers use to generate a sense of evocation that is in fact only a passing mood of trivial regret. The tension between radical intellect and conservative instincts is, of course, often a rich source of creativity, and Hazlitt can never be boxed up in the righteous rigidities of more mundane political prose. There is frequently a menacing ambiguity about his work, a perpetual suspense, the sentences stretching taut with a carefully delayed and exquisitely timed sting, the final battery of adjectives twanging at the end (usually in groups of three) with a deadly resonance. It would now be tit-for-tat to use Hazlitt's description of the apostate Coleridge as an example:

> ...His complexion was at that time clear, and even bright – As are the children of yon azure sheen. His forehead was broad and high, light as if built of ivory, with large projecting eyebrows, and his eyes rolling beneath them like a sea with darkened lustre. 'A certain tender bloom his face o'erspread', a purple tinge as we see it in the pale thoughtful complexions of the Spanish portrait-painters, Murillo and Velásquez. His mouth was gross, voluptuous, open, eloquent; his chin good-humoured and round; but his nose, the rudder of the face, the index of the will, was small, feeble, nothing – like what he has done.

I have used this cool and impertinent quotation from probably the most famous of all the essays for several obvious reasons. But the first is personal and perhaps sentimental or even irrelevant: these were the first words of Hazlitt that made any impression on me, and I came upon them not (as should have been so) in the original essay but quoted at length, and icily, in a book about the poet. In my teens, doped by the mysterious perfumes of "Christabel" and held in the clutch of the grey-beard loon, such a description seemed tantamount to blasphemy. I had probably dipped into one or two of the essays without feeling particularly impressed or eager to explore further. Hazlitt was just a spiky figure on the fringes, a man admired by Keats, and – oh yes, oh of course – a 'great essayist,' said in the tone of voice which relegates the table-talk essay to an antiquated form of limited range and little present relevance.

Thus, as seems so often to be the case with Hazlitt, my first meaningful acquaintance with his writing was only to experience a sort of distaste, to recoil from that swift, bone-crunching brutality so characteristic of some patches of his prose. Any subsequent encounters with the essayist would inevitably be tinged with the residue of an adolescent prejudice. Hazlitt had been given his label.

But about seven years and maybe a thousand books later, when in the first and so most irrationally terrifying grip of an illness which still flickers hotly at my limbs, and when also walled-up in a near-suicidal depression which apparently had more to do with biochemistry than the more attractive lures of self-judgment, I was fortunate enough to be the beneficiary of a deviant volume in an otherwise orthodox hospital welfare trolley.[135] Tucked almost shamefully away on the bottom layer was a well-worn, orangey-brown collection of Hazlitt's essays, which I took with a graceless reluctance designed less to pull myself out of a hole than to fend off the formidable trolley-pusher, who had Good Deeds shining on her face like a badly applied cosmetic.

Graham Greene has written that it is only in childhood that books have any really profound influence on our lives, for only then can their magic work at full potency. But occasionally – even if usually at some crisis – the gift can also be accepted in adulthood, and this now was the case with the grubby volume of essays on the trolley. I record the experience here because the main purpose of my article is to attempt to communicate an enthusiasm – and Hazlitt, at that time, seemed to me at least as emancipating as a mouthful of steroids. He is a writer who demands an almost physical reaction from his readers, an essayist who might well be sitting in the same room, prepared to join in an argument, throw in an opinion or offer a comfort tinged with necessary anguish.

We walk through life, as through a narrow path, with a thin curtain drawn around it; behind are ranged rich portraits, airy harps are strung – yet we will not stretch forth our hands and lift aside the veil, to catch glimpses of the one, or sweep the chords of the other. As in a theatre, when the old-fashioned green curtain drew up, groups of figures, fantastic dresses, laughing faces, rich banquets, stately columns, gleaming vistas appeared beyond: so we have only at any time to "peep through the blanket of the past," to possess ourselves at once of all that has regaled our senses, that is stored up in our memory, that has struck our fancy, that has pierced our hearts:– yet to all this we are indifferent, insensible, and seem intent only on the present vexation, the future disappointment.

Hazlitt frequently and successfully raided that store, forced to record that his earliest hopes were also his last regrets. I responded eagerly and almost immediately to the unhurried and yet somehow urgent rhythm of his conversational prose, the delicacy of his sensual impressions, the knowing mockery of his memory, the vigorous clarity of his opinions, and the continuing sense of a person prepared to dig into himself to expose the full dimensions of either an enthusiasm or a sadness. And, above all, I suppose, I grabbed at the superb invective, abrasive and tingling still, which has ever since seemed to me far more open, useful and dignified than the slippery evasiveness or underhand, over-cautious snidery which nowadays so often passes for combat or controversy. Hazlitt was gifted enough to give not only the sense of a landscape or of a walk in the morning frost but also the weight and feel of a genuine argument or the insistent power of an overwhelming mood.

'There can be no question that Hazlitt the thinker is an admirable companion,' wrote Virginia Woolf, perhaps rather unexpectedly. 'He is strong and fearless, and he speaks his mind forcibly yet brilliantly too... He will live in a volume of essays in which is distilled all those powers that are dissipated and distracted elsewhere, where the parts of his complex and tortured spirit come together in a truce of amity and concord...'

I call in Bloomsbury because of a persistent suspicion that my enthusiasm for Hazlitt is a little too obsessive and personal.[136] Often over the past few years I have played with the idea of attempting his biography[137] but have always abandoned such grandiose thoughts in the almost certain knowledge that it would be even more disastrous and unbalanced a project than Hazlitt's own four-volume *Life of Napoleon* (1828–30). Meant as Hazlitt's major work, his message for posterity, *Napoleon* was a huge failure. 'As a little child,' he recorded, 'I knelt and lifted up my hands in prayer,' for the success of the French Revolution, and the hope for a new order was never to leave him or be long absent from his work. In this, at least, he showed some of the characteristics and much of the devotion of his father, an Irish Unitarian minister who had settled at Wem in Shropshire in 1787.

> Here he passed his days, repining but resigned, in the study of the Bible, and the perusal of the Commentators. – huge folios, not easily got through, one of which would outlast a winter!... Here were 'no figures nor no fantasies,' – neither poetry nor philosophy – nothing to dazzle, nothing to excite modern curiosity; but to his lack-lustre eyes there appeared, within the pages of the ponderous, unwieldy, neglected tomes, the sacred name of JEHOVAH in Hebrew capitals: pressed down by the weight of the style, worn to the last fading thinness of the understanding, there were glimpses, glimmering notions of the patriarchal wanderings, with palm-trees hovering in the horizon, and processions of camels at the distance of three thousand years; there was Moses with the Burning Bush,

the number of the Twelve Tribes, types, shadows, glosses on the law and the prophets...questions as to the date of the creation, predictions of the end of all things: the great lapses of time, the strange mutations of the globe were unfolded with the voluminous leaf, as it turned over: and though the soul might slumber with an hieroglyphic veil of inscrutable mysteries drawn over it, yet it was in a slumber ill-exchanged for all the sharpened realities of sense, wit, fancy or reason. My father's life was comparatively a dream: but it was a dream of infinity and eternity, of death, the resurrection, and a judgment to come!

The arrival of a new edition of *Tom Jones* during his schooldays in damp but palm-treed Wem penetrated the spell of his father's household by showing the young Hazlitt a different sort of world beyond those ponderous and unwieldy tomes. Later came the theatre (and dramatic criticism) and, especially, art to attack further his senses with 'a joy unutterable.' As Hazlitt was to say when he first saw Mrs Siddons at Hackney, 'the gates were unbarred, the folding doors of fancy were thrown open...' He passed eagerly through those doors, initially to become an accomplished painter until turning to literature in 1811. But even when farthest along the road from Wem and his childhood one can still glimpse in Hazlitt the lineaments of his father and some sensually mutated version of his father's dream.

In 1820 Hazlitt became wildly infatuated with Sarah Walker, the second daughter of a London tailor in whose house he lodged. Three years later, under a thinly disguised anonymity, Hazlitt published his *Liber Amoris*, a cruelly underrated, unusual, self-exposing and bitterly painful account of the whole wretched affair. The book was to delight his political and personal enemies and cloud his reputation through the long Victorian years of imperial grandeur, repression and hypocrisy. It is heavy with the pain of love rejected, resonant with humiliation, too close to the experience to be anything like fair to Sarah. Yet the passion survives the futility, the candour gives it its own dignity, and it even bears comparison with Stendhal's *De L'Amour*, which was published just a year earlier.

Crabb Robinson called the book 'disgusting' and said that 'it ought to exclude the author from all decent society.' Others have called it silly, revolting, and unmanly. Certainly *Liber Amoris* is a peculiarly vulnerable work, extreme in detail and emotion, utterly obsessive and full of passages which can easily be quoted in derision of the middle-aged Hazlitt. But in it we can catch at a considerable man being driven to the point of insanity by his feelings, and there is about it the pressure of genius, the full and horrible anguish of unrequited love.

> I am now enclosed in a dungeon of despair. The sky is marble to my thoughts: nature is dead around me, as hope is within me: no object can give me one gleam of satisfaction now, nor the prospect of it in time to come. I wander by the seaside: and the eternal ocean and lasting despair and her face are before me. Slighted by her, on whom my heart by its last fibre hung, where shall I turn? I wake with her by my side, not as my sweet bedfellow but as the corpse of my love, without a heart in her bosom, cold, insensible, or struggling from me; and the worm gnaws me, and the sting of unrequited love, and the canker of a hopeless, endless sorrow.

Hazlitt recovered after a fashion to sip his endless cups of strong tea, argue with his companions, waste himself on Napoleon, meet the cancer in his stomach and die in poverty at 6 Frith Street on 18 September 1830. He was buried in St. Anne's churchyard, Soho, with Charles Lamb and P.G. Patmore (father of the poet) as the only mourners.

Somehow it seems the right sort of end for a man so 'brow-hanging, shoe-contemplative, *strange*.' But there is a better description of Hazlitt in full flight, by John Reynolds:

> Warm, lofty and communicative on everything Imaginative and Intelligent... Passing from grand and commanding argument to the gaieties and graces of wit and humour – and the elegant and higher beauties of Poetry. He is indeed great company, and leaves a weight on the mind, which "it can hardly bear"... His countenance is also extremely fine – a sunken and melancholy face – a forehead lined with thought and bearing a full and strange pulsation on exciting subjects – an eye, dashed in its light with sorrow, but kindling and living at intellectual moments – and a stream of coal-black hair dropping round all.

That strange pulsation and commanding argument have been adequately preserved in the prose. Hazlitt's companionship is still there for the taking; the experience is a rewarding one, leaving the same sort of weight on the mind. There is no need to draw the curtains.

Back – to weave dreams out of my own wallpaper
Sun, 21 October 1968

For at least an hour I talked with brilliant eloquence. Blustering, cajoling, threatening, pleading.

'But all hospital patients say this,' slyly infiltrated the amused doctor as my rhetoric momentarily faltered. 'They all say they would like to go home.'

After six weeks in the alien, clinical, trolley-clanking, pillow-plumping, needle-jabbing, thermometer-sucking surroundings I was not going to be put down quite so easily.

'Oh,' I said bravely.

The doctor seemed to loom up like a white-coated monster at the foot of my bed. Any moment now I would be chewing my pyjama cords and contemplating defeat.

'Yes,' he said ominously, 'they want to go home as soon as they come in. Now I think it would be better if you stayed here another –'

'No!'

My bed creaked with indignation. It was the quickest possible interruption. No, no – home or nothing!

'If you go home…' he began, cautiously.

I beamed up at him, preparing to nod at the right moment, to look grave at the right moment, to smile at the right moment. This was a no-holds barred contest, with liberty as the prize.

And then, like a magistrate lifting the terms of a probation order, the conditions for my release were spelled out in cold, precise detail. I was to stay in bed for a while. I was to stay indoors for much, much longer. No working trips. No social jaunts. No unnecessary stress or tension. A weekly blood count. And assorted bottles of biliously coloured tablets to rattle about like the counters in a game of snakes and ladders.

All this was supposed to browbeat me into submission. Instead I responded with an eagerness which probably tempted the poor man to call in an outside opinion, preferably psychiatric.

'I have to stay indoors?' I chuckled. 'Housebound for months?'

He stared at me, stepped back half a pace, and nodded carefully.

How was he to know that one of my secret ambitions has been to be placed under house-arrest. That he was giving sanction, with all the massive authority of a physician, to my perverse desire to be like the hermits of childhood fairytales?

Travel nauseates me. Hotels are a damn sight worse than hospitals. The conversation of strangers is, for me, a mixture of boredom and foreboding, triviality and terror.

I am almost certainly the only Oxford graduate of my generation who has never been abroad. April in the Forest of Dean is, for me, an infinitely sweeter prospect than the same month in smelly Paris.

The furthest I have ever ventured from home was a three-day stay in Hartlepools,[138] about eight years ago. And I still remember every moment of the nightmare. Strange sights and sounds, weird speech patterns breaking about my startled ears, and a lady in a billowing blue nightdress demonstrating the comforts of a new mattress in a store window. A small crowd gathered in pop-eyed silence to watch as she jumped madly in and out of the bed. Nobody spoke. Nobody moved. Our breath hung in the cold, steely grey air in small toxic clouds of helpless bewilderment.

Is it always like this in Hartlepools? Are the people still there, breathing anxiously against the smeared plate glass? Well, I shan't bother to find out. How much nicer it is to weave the dreams out of your own wallpaper, and populate the world with characters coaxed out of your own imagination.

O, hustling, bustling, chattering, chanting world, I withdraw gratefully from your buses and trains and headlong imbecilities. It is enough, surely to tip-tap on a stick from one room to another – especially with winter about to flex its muscles.

And as you shoulder or strap-hang your way to work this morning, think enviously of me and my small kingdom, and reflect that of all the passions memory is probably the most potent.

'Are you sure I have to stay indoors?' The question was repeated with genuine gaiety. And the answer, again, was reassuring.

So here I am, back home again, the great drama of family life once more encasing me like a huge protective shell. This column can pick up where I dropped it, a mixture of self-revelation and opinionated comment delivered from the same armchair as before.

'If you don't do anything and if you don't go anywhere,' said a friend on the telephone yesterday morning, 'what on earth can you write a weekly column about?' Silly man. Anybody would think that words were places and thoughts were things.

What is this life if,
full of care,
We have no time
to stand and stare?[139]

Normal service will be resumed next week,[140] if you and my friends would care to wait and see.

Lightning over a dark field
Times, 7 December 1968

Bomb Culture by Jeff Nuttall (MacGibbon and Kee)

I remember the huge thrill in the playground when the A bomb was dropped. One of the bigger boys – an 11-year-old who could strike sparks on the tarmac with his boot studs – claimed that, according to his Dad, the bomb was no bigger than a broad bean. Wow! Everybody seemed very pleased, especially the grown ups.

Soon there would be a VJ Party for all of us kids, with a decorated mug and a balloon to take home. Booty – after the usual hectic scrabble called musical chairs. 'Right at that point,' says Jeff Nuttall, who was then two years older and presumably more observant, 'the generations became divided in a very crucial way.' Didn't he get a King George VI mug then, nor even a pretty balloon? The piano stops suddenly. *You are my sunshine, my only sunsh...* Now there's one chair less, then another, then another...

And grinning at the back of the church hall is the survivor. An agile child with red hair, blue eyes and a pretty face. Me. The bomb had dropped and I won a clockwork soldier.

Now, all of 33, I often need a stick to walk. Arthritis twists at my joints. I have chronic psoriasis: a manic-depressive getting through the day on steroids and librium, the night on sodium amytal. Five times in hospital and they want me back in again. 'Classic stress illness,' says a specialist, the tips of his fingers together, making me want to apologise.

But I have gone through and beyond the despair and even the hatred which has so often powered me in the past. After a particularly harrowing year of physical illness and mental self-exploration I clutch at the realization – call it intolerable arrogance if you like – that I might one day write something which will 'survive.' A vocation rather than just a perpetual therapy to exorcize personal hobgoblins; a writer alive and alert rather than a cripple squirming on the end of a pin that grows out of guilts too dark and obscure to explore here.

And if or when I ever meet Jeff Nuttall, who has also gone beyond despair, I should like to put my arm around his shoulders – one human being to another, one writer to another, but primarily the grateful, inadequate gesture of a reviewer to an author who has written the sort of book which triggers strong emotions in the reader. A book which you must read, as soon as possible.

Bomb Culture is an abscess that lances itself. An extreme book, unreasonable but not irrational. Abrasive, contemptuous, attitudinizing, ignorant and yet brilliant. Whole chapters can be rejected by squares like me. The author uses the word 'square' like a farmer talking about pigs. There we are, wallowing in the mud of our mortgages, slurping down our contaminated mash, our pink snouts grunting out the deceitful platitudes which keep us in the white-washed sty. His hatred spikes out like forked lightning over a dark field, and it is no use cowering under the poisoned foliage.

Nuttall has the bomb in his chest. The overwhelming obscenity of it coats everything with slime – and I know the feeling. Emotions which led him, as others, into nihilism and the kind of despair which, had it spread wide enough, might have touched off the Holocaust. The squares kept their nerve because they cherished their lies.

Meanwhile Nuttall was discussing the possibility of disembowelling a human corpse and hurling the messy entrails at the audience. The Underground was turning avidly to sado-masochism. Sick jokes and filth splattered the customers as well as the broadsheets. 'Moral shame, moral absurdity, moral abuse, moral paradox and moral outrage had frozen us at a point of almost total negativity. The way out was the numbing of the moral sense and the use of the sensation, the pain, and the anger as propulsion.'

This is a terrible statement. Not only an admission of sickness, but almost a glorification in it. Alienation could not be more complete.

At this point in the book I could hardly bear to read on. My own elaborate and hypocritical defence mechanism was being threatened. Never part of that scene, I had nevertheless recognized similar symptoms in myself at about the same time and crawled into hospital with profound relief, embracing a passionate but (unfortunately) godless puritanism. The cool hipsters disgusted me. The whole psychedelic and pop swirl affronted all my sensibilities, answered none of my yearnings and seemed only to lead back into the old, old tunnel. I am so square that I prefer Lew Stone to Rolling Stone, so *Bomb Culture* is, for me, a guide book.

But it is also so much more. Having gone to the core of disgust, Nuttall has clambered back into our shared half-light. The book becomes autobiography of a peculiarly intense, honest and challenging type, demanding an equally honest response from the reader. He has got through to me, all right. I felt cleansed when he struggled through to an affirmation of life, the ecstasy of 'perpetual inner illumination.' He wants his offal-throwing friends of yesterday to turn into real craftsmen. The Freakout is over, he says. We must now 'call upon the native European sense of classic form and rational serenity. It is time the hipsters learned how to count.'

If, at that, I held out a hand and said 'welcome' it might seem intolerably condescending. But it isn't. I, too, have been in the pit. Jeff Nuttall helped me to see that even more clearly than before and he managed to do it without putting the tips of his fingers together. There is no need for either of us to apologize.

Part Two
Telling Stories

'It is laughable to sit down and try to write a masterpiece. It is degrading to sit down and try to write anything else.'[141] This comment from the 1971 column "Acid drops" was Potter's latest expression of his desire to write 'something which will "survive,"' and this sense of 'vocation' as a television writer had sustained him through illness.[142] Building on this, Potter's non-fiction in the 1970s engaged particularly strongly with the opportunities and restrictions faced by programme makers. His concern that television would narrow its ambitions in response to a 'puritan pressure group' or the 'overpaid charlatans and memo-grinders' who ran the industry, and his desire to find new techniques, culminated in his response to the banning of *Brimstone & Treacle* in 1976 and his lecture "Realism and non-naturalism" in 1977.

The scale and nature of Potter's profile in this period were evident in press coverage of his first two plays transmitted in the 1970s: *Lay Down Your Arms* (1970)[143] and *Angels are so Few* (1970).[144] Previewing *Lay Down Your Arms*, the *Sunday Times* set its readers a quiz: 'Tonight's autobiographical play is about a miner's son with an IQ of 165 doing his National Service as a Russian interpreter in the War Office before going to Oxford and clashing with the upper class in the persons of his officers: who is the author?'[145] It assumed an answer – 'Quite right, Dennis Potter' – which is a sign of the major role that *seeming* autobiography played in Potter's writing. Potter discussed his National Service in various pieces including a 1961 column in which he recalled an Intelligence Officer who failed to find 'accelerator' in his 'blawsted dictionary' despite having 'been all through the EXes.'[146] In a 1970 book review, Potter virtually trailed the play's themes in his mockery of military life and description of Britain as having declined from imperial power into narrow prejudice.[147] *Lay Down Your Arms* was criticised as anti-Army propaganda,[148] but Potter's later review "Kafka and Brasso" returned to these themes, drawing parallels between his experiences in the military and hospital: 'Each place compresses a version of sickness or distortion.'[149] Those reviewers who criticised *Lay Down Your Arms* as 'a somewhat undigested piece of autobiography'[150] were part of an increasing tendency to identify patterns across Potter's work.

Angels are so Few is recognised as an early example of Potter's use of the 'visitor' motif through which an outsider arrives and 'triggers off intense introspection within the central protagonist,' becoming in Potter's phrase the 'stranger at the door who's really inside your head.'[151] The outsider here is Michael Biddle (Tom Bell), a young man who believes himself to be an angel, and the door leads into the domestic prison of frustrated housewife Cynthia Nicholls (Christine Hargreaves). Cynthia's seduction of Biddle resembles an assault that causes a fall from innocence, which anticipates Potter's observation to Derek Hart that 'a lot of my plays have been about people whose lives do not match their fantasies.'[152] Biddle's arrival seems to offer Cynthia liberation: her husband's disgust at explicit scenes on television draws her response that 'it's the sick people who are scared of sex.' However, the Nicholls' heated conversation about permissiveness was echoed by complaints about *Angels are so Few* itself.[153] T.C. Worsley speculated that 'it takes a certain degree of toughness to send back a Dennis Potter script since, rightly or wrongly, he has become established as an important and controversial writer,' and criticized the *Play for Today* (BBC1, 1970–84) strand of which *Angels are so Few* was a part.[154] Worsley's piece was just one example of how single play strands remained a contested space, which Potter as critic recognized and challenged in his evocative descriptions of *The Wednesday Play* and *Play for Today* as the 'irritating but reassuringly authentic lump of white gristle buried somewhere beneath the skin' of a pork sausage[155] and 'the major area left on TV still capable of transmitting the nourishing zest of an individual imagination which necessarily cares not a Controller's fart for ratings charts or conveyer-belt packaging.'[156]

Potter's next transmitted play, *Paper Roses* (1971),[157] was also read for autobiographical traces, but this time in terms of his experiences in journalism. *Paper Roses* discussed changing newspaper cultures through its depiction of the final days of old reporter Clarence Hubbard (Bill Maynard). Reviewer Peter Fiddick praised the play as 'the most accurate, detailed re-creation of a newspaper office and newspaper people that I have yet seen,'[158] but it was not the naturalistic exposé of tabloid newspapers that producer Kenith Trodd had hoped for. Potter wrote more openly on the subject in his non-fiction, from a light-hearted discussion of the faking of readers' letters[159] to the descent of the *Sun* into a 'tit-and-thighs' tabloid[160] after it was taken over by Rupert Murdoch in

1969. The play was attacked as a 'sour caricature' that distorted the 'real experience of real journalists' despite its makers' claim that 'the author used to work in Fleet Street.'

Intriguingly, however, that attack on *Paper Roses* came from *Paper Roses* itself: a fictional critic in the play has been watching the play and dictates a scathing review written, of course, by Potter. This device demonstrated some of the ideas that Potter developed during this period. Firstly, it showed his certainty that drama can capture experience without needing to use conventional naturalistic means. Secondly, it underlined his dual status as writer-and-critic,[161] which was often mentioned by critics, who sought evidence in his plays that 'His hero was plainly himself'[162] or wondered why someone whose reviews could be so 'rigorous and unforgiving' was 'unduly concerned to anticipate and reject conceivable criticism.'[163] Potter as critic engaged with the practices of other critics, especially when they commented on the work of Potter the author.[164] The fictional critic in *Paper Roses* distractedly plays golf during the programme, which reflected Potter's interest in the domestic conditions in which people watch television,[165] and underlined his concern that neglectful reviewers were helping to make this the 'youngest and most sniffily derided of the media.'[166]

Another discredited storyteller featured in Potter's next play, *Traitor* (1971).[167] Journalists visit Adrian Harris (John Le Mesurier), a former controller in British intelligence who has defected to the Soviet Union. Critics discussed *Traitor* in relation to Kim Philby, who had been mentioned in *Lay Down Your Arms* and inspired *Traitor*,[168] but Potter did not want 'to make it directly Philby' because that would require a biographical approach, which was 'a sphere of writing that I am just simply, matter-of-factly, finally and emphatically, not interested in.'[169] Instead, Harris's motivations, and his argument that he had betrayed his class but not his country, were interspersed with memories, as Potter, according to Carpenter, 'developed the device of subliminally swift and repeated flashbacks or cutaways to suggest what is passing through a character's mind.'[170] Critics also read *Traitor* in terms of autobiography, relating its questioning of whether 'the child is father to the man' to *Stand Up, Nigel Barton* (1965) in order to argue that *Traitor* was 'passionately personal.'[171] However, other critics argued that autobiographical readings had their limits: for Raymond Williams, discussing *Lay Down Your Arms* in terms of

Potter's life meant neglecting the work by 'writing it off' with 'irrelevant' details.[172]

Like *Traitor*, *Casanova* (1971)[173] stitched together past and present through the experiences of an unreliable storyteller. In this, his first serial, Potter 'wanted to do a portrait, if you like, that accumulated, that sifted through layers of various incidents and how they changed perspective' because 'we're walking compendiums in a way of memory.'[174] Potter 'didn't want to write a costume drama'[175] and though the project began as a response to books that Potter received as a reviewer,[176] he claimed to have used their details as merely a starting point because 'memoirs are self-serving and adorned with lies.'[177] He claimed that the biographer was 'tempted to trespass into places where only the novelist can properly walk,' given 'the huge, shifting dimensions within which a character lives, dreams, acts and dies.'[178] Imprisoned and at times ill, Casanova (Frank Finlay) digs into his memories, where scenes and images interact across six episodes, bearing out Potter's belief that 'we know from our own experience of ourselves that any man is likely to be a tangle of contradictory motives, warring emotions, habit-ridden responses, fearful apprehensions and improbable longings.'[179]

Mary Whitehouse complained about the third episode's 'lewdness and gross indecency,' in response to which Potter described her as 'an ignorant and dangerous woman' who should 'hold her tongue' until the end of what would be revealed as 'a moral work.'[180] Finding it ironic that Whitehouse's words resembled 'those of the people who eventually put Casanova in prison,'[181] Potter argued that the 'same fear of sex as a liberating agent is abroad now: we even have our own Inquisition.'[182] Potter was aware that he was eventually 'going to get into some sort of trouble' with plays that discussed politics, religion and sex, areas on which television was never 'quite sure of what is at any one stage permissible,'[183] but he was becoming regularly and reductively associated with sex and controversy in the introductions given by his interviewers and in the abusive letters he received, some of which were quoted in his non-fiction.[184]

John R. Cook pointed out that *Casanova* was written 'during a bad period in Potter's illness,'[185] but before his next plays were transmitted, his illness became even worse. In March 1972, having been taken off steroids as a result of severe psoriatic fissures, he experienced an extreme attack and high temperature and was rushed into Cheltenham Hospital.

He returned home after being put back on steroids, but his GP observed that Potter's hands were 'acutely painful, swollen and fixed,' and that he 'has borne his illness with great fortitude, but now feels no longer able to carry on as things are.'[186] In May, Potter was admitted to London Hospital in Whitechapel to start methotrexate treatment for his psoriasis, where he remained until August. He was able to write by October but methotrexate caused unpleasant side-effects and he temporarily stopped taking it in April 1973, only to recommence after a severe relapse.[187] Pieces in this section refer to the impact of having to spend so much of the year, indeed the decade, in hospital, depending on methotrexate and liver biopsies and undergoing the weekly vomiting induced by the drug.[188]

Potter explored these experiences in his non-fiction in this period, but not extensively in his fiction until *The Singing Detective* (1986). As a result, several pieces here resemble in retrospect a work in progress toward that serial, such as an event described in "A Frosty night" in 1977:

> One man in the next bed reached up in the night for some boiled sweets on his bed trolley, scattered them accidentally on the polished floor, muttered something like 'sod it,' sank back, and died. A nurse picked up the sweets next morning, and told me not to be so untidy. It seemed only polite after that to suck them without remonstrance[189]

It would be problematic to take such moments in Potter's non-fiction as evidence of autobiography in his fiction. Potter recognized that 'the "autobiographical" convention is an extraordinarily powerful one' because the dominance of naturalism meant that people ask 'Is this *true?*,' but he thought that 'a very curious question to ask' about fiction.[190] In his vital *New Society* column "Telling stories", Potter drew out one of his core ideas, 'the relationship between fiction and lying,' with the story of his childhood betrayal of a classmate, in an anecdote that was familiar from *Stand Up, Nigel Barton* and which would be reinvestigated in *The Singing Detective*.[191]

Potter's illness in 1972 affected his output but this was masked by a backlog of as-yet unproduced work. *Follow the Yellow Brick Road* (1972)[192] and *Only Make Believe* (1973)[193] were his next two plays to be transmitted but the scripts had been delivered in July 1971 and January 1970 respectively. Reviewers of *Paper Roses* who wanted Potter to turn his satirical attention to television almost got their wish.[194] In *Follow the Yellow Brick*

Road, actor Jack Black (Denholm Elliott) rails against television drama's obsession with sex and, convinced that he is in a television play, tells the cameras to stop watching him. Like Daniel Miller, a character in Potter's novel *Hide and Seek* (1973)[195] who knows he is a character in a novel, Black feels controlled by a malignant creator who may be the writer or God. The novel's game of hide and seek – as we hear from an 'Author' afraid that we will take the superficial similarities with Potter's background as proof of autobiography – makes it central to Potter's body of work.[196] The game would be extended to *The Singing Detective*, in which psychiatrist Dr Gibbon reads a bleak passage from Philip Marlow's book *The Singing Detective* that is actually taken almost verbatim from Potter's *Hide and Seek*.[197] One example of Potter's capacity to reuse and reimagine stories came in "Boy in a landscape", when he found evidence of how 'The place where we grow up, where we learn to speak and then not to speak, is always beyond the reach of the cartographer,' thereby reusing phrases from *Hide and Seek* and an earlier book review.[198]

Telling stories, revisiting memories, lying: all showed Potter's belief that the 'most beautiful part of being alive is our capacity to shape our lives by language, by stories' because the 'world is full of the murmur of human beings trying to reshape reality.'[199] These themes and seeming self-awareness continued in *Only Make Believe*, in which sections of *Angels are so Few* were re-enacted, but this time interspersed with writer Christopher Hudson (Keith Barron) dictating those scenes. *Only Make Believe*'s use of *Angels are so Few* is recognized as one of Potter's most direct attempts to draw connections across his body of work,[200] as the earlier play's scenes now paralleled Hudson's own yearnings, an effect partly undermined by the delay in production. Like characters in *Hide and Seek* or *Karaoke* (1996), Black, Hudson and Casanova struggle to balance the flesh and the spirit and their place under a creator: Potter described Black's awareness of the cameras as 'a metaphor both for paranoia and for a world without a loving God.'[201] Potter argued that 'the very act of writing is an affirmation of our distinctness as imaginative, fantasizing, and therefore *creating* human beings, which makes it the inheritor, I think, of religious acts.'[202]

Building on his long-standing dissatisfaction with the marginalization of religious programming into a 'Godslot' that 'makes you look for religion in the obvious places,'[203] Potter argued in 1977 that all of his plays since *Son of Man* had had a religious dimension.[204] For Potter, the concern with religion in *Casanova, Only Make Believe* and *Follow the Yellow Brick Road* had been neglected by critics and Mary Whitehouse.[205] *Joe's Ark* (1974), another play delayed from 1971,[206] shows pet shop owner Joe Jones (Freddie Jones) struggling with his faith while his daughter Lucy (Angharad Rees) lies dying from cancer. Instead of television and film treatments of religion which he felt relied upon easy symbolism,[207] Potter sought to incorporate doubt and pain and discussed various kinds of religious language. He sometimes used his non-fiction to draw out the less overtly expressed religious elements of his fiction. Potter explained in his radio talk "And with no language but a cry" that 'I say "art" when I might say "religion" because I want to indicate the sort of symbolic framework it is that brings me, time and time again, to that momentous "if" which perpetually trembles on the edge of triumphant resolution.'[208] *Where Adam Stood* (1976)[209] helped him to show the 'often horrifyingly dishonest' way in which religious people, he felt, misused signs. This concern would be at the core of his banned drama *Brimstone & Treacle*.

Writing more regularly after illness, Potter delivered adaptations of Thomas Hardy's *A Tragedy of Two Ambitions* (1973)[210] and, as a serial, Angus Wilson's *Late Call* (1975),[211] plus two new plays continuing his 'visitor' motif. In *Schmoedipus* (1974),[212] Glen (Tim Curry) invades the suburban home of Elizabeth Carter (Anna Cropper), claiming to be her son and opening up repressed secrets; in *Brimstone & Treacle*[213] the visitor is a fallen angel, the demonic Martin (Michael Kitchen), whose sexual assault of brain-damaged Pattie initiates her recovery, rewarding the glibly-expressed faith of her mother and opening up repressed secrets around her faithless father. The script was not made until 1976, and then not transmitted until 1987.

Potter used his profile as writer and critic to respond to the BBC's handling of *Brimstone & Treacle*, most directly in this section in "A note from Mr Milne",[214] and to defend the play as a serious work that was part of a thematic trilogy with *Where Adam Stood* and *Double Dare* (1976).[215] Potter attributed the bleakness of some of his work in this period not only to 'the dull grind of a painful and debilitating illness' but also to 'unresolved, almost unacknowledged, "spiritual" questions,' and this despair led him to destroy 'one complete play' and 'several false starts.'[216] Acknowledging this despair was 'the slow beginning of the journey back.' The ban coincided with Potter still coming to terms with the loss of his father, who had died on 23 November 1975.[217] In April 1976,

Potter stated that 'incredulity and grief still hang in the air. This feeling has to be expressed, not just assuaged, in my work, which is probably why I can't get on with it.'[218]

Potter could be scathing about people working in television,[219] but critics noted how he 'embraced television, using its technology as its instrument,'[220] to produce work that was 'peculiarly televisual.'[221] This section shows his developing engagement with television's potential, whether thinking about the connection between 'content and form'[222] and 'suffocating "naturalism"'[223] or lashing a book that he found sloppy in its scholarship on the subject[224] or thinking about the neglected potency of television's place in our homes.[225] His 1977 Edinburgh International Television Festival paper "Realism and non-naturalism", which concludes this section, distilled years of thinking about, watching and making television. Many concepts and phrases were therefore familiar from his reviews and interviews: television as a domestic appliance, programmes that trickle into each other in such a 'flow' that dramas and advertisements for a dozen brands of dog food are in danger of forming the same experience. However, he was making an important intervention into a set of debates, proposing different ways of talking about television, most of all among programme makers.

Criticising the slippery use of words like 'realism' and 'naturalism,' Potter called for 'a genuinely alive and pertinent debate' about the 'relationship between art and the world "out there"' that accepted that myth and metaphor could produce at least as valuable an insight into human experience as those naturalistic techniques that were presently more respected. This often personal lecture – 'I am not yet sure whether I love God or the idea of God' – became a heavily-quoted source in academic debates on television, in particular his statement that

> most television ends up offering its viewers a means of orientating themselves towards the generally received notions of 'reality.' The best naturalist or realist drama, of the Garnett-Loach-Allen school for instance, breaks out of this cosy habit by the vigour, clarity, originality and depth of its perceptions of a more comprehensive reality. The best non-naturalist drama, in its very structures *disori-*entates the viewer smack in the middle of the orientation process which television perpetually uses. It disrupts the patterns that are endemic to television, and upsets or exposes the narrative styles of

so many of the other allegedly non-fiction programmes. It shows the frame in the picture when most television is busy showing the picture in the frame. I think it is *potentially* the more valuable, therefore, of the two approaches.[226]

Potter's contrast between 'two fundamentally different ways of seeing'[227] illustrated his passion for television as viewer, critic and programme maker: within a few days, filming would begin on *Pennies from Heaven*, a serial in which these ideas would be put into practice.

DAVID ROLINSON

Acid drops
Plays and Players, November 1971

'You will see,' the letter said, 'that we have restyled the *Plays and Players* TV Drama column and have abandoned the practice of inviting a critic to review the month's productions in favour of asking a television writer to write about writing for the medium...'

Ever willing to take bread out of the mouths of babes, or blood from the bellies of bugs, I am of course ready to oblige.

But consider how few are the possible permutations of even the most extravagantly paranoid testaments on such a sickly subject. Consider, too, the narrow and yet narrower parameters set in this electronic land by the laws of libel on one side and the fire-flickering eyes of the puritan pressure group on the other.

Write about writing for the medium. Honestly?

Perhaps this means I should recall with sour hilarity the malachite-lipped drama executive who said '*Who?*' when some twitching fool with a scotch in his hand inadvertently mentioned the name of Strindberg. Or imaginatively reconstruct the two-hour meeting in some grey-radiatored ITV warehouse which finally agreed to substitute the word 'knackers' for the then totally unacceptable (but surely weightier) 'bollocks.'[228] Or renegotiate my way through potential misunderstandings created when the inevitable suggestion seeped into speech that the BBC should cash in on the (paste) crown jewels of Henry and Elizabeth with a series 'about the Georges.'[229] I offered to write a 90-minute script complete with period music about George Formby or, if that had already been proposed, a black melodrama about George Brown ('I was tired') or George Raft or George Orwell or...

At Orwell the nervous smiles faded. 'Who?' they said.

Write about writing for the medium? Honestly!

Maybe I should recount the inspiring and authentic tale of an acquaintance of mine who sent in a script for *Dr Finlay's Casebook* which had been written on the innocent assumption that Dr Finlay was the older of the two improbable medics. Apparently nobody in the production office was quite able to identify what was wrong with the script, proving yet again the surely by now unassailable point that one might as soon expect compassion in an abattoir as delicacy of discrimination in those responsible for running (and running) a formula series.

Write about writing for the medium…?

But (as script editors tend to say, spreading their otherwise manacled hands), but hold on a minute.

Just as no theory of evolution is able to explain how it is that a frog taken into the bed of a fair lady is able to turn into a prince so no description of the mind-rotted labyrinths within the rancid electronic palaces of TV can ever properly account for the equally astonishing manner in which a few plays somehow manage to reach the screen with all their passions or truth or insights still intact, still coherent. Maybe we actually need all those piles of *Softly, Softly* in order to allow better or braver things to sprout for their brief hour or so.

When a good play works, on whatever level, you are duty bound to respond to it on its own terms and not by analysing the nature of the medium. The most depressing and dangerous of the many intimidating phrases which pass for informed conversation above the melamine tables in dream-factory canteens is the one which contrives to put capital initial letters into 'Good Television.'[230] You know just what they mean with this terrible phrase, pronounced in idiot monosyllables out of minds capable of transforming the 'live' spectacle (!) of a public execution into, ahem, Good Television. When such people eventually stumble, as is their wont, onto the concept, the idea, the mechanism or the word 'medium' the only possible defensive manoeuvre is to hold their hands, put out the lights, think of fairground canvas and explain that, yes, your balls are indeed made of crystal.

I cannot see what profit there is in any too prolonged discussion, for example, of whether the television play is by its intrinsic nature closer to the theatre or to the cinema or is – poor thing – merely a miniaturized hybrid collapsing somewhere between the two older forms. I *can* see a great deal of meaning in discussing or analysing whether this or that particular piece of drama which happened to be shown on several million small screens in several million living rooms actually *worked*, and whether or not the peculiar means or nature of its distribution added or detracted to the ways in which it worked.

(And this, in turn, is not to collude with the ever-present English vice of refusing to theorize at all about 'art' on any real level, especially the political, but rather, by placing sequences of argument the right way round or by putting the individual work in the forefront of such discussion. It is to defend oneself against that same endemic philistinism of our national life as it finds its most odious expression slaveringly chomped out in the halitosic mouths of the overpaid charlatans and memo-grinders who so matily infest the circular corridors of the various TV centres. I am, by nature, a gentle soul, not given to polemical excess.)

In talking about whether a play 'works,' or how it works, you are of course talking about content and form, both. You are also talking about your own times, your own responses, your own sensibilities, prejudices, expectations and often (because people are lazy) the mere fashions of the hour. But the important point is to approach the work as a finished, made thing which is making claims upon your attention. If a play about, say, an old man in a pet shop talking to terrapins and tortoises is immediately discussed in terms of the camera work, the 'mobility,' the time sequence, the lighting, the set, the mixes, the cuts – then it will have failed.[231] Cinema critics have all but destroyed the film because this is so often the way they talk: deflecting all their intellectual energies into analyses of technique at the expense of the harder but surely more rewarding confrontation with the actual substance or life of the work.

It is a useful academic exercise to note that a great essayist like Hazlitt often used adjectives in batteries of three, frequently exploding in a lethal sequence right at the end of a sentence. Helpful and illuminating, too, to measure the simple hammer-like repetitions in a poem by William Blake. But prior to all that, long before you can even get to that stage, you have to read the essay or the poem and fence with, or submit to, or fight against, the arguments, emotions, hopes, loves and indignations of the writer.

I use those two great names deliberately. Anyone now writing an essay or a poem will know that behind him, stretching back beyond his mind and beyond his soul, are mountains of achievement, impossible standards, wondrous strivings, all of which (however unconsciously) inform him of the indignity and terror of what he is trying to do. It is laughable to sit down and try to write a masterpiece. It is degrading to sit down and try to write anything else.

But television (dear God, how dully the very word plops onto the page) has no critical heritage, no distant peak, no sense of its own tradition, no real history, no real pride. The writer who thinks he is writing a 'television' play is almost bound to trip over the cables and deserves to break his neck. He should not confuse what he wants to write with the way it happens to be distributed. He should simply (simply!) commit himself to what he wants to write, and that, as Ibsen once scribbled in a fly-leaf, 'is to sit in judgment on oneself.'

I choose to write for television, not because of any regard for the ignorant fools who happen at this point of time to be in control of its capital equipment, and not because I think there is something of momentous artistic importance in the fact that blobs of light cross and recross a screen in sequences of 625-lines or less. I choose to do so because, by the accidents of technical innovation, we are now in a situation where a writer can communicate to more people in more open circumstances than has hitherto been possible. And I cannot even begin to understand those who do not acknowledge this innovation to be hugely momentous.

'Theatre' was once defined in terms of the buildings or structures housing 'drama.' What we have now is 'theatre' that, at the same time, reaches out to millions of people of all kinds in their most unprepared or relaxed or indifferent state – sitting in their own chairs on their own carpets behind their own doors. They can fidget, interrupt, talk, scratch themselves, fart, switch over, switch off. No extraneous social ritual is involved, no snobbery lurks in the set of the 'public' face. They have a domestic appliance in the corner which shows pictures.

This thought can be emancipating as well as intimidating. Ibsen and Chekhov would now be writing 'for' television because they thought of themselves as writing for people. The conventions of 'the stage' are not in themselves limiting but they have been made so: theatre that is too stubbornly defined in terms of theatre, the building, the social gathering, is too often trivial and often redundant. The only overwhelmingly valid reason for *not* writing first and foremost for TV would be if its structure absolutely refused to accommodate the sort of things one wanted to write – and although this does of course happen (as in the theatre or in the cinema or in publishing or on walls) it has not *yet* become the norm.

It will be the norm if writers are so seduced by what they take to be the more prestigious cultural status of the older means of distributing their work that they do not strive 'to sit in judgment on themselves' in there among the hair-sprays, the astronauts, the party politicals, the striped toothpaste, the gunmen, the assassins, the football teams and the chit-chat crap of this new, old market place, these millions of homes, this National Theatre, this domestic appliance.[232]

The sweetest music this side of heaven
Times, 2 December 1971

The Dance Band Era by Albert McCarthy (Studio Vista)

A canny fellow called McCarthy once tapped out lines which began 'You made me love you, I didn't want to do it, I didn't want to do it.' A curiously potent complaint when taken up by dance band saxophones sobbing out blue ribbons of spurious melancholy, especially when the caressing sounds drifted up in a syncopated perfume to rub against the chipped alabaster cupids on the ballroom balcony. But the day came when alert dance hall proprietors replaced the glugging Brylcreem dispensers in the gents with contraceptive machines and, suddenly, "Keep Your Last Goodnight for Me" turned into a much more sensible sort of leer. Never mind: the old sweet smile can now be put back in its sickly place by all nostalgiacs willing to wallow in the rhythmic moon-and-June delights of *The Dance Band Era*, a splendid compilation by an equally canny McCarthy who I would like to think is related to the mildly protesting bard who didn't want, really didn't want to do it, pom-pom.

Albert McCarthy obviously wanted to write this book. 'After all,' he says, 'the basic factor governing individual taste is generally commitment to the music with which one came in contact during one's youth.' Sufficient licence, indeed, for this respected jazz critic to allow himself the pleasure of toe-tapping back into the lost worlds of the kind of dance bands which once claimed to provide 'the sweetest music this side of heaven.'[233]

By the rivers of a tinsel Babylon, there we sat down, yea, we wept when we remembered Zion (or, rather, the Palais), but it was not the harp that was hung in the painted willow. The shoe shuffle of *this* Zion was built on simpler psalms like "Lover Come Back to Me" and even the lugubrious crooner with slicked-back hair had to insist that it was raindrops and not (sob) tears in his eyes.

The Dance Band Era is a wholly delightful book because it somehow succeeds in throbbing out the harmless pleasures of chalked-floor nostalgia and 78 rpm romanticism without ever losing the edge of a genuine musical discrimination which necessarily keeps at least one ear cocked for the ridiculous. For every Cole Porter number there were a dozen or so forgettable hits like "Does Santa Claus Sleep with His Whiskers On?" Every decade, it seems, has to endure its Neville Chamberlain and its Rolf Harris.

The great age of the big bands petered out at about the same time the former gentleman was informing his audience that Hitler had missed the bus. The blue, blue heaven of the crooners had by then darkened with shapes and sounds which could not quite be orchestrated into the showcase sentiment where roses remember and paper orchids forget you not. And yet we all sometimes need to dip into that rainbow world parallel to the real one, the almost furtive dreamland where love is made of sugar and moonlight softens every jagged outline. Somewhere between Dante and Genet there is a place in my-um-heart for Al Bowlly.

Indeed, the first thing I tested in this sumptuous and beautifully illustrated volume was McCarthy's response to Bowlly, the smoky voiced singer killed by a German bomb in 1941 but still celebrated by a weird fan club which insists, predictably, that although the song is ended the melody lingers on...so sweetly, in fact, that a Bowlly buff once wrote to threaten me with an axe because I used an old Bowlly record as a counterpoint to what he called a 'sordid' scene in a TV play. 78 rpm love had nothing, but nothing, to do with creaking bed-springs.[234]

McCarthy is reassuring, though. 'In the course of listening to hundreds of records of the period I have encountered all the leading band singers, many of whom, it must be said, are extremely mediocre, and I am left with the impression that in his day Bowlly was virtually in a class by himself.' Better still, McCarthy goes into the reasons: he can pick out the astringency or melodic wit in a Lew Stone arrangement that kept such numbers well this side of patent-leather bathos. *The Dance Band Era* never descends to the sub-literacy of record sleeve prose.

The book moves from ragtime to swing, from 1910 to 1950, alternating by chapters between America and the British or (less importantly) European scene. It is scholarly, entertaining, shrewd, and broad enough to interest the sociologist as well as the discographer. And the photographs are delicious and evocative enough to have been taken from the top of Blueberry Hill itself – the book is worth every new penny for these alone.

At another, more oblique level, the book even manages to touch gingerly at the wisp of nostalgia itself, that second-order emotion which at times can well up into something genuinely disturbing. Songs heard in early childhood can return unbidden in vague outline, strange dancing words and sounds bumping out with obscure unease to arrange themselves in fragmented sequences out of the furthest recesses of memory.[235] I suspect that my own fascination for Albert McCarthy's subject can be traced back to that smoky voice on the wireless drifting up the stairs, infiltrating strange words into a mind far too young to grasp how these syncopated murmurings had disguises in or on them – words mixing up deep purple and mist and stars and sleepy walls and someone coming back, coming back...[236]

Does Santa Claus sleep with his whiskers on?

Tsar's army
New Statesman, 13 October 1972

Every week now the Band of the Welsh Guards plays us into *War and Peace* and the big questions must be faced by every viewer in the land. Is this 'wonderful love story faithfully retold' (Robin Scott, Controller, BBC2) as good as *The Onedin Line*? Can savage old Prince Bolkonsky be as intimidating as Chief Superintendent Barlow? Will we miss the foggy-voiced scraps of 78 rpm Al Bowlly records as the soldiers go to war? *Dad's Army*, Tsar's Army: which will capture our hearts?[237] And if viewers can adjust to the idea of Stewart Granger moving in to Shiloh Ranch[238] will they take as readily to the mutation of poor old Maigret into bumbling Count Rostov?[239] On Saturday, too, Ronnie Corbett and Ronnie Barker (the two charlies) added yet more complication by giving 'the last performance in this country of the St Petersburg State Choir.' Somewhere, my love, somebody is rehearsing "Black Eyes".

Understand, though, that this tone depresses me. Eight years of writing 'original plays' for television have left me exceptionally vulnerable to easy sneers about a medium I want, perhaps need, to think of as one of the great emancipating forces of our society. The above paragraph is a parody. But the parody – as happens so often – inadequately masks an undertone of sniggery complicity. In what way *is* TV's *War and Peace* 'better than' series horsehair like *Softly, Softly*? Speech – texture – spectacle – intellect – purpose – what? Astonishingly, miserably, the answers are by no means so obvious as they should be. Leo Tolstoy might become as good as Elwyn Jones.[240] Christ in heaven: is this, then, because it is the curse of television to reduce all its material into the same *kind* of experience? Personal pride (or its remnants) makes the question bitterly painful, yet I must address myself to it.

In the first episode the camera panned slowly along the Rostov's endless table observing the soup plates being meticulously placed all in a row. Naturalism might well demand that life be turned into just one damned dish after another, but the insights of a great novelist are rather more interesting than the eye-line of a head waiter. A similar proliferation of seemingly authentic detail measured out its slow tread, yet crucial subtleties – notably in Pierre's reaction to Bezuhov's death – were strangely absent. Natasha, alas, was a gurgling embarrassment. Everyone moved under a great glass dome of stuffed museum detail. The tyranny of things, the bluster of objects, the rhetoric of design made sure it was pretty and dead.

Alfred Neumann, Erwin Piscator and Guntram Prüfer made an adaptation of Tolstoy's masterwork for the Schiller Theater in Berlin about 18 years ago. Granada bravely televised this version in 1963.[241] The play dispensed with soup plates, but it had a narrator. 'Why are we doing all this?' he asked, looking at his watch:

> ...we are not so presumptuous as to take the huge sweep of the novel, the scope of its ideas, the richness of its characterisations and its final moral, and try to make a play out of the whole thing. We have tried rather to arrange, select, alter, reform and even invent – and hope thereby to have served Tolstoy's idea and purpose.

The result was something lucidly didactic, a work in its own right, inside translation not surface transliteration, boldly dispensing with the suffocating 'naturalism' so beloved of BBC classic serials and yet cutting cleanly through to the bigger bones of the original.

Arranging, selecting, altering, reforming, inventing are, when ventured upon by the right hands, acts of creative respect rather than philistine vandalism. 'Why are we doing all this?' is *always* the first question to ask. Any pictorial dramatization of *War and Peace* is by its very nature bound to be a thin little wafer of an offering when measured against the novel itself. Accept this, rather than fight against it, and you can safely smash up the authentic crockery or even the Band of the Welsh Guards in favour of catching at the informing intelligence or purpose of the story. What is there *so far* (hopeful italics) to make us accept this as an achievement on an entirely different level from, say, Galsworthy? Very little. We sit back to watch a 'wonderful love story' bathed in detail, but are not compelled by the drive or passion or demand of it all to respond with our own intelligence and discrimination.

Is it, then, to go back a bit, the curse of TV to pap its material into the same kind of experience? I cannot willingly answer yes, not yet. One sort of reply, though, would be to compare *War and Peace* with Granada's recent *Country Matters*.[242] No doubt at all which is the better, nor why. The brilliant ITV plays were, of course, adaptations of short stories, without anything like the same problems of scale or the same debilitating awe. But they established their own kind of truths, made their own distinct claims, often movingly, always creatively. Original drama, in fact. And it is now only in the rare, fiercely independent documentary or in the so-called one shot play not written to a series format that we still pick up the no doubt irritating cadences of the individual voice.

Alf takes over
New Statesman, 20 October 1972

I spent the whole dreary summer on my back in a sprawling East End hospital where every other bed in the ward (including mine) seemed to be occupied by one or other sickly manifestation of Alf Garnett. Upright and home again in the sweeter environs of Ross-on-Wye I now sit through *Till Death Us Do Part* with much the same tight smile of discomfort, embarrassment and relief which I used to feel upon being lifted onto the bedside commode. Johnny Speight's not altogether comic dialogue is at times so devastatingly authentic that I hear again the rodent squeak of the drug trolley coming down the passage, full of pills and poisons momentarily interrupting the overlapping monologue of assembled Alfs addressing themselves to the unpalatable fact subdued Pakistanis had somehow managed to infiltrate into the ward under the pretence of chronic sickness. We all knew as a matter of course that these cunning brown bastards were only there to draw social security payments, an argument which temporarily wavered when one of them so miscalculated his ruse that he actually went so far as to die. 'There's yer bleed'n curry for you,' observed my nearest Alf, not entirely without compassion.

I am pretty sure now that *Till Death Us Do Part* has become by far the most popular programme in the land because it offers otherwise illicit opportunities for enjoying and even sharing the base prejudice of the British people under the flimsy guise of satiric comedy. The objections to it came in large part from privet-protected worthies who cannot bear to hear what they take to be their dearest principles rolled around in the dirty great big mouth of an uncouth yob. Thus, an outraged viewer wrote to the *Daily Mail* to complain that he had counted 78 'bloodies' in the very first episode of the present series – and I agree that we do not need to laud our Queen, our country and our whiteness with quite so much bad language. The Alfs in the hospital always modulated their own speech when the ward sister was in earshot. If Speight ever applies the same self-censoring process to his own creation we shall be forced to see the programme for what it really is, an increasingly nasty mess spilled out of a gifted writer who seems for the moment to have lost control over his own gut reactions. The last two programmes were especially brutish, stirring together so many different kinds of bigotry that they took on a manic hatefulness impossible to chortle away without some collusion in it all. I object, of course, from behind my own nervous privet.

But what is happening, surely, is that Garnett is gobbling up his own creator, bones, brains, marrow and all. Only Speight's tape-recorder ears are still unchewed. *Till Death Us Do Part*, partly composed in defiant bravado of the monstrous hordes of prudes and censors, has lurched in ugly staggers from what it began by satirizing into the very thing, the exact process satirized.[243] An awkward ambiguity of response from liberals has prevented them from seeing just how much the writer's stance has changed on the way to making Alf altogether the hero. Speight is at present feeding what we must believe he set out to mock, hence his increasing difficulty in giving lines let alone shape to the subordinate characters around the all-consuming central figure. Personally, I don't mind just so long as we know *why* we laugh, if laugh you still do. There is room for a populist half-hour on the box, but there is no need to pretend that it is anything else. I still think the bald bigot is the funniest character on television, always excepting Philip Jenkinson.[244] Indeed, I laugh until I'm (let's be exact) sick.

All last week on the little screen, spruced-up Garnetts were multiplying before our eyes like figures in a funfair mirror, what with live coverage of the Conservative Party conference and *Panorama* digging away down among grass-root Tories in Bristol. A garage owner called Tribe quoted 'my old RSM' approvingly: more discipline (pronounced dis-kipling) is what we all need. Old ladies' handbags (violence) and quarts-into-pint-pots (immigration) recurred like a chorus. A Tory MP, face as smooth and pink as the front page of the *Financial Times*, informed a polite throng of docile supporters that 'we don't have top people in the Tory Party,' while another saw great felicity in 'smoking your pipe and digging your vegetable garden' as a sensible substitute for the anxiety-making ideologies which so afflict the malcontents of the left.

"Small Earthquake in Shepherd's Bush Where Not Many Are Alive": footnote space only left for headline start to *Play for Today* (BBC1). Arthur Hopcraft's *The Reporters* was beautifully cobbled out of old newsprint and fresh eyeballs. Robert Urquhart as the phraseworthy journalist sagging into the final stretch of a disastrous career gave a stupendous performance, old boy voice struggling through to the cigarette ash which grew and grew like an extra muscle out of his beer-washed tongue. Quote Enough to give any critic the jitters End Quote Full Period. Thank God I'm not doing this for very long...

Switch on, switch over, switch off
Times, 15 March 1973

The Least Worst Television in the World by Milton Shulman (Barrie & Jenkins)

Only during a gas strike does any other domestic appliance seem to give such cause for scandal and concern as the television set in the living room. The bright glass tube has long since displaced the yo-yo, the pogo stick, the Charleston or even the wireless as an infallible indicator of the nation's bog-headed preoccupation with chronic frivolity/mindless triviality/dum diddy dee. The three most important things you can do to the box are to switch on, switch over or switch off, yet there are people in our midst more worried about television than about bad housing, unemployment, overcrowded schools, child poverty or any one of the many other casual brutalities which determine the way large numbers of our fellow citizens live. The populist wing of the anxious puritans is led, of course, by Mrs Whitehouse, but the 'intellectual' nagging has for long been the especial noise of the omnipresent Milton Shulman. He was recently seen on an ITV programme stoutly delivering himself of the observation that 'it's very important that we make television duller,' simultaneously proving that the exhortation can easily be made flesh.

Shulman's latest treatise, *The Least Worst Television in the World*, is unfortunately by no means the least worst of the many inadequate books which have been written about British television. The youngest and most sniffily derided of the media has few resilient traditions, uncertain critical standards, snobbish enemies, philistine bureaucrats and a bibliography of informed enthusiasm which is not much bigger than the mote in a newsreader's eye. All the more pity, then, that this new book, which has some rough and true points to make, should be quite so sloppy and scrambled as it is.

Only Peter Black, Stuart Hood and Philip Purser have written at length in terms which show that they actually *like* some of the stuff they see, a minimum qualification for intelligent critical response to the bad as well as the good programmes.[245] Milton Shulman, by contrast, gives scarcely any indication that is his own of the style or scope or texture which make one slice of television better than another: you do not feel he is overwhelmingly concerned about discriminating between the many levels within any programme or with elucidating the differing functions of a medium which is film, theatre, concert hall, newspaper, sports arena, schoolroom by turns and yet also none of these things. Instead, he sits back, preacher not critic, and rumbles on and on about 'the mental and social health of the nation,' a phrase which in this context should always be spoken out loud with a mouth full of cold, wet melon.

Milton Shulman has been a television producer and a television critic and he must know how some of the machinery works. *The Least Worst Television in the World* might almost have been concocted out of his own envious memories of the whirring little machine in the cutting room which can run a spool of film backwards and forwards, fast or slow, garbling the speech, slurring gestures, reassembling exploded vehicles, repeating facial twitches or giving the gift of tongues to the manager of the England soccer team. The ponderous tread of print, plodding on line by line from the top left to bottom right of each rigidly numbered page, rarely offers such push-button opportunities for dislocated argument or incoherent adventure. But this book with its repetition, its misprints, late footnote, statistical mash, flick-flick-flick rhetoric and unsynchronized angers can rival any editing machine for serendipitous delight. It takes a gremlin of genius as well as a happily slipshod proofreader to turn 'advertising' into avertising, for instance.

There is a key passage in one of Shulman's seven familiar chapters which, by changing one word, can be dropped into many other sequences in the book rather in the manner of an establishing shot in a dire TV series: 'By its indiscriminate and undue emphasis on xxx, the BBC presents an unbalanced picture of life in Britain. If, as a consequence, many young people get their social priorities wrong, can we not detect a probable TV factor in that process?' You can fill in the missing word: violence, say, or sex, or, to pick from Mrs Whitehouse's alliteration, dirt, doubt and disbelief. Everything then hinges on the unproven, unlikely 'if.' But note the clumsy tautology of Shulman's second sentence which really says, 'if, as a result of television, many young people get their social priorities wrong, can we not detect a probable TV factor in that process?' You betcha. Shulman's use of statistics is similarly lazy, for not even a very late errata slip sent out on the eve of publication can wipe the tape in time. An afterimage persists of a bull in a magistrate's court.

And yet Shulman is right to complain bitterly about the amount of trash which gets on to our screens. Certainly, as he suggests, we need to re-examine the structures of the TV bureaucracies and of course we must ask what the medium should or could be doing as well as argue about how it should be financed. He wants a Broadcasting Council whose 'prime duty would be to ensure that the most powerful medium of our time conscientiously reflected the true values, the cultural heritage, and the lifestyle of the nation.'

What are these things? They are words to roll about on the page, not prescriptions for good programmes. Let the critics concentrate on identifying what they think is worthwhile and be mercilessly contemptuous of what they think is bad, dishonest and untruthful. Their role is far more crucial than even they dare to acknowledge. Shulman does not bother here with such healthy labours; he bangs away at the 'if' of the first quotation, the missing word of which, dear Clough above, is 'sport'!

Kafka and Brasso
Times, 14 May 1973

All Bull: the National Servicemen edited by B.S. Johnson (Allison & Busby/ Quartet)

Left, right, left, right, arms swinging, heart pumping, toe-caps glistening, eyes set in fear-flecked marbles in your cropped head, left, right, dear God, left, right, the brutish rhythm of gravel shouts, obscene abuse, blanco, Brasso, boot polish, squared-off kit and waste, waste, waste. Ten years it is to the month since the last British national serviceman was discharged. *All Bull* brings it all back: or, rather, in the honoured tradition of the demob binge, brings it all up.

> The perspective of 10 years is a good one from which to look back on 18 years of conscription in peacetime: not sufficient for the distortion caused by real nostalgia, short enough for incidents to be remembered with a reasonable degree of sharpness, yet time for its effects to have begun to be noticed and isolated.

Thus B.S. Johnson, the editor, in his introduction. But this, to me, seems uncomfortably close to the woolly cadences of the Commanding Officer's welcoming address: it sounds reasonable, is delivered in hopeful tones of justification for what is yet to come, but in the event promises far more than is actually fulfilled. How about the perspective of 11 years, then? Most ex-national servicemen know how to ask irritating if not quite insubordinate questions, and predictably the squad Johnson marches into print has not bothered too much about the editor's ponderous introductory speech.

Twenty-four men give their accounts of the compulsory years and the book reads best, says most, when the itch of uniform rather than the silk of hindsight rubs against the words. The nearer it gets to the parade ground and the barrack room the more astonishing, comical, moving and heartening the collection becomes. Perhaps we all have the capacity to write or speak well about one or two heightened or dislocated periods of our lives – and those two years after 18 are in any case a time of personal shock, exhilaration and sometimes humiliating self-discovery. Young men like to feel they are breaking out of cages even when they are simply pacing out the real dimensions of the lifelong cell. The genuine temptation of nostalgia is that it makes you believe there was a time when the secret words in your head were strong enough to break the bars. 'When I get out of all this' was said so often, with such vigorous yearning, by so many conscripts that the receding pulse of it still sends out a subdued, complicated tension to the pages of *All Bull*.

Men on the edge of middle age, maybe submerged already by partially mortgaged property and wholly mortgaged aspirations, are prone to look back on their younger days with edgy affection or envious complicity. Thus, many of the moods and judgments made here have little to do with National Service as such. But the evident absurdities, the regimented fevers of military life, become a brass-hinged showcase, ceaselessly polished, breathed on and polished again until some very clear images glower back across the years. Kafka and Brasso make a great double act with a NAAFI piano.

Put each man from this book in his own bed-space around the buffed and bulled hut and despite the quirks of style or the wildly differing levels of expression he sooner or later crashes with banging studs into the familiar conscript family: the nervous one, the boaster, the sullen lout in the corner mumbling vengeance, the comedian tangled in his own webbing, the accomplished idiot with knife-edged creases, and the helplessly dogged failure who can no more keep wayward fluff off his beret or stains from his gaiters than he can avoid standing slap in the middle of the exposed front rank on the day the inspecting officer is out for blood.

All Bull, in consequence, has many splendid stories and unlikely hilarities packed into its pages. When the contributors recreate the claustrophobic jumble in direct, necessarily shamefaced honesty the bad dream seems only an eyelid away. When they pontificate and moralize, years late on parade, the tight language of real memory breaks ranks into the predictable shambles of a liberal leader-writer's prose. We surely do not need to be told how silly or monstrous such deprivations of liberty were then and would be now: any remaining thugs or idiots who advocate any form of compulsory military service in today's Britain should be themselves locked up in a regimental museum.

Only one of the contributors refused to submit to military service. David Hockney served his time in a hospital instead, nauseously retching to the Dettol and Lysol smells in much the same way as the rest of us got boot polish and metal cleaner in our nostrils. His piece reminds me that it is only in the similarly reluctant stretches I have since wasted in hospital that the old sense of indignation, of frustration and giggly anger returns, that moment when the lights go out and the snores, grunts and pent-up dreams bubble around the sparse walls of hut or ward. Each place compresses a version of sickness and distortion; but the nicest thing about National Service is that it is now long gone, leaving only our service numbers like a scar, totally unforgettable numbers, here again dancing back *hup-two-three!*

The Hart Interview
Interviewed by Derek Hart
BBC1 (West region),14 August 1973[246]

HART: Few decades have had so profound an effect on almost every aspect of British life as the 1960s. And it was during this period that television, itself the most powerful social influence ever known, finally moved out of its novelty status and started to grow up and flex its muscles. It provoked and it probed, it experimented and it explored, in a wide variety of fields. It also spawned its commentators and its comedians and its light entertainment and its documentary films. But it also brought drama to more people than ever really knew it existed, and, at the same time, it nourished new playwrights. One of the most provocative talents to emerge and mature during this time was that of Dennis Potter, a young writer and journalist from the Forest of Dean, and now the author of some twenty television plays. The best remembered are probably the Nigel Barton plays, his dramatization of the life and loves of Casanova, and that startling and realistic portrayal of Christ in his play *Son of Man*. And one can't help reflecting, as one looks back over them, Mr Potter, that most of them – the production of your plays – were surrounded by dramas or rows of one kind or another. Sometimes they were postponed; one or two of them were actually banned altogether. Now, was this accident or design on your part?

POTTER: Well, it wasn't design because, when you write something, you want it to be done, and you want it to be done as you've written it. In the sense that they sometimes dealt with issues, either political or religious or in terms of people's fantasies or sex, it was inevitable that television, never being quite sure of what is at any one stage permissible – it's constantly redefining itself; it's constantly feeding upon its own programmes in order to see what it *can* do – that if you are accidentally working out somewhere along the lines of what is being defined, sooner or later you're going to get into some sort of trouble. In any case, television creates its own guardians outside, in the viewers, who are more offended by things on television than they are in newspapers or novels or in the theatre, because the peculiar and valuable intimacy of television – this thing in the corner of your room spilling out pictures over your carpet – is somehow infinitely more disturbing and potent than any other medium yet. And so it's inevitable, and one accepts it, that there are going to be some clashes at some periods. But to do them deliberately? No. I think that adds a spurious element to a play, particularly. It then becomes defined in terms of its row, and not in terms of its content, and that would be a pity.

HART: Does it happen in the reverse effect: that the row does actually damage what it is you are originally intending to do?

POTTER: Well, it...it could do. I'm not aware... I don't think that it has. The greatest danger is that it may make you – or me, as the writer – more self-conscious than I need be. Obviously, you must be self-conscious when you're writing, but that's an element between you and the page and the pen and the marks that you make; and between your own tensions and the outside world. But if you have to think about Mrs Whitehouse or a particular philistine in the bureaucracy of this or that television organization, then you're starting to think about 'What can I get past? How can I shape this scene?' That's dangerous and corrupting and wrong. But it doesn't really happen. I think television has grown more liberal. But it always has these public relations battles, really. I think the writers who try to do what they want to do, on the whole, can get it by if their intention is clearly serious. And then, if their intention, on the other hand, is to whip up a row, they'll very soon get one, and deserve one.

HART: I was really thinking – recently we had the case of the David Bailey film about Andy Warhol,[247] which was made perfectly simply, with certain things in mind, and it was completed. By the time it actually came to be transmitted, it was totally impossible for anybody to view the thing as anything other than a great cause célèbre. You couldn't have a simple reaction to it. I wonder if you felt that any of your plays have suffered for similar reasons?

POTTER: With the Warhol thing, it wasn't a programme any more by the time it went out; it had been redefined. I don't think, with the possible exception in 1965 of the Nigel Barton plays, one of which, being about party politics, had to be postponed; the ending had to be rewritten. I was then very new. It was in my first year as a television dramatist. I think that might have been affected in that way. Not since, I don't think, because the row has been either after, or on the night of. The thing has happened in the normal course of television programming. The pictures flow on like tap water. Then suddenly there is this picture, then that picture; there's a play which you've got to react to. Some of the reactions have been exaggerated. All of which is inevitable, because of the nature of television – because of the subjects one is writing about.

HART: But it's always seemed to me slightly that you've had a love-hate relationship with television. You were actually involved in it yourself, weren't you, as a general trainee in the BBC, at the beginning of the Sixties?

POTTER: Yes. For a year, yes.

HART: And then you got out of it. You couldn't really stand it too much.

POTTER: Well, I didn't like all the ironmongery of television, and the bureaucracy of television. When I came down from Oxford, I was a general trainee – 1959–60 – and I worked very briefly on *Panorama*, I was shifted around, as a trainee is, between this or that department of what was called Talks, at Lime Grove. And there was something…antique, almost, about these great trundling cameras, cables you tripped over, the things you could and couldn't do – the artifice of television, in current affairs, anyway. Drama then wasn't all that possible in the same way that it is now, with videotape and film and redefined subjects. But I didn't want to be involved with the production of programmes. I didn't want to be responsible for transmitting other people's opinions and other people's attitudes: I really wanted my own opinions and my own attitudes, my own emotions, my own…thing, if you like, to be taken from me and put on television. I wasn't then responsible for it. I had withdrawn from it, and I was freer than if I was walking about a studio – a big studio like this – which I didn't enjoy; wouldn't enjoy.

HART: This was the period when you came down from Oxford and you published *The Glittering Coffin*. I well remember talking to you thirteen years ago,[248] on the day of publication of that book, which was a very savage, swingeing attack on the complacency of the 1950s and most of the values which seemed, to you at that time, to be in radical need of reform. And, indeed, I remember your being hailed in that well-known, overworked cliché of the time as an 'angry young man.'

POTTER: *(Sighs.)* Yes.

HART: It seems a century ago that people could have used those kind of phrases.

POTTER: Quite. Yes.

HART: But I'm wondering how far this was involved in your attitude towards television at that time: did you feel perhaps you weren't able to get enough out of it or put enough into it, to change things in the kind of ways you obviously wanted to do?

POTTER: Well, yes… I've never had any sort of missionary sense, or anything like that: I've never really wanted to change things as such.

I mean, I've wanted to change them as a citizen, and I've wanted to change them because I don't like things, but I never really wanted to say, 'This piece of work will be responsible for changing *that* abuse.' Television then was very restrictive, in a way we've forgotten, I think, now; and very cumbersome too, in a way that we've forgotten now. And to be part of the production side, or the bureaucracy of television at that stage I found very frustrating and inhibiting in all sorts of ways. But I always wanted to write. The thing about television *is*, as you said in your opening remarks about it bringing theatre – or drama, rather, would be a more accurate word – to people who have never seen it, never been to a theatre: the sense that you get of all sorts of people of differing backgrounds, different ages, different assumptions about life, all sitting down at the same moment of time to watch the same sequence of emotion or argument, is something which has always made my adrenalin slop about, as it were. For example, in the first two weeks after *Son of Man*, I had something like 400 letters which would vary from the abusive – like 'You are going to go to Hell' and so on – to a Salvation Army man in Lancashire saying, 'I spent the night on my knees because I saw the way my God died' and so on, to literate, oversophisticated reactions like 'Are you aware that the Gospels give you no justification for this or that?', to teenagers, to old men, to coal miners, to dons: you would realize that, to get any such gathering in a theatre would give that audience a very peculiar flavour, because we do have large audiences, but we group them together according to category: a football match, a West End theatre. Television breaks through all of that. And, although it loses things in doing so, because it means that everything seems to have the same quality of response, whether it's a panel game, *Panorama*, a play, it is just tap water – pictures going on and on and on – nevertheless, if you can put a bracket around an hour, two hours, and say, 'This is a play making demands of you,' those demands are far more powerful amongst your chairs and carpets and cups than it is if you dress up and go out or buy a book. That's so much more intimate – which is why we get rows about television. It becomes…it becomes…it has a potency which we haven't really realized, or come to terms with enough, quite honestly, I don't think.

HART: You were for a period, of course, a television critic yourself, weren't you? Did this sour you towards it, or was it this that perhaps helped you to realize the potential?

POTTER: Well, I became a television critic out of necessity. I'd left the BBC to work on a newspaper. Mistakenly I thought I would be allowed to express a sort of socialism in the *Daily Herald*, which was a great mistake. But in 1961 and 1962, the winter of '61–'62, I became ill for the first time, and immobile. And I had either to give up my job – and I didn't have anything else to do – or become a television critic, which meant I could work from... Because, in those days, the cripples, the has-beens, the deadbeats and those due for retirement were allowed to be television critics. I think it's changed *slightly* – you still get a lot of deadbeats, but not so many cripples. I became, therefore, a television critic for two years for want of else. And watching it, having been concerned with the studios, and still wanting to write for people – that sounds pretentious, but in ways reacting against an elitist education, I still wanted to get across... I still believed that I could write for the majority, or the mass, of people. And those two years made me – when you had to sit down and watch programmes and react to them, you had to have opinions about them – having to have opinions made me sharpen my appetite for television, in a way. I was aware that there was an unnecessarily high amount of awful television, of sloppy television, of conformist television, of wasteful television, but nevertheless you did see, every so often, something which clearly got through to you as the viewer, something that clearly addressed you as an adult, thinking being – and then it was better than anything. I've always had a prejudice against the theatre. I'm uncomfortable in the theatre, and I get embarrassed about those flesh and blood lumps jumping about in front of me and making the boards sound and all that, and the fact that you can't react in an absolutely normal way. An audience is a conspiracy. We all conspire with each other to clap, to laugh, to be silent together, which means that already your sovereignty as a consumer of this work is being affected by who is sitting next to you, and who is sitting three from you, and so on. And those two years, combined I think with my immobility, with my withdrawal, my...in a sense, my panic about myself – the two things coming together made me want very much to write for television, in a way. When I first came to television, it was about politics in the conventionally defined sense of the word, about current affairs: all that area of television. But that fell away from me much more so. I realized that it was still about imagination and people's fantasies, people's wishes, people's pains, people's anguish that really was the stuff and substance of what we could write about, and television has that peculiar power when it is dealing with what people actually dread, think, want, are joyful about. Which is why, I think, as time has gone on, the current affairs, the purely journalistic side of television has become less effective, more and more habit-ridden, more and more predictable. I mean, I would much rather see *Alias Smith and Jones* than *Panorama* on a Monday, simply because there is a slot to be filled with a signature tune with people sitting in their chairs addressing each other about issues that are all present in our minds, but present in a way that programmes like *Panorama* can't really get to.

HART: You feel that you can make more comment, in a kind of way, and a greater contribution, in a dramatic form or in a television dramatic form?

POTTER: Yes. This is what I *think*. Whether it's true or not is another matter.

HART: It's true for you.

POTTER: It's true for me.

HART: I also wonder that, when you left the BBC, you went under the mistaken idea that you'd be able to write about socialism in a socialist newspaper, the *Daily Herald* –

POTTER: Well, it wasn't a socialist newspaper, as I discovered. *(Laughs.)*

HART: *(Laughs.)* Yes. An allegedly socialist newspaper.

POTTER: Yes, well, it was a popular newspaper with all the shibboleths of Fleet Street, and it deserved to die, as it did.

HART: But I wonder whether, at the same time, that you tried to impose the same kind of attitudes – the same kind of socialism, if you like, in its broadest sense – in your television plays?

POTTER: Well, no, because –

HART: Less consciously, as you did in Fleet Street.

POTTER: Not consciously, except maybe with the…the Nigel Barton plays were about a political candidate, a Labour party candidate meeting all the pressures and compromises and stresses of being a Labour party candidate at a particular time.

HART: Which you were.

POTTER: Which I was, in 1964. Then, of course, the subject was explicitly political. Now I don't write so much about explicitly political things in that easily identifiable way, but I think, you see, politics is too narrowly defined: politics is about what we would want to be. It is about what we fear. It is about our fantasies. Now, obviously this isn't party politics, but it is about what kind of society liberates us and what kind of society doesn't, what kind pushes us down and what doesn't. So I don't begin explicitly by saying 'This is a political subject and I want to get this lesson out of it.' I'm not aware of writing messages, but merely of exploring certain characters under certain kinds of stress – often – or fantasy or mistake, people living certain kinds of illusion. Whether this is political, I…it's political to me.

HART: I understand. But, you see, you say, in effect, that you do not have the Messianic approach to writing television plays, but in a kind of a way, you did have it, didn't you, in terms of your political aims? You were politically ambitious when you left Oxford. You did wish to become a Labour Member of Parliament.

POTTER: I did. When I wrote *The Glittering Coffin*, I began it by saying what now seems a very lukewarm…what seems a ridiculous thing to say: that I wanted to be a Labour Member of Parliament because I believed that the things that I believed in…that was one of the best ways of getting them. To me, that no longer even begins to apply. The sense in which party politics has fallen away in this country, the sense of choices that the parties give us, the dishonesties and evasions of party politics no longer interest me in *that* way, but I believe the parties have to react to what we create around them, and that creating around them is the most useful thing. But, again, this is making it seem too utilitarian. I mean, I *have* changed in that sense: that I no longer have public ambitions. Partly this is due to health. Partly this is due to my own withdrawal that has been forced upon me.

HART: Yes, I wonder – could I be a little bit more explicit about this, because people may not know – but you had this savage misfortune to be afflicted with arthritis and a virulent form of psoriasis as well. And, of course, this has had a very profound effect upon every single aspect of your life. Now, you said that this has forced you to withdraw to a considerable extent from social life and life around you, and that you are, to a very great extent, immobile. Now, this must have some bearing upon your attitude towards the whole political scene and your involvement in it.

POTTER: Well, no, it has brought home to me the things that are bigger than politics. I would still call them political, but we have to use these words as they are ordinarily defined. The fear of pain, all sorts of personal anguish, our behaviour as mortal beings who know that we're going to die, all that sort of thing isn't defined politically and yet it defines really the way we react to each other much more than party politics would, you know. It introduces you to areas of life which you have pushed aside or been unaware of or considered as something that you would have to come to much later. Whereas, you see, over the last 10 or 11 years, something like seven periods in hospital…in the last 12 months, I've spent five months in bed, which means that you are gnawing at yourself all the time. You are chewing your own life all the time, in a way that *can* be very destructive. But if you're fortunate, as I am, not to have to worry about the morning train to work, not to have to worry about my hands being as they are – in that I can still function – there is therefore a relationship between whatever pain or upset or anguish or fear that I went through is now…it can be translated into work. Not translated in a miserable way, or a wretched way – I hope – but in an emancipating way. Because, to one degree or another, what we don't realize, in the flush of adolescence, and in the vividness of adolescence, we theoretically know that life is shadowy too, but we push all that away. We don't have to grapple with demons that early. When we do grapple with demons, sometimes it comes as such a shock that people go under, or become sour and crabbed and vindictive or whatever – you know – all those things, those standard reactions to distress. But distress can also be very creative, in an odd sort of way. I mean, I believe there is a sense in which we do choose our illnesses. It's a paradox which is acceptable to me because, in many ways, I am living the sort of life I would *want* to live now: in not

143

seeing nuisances, not having to pretend so much publicly. When I do go out, it's that much more splendid for me. The sorts of people I've met in hospital…for example, three months in the summer I was at The London Hospital in Whitechapel.[249] The East Enders in the open ward – those are people who, if I had met them in outside life, it would have been on a very superficial level, whereas every conversation in hospital is distorted to a degree by sickness and by fear of one kind or another. And so everyone's fantasies and hopes are thrown up in high relief when you're in for a long period in hospital. You get to know what drives people and what moves people that much more readily, because all sorts of barriers are down already.

HART: Have you had to fight any bitterness in this affliction?

POTTER: To a certain degree. In 1964, I thought things were lifting, and I was a candidate in the General Election. That was the turning point because I so exhausted myself physically and, I think, wearied myself mentally as well – disillusioned myself, in a way – that I found I was unable to go back to the newspaper. It was then the *Sun* – not the dreadful Murdoch tit-and-thighs *Sun* of now,[250] but a *Sun* that attempted to be a good newspaper. I was appointed leader writer at that stage, having looked as though I was getting fit again, and that October of '64 ended all that. I became ill, severely, again. And in 1965 I knew I had to take my life into my own hands at that point – I knew there was no job I could hold down any more – and then it was not a question of 'I will write one day' or 'postpone this,' it was a question of *now now now* with the children, with the mortgage, with marriage; with all the ordinary pressures that everybody has. You knew that the problem of income was going to be very real and very immediate. And so I left the newspaper and, from then on, I've been working for myself, as it were. There's been no salary, there's been no security, so I've had the double threat of long periods out of action altogether, but nevertheless the immense personal freedom of being *forced* to choose what I really wanted to do. Not of waiting for the ideal moment; not of waiting for it to be right and opportune, and making sure I had enough savings and so on – and, in fact, I didn't have any.

HART: But do you feel that you are, again, consciously – this is perhaps a misleading use of the word, but I think you know what I mean – do you consciously attempt to translate this into your television

144

drama? Do you see, do you detect in yourself, a way in which this is being translated into a more universal experience, as expressed in your television plays?

POTTER: Yes, I think that people get clobbered, get put down, get humiliated by things that they have no control over... Illness is merely a melodramatic, very vivid, very immediate and recognizable external force acting upon you, and the sense in which there is...the most terrible sense of all, that if there is a God, that God is an indifferent God playing with people: sometimes I feel like that. I suppose that would be a sort of bitterness. And yet even as I say it, I'm able to recognize it as a useful thing: a thing to manipulate and use. So a lot of my plays have been about people whose lives do not match their fantasies, whose wishes cannot be translated into social realistic terms, and I suppose that has been more immediate to me, because that has happened in a sense to me, except I am now living the sort of life I believe that I wanted to live.

HART: But have they had the effect that you would hope they would have had? I mean, in terms of critical response, many of them have been pretty savagely attacked, haven't they, of your plays?

POTTER: Erm...some of them have, yes.

HART: What effect does this have upon you at the time?

POTTER: I dislike... I think everyone who submits something for the public mauling, as it were, is affected by... You see, in television, you have no feedback, you have no audience around you reacting in a way that you can see and know. So criticism, as such, becomes exaggerated: it has bigger importance to you, because you haven't had that reaction. And I think anyone who writes is affected by criticism. I don't mean 'affected' in the sense that it changes what you do, but simply that you –

HART: It hurts.

POTTER: Yes, it hurts. Yes.

HART: But this is something which you use, again, as a spur, perhaps?

POTTER: Yeah. I think it goads you in a productive way, very often.

Receding dreams
New Statesman, 15 March 1974

The garrulity of old men suggests that the desire to tell stories increases with age but the pensiveness in our own eyes shows that the ability to believe in the best and most beautiful tales diminishes in like proportion. Only a sick adult can accurately reproduce a world where animals speak, trees whisper, mirrors send back words in verse and wisps of hay turn into threads of gold. Growing up dwindles down the witches' bogles and boggarts of the night into humdrum paranoia, and the furiously thrilling foot stamping of a gesticulating Rumpelstiltskin into the prosaic mouthfroth of a Levin. This loss of wonder, or expulsion from Eden, is part of our metabolism, so it is very brave of the BBC to ignore biochemistry and memory in launching a new Sunday night series of plays 'based on' old fairy tales. Six writers of good repute are daring, in effect, to bring their boots hard upon a child's skull.

There was a time, bless your furrowed *NS* reading brow, when the great thaumaturgical chamber behind your now stale eyes was hourly filled with wonders beyond the reach even of a party manifesto or an estate agent's prose. And I suppose it is every writer's dream to occupy that space with some of the potency of the nursery tale, an ambition not unlike the desire of the frog to enter the bed of the fair lady. *Bedtime Stories* (BBC2) is a series that is inevitably doomed to failure when measured in these terms, but so is everything else. What we have instead, to judge by the first two plays, is a gentle and diverting exercise which measures the gap between wonder and entertainment, or awe and relaxation. A long way to fall?

On Sunday night Andrew Davies deftly transposed *The Water Maiden* into a melancholy but photogenic love affair between a taciturn used-car mechanic and a beautiful dropout mouldering in a contemporary haze of pot and sex on a painted barge. The mechanic pursues her with humourless I-love-you tenacity, even after he has found her in bed between two long-haired louts. He persuades her away from the canal and into a brand-new council house. 'Can I do anything?' she asks as he starts to nail wood cladding to the walls. 'Just sit there. That's enough.' So how can it last? The enchanting water maiden is soon pushing a pram slowly through cringing streets, the tears coursing down her cheeks, the resolve to escape from such an alien element hardening at every crack in the pavement.

Every now and then the original was dangerously invoked by an oblique out-of-vision narrative which allowed an unknown woman to read the story to an unknown child. And within the dialogue itself rather heavy references were made to the impulse or structure of the older fantasy. 'I don't believe in her when she's not there,' said the man in the motor trade. 'Maybe you made it all up. Perhaps it never really happened,' replied the wise woman in charge of the petrol pump. Moments like these provide the measuring rod and are therefore like self-inflicted wounds: a play that was touching and often truthful in its own right was seen to buckle and wilt under the still magical spell of childhood ache or the receding wonder of dreams never again recoverable.

Similarly, *Goldilocks and the Three Bears* by Alan Plater the week before was too good, too amusing to have to depend upon awkward transpositions from the simplest of nursery yarns. Goldilocks became a pert young social worker with wide eyes and a bulging file trying to straighten out three 'bears' who were more than content with idle scrounging, shoplifting and truancy as a way of life. 'Who's sitting in my chair?' or 'Who's been eating my porridge?' were lines inserted in mock obedience to the format of the series but, for me, perhaps ludicrously over-solemn about guarding or brooding over the lost garden of childhood, they seemed to waste stored goods in too easy a manner. Mind you, I have done the same thing myself, time and time again.

These two plays would have been better, because less self-conscious, as single productions free of the yoke of the umbrella title which is increasingly imposed on television writers. Each of the six productions in *Bedtime Stories* is compelled to bare the bones of its own origins by the tyranny of the collective format. And after the first each is subjected to the law of diminishing returns, where surprise and discovery are blunted into predictability and familiarity. Producers and story editors may well be right in their assumption that viewers prefer it so, but writers should still resist them for as long as can be afforded. Perhaps Davies and Plater would not have written their stories without the stimulation or reassurance of this particular series idea, or perhaps they would have come upon their themes later.

Imagine both these plays as single productions free of the *Bedtime Stories* imprimatur. The potency of their source would surely have been buried much deeper and yielded the richness more slowly, more satisfyingly. The deviations into discovery would have been less dependent upon the over literalness of the format. Plater's observant wit did not need the clutter of the surface transpositions here demanded. Two good plays could have enjoyed the infinitely greater resonance and sharper challenges of their own independence. And the storehouse of childhood (the source of most good writing) would not have been plundered with such careless ease. It is long since time for television to pull down the umbrellas and put away the wrapping paper. We shall have to tell those who sit and scheme in the production offices to stop eating our porridge.

Boy in a landscape
New Statesman, 29 March 1974

Whoever created 'TV snacks' for the supermarket shelves had just the right kind of ingredients in mind to go with the peak-hour pap: monosodium glutamate,[251] hydrolyzed vegetable protein, caramel colouring and gum arabic. Chomp, chew, swallow. And down goes another evening's viewing, so bland on the palate, so easy to digest, the flavours and colours seeping together in a tacky slop soon unrecognizable by any remaining faculty of discrimination. How many minds are touched with the pale fire of wonder when the television picture collapses into a single bright dot at the end of the day's transmission? The question, for me, is not merely snide rhetoric delivered with a jutting lower lip but comes out of nine years of work in my chosen medium that seems to have left me with a feeling of waste and despondency which cannot be due entirely to present depression and sickness…

So began the bilious contribution I was fortunately unable to finish and deliver last week. I lead off with it again not to be like the biblical dog which always goes back to its own vomit but to place in perspective the eagerness and the gratitude with which those who demand much of television respond to any sign that complexity, density, audacity and originality of both scene and exposition have not been entirely machined out of the schedules. David Rudkin's *Penda's Fen* (BBC1) demonstrated that the *Play for Today* slot has become, together with the occasional documentary, late-night arts programme or specially mounted 'prestige' production, the major area left on TV still capable of transmitting the nourishing zest of an individual imagination which necessarily cares not a Controller's fart for ratings charts or conveyor-belt packaging.

In prospect, Rudkin's play seemed about as uninviting as a meeting in a cul-de-sac with a fellow evangelist taking his pamphlet out for a walk. Functioning at the moment by the biochemical courtesy of methotrexate, and anxiously awaiting another liver biopsy on Monday, I find I am more willing to discuss practical questions about the body and its potential delights than to exchange those endless, whining abstractions on Good and Evil which come better out of the healthy pink cheeks of impertinent clergymen. And so a play which dares to begin with the old raspberry-inducing challenge 'What is to happen to my soul?' does not exactly grab my attention, and cannot in the present state of electronics provide much of an answer anyway.

But it did not take long to realize that *Penda's Fen* was offering far more than a mere chicken-scratch on that well-tramped top-soil. There are older coins and juicier slugs deeper down beneath the snuffled ground of platitude and tufted banality. Any intelligent adolescent finds that the fissures opening at his feet also crack open most of the hard little kernels of received information clunking about inside his brain. Rudkin made his central character just such a being, alert to sudden dissonance, troubled by sticky revelations, religious premonitions, sexual confusions and intense anxieties about the purpose (if any) of human life.

Better still, the boy was seen to be struggling in a real place, a patch of landscape and so of mindscape that kept bringing any wild and whirling abstractions back to the sounds and shapes of the English countryside. The place where we grow up, where we learn to speak and then not to speak, is always beyond the reach of the cartographer and forever charged with the intensity of those first perceptions which turn words or songs heard in the head into particular configurations of local topography, and are even capable of turning someone else's elaborate metaphor back into locatable reality. The strength of the play, and its ultimate brave 'failure' lay in the precision and indeed literalness with which the images of light and darkness warring in the young man's mind were exposed in the cold flat glare of the television tube.

The virtues of the writing were often demonstrated by this realistic foredrop, from the halogen fire of headlamps sweeping against a cottage wall to the especially English grace of a damp, thick light reluctantly fading upon the blue flanks of the hill. When dog-collared father and earnest son walked by the river talking of old gods and new technology, the big fat globe of a dying sun spiked itself on the horizon to give uncanny pertinence to the ancient yearnings and renewed conflicts which might otherwise have stayed on the tip of the tongue or sidled off into a twitch of face muscle. So much of this was beautifully done, gloriously resonant.

But it was a mistake to give literal solidity to the way in which, when sleep drifted out of the boy's limbs, the dream it had carried stayed a moment longer in the room. We had to contend with an all-too-visible demon or devil sitting on his chest, terrifyingly real when trapped behind the eyelids but on the screen little more than a comically inflated carnival novelty. The play eventually teetered on the very edge of risible farce, because of this determined literalness, but long before the end Rudkin had fetched up so many striking images, so much intensity and buried wealth that one wanted to see it again immediately. The idea that a 'repeat' is somehow a dereliction of duty by the TV organisations is itself an indictment of the kind of fare which occupies the bulk of almost every evening: it simply is not worth seeing again, nohow. Thus, London Weekend's promise last week that there would be 'no more repeats' in peak time is not a boast but an apology. *Penda's Fen* will have to be shown again, reassuring all of us that the wide spikes upon the millions of housetops can pluck far more out of the air than expanded hucksters or narrowed down diversions, the stunted dreams of greedy little men.

Mimic men
New Statesman, 13 September 1974

Time was when even a penny-ante gumshoe looked at you down the length of his hard nose, jiggled a cigarette between the slit in his face and came across with lines which had more salt than a bag of cooked peanuts. But not now, not on the dwarf movies made to shift fancy deodorants or instant doodahs and then dumped in the soft lap of some out-of-town sucker from the BBC. White meat to the heisters, these tweedy patsies who willingly hand over Bank of England funny for garbage called – phut! phut! – *Ironside* and *Harry O* and *Cannon* and *Kojak* and Jeez-us holy Christ you name it. This used laundry will rot your grey stuff so watch where you're putting your eyeballs when gat-time comes on nights. Which is every night, no kid.

Now I may be big, fast, tough and full of pickles but I'm not getting twenty-five a day plus expenses and I can't snick a match on my thumbnail and it's a heck of a job to get my lower jaw up off my chest after watching *Harry O* last Friday. I should write out of the other side of my mouth. And like Philip Marlowe I should be wearing my powder-blue suit, dark blue shirt, tie and display handkerchief, black brogues and black wool socks with dark blue clocks on them, 'everything the well-dressed private detective ought to be.' Not to go calling on four million dollars, you understand, but so as to feel right in the ventricles before penning the lament I have to write on this length of classy wood-pulp.

But – oh, dear – frozen British prose is needed hereabouts to describe the debilitating situation in which British television viewers spend a bigger and bigger proportion of their evenings staring with bottle-top eyes at the debased remnants of what was once a lively and occasionally magnificent art form made out of an admittedly half-alien culture. We are thus twice-removed from a source of urban melodrama that in its high days provided us with a compulsive city of the imagination to set the sprawling conglomerations of cosy villages which so much of our own writing offers us as the supposed city of reality.

There are at least half a dozen series of American private dick-cops-gangster stories presently slicing out chunks of BBC and ITV prime time. In most of these busy concoctions there are, of course, fleeting moments which recall the efficient B movies of decades back, and the dialogue sometimes picks up the stylized zing of sidewalk combat which Chandler and Hammett turned into literature. *Kojak* is, so far, the best of the heap, but as Marlowe might have said had he survived into the videotape age, you can grow a beard waiting for the genuine package when these programmes are on the air.

Take a look at *Cannon* on BBC1 tonight for instance. He seems at first glance the kind of heavy who could pull his own fingers until the knuckles crack, but five minutes in and you'll place him as someone out on parole from a health farm. The flurries of suspense (to murder a word) owe most to the need to find stay-tuned slots for the plagues of commercials which shape all stories imported from American TV studios. Down these mean streets a salesman must go. And the result is that the evocative conventions of the gangster film slip and slide away into the adulterated mash which American TV writers make of almost all American experience. There's nothing *we* can do about it, except stop buying the stuff.

We won't, though. Like the mimic men of our old Empire who carried furled umbrellas in the middle of a dry season we, too, have slowly taken on the mental inflexions or infections of a provincial and colonialized people. Somewhere in the invaded landscapes of our imagination cowboys silhouette the dusty horizon, gum-chewing cops sweat under the armpits and a laconic shamus chats up a blonde in a bar or a diner. It's all got mixed up with the music on old radios and the warm, dark interiors of those cheap cinemas which seem to have come after the womb back there in growing-up time. American TV writers evidently have no sense of responsibility about nourishing the silvered images in my head, forever fixed there by a shining, slanting beam in which the blue cigarette smoke swivels. How come they don't write the crackling backchat anymore?

Last week's *Harry O* on BBC1 was definitely a big sleep. This new private dick is a slow mover because, like *Ironside* the cop, he has a bullet in his back. But everything else was slow too, and bits of the dialogue must have been lifted from Patience Strong. Irritating electronic music, soft out-of-focus shots, meaningless jump cuts, half-lit sets, still frames dropped into the action like seltzer tablets, and even a picture dissolving into dots. About as far from the real thing as Cliff Richard's supposed imitation of Elvis on Saturday. *Harry O*'s director clearly realised that the script had nothing to say, so he played around with utterly insignificant close-ups of things rather than faces, none of them seen with a pair of ordinarily level eyes. Big Louie would have vomited.

Watching the news on Sunday night, however, I caught some of the old certainty of style. President Ford, it said, had given Nixon *a free pardon*. Slow Gerry moves his lips when he reads but this was the first sight of him writing at his desk. The way he held the pen, sort of attacking it from the long way round as though trying to creep up on the gold in the nib, was an absolute give-away. He's not the big guy in *that* organization. A still of Nixon followed, bleak-faced, granite-eyed, the deposed head of the syndicate. 'Mother of God,' he might have been saying, 'is this the end of Rico?' So that's where those old B movies have gone.

Second time round
New Statesman, 27 September 1974

The leaves spontaneously rot on the aching trees and the long grey summer of repeats subsides equally naturally into the season of mists and whispered bankruptcies with the biggest re-run of them all. *Election '74* the studio captions said back in the dark ages when a week had only three days.[252] *Election '74* they still say, scarcely curling at the edges.[253] The same words are being brought back to the boil by the same gaggle of dissenting cooks. But the convenience of using second-hand camera cards is matched at times by splendid economies of phrase in the studio, where once again the well-balanced chairs are carefully placed in groups of three. 'What I want,' said Heseltine on Sunday's *Weekend World* (ITV), 'is the policies the people want.' And what do the people want? Well, for a start, they don't want their favourite TV programmes shunted about to make room for talking-heads-in-groups-of-three. Hence, the first welcome fact to register about this renewed TV election is that it occupies less space and comes on at a later hour than seven months ago. The whole shindig has been electronically shrunk to proportions rather greater than Cruft's dog show but smaller than the recent football tournament in rain-soaked Munich.

'We're half a century behind West Germany,' said Lord Byers on Sunday, not talking about football. Our Hitler, in other words, is yet to come. Meanwhile, the best bet while the words thunder and flutter against the lens seems to be to stock up on tinned food and rock salt. Future catastrophe will throw up a leader, said bow-tied A.J.P. Taylor to bow-tied Robin Day on Thursday's *Newsday* (BBC2). 'When the appalling crisis comes, as it will, and there's no unless about it,' twinkled the historian with every semblance of relish, 'the crisis *will* demand a man...' The natty neck gear was so much at odds with this sudden chill that one suspected an elaborate joke with squirting water and mock buttonholes, a feeling confirmed when Taylor went on to offer the name of the avuncular Callaghan as the man who might yet rally the stricken nation. Help it or not, traces of black farce are seeping in between the speeches and the handshakes. Sooner or later, surely, someone is going to be led out of the hot studio strapped in a straitjacket, laughing hysterically across a carpet of soiled manifestos.

On Friday, for example, the travelling cameras picked up Jeremy Thorpe in Edinburgh gesturing warmly at some extraordinarily passive figures on the other side of a stretch of plate glass. 'They're all dummies in there,' advised a dry Scot on the pavement outside the dress shop. It didn't seem to matter. 'There is a great and growing militant middle,' the Liberal Chief Whip had said on the box a few days earlier, and this is presumably what they look like: stiff-limbed, blank-eyed and utterly helpless. 'The Conservative Party are occupying the middle ground,' insisted St. John-Stevas on Thursday's *Midweek*, also addressing the same plastic dolls in much the same plastic words. It is already clear that the two opposition parties are scrapping over their allocation of shop-window dummies: a re-run, yes, but this election as seen from the TV screen is astonishingly unlike the February affair. The Labour Party is in a situation where even its own timidities and perpetual lack of passion cannot snatch away the prize.

The change in Edward Heath is greater than any worked on Dr Jekyll. Seven months ago his massive head loomed menacingly out of the box like a hunk of raw meat with the hook still attached, but now his features have slid together in a meek, smiling affability closer in texture to a soft omelette that has been tossed once too often in the pan. 'He will consult anyone and everyone who has a part to play,' promised one of his henchmen on Monday's *Campaign Special* (BBC1), a statement that could only be delivered with a simper or a frown but in this case, somehow or other, with both. The harsh rhetoric of confrontation has burnt out into the softest of ash and you can almost see the taste of it in Tory mouths. Their party political on Tuesday abandoned the snarling aggression of the last batch in favour of a tactically discreet whining over patently manipulated statistics. Mournful Geoffrey Johnson-Smith seemed perpetually on the point of wringing his hands, or, better still, washing them.

A week before the last polling day I was able to deduce in this column 'from the pictures alone' that the Conservatives would not get their majority. There is a metalanguage of gesture and face muscle and bodily starts which the cameras exaggerate in the manner of an echo chamber, and by the last week of the campaign the signals of fear, even panic were beginning to twitch across too many sleek Tory limbs to be ignored. Sometimes, indeed, it is sensible as well as kindly to turn down the sound and watch the expressions with a clinical eye. You may object that this procedure is even more metaphysical than the social contract (which was not mentioned, incidentally, in Labour's opening party political on Monday night) but I can prove with triumphantly earned Ladbroke's cash that the infant skills of semiology have more rewards than an opinion pollster or a word-bound leader writer could ever acknowledge. Television has the scary knack of catching the mind naked behind the face, and so far the election programmes show that the Conservative spokesmen have already given up their hopes in the inner recesses of their beings. Unfamiliar words of compromise and even remorse scrape out from between their bones as the merest patter of a thankless ritual. There is no need to listen.

Wilson, by contrast, is coming across with the cocky bounce of the leader of the band. And the tune he most likes to play has more than passing resemblance to that old one about the lights coming on again in London. The band itself is presented with the dated panache of Lew Stone at the Monseigneur. 'Teamwork. That's what counts,' crooned Edward Short in Monday's party political immediately following an opening sequence of stills featuring the trombones, saxophones and trumpets of Foot, Jenkins, Healey, Benn, Williams, Callaghan and Wilson, in that interestingly syncopated order. A rosette crashed onto the screen insisting that Britain will win with Labour, a fetching optimism when measured against what Mellish sternly described later in the evening as 'the tone of gloom coming from the other two parties.'

The more that the opposition parties try to point shaking and bony fingers at the bad days ahead the more cosily secure the Labour position seems. It is this cruel dilemma which is causing Heath to be so subdued and Thorpe to perform with the stylized gestures of an Edwardian undertaker, flinging out his right arm, pinching his brows and bending sharply forward at the knees at one and the same moment. But there is a directness about him which at times can be splendidly disconcerting and is much more attractive than the mannered solemnities of his set speeches. 'What are you going to do for Scotland?' demanded an aggressive woman with an SNP badge on her coat. 'I'm going to keep Scotland in the United Kingdom for a start,' he snapped, where Wilson would have given her a rapid blink of the eyelids and Heath a heave of the shoulders.

But the mannerisms and the words, from wherever they come, cannot shift the weird sense of dislocation and unspecified fear that hangs above this election in a pall of mockery. The participants seem to be moving about in a long, slow dream stuffed with redundant words and innocent stupidities. Ads for toilet rolls have reappeared between programmes but the days of wine and roses have dribbled away. 'Britain is sick,' said the omnipresent Professor Milton Friedman to Robin Day last Friday, 'and you're going to pay a price whether you cure it or you don't.' The fatalism is infectious, and may well account for Labour's lead in the polls: somewhere in the forest of Healey's eyebrows salvation waits like a tyger or a bromide. He has already accused the other parties of a lack of patriotism, a device which is depressingly rewarding even in the era of Monty Python and Alf Garnett.

The Italians, for example, are here in force to observe the fun because 'we are both in the red.' On Monday's *Campaign Special* these brave Latins attempted to interview a middle-aged English woman in the street. 'It isn't a bad country,' she said. 'Too many foreigners have got their eyes on it.' The cunning wops thanked her and closed the camera shutters not at all abashed.

In a rut
New Statesman, 22 November 1974

Higher and higher he sets his sights, and nothing can stop him now. Kingsley Amis turned in a *Softly, Softly* script last week that was worthy of Elwyn Jones himself.[254] Resisting the easy temptation to write a topical yarn about family trouble in the jury room, Amis came up instead with a weary piece of antique sleuthing in which the criminal was eventually unmasked because he delivered 'lots of set phrases used without meaning.' Impossible not to hear the vulpine snarl behind the lines, for such a ghastly crime would knock out all critics at, er, one fell swoop. And bang goes Denis Healey, too, trying out his compassionate pig-farmer act again last Tuesday night, as well as Robert Carr exercising what is called his right of reply on the following evening by rolling set-piece solemnities round the screen like loose false teeth in an undertaker's mouth. The retiring Archbishop of Canterbury popped up on all channels to give further substance to Amis's catch-all accusation, but I don't think the dear old soul actually managed to finish a sentence while I was watching. All week, indeed, the tendency for 'lots of set phrases used without meaning' seemed to be even more criminal than usual, especially when Ludovic Kennedy talked to coal miners on *Midweek* or Ian Ross talked about them on the BBC News. It must be a long, long time since *Softly, Softly* provided a line of dialogue capable of such malevolent resonance. 'One mustn't get into a rut, you know,' chuckled Amis's bright-eyed madman for good measure, truly his master's voice.

Ruts, however, are nice for programme planners as well as stags. They like nothing better than a series which dribbles on for years or, failing that, 'an idea' that can be stretched over 13 weeks and costed like a quarterly gas bill. Expensive hot air will fit all too well as a description of the new Tuesday night slot-filler *The Mighty Continent* (BBC1) if subsequent episodes are going to be anything like as flatulent as the first. A bad case of the K. Clarks, this, illustrating the eccentric passion of the BBC for spending their way out of a financial crisis with big dollops of 'location colour' to brighten familiar words about overworked subjects. I see that Mrs Whitehouse has pointed to my *Casanova* as an example of extravagant waste, but she seems to have missed the complicated bit of film about the sea cucumber in one of David Attenborough's programmes. The sea cucumber, you may care to know, is a small animal principally distinguished by the fact that alone of all creatures it breathes through its own anus. Well, almost alone.

'History belongs to us all,' said Peter Ustinov in a pink shirt and butterfly tie at the start of *The Mighty Continent*. You knew he was moving about Europe because his shirt, jacket and tie changed colour several times even though he could have done it all with a pack of postcards. Billed as 'a view of Europe in the twentieth century' and decorated with busy graphics, the opening episode was memorable mostly because of film of the beautiful Zeppelin which has already been seen on, I think, *Blue Peter*. 'There was fever on Europe's brow,' Ustinov told us, sitting over a cup of coffee with a melancholy air. Perhaps there was something in the water. Back in the studio John Terraine spread his hands as he talked, but the gesture was hardly wide enough to span the number of clichés he managed to cram into this disappointing opening.

Relief came within an hour or so when B.S. Johnson imitated some of the same mannerisms in his valedictory *Fat Man on a Beach* (HTV), changing his clothes from shot to shot in the middle of a single sentence to point up what he called 'the little deceits' which establish continuity in clapper-board land. 'This is a film about a fat man on a beach,' he began in all insolence. 'Do you really want to sit there and watch it?' Imagine Terraine or Ustinov opening in the same manner, or the eager response switchwards such an invitation would provoke in the most apathetic breast. The merit of *Fat Man on a Beach* lay in its insistence upon showing the mechanisms of a trade where 'to cheat' is actually a verb of standard convenience used about the camera.

Johnson has previously written that 'telling stories is telling lies.' Here on the beach, where the pebbles were as big as eggs and a dead sheep lay on the foreshore with its eyes pecked out by screaming gulls, he kept prowling heavily round this obsessive theme. The few square yards of flotsam at his feet were 'full of images and metaphors and things happening' but he wanted to celebrate these accidents rather than turn them into 'a story,' which he saw as a device to tidy up life. But no fictive device – film, play or novel – comes *ex nihilo* and even a selection of accidents is inevitably a tidying up.

Jokes with fireworks, stones, bananas and mirrors made this a funny and a disturbing film, though it could not only be the cruel hindsight provided by B.S. Johnson's suicide which left a sense of desolate contradiction beating against the shore. He described a road accident he had once seen in which a motorcyclist was catapulted onto a wire fence by the side of the road, and offered it as 'a metaphor for the way the human condition seems to treat human kind.' This story would not quite dissolve into 'a lie.' Despair was once castigated as a sin: Johnson turned it into an elaborate prank and at the end of the film walked straight out into the sea.

And we forget because we must
And not because we will

Violence out of a box
New Statesman, 29 November 1974

'I count only the hours that are serene': what sweet relief it would be to have even temporary possession of the kind of mind which could act in the spirit of the inscription on the sun-dial celebrated in one of Hazlitt's gentlest essays, or to be blessed with the sort of temperament which could scorn the accumulating miseries of time by measuring only what is dignified, just and compassionate in oneself and one's fellows. Failing that – for it *is* an impossibility, of course, as Hazlitt was quick to see – how tempting to wish for a return to those days of pretended calm when a mellow voice on the wireless once started and finished the news bulletin with the most comically inept sentence ever to be composed by comfortable men about the affairs of the troubled world beyond the microphone: 'there is no news tonight.' That's all right then, we could say to each other, switching out the light and climbing the stairs, that's all right, nobody is crying out for food, no limbs are being broken by atavistic nightmares, no prisons hold the innocent, no insolence disturbs the mighty, no flies crawl in the eye-sockets of a dead soldier, no child mouths by rote the hatreds of its ancestors and no family tries to rest without a roof over its head. There is no news tonight!

The pictures coming out of the screen last Thursday night sent more than shadows into the room, for proximity always increases horror. Birmingham after the bombs was suddenly transformed into that most ominous of words: a newsflash. We were shown bodies in the rubble, mutilated beings covered by tarpaulin, dazed people wandering about with blood on their faces. The first and most overwhelming pictures were hurriedly inserted between *Play for Today* and *Midweek*, taking their place in a sequence of electronic images that lay like lead on the heart and which I hesitate to describe. But it went something like this: the almost wantonly bleak play finished with a young lad sobbing on a filthy workshop floor, doubled up with pain after a vicious blow in the stomach; then came the real misery and shock of a report from Birmingham, then *Midweek* immediately focused on 'a small part of the sorrow and grief caused by the war in Cyprus between the Greeks and the Turks,' a harrowing film which included scores of weeping faces, much evident cruelty, Greeks sobbing at the incomplete family table, wailing Turkish women spreadeagled on the graves of their husbands and children. Back to Ludovic Kennedy for the closing sentence. 'The anguish of Cyprus,' he said. 'Well, that's all from us tonight.'

But it wasn't all. *The Late News* was still waiting for us with blood and frowns and the lunatic autocue: Birmingham, the Middle East, the hijacking, unemployment figures up to 650,000. And then, God help us, with scarcely time for the BBC's model globe to resolve against its pretended firmament, straight into the sixth programme about the cold war in Europe, *The Unsettled Peace*, with yet more grisly film of weeping, frightened and exhausted Hungarian refugees pouring over the border during the 1956 uprising. And then back to Birmingham, with the figures for the dead and injured revised upwards again. If the newsreaders had worn hoods over their heads with slits cut for their eyes, and if the continuity announcers had confined themselves to the simplest of screams, the total effect of such a sequence could hardly have been more devastating. The bright box in the corner of the room can turn itself within minutes into a hell-hole: there, where the dancers cavort and pop singers clean their teeth with the microphone, where lewd comedians snigger and magical detergents remove impossible stains, there, inches above the carpet, is a chopped, edited, summarized version of a few of the terrors and miseries and endless conflicts which afflict our kind. The speed of the reportage, the increasingly violent nature of its substance, the means of its distribution, have taken us to the lip of the volcano. We can look down and see the world boiling, and then we can go and put the cat out.

What effect does all this have on us?

Are we the best informed generation that has ever lived? How is it that we can walk about without being sick on the streets, perhaps the only meaningful sacrament left to man? *He that increaseth knowledge increaseth sorrow*: surely no rational mind in our scientific century could ever accent such Old Testament tosh, but...

No, the suspended 'but' is the last great treason. Even a mind at the end of its tether has to force itself to frame yet one more question and then another. There is now a new class among us, a new elite, who are the custodians of 'the news' and the comment which is not always seen to be inseparable from it. They do not spend their time counting the hours that are serene, but in feverishly allocating stopwatch seconds between disasters or bits of rhetoric or whatever other unlovely item bobs up like scum to the top of the bulletin. Monday's *Inside the News* (BBC1) showed just how fast or even garbled everything has to be, from pictures bounced by satellite across hemispheres to a video-camera maybe a few miles away waiting to feed in a last-minute report. So intense is the scurry, so telescoped the language, so immense the scale that it would not be surprising if the busy people at the core of the news operation have fallen behind the technology. The raw pictures and the sober face in between are somehow permanently out of sync. I am not asking for a guide to take us through the rubble, or a sage to point out solutions where none may exist, or a saint to draw light out of the gangrenous air. What is needed now, more than ever, is the *question* rather than just the image, and a multiplicity of opinions rather than the strangely cool uniformity of tone that assumes the news is something 'out there' in a world that is as it is as it is.

For if proximity always increases the horror, it also increases the danger to liberties and to reason perilously won. The combination of IRA bombs, economic decay, national decline and apocalyptic doom-machine rhetoric is one that *is* going to put immense and sustained pressure on the media and upon all who use public words. Too many of us have been half in love with violence. Too many others have not seen that violence has other, slower guises. Too much hypocrisy passes by unquestioned, on the screen and elsewhere. We are threatened by bombast as well as by bombs. In the days ahead the unique responsibility of the elite who compile the news and mount the discussions is going to be bigger than ever. They must address themselves to the problem of showing a world in a box in a living room not simply as it appears in the tilting lens but how it looks from inside many other people's heads, perhaps of people we don't want to see or to hear, a world that is not a sequence of pictures which suddenly 'happened' but one that is still being made by the questions which are asked or, worse, by those that are not being asked. The technology which can show us murder within the hour and grief by the reel does not and cannot offer 'explanations.' We still need thought for that, and the sort of vigilance which is older by far than videotape.

Switch back
New Statesman, 7 March 1975

When asked in hospital if I wanted to watch any television I pulled the sheet up over my head and made growling noises, thus risking both the incredulity of my sickly neighbours and an unwanted tranquillizer at the next drug round. I admit that I felt like a rest from the non-stop puppet show but the real explanation for such wilful behaviour was my unhappy knowledge that, at the time of the invitation, *Churchill's People* had just started another episode. It was obvious that even a distant glimpse of this wretched saga would set my recovery back by several weeks. And, indeed, while filling my sample bottle the next morning, I read in one of the reviews that I had narrowly missed the sight of rhubarbing King Alfred burning the cakes in a corner of the studio, and my relief was only slightly tempered by the suspicion later that day that the same spoilt dough was being served up for tea. In the event, however, I need not have been quite so terrified, because the television set along the corridor was almost permanently clamped to the commercial channel, the switch presided over by an amiably bronchitic master of ceremonies who between rattling coughs impartially pronounced at suitable intervals that it was all shit.

Back on this beat, however, I realise that paid criticism has to be less accurately succinct.[255] And so when the chairman of a big oil company smilingly insisted on *News Extra* (BBC2) last week that '*any* tax is a deterrent to any industry's development' and the interviewer nodded, when Philip Jenkinson on Saturday's *Film Night* announced that he had always considered Michelangelo enormously 'cinematic,' when Michael Parkinson seemed mildly surprised that Larry Adler had turned up with his mouth organ (cor!), and even when Princess Anne was shown on Monday's news at the Ideal Home Exhibition displaying 'a keen housewife's interest' in domestic appliances, I still need to deploy more than the basic four-letter word. There was also film of Enoch on the rampage again last Thursday evening, stiff white triangle at his top pocket, stiff white rhombus above his Adam's apple, a tight knot on his tie, tighter muscles on his cheeks, three microphones in front of him, the devil not quite behind him. A curious dazzle of lightning flickered suddenly across his deeply etched visage: I thought at first it was a press photographer's flash, but it might well have had its source inside and not outside the bones of his head. Next booking: *Doctor Who*.

The *Play for Today* on the same night, Roy Minton's *Funny Farm* (BBC1) was full of less dangerous obsessives. Hospital again, but this time a psychiatric one. Too long, with too many uninterrupted monologues,[256] this gentle and observant drama was notably successful in catching the pace and moods of any institution for the unwell, such as a crowded ward, an army billet or the Television Centre at Wood Lane. Beautifully acted, compassionately written and intelligently directed, *Funny Farm* placed its damaged characters and underpaid male nurses in a shrinking world of endless passages, pale windows, distant scrabbles of voices, swishing doors and subterranean green colours. The patients didn't seem to watch much television, another disturbing similarity to the inmates whose doors open onto a long corridor that goes round and round the Television Centre and never quite makes it out into the real world. Except in plays as good as this.

Places, as well as people, seem to endure chronic ailments of the spirit, diseases of the circulation, and unsightly growths more or less malignant. Birmingham has been incontinent since birth, Harrogate uncomplainingly geriatric, Glasgow long a suitable case for treatment. *Imagine a City Called Berlin*, which occupied the whole of *2ⁿᵈ House* (BBC2) on Saturday, offered up the sight of a city which has suffered so many coronaries that it languishes now in that intensive care unit at the back of the mind where we barely keep alive the images and the prejudices of the past. 'A city of hints, fragments, echoes,' diagnosed Michael Frayn, going a fair way to describe his own elusive and perceptive narration. Drifting about in front of shop windows and stolid buildings with that terrible smile on his ascetic countenance (which always reminds me of an ageing theology student who has discovered that God is enormously irritated by prayer), Frayn kept plunging his hands into his anorak as though looking for glassy aphorisms in the pockets, chinking about like marbles.

'Why on earth is Berlin in Berlin?' he asked, talking not about Irving's travel arrangements but the strange dislocations we sometimes experience between our ideas of a place and the too emphatic reality of its actual physical presence. Modern Berlin, where two sick ideologies vomit at each other across electrified wire, murderous wall and depressed wasteland, is perhaps not altogether unjust a consummation to follow the years of the jackboot. The Brandenburg Gate was shown as a meaningless triumphal arch in a patch of nowhere. Frayn was right to keep his occasionally elegiac tone for other parts of the lost capital, most of all in a junk shop against the old railway arches where a nun tinkered on a badly tuned piano and scavenging hands picked among abandoned possessions. The rubble of forgotten parlours is always more plangent a sight than fallen stones and decayed abstractions.

One of the best things about the film – produced by Dennis Marks – was the way in which grainy old pictures from the past were allowed to bleed in to the present. Bland, pretty colour would slip away into the patina of monochrome seconds before the old film was laced into position, a mannered but effective technique for reducing the visual shock and tempering the rainbow sneer of hindsight. Superb, too, was the rostrum camera work, pulling the eye along still canvases, and reinforcing Frayn's desire to see a modern city other than Paris made over into the visions of its own art. Indeed, much of the film was so accomplished, and the commentary so intriguing and original, that I even dared to hope that we might get by without a shot of a billion-mark banknote from the great inflation and (especially) without that song from *Cabaret*. But no, they duly arrived. Presumably much to the pleasure of my former colleague, the bronchitic in charge of the switch.

Telling stories
New Society, 15 May 1975

I did not want to go to the gathering at all, and I was worried about the talk I had agreed to deliver. My notes had been hurriedly plagiarized from the few volumes of literary criticism which glower down in disapproval from my open bookshelves, preachers at a carnival. But I had to go, trapped for once by a wheedling and flattering voice on the telephone. 'Talk about writing,' the man said. These people, my audience, met at a hotel in the Forest of Dean. They had followed my career with interest (I was told) because I was a native of the same patch. But the people I grew up with were surely not the sort to meet in a hotel for dinner and then listen to a talk 'about writing' while they picked the food out of their teeth. Depressed, I cast my eye over the scrawl of utterly tedious speculation which stood between me and total embarrassment. At least – I reassured myself, in the dozen miles of tree-fingered roadway between my home and the hotel – at least, they won't want me again. Dark foliage scudded past, but the taxi headlights picked out tiny paths which seemed to plunge straight into a strange old ache that had inexplicably returned to my mind. In a panic, now, I gave as much of my attention as I could to the opening paragraph of my speech.

'Some writers,' it said 'are so hung up on the relationship between fiction and lying – *telling stories* is a popular description of both arts – that they insist on tightening the noose of theory about their necks. Many recent novels are structured to allow their authors to lean in and out of the sentences, heavily breathing, obtrusive, irritating. They insist on challenging us with the fact that they really *are* there, shaping the words, manipulating the characters, conning and cajoling us, insinuating along each upward loop or downward stroke. These desperate, deliberately self-conscious interventions from the author are not usually appreciated by critics, who, being conventional men with mortgages, rather dislike treacherous questions about the tensions between art and life. Novelists who set out to expose the mechanism of the story even while they are writing it are bound to seem awkward and pretentious to those who have solved the equations between the writer, the writing and the world (or between fact and fiction, truth and lies, "truth" and "lies") simply by taking them for granted. *Look here* – the orthodox can snarl – *I know this is a book I am reading. I know it is a story, I know it is written by someone, I know it is not, well, "true."* But why, then, do they get so upset when a writer goes out of his way to confirm such "knowledge"? It is because the very act of so doing breaks open the form, construction or shape that had seemed neutral and safe and…'

I soon realized that if I went on in this vein I should lose my audience altogether. Already, there was some coughing, sighing and foot shuffling at the furthest reaches of those few cubic feet of hired air. The people nearer to me had picked up my ill-suppressed anxiety. Worse, a few of the more alert sensed my lack of conviction. It was turning into a nightmare: a recurring one, too, because, much to my surprise, at least a third of the diners had been to the same village school that I had. Some of them at the same time, too. The ramshackle old building loomed up again, mossy gravestones coming right up under its high windows. Bored faces jowling with the years dissolved back to the peck, peck, chicken peck sharpness of colliers' children in the perpetual melodrama of the classroom.

Once more, too, I was in the same kind of situation as the nine-year-old suspected for his 'intelligence,' quick answers, and pretensions; a timid child with flaming red hair and dazzling white secrets. In those days, I protected myself with strategic comic turns, and fantasies labyrinthine enough to pull in my companions, forcing them to lower their fists. My vapid theorizing now needed some similarly instinctive skill if I was to save my talk from complete disaster. I needed to recreate that old collusion, the nearly forgotten conspiracies of desk, blackboard, playground. Surely that one there, in the blue suit and panatela, used to have dried snot on the sleeve of his jersey, a bit like the trail of a slug on a stone path?

Fixing my eyes on him, I moved from the general to the particular, from dry criticism to practical demonstration, abstraction to memory.

I reconstructed the incident which had first signalled to me the way in which a lie is transformed into a 'truth' when reinforced by the assent of its audience. The demonstration would show how I had used a nasty childhood lie of my own – the truth of a real experience – by dramatizing it in one of my first television plays, a fiction. Lie-truth-lie: an irresistible symmetry, open at both ends.

In my play, *Stand Up, Nigel Barton*, I had written a scene in which an unhappy boy yanked a daffodil out of its pot on the classroom table, breaking the stem in doing so, and then carrying the damaged bloom home in strange triumph. I made his motives clearer than mine had been when I did the same thing a few weeks before my ninth birthday. In the play, the boy fidgeted uncomfortably in his desk when the sharp-tongued bitch out front invited the class to find out which evil boy had stolen 'the lovely flower we have watered and tended...' The teacher, in fact, had been young and gentle, the first love of my life, an emancipator. Nigel Barton was asked, in shocked tones, if he knew anything about it... so was Dennis Potter, betrayed by sudden crimson and a jerk of anxiety. Both boys stood up, and immediately told a lie. Yes, I *did* know, Miss, but... Elaborate, plausibly detailed, a story came almost unbidden to the lips, garnished with a fine show of reluctance about giving up the name of the boy I had said had taken the flower. 'Isaac Holt,' I said. (A fictional name which duplicates the conjunction of grand Old Testament and fine old English rhythms in the real one.)[257]

As soon as I mentioned the name, then, and now in the hotel, a tremor of amusement came from my audience. The coughing and shuffling ceased, and eyes quickened back to attention. I had not expected Isaac Holt to be so swiftly remembered. He had been an odd, rather portly child from Standard 4, the oldest class in the junior school. I sometimes used to see him running flat out along a path in the woods, arms thrashing. ('What bist doing, Isaac?' 'Trainin',' he used to gasp, thumping past.) A heavy phlegmatic, rather stupid oaf. The first name that came into my head.

I did not expect the teacher to send for Isaac straight away. But she did. When he came padding down the aisle between the desks from the door at the back of the classroom, I was tingling with fear. Exposure now would be disastrous. But the lie had already grown in this room, and its victim was comically, cruelly unprepared. The teacher did not ask Isaac if he took it; she asked him *why* he had taken it. He blinked, swallowed, gaped about, and said, 'Beg pardon, Miss?'

It worked quite well in the play. It worked better still in my talk, for the smaller audience had a closer feel for the location of the scene and the cadences of the outlandish Forest speech. But it worked best of all back there in 1944. The class had picked up the possibilities of drama. Their eyes, so to speak, raced ahead along the page. An exasperated cross-examination by the teacher and a confused silence from Isaac drew out of the others an inevitable response. 'Please, Miss,' volunteered a girl in pigtails. 'I saw Isaac with the daff outside the bread shop.' She paused for the slightest moment, then added the clinching detail of her own lie. 'Him said as a' was goin to plant'n, Miss.' A hiss of relief or pleasure came from the rest of the class. Voice after voice now gave chase, released from the leash by the girl's corroboration. Isaac, it seemed, had been seen carrying the daffodil at various precise locations between school and his house.

Perhaps suspicion of this sudden flood, or more likely bored by it all, Miss at last re-phrased her question in the proper manner. '*Did* you take it, Isaac?'

He dropped his head. 'Yes, miss,' he said, to my complete incredulity. Moreover, he now obviously believed that he *had* taken it. Pressed for a reason he whispered that it was 'pretty.' A word offered up in alleviation for his non-existent crime, a protection against the coming wrath. He did not seek me out later to thump me. The lie had so enveloped him that he saw no choice but to accept it as the truth, really the truth.

And I discovered in one precocious leap, back there in childhood, what people are like when they sense drama in the air. They want to shape it, control it, entertain themselves with it. I realized how a fiction generates its own heat, moves forward, and compels belief. Plays and novels are accusations, their characters victims, their audience or readers the witnesses. I offered up this account with proper unease, because the incident comes back to my mind again and again, especially when I am tired. But both in the play and at the hotel, the story came out as a schoolroom comedy. I could not make them *not* laugh. Always, Isaac is isolated, then hunted, just as eagerly as before. What are stories for? This is what stories are for!

My talk was a success. Afterwards, relieved and yet vaguely ashamed, I chatted with a few of those whom I had not seen for so long. Did anyone know what had become of Isaac?

'Don't you know!' chortled the man in the blue suit, still utterly crass. 'He's been in the lunatic asylum for years.'

You have probably assumed this to be a truthful account. If it is, you have an example of the predatory skills of a writer's memory, the ravening power of the imagination which cannibalizes all who have entered in. But if this is a lie, fancifully extended, you have – what? A short story? A piece of literary criticism in defence of this so-called New Fiction? I'm not saying, because it is a truth either way. And that, as my teacher neglected to say, is the nature of the relationship between fiction and lying.

The daffodils in the famous poem the teacher read to the class, after Isaac's crime, nodded their heads, manipulated blooms, words in the brain.

Marching to Zion
New Society, 19 June 1975

'You don't want to keep this, do you?'

A battered little book, this, with curling dark-grey pages, floppily soft covers once the colour of flame but now closer in more than just the mind's eye to that of dried blood, and, on the back, an injunction in the shape of a shield to 'read *The Christian* every week, published on Thursday, twopence.' A mighty and righteous indignation made me straighten up from the lid of the trunk. Not keep it? A chorus of radiant voices broke at the rim of memory, teetered for a fraction of a second on the verge of the sardonically dismissive, then pulled me back to the long, split benches of the square stone chapel at the top of the steep hill. 'Look inside!' I almost shouted.

'Presented to Dennis Potter, Whitsun 1942. Salem Free Church Sunday School.'

Almost seven years old, I had been very pleased to own Sankey's *Sacred Songs and Solos*, in which are found 'most of the old favourites sung by Mr Sankey in the great Revival Meetings conducted by Mr Moody during their three notable campaigns in this country...the premier book for use at Conventions, Evangelistic and Fellowship Meetings, in Places of Worship, Sabbath-Schools, and Mission Halls. It is almost superfluous to add that *Sacred Songs and Solos* has found favour in all parts of the world where the English language is spoken. THE PUBLISHERS.'

Memory has been variously described as an idiot, a deceiver and a vengeful predator. There are times when we fetch up the past like something curdled and sour we have unwittingly eaten, sickening moments when a look, a smell, a repeated sequence of words, coats the mind with a grey and furry nausea. But most of us are adept Stalinists when it comes to re-writing our own personal histories, blotting out this or sifting away that, a near-pathological confabulation determined upon adjusting the habit and expectation of self-regard against an accumulating heap of evidence which demands a more humble response or (what is the word? come now, it presses against the tip of the tongue in much the same manner that the wooden bench of Salem used to press against the back of the legs) or – repentance.

What shall I do? What shall I do?
Oh, what shall I do to be saved?

The evangelical chorus which spaces out the evangelical verses (hymn No. 496, the harmonium holding the starting note with a peculiarly tremulous wheeze, a mechanical voice about to break down into more complicated sobs and confessions) is rarely a dreary sound, even when the rain bounces against the slate roof above. A thump and a bump and a desire to beat out the simple rhythm with banging palms, a swing of the shoulders, a lift of the chin, a quickening pulse, a genuine exultation. It is a bit like being in the middle of a crowd behind the goal, celebrating a shot as it whoops into the back of the net. The repeated question comes with an upturned intonation, repeated yet again, bringing the singers to the triumphant answer, the rock at the end of the thrashing tide where we are invited to cling and thereby find salvation. Thus, 'What shall I do?' which has been thrown against the rafters no less than twelve times in the hymn, is emphatically resolved at the very end with the same plain beat amplified into the noisy serenity of absolute certainty:

That will I do! That will I do!
To Jesus I'll go and be saved!

A rustle of Sunday best, a scrape of boots and shoes on the planked floor, a few coughs and subdued murmurs, and the congregation sits.

I am trying now to peer back, seeing the vases of flowers in the deep window sills, the embroidered banner with the shimmering angel behind the pulpit, the face of the waiting preacher, the fat Bible open (you betcha!) at the prophets, the images evoked by song and prayer and sermon as they then presented themselves to an attentive child, tender in my adult thoughts.

I don't want to keep *any* of this, do I? For even then – surely? – there was a counter-rebellion of the spirit against the sanctimoniousness, the sometimes evident hypocrisy, the claustrophobia and airlessness, the insistent cant and gory wash-in-the-blood-of-the-saviour repulsions, which made Sunday mornings and Sunday afternoons an imprisoning depression of duty separated by the smell of boiled cabbage and the alternative mysteries of the *News of the World*, mixing as it did the heroic exploits of the Eighth Army with the less noble mishaps of other soldiers home on leave. 'What is indecent assault?' 'Never you mind.'

Have we trials and temp-ta-tions?
Is there trouble any-where?
We should never be dis-cour-aged;
Take it to the Lord in prayer!

Turning the pages of the rescued book, where almost every question mark has an answering exclamation, I find, as most people do when faced with tangible evidence from their own past (whether in an old snapshot, a letter, a forgotten object, or a resurrected paragraph from something once read and pondered upon) that memory refuses to own to a consonance or an affinity with the cautious movements of a logical and reflective mind. It is, rather, an imperious force that addresses you not from 'the past' where it would seem to belong but out of a present that is parallel to your own sudden blink of recognition. You have no means of finding out what you were, so to speak, but only another and yet more awkward than usual glimpse of what you now are.

The present tyrannizes the past, for memory, by the pointedness of its selections, seems to make you think and behave in years long gone not so much in response to the situation you were *then* in, but at the behest of the future person you have since become. I own myself in a special trajectory that allows me to cast a half-amused eye on the italicized chorus of an old hymn, sense rather than recall the boy who once sang it, more accurately recollect the place and some of the circumstances which gave added resonance to the strident voices, and at the same time fence with the very complicated ambiguities of my present mood.

The tangle of the preceding paragraph – now that I think about it after a small interval and a couple of unnoticed cigarettes – probably shows how much a chapel upbringing determines the cast of one's language and personality. Perhaps the proper answer to 'You don't want to keep this do you?' is 'I can't get rid of it.' Sankey's lugubrious collection simply brings me up against that implanted sense of acute self-consciousness, or of personal destiny, in which the determined solitude of what I once found simple to call my soul has been 'given' to me as the secret and quiet place of inner struggle where I can (must) find meaning, purpose and grace in the clangorous passage of the transient. Nothing could be further from an envied spontaneity, or from the liberations of a so-called permissive morality.

I am perforce still marching to Zion,[258] even though the holy city on the crown of the hill has long since been plundered and razed to the ground. It is too late to get off the path now and hide in the rocks which tower alongside in great slabs, baking and cracking under an alien sun, the landscape of the perpetual wilderness which still awaits those who wander off in search of vain whims and fancies, the butterflies of the mind.

Far on the mountain, why wilt thou wander?
Darker and darker thy pathway will be.
Turn from thy roaming, fly from its dangers.
While the Good Shepherd is calling to thee!

Protestant evangelism is close to the mind of a child in its clear and simple images of rock and sea and mountain and the knock, knock, knocking at the door, but very distant from him in the demand that he shall take personal responsibility for the weight and meaning of his individual thoughts and actions. The scenes and the demands do not go together until the damage has been done, so that the natural movement towards maturity is inevitably tinged with the hideous melodrama of an especial landscape.

Aspirations and even just growing older itself is cast in the form of a journey, a pilgrimage, in which the 'true' self leaps on ahead and beckons urgently to the idling dullard within to follow. The hymn book I have been looking at is arranged in a similar progression, moving from

Invitation to Warning and Entreaty; Divine Guidance and Protection; Service and Reward; Heaven Anticipated, and finally the great release of Death and Resurrection.

There shall sorrow, pain and parting
Grieve our hearts no more;
Soon, soon we'll meet beyond the river,
Safe on the Home-land shore.

I am working on the top floor of an old house and through the quartered window I can see in the middle distance a man in the long grass playing with a small paper kite. He seems to be totally absorbed, launching it again and again into the small breeze of a rare and golden summer's afternoon. My son comes into view, tooting on his new bicycle. The man immediately becomes aware of the child's presence, and something about the configuration of his adult movements suggests that he is suddenly conscious of being absurd. I look away, but there on the desk are these half-remembered hymns, paper kites to flight into a vacant and uncaring void. If I had been caught with them, and if I had no time to explain, the same sort of shame would have undoubtedly hunched itself into my ligaments or pricked at the pores of my skin.

But, then, the man out in the long grass, the boy on the bike, the birds yammering in the bright air, and the writer bending over the floppy remnant of a chapel legacy will all eventually perish. The things we do have only a temporary meaning, and in any longer perspective are swallowed up like gnats in the sharp beak. We have to *pretend* that our actions have purpose, because reason suggests none that will measure up to the absence of that place 'beyond the river.'

The pages turn, back and back, a last flip through – and what had just started out as a mildly amusing exercise (in intention, that is) has turned into a rather desolate and even bitter experience. I can smell the cabbage again and see those upturned faces, but the gap between then and now, or between (shudder) now and now, causes an ache at the edge of the 'soul.'

Oh, list to the watchman crying:
Come, come away!
The arrows of death are flying:
Come, come today!

No. Thank you very much, watchman, but decidedly *no*. And quite right, I don't want to keep this relic. But where shall I throw it? It won't stay there, not for long.[259]

One man's week
Sunday Times, 18 April 1976

SATURDAY

'You poor sick bastard, is your play tonight *all* you know about the kindness and sincerity of life??? Let us hope on your death bed it won't be a whore or a ponse with his penus!!!! Shame on you Potter. REMEMBER THIS.'

Abusive letters about my TV play *Double Dare*, which the BBC have sent on to me here in placid Ross-on-Wye, arrive this morning with an ominous plop on the doormat. Huge capitals, full stops and underlinings emphatic enough to make holes in the paper, complete pages fenced off with barbed exclamation marks. Rarely signed, usually sub-literate, hissing venom, their very similarity – even to the giddy slopes of the spidery handwriting – reduces any impact they might have had.

These scrawls are balanced by an approximately equal number of rather more intelligible letters saying much nicer things. But the speakers on *Critics' Forum* today (Radio 3) complete the circle by calling me a rancid puritan.[260]

SUNDAY

I had been up most of the night pretending to work, but in reality diverting myself with such gloomy oddities as listening to the football results at 3.30 am on the BBC World Service. The poisonous methotrexate I have to take in order to control chronic psoriatic arthropathy forced me once again to vomit and curse.

Some brass-band music on the radio instantly revived dormant grief for a lost and tender area of the past, pom-pomming me back to the proud child of 30 years ago watching his father in the village band. It was on a Sunday morning four months ago that my father died very suddenly, and incredulity and grief still hang in the air. This feeling has to be expressed, not just assuaged, in my work, which is probably why I can't get on with it. Meanwhile, reactions are still coming in to what has already been finished: I nervously await the Sunday papers and their reviews of *Double Dare*, hoping the critics realize that Palm Sunday is a proper time for Hosannas.

MONDAY

Kenith Trodd, embattled producer of *Double Dare*, the banned *Brimstone & Treacle*, and next Wednesday's *Where Adam Stood* (all designed to cohere together), telephones to say that he plans to bring down a video-cassette recording of *Brimstone* for me to see very soon. He tells me that Mrs Whitehouse has announced that she is approaching the Director of Public Prosecutions about last week's play, which 'perfectly illustrated the decadence to which Solzhenitsyn referred in his TV interview.' Does this help the campaign within the BBC to get *Brimstone* shown?[261]

Trodd is hopeful, on the argument that farces always have happy endings, so I outline to him my new book about *The Last Days of Alasdair Milne*, which has the Director of Programmes, Television (who banned my play) sobbing on his office carpet and inviting Mrs W to pray with him. I have to break off to be sick again, and presumably Trodd does too.

TUESDAY

The weekly methotrexate nausea duly passes and I am again convinced that dialogue will flow more easily under my fist. My skin and joints are improved enough for me to signal Elizabeth Thomas at the *New Statesman* that I will return as their TV critic next week.[262] I have a dread of giving up the column in case my health gets much worse, for we all know that even a raving cripple can still be a critic if nothing else.

Even so, I am rather disconcerted by the results of a readership survey in this week's issue. Anthony Howard claims that: 'The replies plainly demonstrate that the familiar picture of the *NS* reader – the gangling Fabian vegetarian, usually with glasses and rarely without a worried frown – is not so much a caricature as a total distortion…' I hope not, for I write my column with gusto and relish precisely because I imagine myself addressing just such a nincompoop readership.

WEDNESDAY

In the middle of a grey and rainy afternoon which seems to have come from inside my head my 11-year-old son Robert suddenly clutches his stomach and nearly shouts aloud with pain. Within an hour or so, he is in an ambulance with my wife Margaret on the way to Hereford

County Hospital. I stay with his two older sisters, dry-mouthed with foreboding. 'Get me out of here!' Robert insists in the unfortunately-named Peter Pan Ward, unimpressed with its fish-tank, toys and happy pictures. He is given an enema and the usual battery of tests. The doctors are reassuring, but we are sleepless and terrorized. I find myself silently intoning 'Please' over and over again, the nearest I can get to the prayers I so often want to make.

THURSDAY

Robert's pains have gone, thank God. He has slept well, and he can come home if the result of the last urine test is all right. He is here by tea time, immensely proud of himself and brandishing one of the local papers. 'They're having another go at you, Dad.' Mrs Louise Shepherd, wife of local Tory MP Colin Shepherd, has released to the local Press an ill-written and ungrammatical letter of complaint about *Double Dare* which she had sent to the Director-General of the BBC. Poor Louise (as some of us call her here with dreadful rural familiarity) thinks, among other things, that 'media' is a singular noun when used about television. Lord, deliver up to me mine enemies – especially if they need a dictionary.

FRIDAY

My chapel-going in the Forest of Dean has left me with vague yearnings and puzzled restlessness on every holy day. The depression and anxiety which has been dogging me recently is no ally of religious aspiration, which I always understood to be drawn out of the deepest human impulse towards gratitude.

Bemused and sardonic, I empty my mouth of spicy hot cross bun to address my less than attentive family. I look from chewing face to chewing face, at Margaret, Jane, Sarah and finally Robert. A leap of joy, of praise and thanks, suddenly uplifts me, and there aren't even any trembling violins in our kitchen. I still need the methotrexate, though…

A note from Mr Milne
New Statesman, 23 April 1976

I have always found it a pleasure to watch someone cooking his own goose so it is only fair if I open up the oven door on my own plucked and basted carcass to explain why the same team of BBC bureaucrats that didn't bring you *The Naked Civil Servant*[263] has also decided, with similar noises of shock and horror, not to bring you my play *Brimstone & Treacle*. You will have to excuse me, therefore, if I resume this feat in front of the twinkling set with a description of what is going on behind the double-glazed windows at the BBC's pap factory rather than with a review of the Easter holiday programme. I cannot tap at the shell of that particular egg because this is the first chance I have had to set down an account of the way in which *Brimstone & Treacle* was castigated as unfit for the public to see, a decision which in more than my not entirely disinterested opinion reveals a lot about the changing nature of the BBC and the sort of television we're going to get in the future.

'I found the play brilliantly written and made, but nauseating.' said Alasdair Milne, the Director of Programmes, in the one brief and insolent letter he condescended to write to the author:

> I believe that it is right in certain instances to outrage the viewers in order to get over a point of serious importance, but I am afraid that in this case real outrage would be widely felt and that no such point would get across.[264]

Try reading that out loud, and the intonation will comically approximate to the injured tones in which Neville Chamberlain declared war on Germany. But the paragraph, amusing though it is, represents the argument in its entirety as put to me by the BBC hierarchs. Milne cannot bring himself to say which scene, or which shot, or which passage of dialogue made him plunge retching to the sixth floor lavatories at the Television Centre. Nor does he make any suggestions for cuts, or indicate that he will listen to any contrary argument. Instead, when the fuss begins, this Reithian Scot packs his bags and goes off on holiday, presumably to some place where nobody tries to sell him a comic postcard.

Yet if the test of what is to be forbidden to viewers is the possible nausea and outrage the programme might cause, then how come that in the same drear week that *Brimstone & Treacle* was due to be shown we had to put up with such proven emetics as *Jim'll Fix It*, the 400th repeat of *Star Trek*, two uninterrupted hours of the *Eurovision Song Contest* or (even worse) ten uninterrupted minutes of the Rt. Hon. Sir Geoffrey Howe, MP? For answer one might well quote Cilla in one of her recent Saturday night 'interviews' with a startled family outside their front door:[265] 'How can he say anything,' she protested when a toddler made an obscure noise, 'if he's got that dummy stuck in his gob?'

Any television company which pumps out programmes every night of the year, for ever and ever, is compelled by its own narrow logistics to accept that it is right in certain instances to outrage the viewer in order to get over a point of no importance whatsoever. The same penny-pinching misfortune or quotidian exhaustion accounts for the fact that no matter how scornfully the BBC sniffs about the degraded commercialism of American television, it is obliged to ship over so many of the worst examples of just such electronic chewing gum. There seems to be no other way to feed the insatiable machine, and therefore necessity has become the mother of hypocrisy: senior programme executives who like to think well of themselves do not spend much time at their desks agonizing over tawdry variety shows, alien thrillers, idiot back-chat or the wearily mechanical smut which sustains the worst of the regular comedies. They point instead at the ratings, and wash their hands.

Unfortunately, though, the bilge-water seeps under the office door. Those who use up a lot of their time fastidiously averting their eyes and minds from so much of what is actually produced inevitably find it difficult to look at *anything* with a steady gaze. The characteristic approach of the better programme makers to the programme controllers, therefore, is one of cautious double-talk and protective secrecy. The BBC, in consequence, is an uneasy confederation of cunning groups, each pushing and concealing its product until the moment when it gets on the air. Memoranda drift up from one floor to another, and back down again, or sideways, and in the spaces between the words, so to speak, programmes get made.[266] The ramshackle anachronism which the Corporation has become offers marvellous opportunities if the game is played with properly Byzantine skill, but occasionally a Controller loses his head, froths at the mouth and exposes himself and the whole system to ridicule.

Brimstone & Treacle was delivered to the BBC in early December 1974, discussed, praised, accepted and paid for in January 1975,[267] assigned to a producer (Kenith Trodd, thank goodness), discussed again in long and involved meetings, given the crucial nod by the Head of Plays, handed over to director Barry Davis, discussed yet again, then cast, rehearsed, brought into the studio, videotaped, dubbed, scheduled for transmission, and announced in the *Radio Times*.[268] Everyone along the labyrinthine chain of command which makes the BBC so delicately elephantine had a chance to throw in his or her two pennyworth of unhelpful comment. Actors, designers, wardrobe, lighting, cameramen and sound engineers – and about £70,000 – were deployed to bring it from the stage to the screen. You could be forgiven for thinking that a more appropriate point of rejection might have been found during 15 months of work, discussion and expenditure. After all, it's your licence money.

The final outcome of the process, however, was a miserable letter on one sheet of paper which talked about 'nausea' and brazenly closed the door on any other discussions. Yet leaving aside the lack of grace or tardy obtuseness of such a communication, the awkward fact remains that Milne and his immediate subordinates are, of course, entitled to exercise editorial control over what is to be transmitted by the BBC. I have had scripts mauled or rejected before now, and not even the most rabid paranoia, nor the worst excess of arrogance, can allow me to argue that the BBC should be compelled to screen my work. In the last resort, I would not even rest a case on the ludicrous delay, wasteful extravagance and bureaucratic inefficiency which bans a play when it has already been made: such ill-mannered nonsense is a matter for accountants, management consultants, the parliamentarians who fix the licence fee and an Annan Committee examining alternative structures for getting stuff on the screen.

The case is simpler: Milne is wrong. Television critics from the *Guardian*, *Daily Telegraph*, *Sunday Times* and *Time Out* who have by accident or subterfuge seen the tapes say it is at the very least an interesting play that should be shown. The Head of Drama thinks so, too. And the Head of Plays, who has just left the job. And the new Head of Plays. The Drama department, the Arts department, many directors and writers, and all those concerned in making the play are of similar mind. They are not so much angry on my behalf as on their own: the programme makers detect signs of a loss of nerve in those set above them. Indeed, a deputation of drama producers has been to Milne to tell him so. But there is no one more stubborn than a puritanical Scot in a corner and it is because I realize that his elusive half-suggestion that the affair might be reconsidered has not yet been taken further that I am writing this piece.

Brimstone & Treacle is near to my heart (or liver anyway) because I think it may be the best play I have written. The fast diminishing residue of what was once an almost evangelical passion about the place of drama on the television screen, rather than simpering self-love, makes me demand that you should be *allowed* to see the play. Unlike Alasdair Milne, I am assuming, of course, that you are grown up and know how to work the off-switch. You can reach him if you wish to object to his censorship by telephoning the BBC on 01-743 8000 and asking for the Ghost of Lord Reith.

Poisonous gas
New Statesman, 28 May 1976

For days now, the irritating words of an irritating tune have been going round and round the mouldering interior of my head like tired wasps circling the remnants of an abandoned cream-bun. 'No Two People have ever Bin so in love Bin so in love, Bin so in love, No Two People have ever Bin so in love as my lovey-dove and I –' and then all over once again, her lovey-dove, his lovey-dovey and me. I do not wish to deny the manifold pleasures of such great passion, but its tinkling repetition is surely an excessive punishment for watching *The Black and White Minstrel Show* (BBC1) right through from sugary beginning to sickly end on Saturday evening.

It is not so much the potency of cheap music that alarms me as its promiscuity: the plink-ploink of the off-screen band and the ban-an-an-ality of the lyrics have since intruded into the most guarded recesses and the most private moments, a chime of 'Bin-so' like a call from the great icecream van on high. There was, for example, an affecting programme about cancer patients on BBC2 on Monday (called *Dying*, rather to the delight of the other channels) which ended with a dressed corpse in a coffin, a glisten of tears in the eyes of my wife and eldest child, and a dumb stupor on my own part in which 'Bin-so in love' tripped gaily across the back of an addled brain. The nearest and most horrible analogy to the effect of this maddening chorus, perhaps, is to the original nerve gases developed and stockpiled by the Germans during the last war, all of which so successfully devastated the microchemistry at the nerve endings that a victim was left with no means of stopping muscle action once the muscles had been activated. (They even had ways of making us dance, it seems.)

The Black and White Minstrel Show is a programme specializing in noxious syncopations which are all made to sound as if they come from the palsied hand of one and the same cretinous tunesmith. There are no real distinctions, therefore, between a jolly dance, a lugubrious 'country' number, a sweet old folk-song or even an evangelical hymn. On Saturday, for instance, the renowned West Country song "Widdicombe Fair" was delivered in bland mid-Atlantic accents by a choir standing on a polished stairway that led from nowhere to nowhere missing out old uncle Tom Cobley and all. Blacked-up minstrels and stripped-down dancers prance and mime around a vaguely geometric set under a paper moon and ochre skies, lacking any sort of vigour which might otherwise overcome the contradictions of place and time and mood and music that make the programme so laughable.

But why on earth expose my precious self to such poisonous gases in the first place? Or even compound the distress by tuning in to (and staying with) *It's a Knockout* (BBC1), *Husband of the Year* (ITV), *The Money Programme* (BBC2), *Crossroads* (ITV) and other such low-minded drivel?

I decided that my last column for a few months would have richer flavours if I took heed of some characteristic sentences from Martin Amis which I came across while shredding a back number of the *New Review* the other 'Bin-so' day. The splinter off the old block was confiding what he called 'a mild suspicion' that

intelligent people would rather watch anything at all than intelligent television – that indeed they pine for the rubbishy, frivolous and ephemeral…it is only the TV critic, that unhappy figure, who actually wants to watch all those documentaries on the recreation facilities for Stuttgart-based immigrant workers, all those regional plays about the illegitimate offspring of paraplegic pet-shop owners.

The tone of voice is recognizable in others, the attitude of mind is shared by many who work in television, and the level of its response helps to explain why a derivative and second-rate novel can often lay more claim to attention or respect than good programmes which shunt and bump across the schedules before disappearing for ever into the night. The latest of the many treasons of the clerks, in fact, lies in just this amused disdain for a box that can be plugged into the same socket as a hairdryer or a coffee percolator. The rubbishy, frivolous and ephemeral are fit enough for such a contraption, are they not? Certainly it would not be possible to advance the mildest of suspicions that 'intelligent people' (hello there) would rather read anything at all than intelligent books, or at least not to put it forward in a literary journal which in other matters accepted that the task of the critic is to attempt to discriminate (with reasons) between what seems to be good and what feels to be bad.

The unhappy television critic lost in the arid Stuttgart of the soul occasionally ends up clowning with his readers because he, too, is infected with the mild Amis suspicion about what the intelligent want to see on their screens, and so turns his pieces into complicit sniggering about precisely those vast areas of television which tend to make it a mere device to pass the time. I believe the ailment is also called the Clive James syndrome, but only in its more chronic manifestations.

'Do you mean,' quavered an incredulous crew member on the starship, 'that one of the people who threw the Enterprise a thousand light years is on board and killing our people?' 'Exactly,' came the answer, on the nod, tightening the tension in the *Star Trek* episode celebrated here last week.[269] A useful scrap of dialogue which emphasizes that the best thing to do in such circumstances is to get off the ship for a while, even if it means leaping into the summer doldrums with only an excruciating pun as a life support system – and that ('Bin-so Bin-so Bin-so') is what my present aim is.

Puppets on a string
Sunday Times, 5 December 1976

Frivolity is at its brightest and best when it finds a strain of banter or a few radiant bubbles of mockery in the dead, solemn, suffocating weight of things. Far less palatable – and, alas, much more common on the beaded tube – is the po-faced solemnity which reduces what was meant to be exhilarating, or at least trivial, into the crabbed dimensions of morose earnestness. Thus, although dutifully down-in-the-mouth *Panorama* and *This Week* would both be immeasurably improved by a strategically placed cuckoo clock in the studio, it seems even more important to demand a wooden rattle, a cascade of coloured toilet rolls and an occasional sharp witticism from the heavy-headed souls who present *Match of the Day* (BBC1).

The plight of English football might almost be represented at the moment by the apparently ever-increasing length of Jimmy Hill's pendulous chin. Down, down, it goes, as though about to hit the studio floor with a dull clunk of sickly grinning depression. And yet I remember him from distant Saturdays at Fulham as a vivacious and spontaneous player, all flailing arms and splendidly bad passes, the sort to chuckle as he missed an open goal. He should summon up the same refreshing impiety to mock the lugubrious administrators and fearful managers who try to turn league football into a 'game' of dour attrition and leaden plod.

Last Saturday's *Match of the Day* took a trip to Middlesbrough and the sights discovered there cried out for a prolonged yelp of derision. The home team is managed by Jackie Charlton ('I'm a negative thinker, I am') and their play – to misuse a word – exactly fitted the weird advertisements plastered round the drab stadium: Strongarm Ale, Machine Tools, Steel Stock, Geordie Home Brew and an ominous but mysterious substance called Guld Barre. What on earth can it be? Even the names of the Middlesbrough players sounded like tin tacks lodged in the windpipe when the ball went from Platt to Craggs to Souness to Armstrong then Cooper and Hickton.

'Hick-ton! Hick-ton!' chanted the shivering crowd sourly, trying to imitate the sound of hailstones on a factory roof.

The tackles were delivered with the sort of crunch that used to advertise cornflakes, and the home fans cheered every foul committed against the ankles and shins of the Ipswich visitors. They also sang the standard, vaguely low-church dirge "You'll Never Walk Alone" but banged their palms hard together as they did so to make it clear that they really meant "You'll Never Walk Again." The gloom which slowly descended upon the ground as Ipswich scored twice could not be lifted by the floodlights that make each player walk in a small puddle of four of his own shadows. Nor did ecstasy leap unbidden to the brim of the Strongarm Ale at the monstrously solemn interview which followed this penance. A Middlesbrough player mumbled: 'We've just got to knuckle ourselves down and play to a rigid pattern' – just the sort of promise to rust the turnstiles.

Jimmy Hill would do soccer a great service, and add considerably to the hilarity of the nation, if he for once ignored the suspicious eye the Football League fixes so coldly on television and turned his Saturday spot into a scornful blow-by-blow demonstration of the joyless inadequacies of a game which ought now to be billed under the title When the Boot Comes In. But I was grateful for the concluding montage of George Best at play which showed just how entertaining and zestful football can be at the feet of a genuine master. The way he teed up the ball and then flicked it over the head of an open-mouthed defender, was a sight that would make even the Sex Pistols swallow their dirty little tongues.

Comedian Dave Allen could do with a mouthwash too. His fortnightly *Dave Allen at Large* (BBC2) is the nearest equivalent yet to the wink and the nudge on the bar-stool, a form of signalling that always makes me look for the nearest exit. He is one of the many comedians on the box who somehow contrive to have more writers on the final credits than jokes in the script.

But more delight came in *Parkinson* (BBC1), in which mine host – his nervous fidgeting and fawning long since flattened into weary ease – played the perfect straight man to a puppet emu. This horrible bird comes menacingly alive on the end of Rod Hull's arm.

It has bright blue feathers, a yellow beak which curls into a snarl, long loose legs and eyes which Angela Rippon keeps for news of the pound sterling. I thought Parkinson was overdoing it more than a bit when he greeted this bizarre creature with such an uneasy simper, and I scribbled the single word 'fool!' to help find a way through my brief, exclamatory notes. But there followed a scene so manically aggressive, so outrageously funny and so perfectly staged that I managed to cross out the premature abuse before collapsing into the longest and loudest laughs which the glum old screen has provided in months.

The mad emu launched itself on Parkinson, grabbing tight hold of his nose, tearing at his hair, pecking at every available limb, the swift jabs eventually knocking him bodily out of his chair and onto the floor, where the rising and gurgling Parkinson, still under attack, lost his shoe, his dignity, his breath and his last enemy. By the end it had become the nightmare of a child being tickled half to death, and there was even a note of cruelty and hysteria beating out from the helpless studio audience. A very strange and, ultimately, unsettling affair which, in the context of the surrounding programmes, took on the peculiar hues of all those secret fears and aggressions waiting to be projected onto the nearest unlikely dummy. I hope Benn and Powell were tuned in to something else.

A place could have been found for a psychotic puppet in any one of the dazzling episodes of *I, Claudius*, Jack Pulman's happy decoction of the Robert Graves novels. Indeed, almost anything goes in this BBC2 serial. The final episode is screened tomorrow night, and I shall be downcast when the snake slithers across the mosaic for the last time. The panache of Herbert Wise's direction, the swift economy of the narrative, and the lurid rubefaction of the settings, has been a triumph for brazen irreverence. *I, Claudius* occupied its chosen territory with maximum skill, and those who sneer at the potentialities of television should ask themselves where else such a mix could have been made to work quite so stunningly.

The acting, in particular, has been a Via Láctea of star turns. Brian Blessed's death as Augustus, Siân Phillips's waspish Livia, George Baker's disgusting Tiberius, and John Hurt's tinselled and spangled cabaret as Caligula made one's eyes revolve incredulously on the end of their popping stalks. But it is the performance of Derek Jacobi as the limping, shuffling, stuttering Claudius which holds everything together – a marvellously slubbered and spiracular impersonation that never quite passes over into the ham specially cooked for all those who too obviously enjoy such meaty parts. F-f-fantastic!

Last week's episode saw the shapely Messalina lose her head with one neat chop of a gleaming sword. I thought of this efficient stroke with longing when watching the woman who sometimes addresses the *Tomorrow's World* (BBC1) cameras. On Thursday, she held up a bulbous and misshapen tuber in her hand and sadly intoned, 'It's been a bad year for the potato.'[270] It's been a good one for raspberries, though. Here, madam. Catch.

And with no language but a cry
BBC Radio 3, 27 December 1976[271]

The gifts which one might wish to lay in the most tentative of gestures beside the swaddled infant in the manger are not those which belong to the realm of language, for the images of the Nativity are of such transparent simplicity that even the mockery of a determined iconoclast can pass straight through without being refracted. It is when one seeks to animate and extend the familiar tableau into the concept of a loving God present then and now, there and here, continually manifest in human culture, that the meagre words twist and buckle and sometimes break apart into evident gibberish.

I don't wish to demean the jots and tittles of my reason when I address myself to the claims of the Christian religion – but as a result, perhaps, I have found myself nagged and buffeted by a disjointed series of thoughts or impressions which resist the ready categorization that would make them more easily accessible to my stranded emotions. We are all of us, at times, like parched beings who dare not stoop to the clear pool of water in case it is a mirage, and the hard work it takes to pull together my scattered thoughts into consecutive sentences which kindly mimic the form of consecutive argument is made even more difficult when I am forced to admit that my ideas and intimations have remained in this random state precisely because the attempt to make them cohere can be carried out only at personal risk and with the absolute certainty of self-exposure.

But this paralysing combination of anxiety and laziness can always be passed off as modesty, and is not the sole reason for the lip-chewing which preceded acceptance of this surprising invitation to talk about my own understanding of the significance of Christmas. A priest, a theologian, or, at the least, if not the authoritatively required very least, a committed Christian not only seem to have a better claim to your attention at this time, but would (I presume) be far less likely to carry the hesitation and unease right into the substance of the talk.

In truth, I am compelled by my present condition or understanding to be evasive and uncomfortable about the very things which seem to me to be the most important in the world. A fretful scepticism grates at my mind with the noisy insistence of rooks at dusk, and although I often settle upon the thought of 'God' in the silence of my own head, and although I yearn for God in the speechless ligaments of my being, I find the word 'God' and the words 'Jesus Christ' in my mouth a genuine embarrassment. My tongue, already dipped and coated with the acid of hypocrisy, feels no more than a sliver away from cant and sanctimoniousness. Again, I do not yet know how to pray – except, perhaps, for a monosyllable squeezed out between clenched teeth: perhaps this, too, is because in the last resort, at the moment of encounter, it is not really possible to be evasive with God himself no matter how wary and oblique the approach. Even when brought by something quick and compelling inside myself that can be identified, peculiarly enough, as both anguished and light-hearted, I find that the door does not in fact swing open as promised – no more than the length of a chain, anyway. If there is such a door, and if it's the right door, then my knock is not firm enough.

But I *do* know that doubt, even doubt malignant enough to drain life of colour and purpose, is part of the provenance if not the language of faith. Its shifts and stirrings take their stubborn power from that way of seeing existence which is called religious, and therefore are not only against the grain but the whole weight of the utterly secular comprehension which has become the dominant mode of perception. These dark flutterings conceal a double-edged blade that can also be turned against the materialist and determinist formulations which have almost inexorably driven back religion from the minds of men and women. Most of the modern views of the place and purpose of man in the world can be reduced to the bleak assertion that we are here because we are here because we are here and the emancipations wrenched from the now supposedly empty heavens have narrowed down into increasingly deterministic language which leaves scarcely any space at all between one programmed gene and another where the tiniest flame of personal freedom is allowed to flicker awhile before being permanently extinguished.

It seems to me that we are enslaved more completely than ever by such quasi-mechanical perspectives unless we again take flight on the wings of doubt. An inch of knowledge gained is not necessarily convertible into a yard of hope lost. Nor must we be so brow-beaten by disguised metaphors as to suppose that there is any difference of status between the statement that there is no God and the statement that there is God, or, rather, that God is. Both are assertions and neither is amenable to disproof, and so neither of them has the function of those kinds of knowledge which 'explain' thunder and lightning and the boiling point of water.

The doubt which hovers between both of these opposing assertions is always likely to seem irresolute and evasive, and sometimes even cowardly. But from where I find myself on what feels like a voyage, it keeps open a porthole of grace and light that looks beyond the oceans of chance and death which bound us in on all sides. Even when grief and pain and despair are carried in the hold, there is still this glimmer of light, or thread of grace, pointing away to an alternative. The only possible alternative, and one that gathers up all those other luminous concepts such as justice, pity, mercy and, especially, love, which are also forms of knowing or ways of seeing that fit so awkwardly into the dominant modes of perception.

A way of seeing which needs constant attention if it is not to be blanked out and shuttered. I am aware that 'prayer' is the best name for this attention, but joy also, light-heartedness, or even the frivolity which finds a smile in the dead lump of things, can demonstrate this necessary attention. And it is here that I look for the significance of Christmas, a festival inextricably enravelled in the mesh of hope and doubt, memory and longing, in which (of course) childhood carol, crusted dogma, secular glitter and the sparse narratives of Matthew and Luke are oddly mingled. It takes a stern heart to banish every trace of sentiment from the backward look at childhood, and one would have to suffer from a very wintry disposition not to welcome the chance to be of good cheer for a few days in the colder stretches of the year. But sentimentality and spangled excess can make a particularly mindless paste, or mince, and I am not here to give the goo more than a haplessly grinning nod in passing. The pagan bravery of 'eat, drink and be merry' will persist even when modern minds more used to euphemism leave out the 'for tomorrow we die' which gives the injunction its force.

Yet on some tomorrow we do indeed die. The great Christian festivals take their beauty and their tension from the revelation which, if it is to be trusted, has conquered death. If. Ah, if! A cry that's not simply the vain and empty outpouring of that superstition, fantasy or obscurantism which uses the name of God as a temporary explanation for what cannot be understood, or as a consolation for what cannot be endured. No. The 'if' is poised on the still point of the churning mind, a question as well as a cry, a demand as well as a yearning, a single word trembling on the edge of an entirely different order of speech. A metalanguage whose 'words' parallel the act of divination which first made the human animal struggle towards naming and thereby ordering the incoherent nature that threatened him. An enterprise so successful that we often forget that we are peering and poking about from inside a complicated lattice of signs. A lattice adjusted from age to age, fashion to fashion, in such a way as to make the speed and sweep of everyday discourse appear to be the expression of what is 'natural.' The things out there, the It of the world, is thereby turned into something we can manage and even manipulate, where the sign and the signified become difficult to separate, but there's always a gap between sign and signified, words and things. As we strive to make sense of the universe and our own place within it, we need to be exceptionally alert to the ways in which this gap, this *chasm* indeed, is bridged by any one particular system of language. The bridge is often narrower and flimsier than we acknowledge. Each strut is an 'if.'

The persistence of art in the human world represents not the triumph of illusion in the teeth of advancing knowledge, nor the lingering echoes of impotent cries thrown up at an indifferent heaven, but, rather, the tenacity of other ways of seeing. Art continually restores to human beings a sense of our own passionate involvement with the material and substance of the things out there, the pulse of being. Thus, myth is not in itself a lesser or secondary form of ordering our experience, but the breath and vivacity of it. Stories, parables and metaphors are not, in themselves, merely displaced or shiftily transposed categories of knowledge. They break through the lattice of signs. They re-open the space between the words and what the words signify. And they turn the cry that seems to rise from the suffocating materiality at the dead, blank centre of the blind world back into the spirit which alone has language.

I say 'art' when I might say 'religion' because I want to indicate the sort of symbolic framework it is that brings me, time and time again, to that momentous 'if' which perpetually trembles on the edge of triumphant resolution. Religious people are often horrifyingly dishonest in the way they use concepts because so many of them seem to feel compelled to use one system of signs, one means of knowing, to commend and sustain a different category of discourse. I once wrote a play, using a few chapters of Edmund Gosse's *Father and Son*, to show to myself as much as to others how crippling and ultimately doomed an enterprise it is to subborn and discountenance the facts which our proper search for knowledge will keep bringing into the light.[272] The agony which the theories of evolution brought down upon many Christians showed, as so often before, the frightened contortions and moral dishonesties which follow when the love of God is subverted into worship of a fading shadow.

But I have taken the title of this talk from Tennyson, a great poet struggling with grief and doubt on the eve of the period that was to cause such havoc in the Victorian church. "In Memoriam" shows an astonishing insight into the storms to come, and there is in its anxious quatrains a moving sense of the tensions of a serious mind finding disciplined expression and wholeness in the face of darkness and chaos. Again and again he summons up the hope 'that somehow good will be the final goal of ill,' but:

> *Behold, we know not anything;*
> *I can trust that good shall fall*
> *At last – far off – at last, to all,*
> *And every winter change to spring.*
>
> *So runs my dream: but what am I?*
> *An infant crying in the night:*
> *An infant crying for the light:*
> *And with no language but a cry.*

The language that is the cry seems a long way removed from the confident assertions of the creeds of the Christian church. But it isn't. Faith cannot be confined to definitions of belief, and will always arise out of the cry within each soul, the cry that calls for a light in the darkness. The painted caskets of make-believe gold, frankincense and myrrh which some of us carried as children in a nativity play will sooner or later be found to contain doubt, anxiety and pain. Indeed, the poignant images which cluster about the Christmas story are especially beautiful in the way the strange ache of joy gathers up into itself so many other pains nourished in the winter of the heart.

Imagination, judgment and insight are not necessarily given to us together, nor do they come all at once. They are never complete because they are processes which cannot be completed. By these means, Christian Revelation is demonstrably creative within each new generation. At Christmas, therefore, at each new Christmas, we are trying to celebrate the birth of the Christ of faith who will be encountered, when and if encountered, in fresh ways and by new demands. There is thus little point in fretting about such things as the accuracy of the accounts of the birth of Jesus of Nazareth. We have no means of knowing by any historical method, but we do know from other spheres that few things in the distant past can be translated easily into the present. All the parameters shift, so that an open and imaginative response is needed to understand any one event in history. The gospels, surely, are not simply recounting happenings in an instantly accessible history that allows us clear passage to Jesus as he was in so-called 'real time.' The interpretation and celebration of the Christ of faith is already going on in these brief and exultant 'narratives,' vibrant as they are with the conviction that the night is far spent and the day is at hand.

I cannot argue myself into faith. And I cannot argue myself out of my hunger for it. Like so many others in so many differing times and conditions, I must therefore watch and wait and keep alert. I must give my attention to that which so obviously calls for my attention. I feel the love of God in the great cavern that is the next minute of my life, and I give back what is given in the minute upon minute in which the mystery I call my self is making and being made.

Only in this continuous present does the attentive waiting make sense for me. I cherish the meanings of Christmas because they show to me that God is also in the waiting and in the cry. The humility and gentleness of the Nativity story allows me to comprehend how even what is passive and inarticulate is yet a form of address. At Christmas, God himself has no language but a cry, God is seen as utterly dependent and completely helpless, manifest in human culture in a plea that is at the opposite pole to both the brute idolatory and the vapid abstractions into which the religious impulse so easily degenerates.

The Christ who was born to teach in parables and die in degradation is vivid in another parable in this Christmas story, one which is more radiant than any other in moving the imagination. The crucifixion throws back the shadow of the hatreds and cruelties that make us seek to destroy what is tender and sacred within our own hearts. But the cradle song of Christmas celebrates the birth of God in the hungering soul. And, at this time, even that which is properly cautious and evasive and sceptical in me will not hold back the imagination. I cannot, thank God, do other than strive and hope.

Glop
New Statesman, 22 April 1977

Visions Before Midnight by Clive James (Cape)

Does he narrow his glittering eyes and ho-ho derisively at the little screen across screwed-up piles of abandoned jokes and discarded doggerel? Is his mouth full of salted peanuts, are his lips wet with tinned beer? Do people wander by accident into the gymnasium where he is *viewing* and tiptoe out again, awed and embarrassed? Does he pull up a – what could it be? A chair? A vaulting horse? – and leer at the twinkling tube, his jackaroo's visage a mere snort or two from the action? And when the picture collapses into a whining blob at the end of transmission, can the others who may be trapped behind high windows in the household pick up the sound of someone down below whistling in the dark?

In much the same way (let's pretend) that Keats wanted to know the exact position in which Shakespeare sat when quilling his way through 'to be or not to be,' so I would give the skin of a lemon to have seen the unlikely posture as well as the improbable setting in which Clive James watched the magic box before he tapped out on his worn but neoteric keys '*Mission Impossible* is glop from the schlock-hopper' in that ritzy New York-Cambridge-Rockdale Odeon amalgam he has almost made his own.[273]

One needs to know these crucial details, of course, to help keep at two fingers' length the vigour and comic brilliance of an invented world of jabbering mannequins that is itself made out of the electronic simulacrum of 'real life' beyond the lens. Clive James's television reviews are sufficiently potent to turn the pale glimmers on the set into something like a gaudily lit portable theatre of clacking wooden puppets speaking a splintered language that has never been heard before and yet which is instantly, and hilariously, recognizable. His stunning weekly pieces in the *Observer* readjust horizontal and vertical holds almost before there is time to blink away the images that are actually transmitted. This collection of reviews, culled from four years of self-delighted service in the column, enables readers who can swallow the temerity of such a book to forget the pictures altogether and concentrate on the omnipresent puppet master himself.[274]

He is nothing if not sardonic, so he makes sure that mainly the dross becomes the grist of his flailing mill. He is clever, in the sense that the late Lord Salisbury understood the word. Cute. Sharp. He scoffs lethally, but mostly at that which is generally derided. He stings like a cattle prod, though he imagines it to be an ice pick. No one on the funny farm is more brutally efficient at herding gabbling sports commentators or melamined beauty queens into the ducking pond, but he often takes silent cover when tougher beasts pass by on their way to the trough. And though he does not bleed, he wants, begs you to acknowledge that *he cannot be fooled*. Why, he even saw through Nixon.

Best of all, Clive James is sure that he owns a pair, at least, of panoptic eyeballs, swivelling pitilessly below a brow that can comprehend *everything* between *It's a Knockout* and the *Eurovision Song Contest*. Suspicious of rhetoric, gleeful about glop, frenzied into froth by all speech dislocations except (apparently) his own pronunciation of 'penis,' he is nevertheless prepared to issue the occasional emphatic statement of faith. It is extremely moving: 'Television,' he says, and not out of the side of his mouth, 'is for everybody. It follows that a television critic, at his best, is everybody too – he must enjoy diversity without being eclectic and stay receptive without being gulled.'

Oh, don't laugh, for God's sake. When your technique depends on the deft snigger, your wit on the easy victim, your passing solemnity on assent to what is generally assented to, then it is too much to bear when others are provoked into scorn about your own place in the gazebo. The second person singular may be a hapless reference to myself but I do not intend it so. Newspaper critics, however, have tender skins, for they know that they engage in a trivial activity, one removed from chatter. How much more culpable, then, to do it in a trivial way. And this, for all the pyrotechnics, is what Clive James does. It is the best oiled, most spectacular schlock-crusher in the business but nothing very much more.

Those who get bitten by a critic's vulpine fangs almost always cry out, in the agony of their little death, for the salve of 'constructive criticism' with which to bind up their torn flesh. James rightly dismisses this standard ploy as 'the eternal plea of the kitsch-merchant.' Let him now hold his tongue, then: a manoeuvre that reduces a man to making a noise like glop-glop-*glop*!

A Frosty night
Sunday Times, 8 May 1977

When the unfortunate Rector of Stiffkey was thrown out of his minor office some 40 years or so ago for 'kissing' (as the Bishop called it) a few tarts in Soho,[275] he was reduced to exhibiting himself in a barrel at Blackpool, and eventually to perishing at the paws of a flea-bitten lion in Skegness Amusement Park. Nowadays, of course, the poor fellow would be able to expiate his sins and to provide for his continued pleasures by appearing on television at the small cost of being upbraided by some of his nearest living equivalents. Greater sinners, alas, are reserved for those who have more financial clout: if Adolf Hitler or Martin Bormann were to be found alive if not well while, say, judging *Come Dancing*, then they could expect to be handled (at a percentage) by David Frost's production company.[276]

The first of *The Nixon Interviews* (BBC1) on Thursday night, was, in the event, far more solemn than an hilarious encounter between a crook and a creep which previous incarnations of Nixon as early Cagney and Frost as earlier Uriah Heep had led one to expect. I had had a heartening dream the previous night in which the programme could not get started because both of the protagonists were unable to unstick their sweaty palms from the handshake that presumably began it all. But showbiz triumphed, the bargain was sealed, and the talk duly unspooled itself into the few cubic yards of stale air that separated one comfortable armchair from another in a dead room full of unread books and inexpressible thoughts.

Every now and again, a jet plane passed over the house in a curdling wail that might well have been the passing cry of Nemesis on her way to wipe the tapes. But otherwise there were no intrusions from the outside world, little sense of words being used to describe real things and genuine emotions, and nothing except pity or scorn or occasional amusement to divert attention from two heavy faces sagging into their own collars. One head was sculpted out of candlewax, the other out of blancmange, and I'm damned if I can say which.

Nixon's evident paranoia did not seem a wholly unreasonable stance in the circumstances, but Frost's allegedly 'tough' questioning was a great disappointment. I did not think he would have the gall to depart from his usual soft unction simply because his man had already been disgraced and humiliated. Far better, surely, to have coaxed the ex-President into childhood memories of the grocery store or a tapdance on the shag-pile carpet, or even another rendering at the piano of "My Wild Irish Rose". This would have been much more entertaining than watching Nixon's glutinous visage squeeze out a voice that was alternately querulous and quavering, humble and indignant.

But no. We went all the way through the big Watergate 'cover-up' again, a quag of oozing syntax translated into physical expression when Nixon held up four fingers to tick off three points. There can be no one left on earth who seriously doubts the wretched fellow's guilt, but it ill becomes those who bowed and scraped when the same man with the same faults and the same queasy history was at the height of his power to chop now at the throbbing jugular of his exposed and wobbling neck. It was rather clever of Nixon to refer warmly to an earlier interview he had had with Frost when running for office. The suddenly bared teeth were meant to be a smile, but they could also have served as an accusation.

By the end of the interview, with Tricky Dicky on the verge of viscid tears, there must have been many a tender heart longing for the so-called 'concealment trolley' shown in Tuesday's *Man Alive Report* (BBC2) to be wheeled in. This dread contraption is used in hospitals to cart away dead bodies from the wards in a way that does not disturb other patients. The trolley is euphemism made manifest, so to speak, a conveyance whose design and false bottom shudderingly represent the evasion and hypocrisy by which our society's attitudes to death make even Nixon's tortuous circumlocutions seem to be the plain words of a blunt and simple man.

The *Man Alive* programme made one fear an institutionalized old age much more than the inevitability of death itself. A pitiless scene of geriatric patients sucking and slubbering down their food was, for me, more than just the bad sight of the week; it released dormant horror of being similarly penned up with redundant journalists at the end of my days. I have never seen anything which quite so much resembled an editorial conference at the *Daily Express*, though the dear old man who confessed that 'my ambition is the West London Cemetery' did not look at all like Jean Rook in her prime.

I have watched five people die during my stays at half-a-dozen hospitals over the past 16 years, and in each case the act of leaving has been reassuringly banal and relatively untroubled. One man in the next bed reached up in the night for some boiled sweets on his bed trolley, scattered them accidentally on the polished floor, muttered something like 'sod it,' sank back, and died. A nurse picked up the sweets next morning, and told me not to be so untidy. It seemed only polite after that to suck them without remonstrance, a gift which I am at present receiving in the same sort of form from Charles Wood's six-part comedy, *Don't Forget to Write!* (BBC2).

This series has already been mauled to death by critics who hanker after the delights of Skegness Amusement Park. Wry accounts of a playwright's tribulations are never likely to be popular, especially when there is real hysteria and fear coiled into the repartee. But I am enjoying every minute of it. Charles Wood is a quirkily sardonic writer who is apparently trapped for the moment behind a thorny lattice made out of the loops and whirls of his own words. He looks at a cloud and sees a blank page, listens to a bird singing, and hears a typewriter. The complaint is a painful one, but he makes the symptoms appear to be so amusing that the cure cannot be long delayed.

Michael Frayn is in even more danger of falling aphorism over elbow into the gap between Appearance and Reality which makes writing such an itch of the brain. His elegantly witty essay *Vienna, The Mask of Gold* (BBC2) on Sunday night turned the stones of the city back into the fantasies that called them into being. All great cities are in part masquerades built out of the pretensions of the dead, but here, Frayn, with umbrella and white shoes and disarming clerical smile, so consistently summoned up 'appearance appealing to appearance, illusion beguiling illusion,' that he himself dissolved into a bundle of fleeting epigrams. Let him now try Birmingham.

'What do they think about it all?' he asked the stone caryatids and the zinc busts of the old imperial city. And, do you know, not one of them dared to answer. Nixon should remember that when he, too, is finally immortalised in a piece of sculpture. Even if they make it out of candlewax *and* blancmange.

Whistling in the dark
Sunday Times, 12 June 1977

I was born a few days before the last Royal Silver Jubilee and it is possible that I shall expire out of sheer astonishment a few days after this one, thus neatly spreading my days between cant at the beginning and humbug at the end. Curiosity can kill a critic as well as a cat, and it was this detached or even rather scornful motive which led me to switch on every one of the Jubilee programmes last week. But I am so stupefied by what I have seen on the screen, or glimpsed out of the corner of my ear when walking up and down in the real world, that I am genuinely embarrassed now that I have to record the shifts in my sensibilities – if not my reason – which took place during these last few days of incredible celebration.

'Here comes the flaming Royal cipher,' said Raymond Baxter during *Fires of Friendship* (BBC1) from Windsor on Monday night, echoing my sentiments with unusual precision. The commentator, however, was speaking literally, as befits his always ponderous style. The EIIR was burning on the end of a pole being carried towards the towering cone which would itself soon be belching extraordinarily lurid smoke and flame into the stormy night. Ashes for the stormier morrow, as nobody dared to say.

Princess Angela Rippon had duly enunciated the same drab old news with a bowl of fresh red and white flowers beside her, and even the weather map was decorated with monarchical insignia as well as little white clouds oozing little black drops of predicted downpour. The flags, the bunting and the gush were already streaming in the wind, and my notebook crackled in anticipation of all this sycophantic excess or comical verbal infelicities which help the BBC's Royal commentaries slip down like treacle at its most unctuous.

Who would be the first to exclaim 'The crescendo excitement has mounted steadily'? R. Baxter, naturally. Who would be the first to dip down into the battered old locker and pull out 'adding a brilliant splash of colour to the grey scene'? Richard Baker, of course. Anyone in search of reach-me-down rhetoric or second-hand purple would undoubtedly have garnered a juicy enough harvest of windfalls as the Union Jacks stretched and cracked in the gale. Microphones do not take kindly to wind of any sort.

But this weary old game soon began to pall. Some sneers are an occupational hazard, and others are a civic duty. Last week's "Special Jubilee Edition" of *Saturday Night at the Mill* (BBC1), for instance, allowed only one possible facial expression during the craven interview with someone announced as 'a toastmaster who has officiated at functions attended by every member of the Royal Family.' Gracious me. 'Come on,' inveigled the smirking interviewer, 'give us the low-down – any little insight into Her Majesty the Queen?' The toastmaster complete with scarlet jacket in lieu of scarlet cheeks, leant in conspiratorially and began to croak 'Just between ourselves –' before I collapsed him into a little white dot in the middle of a very blank screen.

What a dreadfully tatty programme this is. The first item had a shameless trailer for a new comedy series from Frank Windsor which, he said, in entirety matter-of-fact tones, 'deals with the collapse of civilization as we know it.' Ha-ha. Ho-ho. 'The total breakdown of society could happen in a matter of months,' the lugubrious actor told us, adding his tarnished two pennyworth of insight to the endless apocalyptic diagnoses which, as a Thomas Hardy character once said, gives us more reason to think we are living in the Book of Revelation rather than midsummer England.

I clung to those words on Tuesday to help explain to myself the truly unprecedented and utterly joyous scenes which lapped around the ludicrously anachronistic golden coach throughout *A Day of Celebration* (BBC1).

No; I am being dishonest. The fact is that, entirely against the dictates of common sense, of logic, or the promptings of intellectual fashion, I found myself with what could only be a *lump* in my throat. Moreover, it was as big as the Koh-i-Noor and as indigestible upon subsequent analysis as one of the Duke of Edinburgh's flaccidly Tory orations. How come?

The pictures for a start, were superb in their sweep and colour and vibrancy, managing both the occasional intimacy of the adroit zoom and the grand panoramic vista that owed more to careful pomp than to accidental circumstance. Antony Craxton's production units were deployed with consummate skill, bringing us a gorgeous pageant whose glittering fluency and costumed postures made the whole city seem a gigantic backdrop to a piece of unparalleled public theatre. As the NBC correspondent rightly said in Thursday's *Tonight* (BBC1), these must number among the best television pictures ever seen.

Yet this, too, was to be expected. The BBC always manages to rise to such occasions, just as ITV perpetually contrives to dishonour itself and its obligations with the usual grubby holiday fare of wrestling and Stork margarine. No matter how skilful the BBC broadcasts, however, their power to move and, yes, enthrall came from something intrinsic to the occasion itself, something far beyond mere atavism or crude glimpery. We were seeing, and participating in, the release of all that pent-up frustration which so much of the exaggerated 'sick old Britain' talk has engendered. The people thronging the streets were determined to shout that we were still alive and well.

Tom Fleming, the main commentator throughout this zestfully assertive spectacle, said that as well as paying tribute to the Queen 'we were also celebrating *ourselves*.' The raucous street parties shown in

Nationwide Jubilee Fair (BBC1), and the sprinkle of revealingly emotional interviews during *The Queen and the Thames* (BBC1) beat out the truth of Fleming's aside. The spiralling cascades of fireworks over London were lit by fuses buried deep in an often artificially fostered despond and humiliation. Some of those rockets literally *were* whistling in the dark.

Even so I am grateful enough, moved enough and astonished enough to record that there was, for once, not a single damp squib in sight.

The spectre at the harvest feast
Sunday Times, 19 June 1977

When you are sprawled at your ease at a flickering hearth the regular swing of a pendulum or the throaty tick-h, tock-h of an old clock can be almost hypnotically lulling in the gentle insistence. Time is ebbing, for sure, but with a placid melancholy that scarce disturbs the indolent soul. One day will follow another in an ordered rhythm. As things are, so they will be. Tick-h, tock-h. Shadows lengthen, and shadows diminish. The teeth of time are not yet ravening at our throats.

How clever, and (I hope) how misguided, of Denis Mitchell to use as polemic the most reassuring images of Time, that old physician, in his deeply absorbing, often very beautiful, plangently nostalgic and yet disturbingly troubled film of Norfolk, 1976–77, *Never and Always* (Granada). He began with the pendulum, the clock, and the tolling church bells across luscious meadows for all the world as though these familiar measures of our mortality were part of the same harmonious dapple of leaf and shadow which glowed upon a lens almost too replete with fecund images of growth, stability and harvest home.

Denis Mitchell is one of television's great innovators. When others thought that 'documentary' meant pointing a camera at a commentator pointing his finger at what we were supposed to see, or that simple juxtaposition of opposing events was the natural rhythm of both wit and irony, his films brought the densities of thought, the nuances of ambiguity and the stretch of tension between sound and picture which made so much else seem so ploddingly literal and predictable. He has always been an author, not a bystander. A dramatist, and not a snoop. Crucial distinctions that are currently in danger of being lost in what might best be called the mud and flotsam of the Thames school of documentaries.

Never and Always paced out the seasons of the year with all the traditional lyricism of country portraiture. Ripe fruit and young brides, howling babies and gambolling lambs, falling leaves and tender shoots, the christening and the grave-digging. Nothing exceptional, indeed, except for the skill of its flow and the sweet ease of its shape. But slowly, then stridently, the film warped in upon itself. The rich images became a hymn for what has been or is about to be lost. The throaty tick joined in conspiracy with an ominous tock, and the pit was added to the pendulum.

Instead of looking at what he could see, Mitchell dragged in the headlines, the voices and the rhetoric of the media mongers. He bounced this diseased blather out of the Dalek-like robots of a seaside funfair, so that from a mechanical larynx the claims of politicians, the black warnings of tabloid newspapers and the panic of currency speculators and other such cheapjacks punctured the soundtrack.

The images of time were now the drama of warning. The steady pendulum and the sonorous church bell were not simply measuring out the minutes of the normal day but carrying us towards bitterness, frustration, doom and chaos. The film was distilling threat out of the meadows, anxiety from the rustling tree tops. And, yes, this perhaps has been, or still is, the mood of contemporary England. There are people among us who look at a sunset and see blood.

'I wouldn't want to be born now,' said an old woman in the film. 'I'm glad I was born when I was.' When I remember the poverty of my own childhood, or the indignities of my father's life, the total illiteracy of my grandfather, who coughed his silicotic lungs up into the grate, the cap-touching, fawning, philistine ache of other days, the waste and humiliation of lives used up in stunting toil, my heart and mind cry out in anger at those who mistake an income tax demand for the disintegration of civilization. As soon as the middle classes feel the slightest pinch, they rise up like a Paul Johnson and quake out their bile through every pore.

I am sorry to say that Denis Mitchell – by far the most talented and humane documentary maker television has yet produced – was not here *observing* a mood, but *participating* in it. An angry or frightened man abdicates the disciplines of his art when he clouds the lens with his own panting.

This was an important film because it showed how far the gangrene of pessimism and foreboding has eaten into the limb. It was at one, in a diagnosis from the Right, with the temper and posture of three of the four left-wing "Playwrights of the Seventies" examined by the metallic voice of Albert Hunt in last week's *Arena* (BBC2).

It is well known that writers hate each other. A BBC drama producer has sniffily cautioned me about the schizoid tendencies inherent in being both a playwright and a critic, and I would be a fool to pretend that I am two different people when tackling these often opposing tasks. But (and I boast, of course) my long struggle against the pain and degradation of illness – now so much easier, thank God – and the reclusiveness thrust upon me during the past decade or so have left me either armed against or indifferent to certain established proprieties. Thus, the loathing I felt when listening to Howard Brenton, Trevor Griffiths and Barrie Keeffe may well have more to do with my actual reason than my too easily presumed rivalry.

These New Reactionaries cannot see change unless everything changes. They glimpse fascism round the corner because they refuse to look at what is capable of repair in the road directly in front of them. Violence and corruption take the centre of the stage, and there is nothing else in the wings. Their wilful pessimism and occasionally overblown rant is shameful to contemplate when placed alongside the Czech writers shown in last week's *Panorama* (BBC1) struggling so bravely against real tyranny.

John McGrath, by contrast, demonstrated how it is possible to break out of the circle (or the stalls) in which comfortable theatre audiences are harangued about the catastrophe ahead. He has taken his considerable talents out to the people with the 7:84 Company and dipped back into narrative techniques that enable his audiences to make connections rather than just bang their palms together in idle assent. He does not renege on hope itself. I wish, though, that he could accept that there is an even more potent location than the village halls and scattered buildings which house his remarkable company. It is called a television set, and there is one in almost every home, licensed like the dog that also barks in the night.

Various kinds of scavenger
Sunday Times, 24 July 1977

An owl can be defined either as a large-headed, small-faced, hook-beaked, nocturnal bird of prey, or as a solemn, wise-looking dullard of the human species. The entrancing sight of David Attenborough steadily and silently gazing at a tame barn owl during Tuesday's *Wildlife on One* (BBC1) would have delighted an economical lexicographer by the ease with which it merged these alternative definitions into one composite image. The question was not so much whether the two creatures actually looked like each other but, rather, which one of them would be the first to emit the characteristic to-whit-tu-who that gives such plangent euphony to dark woodlands and tangled scripts.

The bird kept its dignity the longer. The silence between the two, while it lasted, brought a genuine tension to the screen. It was as though Robin Day and a panda or Angela Rippon and a marmoset were placed eyeball to eyeball. The owl maintained its impassive sobriety of expression with so determined a composure that the solemn, wise-looking dullard was compelled to turn away uncomfortably. 'Owls are among the easiest of birds to recognize,' he said. And so – the owl seemed to add in the depths of its unblinking contempt – are television personalities.

But Attenborough is still by far the best wildlife presenter on the box, and this wholly absorbing programme was not so stuffed with loose-tongued gabble as the comical badger saga some weeks ago. The snoop lenses of the infra-red cameras picked up the eerily silent flight of a barn owl in the darkness, and slowed-motion brought alive old country tales of Will O' the Wisp as the bird with the pale, strangely human face flitted ghost-like above the fields.

Hunters in search of their prey are not always so weirdly beautiful, and when the owl sicked up the skull and bones of a mouse or two just as I was about to bite into a sandwich I was reminded again of how perilous journalism can be to those with queasy stomachs. Fifteen years ago I worked for a while on the old *Daily Herald* and then, understandably, fell ill.

When the Mirror group took over the paper one of the first sights which greeted Hugh Cudlipp when he stared gloomily out of a dirty window in the drab *Herald* offices was your present critic painfully tip-tapping his way to work with a walking stick. 'There's a lot to be done,' Cudlipp sighed as be turned away from the window, less than enchanted by the cripples he had inherited.

In the cobwebbed attics in the middle of long corridors which went on and on like a spiked story, I sat next to the *Herald*'s theatre critic, David Nathan, who chivalrously protected me from requests to write readers' letters, and even the next day's horoscope when the old man called Daphne, or something, was absent on unforetold illness. I have not seen Nathan for the best part of a decade, so there can be no trace of displaced nepotism in recording the fact that his play on Sunday, *A Good Human Story* (Granada) was an excellent piece of work on almost all counts.

He distilled the authentic reek of the British Press at work. In this coldly observant tale of a trio of hairy-nosed reporters picking over a murder in a seaside town windily out of season, Kenneth Haigh, Michael Elphick and Warren Clarke were nauseatingly accurate as the scavengers hustling their way to the nearest deadline, and their knowing conversations over booze in the mausoleum of a hotel were both hilarious and ruthlessly sardonic. The murder turned out, in well-contrived pathos, to be a family affair, and the play itself had the neat efficiency of an inside job. Like a bug in the bowels.

'If you want to expose someone who is evil, wicked and corrupt, you have to do it in a way that's readable,' said the editor of *Reveille* in *The Editors* (BBC1). I switched over at the end of Nathan's play straight into the latter end of a discussion about "Sex and the Press" which made the ink run even colder in my veins. The woman's editor of the *Guardian*, where they misprint four-letter words with what used to be known as gay abandon, confessed that the readers of her paper had been upset by 'a picture which showed two pigs copulating in the background.' The editor of the *Daily Telegraph* was compelled to ask 'what is the virtue of becoming more explicit?', apparently unaware of what goes on in modern farmyards.

After the owls and pigs, one only needed a pussycat to be in the land where the Bong-tree grows.[277] It is here, or hereabouts, that the Ditchley Tripe Works produce sodden face flannels which are passed off as food. Bill Tidy's zany strip, riotously dramatized by Alan Plater in Wednesday's *The Fosdyke Saga* (BBC2) had the emphatic, balloon-like splish! splosh! of cartoon excess and gleeful performances from its cast of six players pungent enough to outrank pig's bladder brawn. It came across like a smack from a wet hand – but as the senior Fosdyke observed, a smart crack across the head never does anybody any harm.

I don't know what such a blow would do to Dorian Williams, but almost anything would be worth trying if it could dislodge the hoof as well as the plum from his mouth. *The Royal International Horse Show* (BBC1 all week) has been a real pain in the fetlocks for this viewer, mostly because of the braying tones with which Williams celebrates a horse jumping over a fence. 'Now David!' he shouts, literally shouts, 'The whole of Britain is behind you!' It is undignified to stand in front of the screen yelling 'Not me, mate' but one cannot always be as wise and as composed as a resting barn owl. Television is by no means a passive medium, as the hapless editor of *Reveille* discovered on *The Editors* when he insisted 'The point I'm making is this–' and then forgot what he was trying to say.

Which reminds me to bid farewell to the last of *Aquarius* (LWT).

Realism and non-naturalism[278]
Lecture delivered at Edinburgh International Television Festival, 1 September 1977

In practical and rather derisive terms which suggest both its possibilities and its disabilities, the television set plugged in at the corner of the living room is just another convenient domestic appliance. The set plugged in at the corner of *the lounge* shows the same pictures to a different audience. In all cases, it is part of the humdrum litter of home life; a laminated, blank-eyed piece of electrical equipment, licensed like a dog, which supplies on every evening of the week, every week of the year, a constant stream of oblong images that merge together many apparently different categories of art, information and entertainment into what so often feels like the same sort of 'experience.'

'What's on the telly tonight?'

'Oh. Nothing very much.'

Switch on for one thing, though, and it's very likely that you will be pulled into the stream. One programme trickles into another, quite painlessly. It takes something like the sight of, say, Humphrey Burton to make most of us switch off.[279] If I did not take notes, I would have difficulty in remembering clearly enough what I had seen. Indeed, I sometimes think that so much time and skill is expended on programme *titles* on the screen for fear that the viewer who sees the twinkling set through an unflattering haze of habit, lulled expectation and domestic conversation will not otherwise be sufficiently aware that an insubstantial line of differentiation between one offering and another is about to be passed. There is such a complex exchange of mutual values between types of programme that it takes a sizeable shock to our expectations to make us blink twice at what we are seeing. Thus, the puzzling excitement apparently engendered by the spectacle of Angela Rippon dancing with Morecambe & Wise owes rather less to the length of her exposed thigh than to the oh-my-my of recognizing a properly bullet-eyed newsreader sandwiched in conventionally lascivious callisthenics between a pair of beloved comedians – though, in truth, the shock was duly tempered by the song that the three of them were murdering: "There May Be Trouble Ahead…", the one tune almost everyone would choose as a matter of course if given the glum task of syncopating the standard BBC news bulletin. Much more interesting, to my eye, was that when the same newsreader appeared on *Call My Bluff* it was quite impossible for the opposing team to guess correctly when she was telling the truth and when she wasn't. An acceptable cross-fertilization in both cases, however. But would we 'see' the news in the same way if Kenneth Kendall or Richard Baker were filmed holding banners on the Grunwick picket line? The ever-rolling stream has rather narrow banks after all.

Television drama – which in all its forms stretches all the way from a cigar called Hamlet to a play called *Hamlet* – has to take its place in the flow of pictures as a segment which tries to make especial claims in its own right distinguishing itself from the news, entertainments, documentaries, outside broadcasts, advertisements and the rest. It may seem unnecessarily insulting to say so, but I think that it is this understandable need to mark out territory which underlines so much of the discussion about television drama. There is an essentially trivial preoccupation, that is to say, with styles of production and modes of technique rather than with the ways of seeing – what you *do* with these techniques – that might belong to drama in general and the embattled television play in particular. You will find, for instance, people ready to talk for as much as 10 minutes at a time (!) about the technical possibilities of colour-separation-overlay but unwilling to engage more than a passing shrug with the question of myth and metaphor as alternative ways of 'knowing' something. Arguments about the use of film in the great outdoors, or electronics in the confined studio (or even that redundant old-time 'live' as opposed to recorded drama) are nearly all about methods of production and very little else. At the crudest level – and on the top floor, it can be very crude indeed – these admittedly sparse exchanges can be swiftly reduced to the standard problem of producer differentiation which television drama shares with other programmes.

A 'problem' that might be placed in its most demeaning perspective if we look at the way some of the miniature dramas in the so-miscalled Natural Break go about solving it.

When there are at least a dozen different brands of canned dog food on the market, for example, the advertisers have some difficulty, to say the least, in making the confused dog owner – let alone the dog – distinguish promptly enough at the point of sale between one tin of chunky-whatever and another. (You already see how close this is to the anxieties of a television producer.) The copy writers have exhausted all the more or less legitimate claims for each brand in turn when they have told us about the protein, the vitamins, the marrow-bone content and general fitness for near-human consumption which makes one dog food better than the near-identical next. They then have to conjure up new solicitations which are not designed to convey basic information about the actual and measurable content of the smelly sludge in the tin. And it is at this point, alas, that the discussions in the agency get closest to the nature of the discussions in television production offices.

At the agency there is an ordered frenzy of 'creative' energy about invoking the right moods of mildly comic amiability or mock solemn urgency in which the purchase might be hastened. The fact that there are so many competing brands leads, inevitably, to the use of appeals which are aimed overtly at the good sense or reasonableness of the potential customer and, covertly, with much more subtlety, at the emotions of the human animal who buys the stuff (of course) rather than the unfortunate beast who has to eat it. A non-canine or, better still, a critical and accipitral eye can find in these commercials a whole gallery of doggily fawning pleas that are directed at the snobbery or anxiety of self-esteem or even nostalgia of the poor creature barking at the other end of the chain. I don't mean the dog, who is illiterate and immune.

These solicitations – or, rather, the *form* of these solicitations – are, when analysed, uncomfortably similar to the tones and impulses of wider and wider areas of television. It is obviously true that the techniques, the conventions and the modes of the commercials are drawn for the most part from the programmes which they interrupt, and vice versa – but I mean more than that. I recall a golden sunset and a few resonantly plangent chords of music (in the middle of an arts film about Turner) which was commending a perfume but might also have been torn bodily out of the film. These accidents will happen, and I expect to see many more such. No, what I mean is the way the general run of programmes share not only the actual appearance of the ads – in an elongated form – but even many of their purposes, at one or two removes. They so often look as though they are selling something – and the verb 'to sell' is used, I might add, in the common parlance of production ideas – but what it is the programmes are selling is not immediately apparent. One frequently sees programmes which seem to be extended trailers for other programmes. There are the same crisp encapsulations and pretended urgencies of the commercials. Spot announcements, signature tunes, identification symbols, certain trade marks in the series, and other such devices space out the schedules in a manner that does, at the very least, suggest that the problems of product differentiation (and brand loyalty) as seen by the huckster are being tackled in similar ways by the programme makers. Just as, paradoxically, competition has the effect of narrowing choice and makes competitors more and not less alike, so the need to make particular areas of television more distinctive, more innovative, more exciting and so on, ends in each of the offerings coming to look and feel more and more like every other segment of the schedules. And the reason, I think, is that they are selling much the same thing: a particular view of reality.

If you come into the room in the middle of a programme, or are watching the set with that half an eye which is the accepted prerogative of television critics in their padded cells, it is sometimes difficult to be absolutely sure of the precise category of what is on the screen. The content differs, of course, but the form can be remarkably similar. There are documentaries, arts programmes which look like advertisements, and advertisements which seem to be the opening shots of an arts programme, and so on, and so on. In general, many of the narrative conventions of drama have been taken over by other programmes. And, as in the song, they are all made of ticky-tacky, and they all look just the same.

A preoccupation with *styles* of production has almost completely blanked out more meaningful debate, such as that about the choices between 'naturalism' and its alternatives – choices that have too often been reduced to discussion about mere techniques.[280] Perhaps the lack of a long critical tradition, the inevitable confusion of roles and purposes which make the word 'television' a plural noun, the severe electronic limitations of its grey, nine-inch beginnings, the continued ignorance and philistinism of its planners and administrators have together brought about this sterility. Among television people, it is noticeable that even the sharpest arguments about the medium perpetually make the shift from 'content' to 'technique,' 'purpose' to 'appearance,' 'meaning' to 'style,' 'way of seeing' to 'ways of being seen.' It is the standard mechanism – and any television dramatist with an ounce of gumption and an unknown producer or story editor facing him across the rubber plant learns to talk in the second rather than the first of these terms: often without realizing it.

Never in the entire history of drama in all its forms has so much been produced for so large an audience with so little thought. There is no rationale behind the decisions to make a play, and none about the audiences that will see it. When *Brimstone & Treacle* was taken off I was not consulted, not asked for my opinion, and the 'reasons' given were couched in two insulting paragraphs, mere assertions of a personal prejudice rather than a genuine explanation. This is the atmosphere in which all decisions seem to be taken. I have been writing for television for almost 13 years, and my experiences lead me to suggest that if one were pressed to define the purpose of the great bulk of television, and television drama, then one would be forced to answer: its purpose is to pass the time, and in doing so to make sure that the viewer – who is a chapel-going hill farmer – is not sufficiently bored or offended or puzzled to opt for the alternative yet strictly similar ways of passing the time offered by either of the other channels.

But I am here to address myself to the ideal of real discussion rather than lamentations about the nature of what is actually talked about in the lifts between floors. And there ought to be a genuinely alive and pertinent debate, certainly about the divide between 'naturalism' and its opposite modes. Heads of drama departments may now leave the room, though not necessarily on all fours.

Unfortunately, the terms 'naturalism' and 'realism' are now notoriously elusive because of continued misuse. They have also been caught up in what might be called the manifesto language of the lower reaches that produce the slipshod, sloganized dilutions of political ideologies. Even so, the ready use of the terms, and therefore negatively of 'non-naturalism' too, seems to show clearly enough that they delineate – however shakily – recognizable modes, especially in the novel where demonstrably flesh-and-blood actors do not, so to speak, confuse the issues with the palpable reality of their presence.

I suggest that the key which will help us to order these terms in our heads is to be found in looking at the relationship between the word and the world. On the whole, the naturalist writer trusts that relationship, as indeed we all must do in our discourse. The common response of those who think of themselves as working within the very wide conventions or assumptions of naturalism and what is popularly called realism is that there is a fixed (but not, of course, a static) relationship between art and the world 'out there' which art is seeking to describe or represent, and understand and perhaps change. This implies a fairly stable and generally agreed or shared idea of reality, a confident enough sense of dramatic form, and a trust in the connection between words and the world of the same kind of order as that between representational art and what is being painted. So strong and so rational is this position that even those who argue the case for 'non-naturalism' must do so in ways that use words in exactly the same manner as the realists.

The 'realist' writer, in effect, takes a piece of the world into his hands and asks us to look at it, to examine it – his eyes are our eyes, as when Victor Hugo said 'When I say me I also mean you.' These writers are saying to us: Look – this is the world as it really is, this is what can be seen, this is the way people talk and behave, and this is why they do so. Look – the houses in which they live, the factories and offices where they work, the families in which they flourish or suffocate, the emotions which sustain or afflict them, the streets where they walk, the trenches where they fight, the bedrooms where they make love and where they sicken and die. Naturalist writing has been and still can be a great emancipating force because it makes no bones about its intention to convey authentic reality to us. It is understandably impatient about the cul-de-sac of 'mere' formalism because it is so much more confident about the nature of its form than any other kind of writing. So confident, indeed, that it seems almost to take it for granted.

Naturalism, as an act of necessary hygiene, strips away the layers of myth and mystification which lie between the world and our perceptions of it. This virtually guarantees that it will always remain, in the best hands, a dynamic and exploratory mode, for there is no end to myth-making (political and religious) in human society. I hope, then, that it is obvious that I am not trying to deride or demote naturalism, therefore: indeed, that would be an ignorant thing to do, betraying the tell-tale disfigurations of empty polemicism or manifesto-mongering.

Nevertheless, I find myself, in writing for television, increasingly pulled towards other modes. This is both because of what I see happening in the rest of television beyond the ever-threatened television play, and, more significantly no doubt, because of my need to relate the changes and the anxieties and the yearnings of my own personal belief to the world as I now apprehend it. I am not yet sure whether I love God or the idea of God, and I am not going to stand up here and baldly announce all the force that makes me translate the human need for order, for justice, mercy, pity and peace into a yearning for God. But that is what haunts me. Put uncharitably, though perhaps accurately on some counts, such terrifyingly incomplete and unadorned statements could be seen as further proof that those with a distorted view of 'reality' will inevitably be more tempted by non-naturalist methods or approaches which, in themselves, so often convey self-absorption, obsessiveness, fantasy, and feverish personal dislocations. The non-naturalist writer who is not just fiddling about with paltry literary fashions is in at least *some* danger of the choice between carrying on writing or seeking the help of a psychiatrist or a priest. For the moment, anyway, I feel quite safe.

The pressures against naturalism are part of a far more general dislocation than what is going on in the narrow confines of my own head, of course. Thus, the 'well made play' of fond memory has curled up and died not because dramatists have suddenly become unnecessarily perverse, or because they have ceased to be capable technicians, but because the self-contained, perfectly enclosed, neatly parcelled and tired artefacts which such plays had become no longer represent the degree of confidence which writers placed in the forms of too complacent a 'realism.' Naturalistic writers have had to acknowledge that literary approaches to the reality 'out there,' and hence the patterns and the structures recorded or collected by naturalism, have gradually turned more and more inwards so that the observer, the writer, is himself in the picture. The self-contained, perfectly formed, extremely confident, almost crystalline drama has become more open-ended, more ambiguous, more uneasy.

This shift has been happening within nearly every form of writing – and not only fiction, not only the novel and the play, but also history and biography and other categories of prose and it subtly affects or agitates the writer who is happier using the naturalist mode as well as those who are eager to break out of it. As the still underrated H.G. Wells put it, the frame within which the writer sees 'reality' has splintered and got into the picture. It is harder than ever to keep a steady gaze, even if a steady gaze is what you think you *should* be keeping. The best and most radical of naturalist writers shift the frame, and readjust its dimensions, trying to get more and more of the world within its view, but non-naturalist dramatists – sometimes far less honourably, and merely because it is easier or more fashionable to do so – acknowledge that the frame itself has fallen to pieces, perforated by dry-rot and woodworm.

Television has learnt not to use the crass simplicity of its old idea of itself as 'a window on the world,' but it is still very much in the business of making window frames.

Sir Huw Wheldon, in his Richard Dimbleby Lecture last year,[281] drew a rather facile distinction between TV news programmes which reflect reality defined in terms of 'what has happened' and TV drama which reflects reality of a different order, that of the 'inward' kind, which he called 'inner experience.' Isn't that nice?

However, most of current affairs, news and documentary programmes – the 'fact' rather than the 'fiction' end of the machine, and the quotation marks are obviously necessary – are replete with solicitations, genuflections, appeals and not-quite-stated argument which, like the tinned dog food, are conveying not simply 'what has happened' or 'what is in the tin,' but a complicated series of images or, rather, signals that make complete sense only as something that is both a reflection of and a reassurance to a largely pre-existing set of social and psychological attitudes that make up the so-called 'inward' reality or 'inner experience' which Sir Huw says is the subject matter of drama. This does not come about because of anything like 'a conspiracy,' needless to say – much more the opposite indeed, for it demonstrates more a lack of thought rather than a cunning excess of it.

The truly astonishing thing about so many of these programmes is that, as if by magic, we somehow always seem to know precisely what it is we are expected to be feeling. The existing censorship within the companies is always based on the desire not to upset this pattern of response. I am not here concerned with the most emotive examples whereby, in the news, a 'terrorist,' say, graduates by a sort of universal agreement into a 'freedom fighter' and then a 'statesman,' or President Nixon clearly crosses over the line from leader of the Free World to a crook, or striking doctors become principled heroes and striking miners greedy oafs, but with how it is we *know* how to alter our responses even as (or a little before) these shifts take place. What is presented as 'fact' is certainly, often heavy with second-order persuasion, usually unconscious, frequently superficial, and using the mannerisms and techniques of the rest of television. The dog-food ad in the middle of the *News at Ten* is a model, not an exception; a general type, not a particularly demeaning oddity. Using the most neutral terms, perhaps all that I am saying is that every society authenticates itself in the most widespread and potent of its media.

A writer may wish to confirm or strengthen the prevailing values of his society, or he may find that the movements of his imagination take him in the opposite direction. Usually, it is a bit of both, of course. But if he is writing for television, and thereby launching his own little raft on the never-ending stream 'that bears all its sons away,' it would be as well if he bore in mind the direction of the flow his play will be sucked into in a general context which can drain it of many of its meanings. It will look like the surrounding programmes, and appear to share in the constant duplication, cross-hatching and meshing of the schedules. And when the viewer comes to 'decode' the complex net of signals that he is receiving, I suggest that it does not then matter as much as it should whether it is 'a play' that is being seen – because there is too little being offered by the bulk of television drama that is not also being beamed out in the other programmes. The first task of the play, in short, is to *be* a play, not an imitation of something else. It can step out of the flow and back onto the bank only by drawing attention to its status as drama, and by demonstrating its own workings.

The television play is virtually the last place on the box where the individual voice and the personal vision is central to the experience. In the bombardment of electronic images, the perpetual blitz of meanings and messages, most of which authenticate the habits and attitudes of society, the play has the chance to show that the world is not independent of our making of it and, more, that the other programmes, too, are engaged in making the world even as they purport merely to reflect it. It follows, I think, that television writers should be prepared, if they can, to give more attention to the *activity* of drama itself rather than just jog along unconcerned about forms, naturalist forms, that are taken for granted.

The simple analysis by which Huw Wheldon can claim that the news programmes offer a view of 'what has happened,' as though faithfully duplicating an exterior reality, has somewhere at its root the trace elements of the realist/naturalist tradition which boldly assumes that it is engaged in making more or less objectively true statements about the world that we can see, and tends to be not over-concerned about the forms and conventions it uses to reveal those truths. The non-naturalist writer, by definition, is much more wary about these forms, techniques and conventions. He often wants to examine them, and lay them bare, in the structure of his play.

He wants to show the workings. He wants to look at our way of looking even as he is looking.

A sentence which reminds me that the greatest danger of non-naturalism is the ease with which it can slide towards gibberish – but the one thing to be said for 'gibberish,' perhaps, is that it is a way of distorting the world which can show up other ways of distorting the world that do not – because of their familiarity – appear to be distortions. As the disc jockey says: get it? got it? good.

I can now put more succinctly the case for non-naturalism in television drama this way: most television ends up offering its viewers a means of orientating themselves towards the generally received notions of 'reality.' The best naturalist or realist drama, of the Garnett-Loach-Allen school for instance,[282] breaks out of this cosy habit by the vigour, clarity, originality and depth of its perceptions of a more comprehensive reality. The best non-naturalist drama, in its very structures *dis*orientates the viewer smack in the middle of the orientation process which television perpetually uses. It disrupts the patterns that are endemic to television, and upsets or exposes the narrative styles of so many of the other allegedly non-fiction programmes. It shows the frame in the picture when most television is busy showing the picture in the frame. I think it is *potentially* the more valuable, therefore, of the two approaches.

And it reminds the viewer, even as he lurches with a growl towards the off-button, that he is at least watching a play A Play A *Play*. Those of the naturalist persuasion may now politely clap their hands, the others can wag their tails – enthusiastically.

Part Three
Ticket to Ride

'I know the way the world works,' announced Dennis Potter in 1989. 'You have to build or invent a certain sort of personality or glow around oneself which means, when you're dealing with people who've got the money or the power or the administration...they blink or hesitate before they push you away. [...] They know when they try and interfere that they've got something to deal with.'[283]

The late-Seventies saw the emergence of this more business-minded Potter, now driven by a desire for control and power. As we shall see, he was intent on challenging the habits and conventions of broadcasting as well as testing the clout of the writer. He remained an innovator and great stylist on the page, but often it was in the use of his persona where he truly excelled. His actions became as reported upon as his plays, and with his 'other hat'[284] of critic largely abandoned after 1978, Potter's chief method of communicating his personal views to the general public was through interviews. Several are presented here. By this stage something of an elder statesman in television drama, Potter could always be relied upon for pungent commentary and an acid quote.

The period covered in this section saw a major shift in the play-wright's ambitions. His innovations were no longer confined to studios at Television Centre, or even television. He worked across cinema, the stage and radio, and devised new models for programme making. Sensitive to the changing wind, Potter proved visionary in his efforts to 'adapt or die' in a shifting media landscape.

The turning point, arguably, was his introduction to the experimental drug razoxane in February 1977. Used to combat his psoriasis, it had immediate, transformative effects. 'Oh yes, this is my year of miracles in terms of my personal life,' he told Roy Plomley. 'The new cytotoxic drug that I'm taking in a clinical trial has brought me considerable, huge, tremendous, emancipating relief.'[285]

Consequently, a welcome streak of optimism entered his writing and this is obvious to anyone who has encountered *Pennies from Heaven* (1978),[286] six plays with songs which marked the apex of Potter's non-naturalism. The serial starred Bob Hoskins as Arthur Parker, a music sheet salesman who dreams of a better life but hasn't the discipline or luck to get there. His obsession with sex, and a tendency to deceive, bring misfortune for his frigid wife (Gemma Craven) and a drastic change of circumstances for a rural schoolteacher (Cheryl Campbell). The serial was punctuated by recordings of popular songs from the Thirties, to which the actors mimed in a strikingly bold, dislocating and sometimes disturbing manner.

Potter's newfound energies and mobility allowed him to deliver lectures, discover travel and play a more active role in the media industry. In the 12 months following transmission of the enormously successful *Pennies*, he was instrumental in forming three limited companies: Judy Daish Associates (an agency, to whom he was a client), Pennies from Heaven (film and television production) and the Gloucestershire Broadcasting Company (local radio).

Set up in order to bid for an Independent Local Radio licence covering Gloucester and Cheltenham, GBC produced a proposal document which Potter had obviously influenced. Severn Sound, the consortium promised, would be a truly local station, determined to break the rigid stratifications of radio: 'It is only habit and presumption, after all, which makes one think it might be odd to have a sharp comment from, say, William Hazlitt between two pop records. We want to genuflect before as few habits and nod assent at as few presumptions as possible.'[287] Idealistic, undoubtedly, but such vision demonstrated a lifelong commitment to community which can be traced right back to Potter's writings for the *Dean Forest Guardian*. The bid was successful and the station launched in October 1980.

A national challenge to broadcasting came with Pennies from Heaven Ltd, formed with Kenith Trodd in the summer of 1978. Such companies had existed in British television before – Kestrel, Paradine Productions – but these were very few in number.[288] In anticipating the independent production boom brought about by Channel 4's launch in 1982, PfH's early experiences demonstrated the ability (or otherwise) of broadcasters to work alongside independents.

An attempt to bring Anthony Powell's *A Dance to the Music of Time* cycle of novels to BBC Television faltered,[289] but PfH made greater progress with Michael Grade, then Director of Programmes at London Weekend Television. Announcing a nine play deal in May 1979, Potter wrote that 'programme makers want to loosen the stranglehold of bureaucrats who have scarcely ever made real programmes themselves. [...] It will be the determined seizure of an independent niche in programme making that best ensures increased vitality.'[290] Unhelpfully for Grade, Potter announced at the press conference that the BBC produced 'the best television in the world' and was in his view the place to be. Indeed, it was scarcely concealed from the press that PfH's deal with LWT was Potter's revenge on the BBC.[291]

A catastrophic mistake in calculating the production costs meant that the budget rose from an underestimated £100,000 per play for nine plays to a total spend approaching £1m for just *three*, and this resulted in an impasse with Grade on the remaining productions.[292] *Blade on the Feather* (1980),[293] *Rain on the Roof* (1980)[294] and *Cream in My Coffee* (1980)[295] had all been completed but in July 1980 what remained of the deal collapsed in bitter acrimony. In a parting shot, Potter bemoaned the quick death of a production arrangement which would have allowed drama practitioners 'some measure of control over their own world and their own destinies.' Instead, PfH had been confronted by the 'stodgily inflexible nature' of British television, and 'the ever-growing difficulties of making decent home-grown films for the little screen.'[296]

'Films' was the crucial word, as the electric immediacy of studio drama – which had first drawn Potter to television – was fast falling out of fashion. Potter's last three plays at the BBC had all been shot entirely on film and Channel 4's *Film on Four*[297] would soon apply an effective bi-media approach to the making of films. Such a formula was at the forefront of his mind when interviewed by Philip Purser in October 1980:

> One of the ways that I'm beginning to think that the single play, the individual play, can survive on television, is by treating television and cinema as the same industry: the same cameramen, the same lighting men, the same sound men, and they work between the two. It has occurred to me rather belatedly, too late in the day in some senses, that one ought to be able to make what I would still call a play for the cinema and television at the same time, that what is

called "theatrical distribution" abroad might be possible in order to make the single play still live on British television.[298]

Even before the LWT/PfH project ran aground, the playwright and his agent Judy Daish were exploring Hollywood, prompted in part by a total lack of interest from 'everyone of consequence'[299] in the British film industry. A cinema transfer of *Pennies from Heaven* was the objective – compressed from its original eight hours to a little under two – and in February 1980, MGM finally bit. For the studio, the film's 1981 release would break a long silence in their production of lavish musicals, recalling their heyday of *An American in Paris* (1951) and *Singin' in the Rain* (1952), but in the event box office returns were poor.[300]

Potter knew that the Hollywood experience would be shortlived, and at $450,000 per script it was prudent to make the most of these 'dollars from heaven' with as many commissions as possible. 'Why do you "need" it?' asked Barry Norman in 1982. 'You can't turn round in England if you want to make films,' Potter responded, 'without either working for nothing and taking the money, […] or, when corporation tax and all those things have been paid, you've got to build up a sufficient sum to be able to say, "OK, we're going to put in half a million pounds: will you put in half a million pounds?" and take the risk that way.'[301] 'Working for nothing' had resulted in the British picture *Brimstone & Treacle* (1982),[302] but it was with the aid of highly profitable script work in Hollywood that PfH could grow as a 'player' back home. Its ambition was to make one British picture every year.

The Eighties saw Potter's first completion of a project for the stage, after years of aborted commissions and authorized adaptations of television plays. *Brimstone & Treacle* at the Sheffield Crucible in 1978[303] was arguably his first 'new' piece for the stage – certainly it was received that way by the general public – but it was with *Sufficient Carbohydrate* (1983)[304] at Hampstead that he realized an entirely original work. Having spent many years decrying theatre, it was the restrictions of limited sets which provided Potter with an interesting new challenge and a disruption of habits. There were to be no escapes to the past via flashback, and he embraced this, just as he did when required to write in an American argot for the remade *Pennies*, or when confined to the inarticulacies of juvenile characters in *Blue Remembered Hills* (1979).[305]

This was the mark of a playwright who had never stood still, although it is challenging to discern a clear line of development in his writing post-*Pennies*. In particular, his film scripts – if made at all – would appear out of sequence. The last to be produced within his lifetime, for example, was *Mesmer* (1994),[306] shot some 10 years after delivery. His cinema output in this period largely had its origins in existing texts – *Alice* (1965) became *Dreamchild* (1985),[307] *Schmoedipus* (1974) was transformed into *Track 29* (1988)[308] – and of the television work, there were adaptations of his stage play and novels too. Those studying Potter are therefore faced with a knotty problem – his own fictions were part of a continuous but apparently non-sequential work, 'ploughing the field' two or three times over, where late works often conversed with earlier pieces.

Furthermore, in Potter's adaptations of other writers' work – *Tender is the Night*[309] being the most high-profile – any close analysis of his 'voice' should be made with caution. His own themes were often detectable but it is worth keeping in mind his description of the process of adaptation as a 'sustained act of loving criticism,'[310] consciously serving the text. To assess such scripts in the context of Potter's entire corpus in fact opens the viewer up to an ongoing conversation about biography and other concerns more usually found in his non-fiction. As his introduction to a 1987 edition of *Tender is the Night* demonstrates,[311] Potter's criticism often provides more clues than the neighbouring dramatic works.

One sustained burst of creativity that is easier to define came between the summer of 1984 and the winter of 1987, during which time Potter composed the six-part serial *The Singing Detective* (1986)[312] and two novels, *Ticket to Ride* (1986)[313] and *Blackeyes* (1987).[314] This same period coincided with the arrival of Rick McCallum as a partner in PfH, joining the core team of Potter and Trodd. McCallum had been executive producer on the *Pennies* movie and returned to the fold for the making of *Dreamchild*.

The BBC had continued to use traditional methods of co-production during Potter's absence, and so the major additional funding for *The Singing Detective* came from the Australian Broadcasting Corporation. PfH would not be engaged directly on the project, but, at the earliest stage of set up, Potter, perhaps in a display of hucksterism learnt from his spell in the US, attempted to insert 'producer approval' into his contract. Aghast, Brian Turner of the BBC wrote to Judy Daish: 'It is out of the question for the BBC to give a writer the right to approve the producer. We are perfectly happy to discuss and consult with Dennis Potter on this point but it is and must be the BBC's decision.'[315] This would not be the last of the playwright's attempts to control the means of production.

In the event, both McCallum and Trodd were involved in *The Singing Detective* alongside an in-house BBC producer, John Harris. Potter's second 'serial with songs' concerned a bed-ridden writer, Philip Marlow, who in an effort to occupy his mind during an extreme, debilitating bout of psoriasis (not dissimilar to Potter's attack of 1972) mentally rewrites one of his trashy and long-out-of-print detective novels. Through association and hallucination the mystery drifts into his own life, rooting out the real terrors and guilts of childhood which drive his adult misanthropy, misogyny and emotional pain. As a result, and in a religious metaphor typical of Potter, the writer ultimately 'takes up his bed and walks' out of the hospital ward.

An unusually close collaboration between Potter and his director ensured that a complex narrative was carefully handled in the filming and then further clarified during post-production. Indeed, Jon Amiel helped tease from the playwright a complete rewrite shortly before production and another when Episode Six still proved unsatisfactory. Despite the finished serial's dense, multi-layered structure, audience and critics alike found it focused, funny and touching throughout, aided by charismatic lead performances from Michael Gambon and the remarkable Lyndon Davies, who portrayed Marlow's 10-year-old self.

The Singing Detective was the subject of a brief press storm when news of the sex scene in Episode Three reached the front page of the *Sunday Today* newspaper.[316] That this 'exclusive' was personally leaked by Potter[317] serves as an echo of the Nigel Barton, *Cinderella* and *Brimstone & Treacle* press scandals of the past, yet despite the fuss almost any article about the BBC or drama in the next three years singled out *The Singing Detective* as the yardstick by which all other television should be judged. It received 13 BAFTA nominations in February 1987 but many onlookers were stunned when it won just two awards at the March ceremony, for Best Actor (Gambon) and Best Graphics (Joanna Ball). More happily, the serial was picked up by Channel 13 in New York for late-night screenings in January 1988. Word of mouth soon spread and, heralding a peak time repeat in July, the *New York Times* was prompted to ask, "Is the year's best film on TV?"[318] By the spring of 1989 there were all day screenings every Saturday at the Public Theatre in New York.

The BBC was inevitably keen to secure Potter's talents on further projects. His adaptation of *The Past is Myself* (1968), a memoir by Christabel Bielenberg, was, like *Tender is the Night*, a firmly naturalistic piece. The difference here was that it was a true story, about an English woman whose German husband became a key player in the resistance movement during the war. Shot in the first half of 1988 and transmitted in the autumn as *Christabel*,[319] Potter's voice had been noticeably muted for the serial, the writer perhaps unnerved about telling the story of a living person who could well answer back. There was a sense amongst critics that Potter's wings had been clipped.

Dour writing might be expected in a drama about the rise of fascism, but *Christabel* coincided with a loss of humour in Potter's writing more generally. As far back as *That Was the Week That Was* and the *Daily Herald* the sardonic notes in his writing had frequently been too sour and combative to provoke real laughter, but it was clear in *The Singing Detective* that he could make even the most misanthropic character crackle with a mix of cruelty, warmth and memorable one-liners.

Blackeyes contained few jokes. The original 1987 novel is a deliberately alienating story of male power, once again with an ageing writer at its centre. Maurice James Kingsley has composed a bestselling novel about a model, called Blackeyes, who is exploited and abused by the advertising industry. It is based on experiences told to Kingsley by his niece Jessica, who he himself sexually abused at a young age. She now seeks revenge on Kingsley and attempts to 'rewrite the book' but doesn't reckon on there being other narrators vying to take control of the story. As Potter told Chris Cook, 'it's that metaphor that women need to rewrite the book, the book that's been written by men. The whole book. The whole world. The pages we're in which is the world.'[320]

A year before shooting began on the television adaptation of *Blackeyes*, Potter experienced an epiphany. On 1 March 1988, he walked out of talks for a cinema version of *The Phantom of the Opera* and found himself close to tears. Sick of the film industry treating the writer as a low status creature, he realized that

> If the producers think a script is a sort of neat, useful accessory for their director to shit upon and scrawl on, without actually sitting down and thinking it through, then there is, indeed, only one place I can go. I will have to start directing them myself.[321]

Visitors (1987), a television adaptation of *Sufficient Carbohydrate*, was to have been Potter's directorial debut in 1985. In the view of the BBC it was a risk worth taking – to give an experienced television practitioner the opportunity to try his hand. If he failed, it would only be on BBC2 and therefore easily forgotten, but in the event and much to Potter's disappointment the initial production was scrapped.[322] His ambition, however, was undimmed, and by 1988 – post-*Singing Detective*, rightly lauded and with an increased international profile – his 'right to fail' as a director presented a far more public gamble for both the playwright and the BBC.

Potter's motives with *Blackeyes* were, understandably, to protect an easy-to-misinterpret tale, and a circle of trusted allies and critical friends might well have guided him through this process. Early planning was not helped, therefore, by the disintegration of the Potter and Trodd relationship, which had stretched back to National Service, Oxford and through their time at the BBC and as partners in PfH Ltd. Trodd had been infuriated by press stories of a new Potter serial for Channel 4, *Lipstick on Your Collar*, a project he had played some part in devising but which appeared to have been commissioned behind his back.[323] As it transpired, Michael Grade was premature in announcing the project but the damage was already done. Suspecting foul play, Trodd also discovered – upon his return from a *Christabel* press jaunt in America – that Rick McCallum had assumed the position of sole producer on *Blackeyes*.[324] In what was later described as 'a rash Christmas stumble,' Trodd resigned, and, despite efforts towards reconciliation, he was out of Potter's life. 'Never go out of town in the early days of January,' he remarked ruefully.[325] The rift remained for five years.

Charges of misogyny will always overshadow *Blackeyes*, and the press response to the serial was certainly hostile. The tabloids, who had celebrated Potter three years earlier, now pilloried him. The serial's overarching criticism of female exploitation was lost on many, not least the *Sun*, home of the Page 3 girl, which for Potter rather smacked of hypocrisy. Even the more 'serious' elements of the media were divided – discussions on the BBC's *Start the Week* and *The Late Show* were measured affairs, but, as Potter highlights in his somewhat wounded interview with John Dunn,[326] traditionally friendly periodicals such as *Time Out* and *City Limits* were now vicious and personal in their criticism. The foundation stone for this new relationship may well have been laid during the press conference for the serial, at which Potter was on particularly belligerent form, telling one journalist to 'fuck off.'[327]

Press hostilities certainly proved a distraction from what was a determined effort by Potter to give expression to decades of thinking about the fundamental nature of television drama. In *Blackeyes*, his strategy of disrupting the usual composition of two-shot, reverse shot and so on, led to Potter presenting viewers with single shots which rolled on for several minutes. 'I just wanted to use the grammar of shooting to be a match or a matte or sometimes a contradiction to the content, to what is emotionally going on.'[328] The male gaze, in other words, with the continuous shot acting as 'restless voyeur,' as Cook argued in his seminal study of the writer: 'Potter's aim is clearly to produce an ambivalent spectator; forcing the audience into the uneasy position of recognizing its own complicity with that exploitation.'[329] Added to this was a narrator – not present in the original novel or the scripts, but a creation in post-production – who comments on the action and fights his own desire for Blackeyes. Potter's decision to voice the part himself created a deep unease amongst critics, but, as he argued, 'knowing the power of film or television, I wanted to enter directly into the complicity and the hypocrisy of it. I wanted to show and comment at the same time, and to make the showing and the telling inseparable.'[330]

With its heady mix of flashbacks, feuding narrators and remote characters rarely entering into anything more than stilted exchanges, *Blackeyes* frustrated many who saw it and led to accusations that Potter had become a 'dirty old man.' What the serial ultimately demonstrates is his attempt to push the boundaries of storytelling in television drama to its limits, employing Brechtian techniques and an intentionally problematic form: '*Blackeyes* was about alienation and I just went too far. It was so successfully about alienation that I alienated *every* fucking person in the world.'[331]

Yet, as an act of willpower, the work had been as emancipating for Potter as his first dose of razoxane. A writer who had always trusted directors and in an earlier age rarely attended recordings was now ever-present. The weeks he spent on location and then with his film editor Clare Douglas represented an extraordinary personal breakthrough.

Faced with such bad press, however, Potter soon descended into a melancholia. His withdrawal from public life for the best part of two years marked an unprecedented silence for the writer,

225

but, upon his return, it was clear that self-determination had not deserted him. He undertook to direct *Secret Friends*[332] – an adaptation of his second novel, *Ticket to Ride* – in 1991, with funding from Channel 4. With McCallum gone and Trodd estranged, it was also time for a new production company – Whistling Gypsy – for which he hired Rosemarie Whitman as producer. He retained Clare Douglas too, who would work on all subsequent projects.

Despite the commercial and critical failure of *Secret Friends*, Channel 4 continued in its attempts to rehabilitate the playwright. He was finally persuaded to cease directing by Michael Grade, who advised Potter he should 'make himself a smaller target for criticism.'[333] He took the hint, and *Lipstick on Your Collar* (1993)[334] – a third serial with songs – brought in Renny Rye and even opened with a joke. Potter retreated into simpler storytelling and familiar forms with this light, linear tale of characters who at last engaged with one another again. Potter also tackled the 'dirty old man' accusations head on via the unsettling relationship between Sylvia Berry (Louise Germaine) and Harold Atterbow (Roy Hudd), but the focus of the serial was youth. Its handling of Fifties popular culture and the looming political crisis in Suez is best viewed in the light of Potter's early journalism, rendering *Lipstick on Your Collar* less inconsequential than it first appears.

The playwright continued to rail against the modern world and the state of the media was a theme he warmed to the most, with Rupert Murdoch his *bête noire*. "Occupying Powers", Potter's MacTaggart Lecture at the Edinburgh International Television Festival on 27 August 1993, was a personal statement of his commitment to public service broadcasting in the face of John Birt and Marmaduke Hussey's recent internal marketization of the BBC. The speech ended with his application to become its next Chairman of the Board of Governors.

The following Christmas, Potter felt the first symptoms of what would become a terminal illness. It was not until Valentine's Day 1994 that he received confirmation that he was suffering from pancreatic cancer and that this was in its advanced stages. The life expectancy was short, perhaps weeks only and, when friends and colleagues were informed of the news, it was Grade who responded by proposing one final interview.

Melvyn Bragg sat down with Potter for over an hour on 15 March 1994, in an unadorned television studio with minimal crew, the programme transmitting three weeks later as part of Channel 4's

Without Walls.[335] It was a major television event, celebrated not just for Potter's bravery but as a summation of everything which drove him. The interview created another talking point in his request that each episode of his final two works – *Karaoke* (1996)[336] and *Cold Lazarus* (1996)[337] – should be transmitted by both BBC1 and Channel 4 in the same week. It was impossible for Alan Yentob (BBC) and Michael Grade (Channel 4) to refuse this 'deathbed wish,' and the call of the Writers' Guild of Great Britain showed that Potter's peers well appreciated the symbolism:

> There could be no more defiant gesture in the face of the constant erosion of our industry. There could be no better way to honour the author's lifelong commitment to making a difference.[338]

The stamina required to direct *Blackeyes* was as nothing compared to the energies called upon to complete the scripts of these two serials, to such an extent that *Karaoke* and *Cold Lazarus* are now chiefly remembered for the circumstances of their creation. Potter chased away death for long enough to fix down details of production and cast, recruiting Trodd to see out his final wishes and protect every line of the scripts.

Dennis Potter died at his home in Ross-on-Wye, at 8.00am on 7 June 1994.[339] To his last breath he had 'used himself, used up himself'[340] to fully express his artistic vision, to overcome the torments of his body one final time, and to protect his family and his work even beyond death.

IAN GREAVES

Trampling the mud from wall to wall
Sunday Times, 6 November 1977

I was swallowing whisky, and shuddering, in a crowded pub in Edinburgh after delivering a paper on television drama[341] when a youngish sort of fellow with a cropped head and cold eyes suddenly came at me like a kamikaze pilot or, worse, a Scottish football supporter. It was the playwright David Hare, the muscles of his face marbling with tension and anger.

'I think you should give up your column,' he snapped, straight to the point of my already quivering jaw.

'Oh? Why?'

'Because you are doing damage – to yourself and to others. Your reviews are mean-minded and malicious. You take your own pain seriously, but not that of others.'

Drinking my cigarette and smoking my drink, and wondering in my confusion whether I had been mistaken for B. Levin, I asked him to give me e-e-examples of the m-malice. Hare quoted my review here of Barrie Keeffe's *Gotcha*[342] and of the *Arena: Theatre* edition which featured interviews with playwrights Trevor Griffiths, Howard Brenton, Keeffe and others.[343] 'They read as though they were motivated by personal dislike. Writers shouldn't be critics,' and so on, until I felt like the Burke to his Hare.

David Hare is not alone in his hostility: I have been told that Jim Allen wants to break my jaw, and several whining letters from other dramatists have all said 'addressing you as a playwright, not a critic–' (a fellow prisoner, not a warder) in terms which insist that I am 'letting the side down.' And all of them, of course, share the curious assumption that criticism is meant to be for the programme makers rather than mere viewers and readers.

This is a nervous and a self-conscious preamble to writing about *Abigail's Party* (BBC1), last week's *Play for Today*. It is unfortunate that, like *Gotcha* it happens to have been produced by Margaret Matheson (Mrs David Hare) – unfortunate as far as diplomacy is concerned but otherwise (do believe) utterly irrelevant. The real question is whether strong dislike for a particular drama is made 'malicious' because I am also a television playwright, and whether this fact in any crucial and distorted fashion somehow mediates my critical response. The nasty word 'rivalry' hovers on the edge of expression, does it not?

Abigail's Party is described as being 'devised' rather than written by Mike Leigh, acknowledging that it was carefully built out of an improvised structure by Leigh and his actors. It was originally performed on stage at Hampstead, and on the screen the lack of knowing laughs was probably more of a help than a hindrance, since it is characteristic of a sneer to waver a bit when too obviously shared by one's neighbours. Something called conscience, or perhaps sensibility, interferes with such a superior pleasure.

'Improvisation,' in however complicated a form, is a fascinating means of sharpening an actor's technique, but only at the expense of diminishing the 'characters' thus discovered to a brilliant puppetry of surface observation. The thin wires of prejudice and superficial mimicry can nearly always be seen, tangled up with the words. What one gets is a portrait – and a very revealing one – of the social assumptions and insecurities of that peculiar group of people who earn their bread by acting. This play was based on nothing more edifying than rancid disdain, for it was a prolonged jeer, twitching with genuine hatred, about the dreadful suburban tastes of the dreadful lower middle classes.

Nothing too much wrong with that, perhaps, if some opposing strands, some new insights, are thereby released. A long tradition asserts that it is enjoyable to get on the other side of the ding-dong doorbell in a new suburban villa and trample mud into the wall-to-wall carpets. *Abigail's Party* was horribly funny at times, stunningly acted and perfectly designed, but it sank under its own immense condescension. The force of the yelping derision became a single note of contempt, amplified into a relentless screech. As so often in the minefields of English class-consciousness, more was revealed of the snobbery of the observers rather than the observed.

But insofar as one can ever separate the values of a production from its content, the performance of Alison Steadman as the dreadful, blue-lidded Beverly was memorably nasty. Her cretinously nasal accents made the hairs prickle on the back of my neck, and every moment, every gesture was honed into such lethal caricature that it would not have been too surprising if she had suddenly changed shape in the manner of the fat, thin or elongated reflections in a fairground mirror.

Bernard Shaw's jubilant mockery of social pretension had the merit (or the hypocrisy) of both stinging his audiences and, at more or less the same time, pandering oozingly to them as well. The hotel waiter with Norman blood, a famous barrister for a son, and a line in ambiguously deferential chatter had the fruitiest part in Sunday's *You Never Can Tell* (BBC1), the opening of a new *Play of the Month* season. Cyril Cusack took it with both hands, without needing to let go of the silver tea-tray.

The confident production had a light, bright swirl that carried it happily through the occasional patch of Shavian lecturing, and the illusion of a string band scraping away among the Chinese lanterns on the Marine Hotel terrace beyond. Robert Powell so far forgot his costive and dreamy Jesus[344] as to sparkle with just the right bumptious abandon as the amorous five-shilling dentist: if the playing of this role is at all miscued, the whole thing collapses into wordy trickery. Shaw was attempting to outdo Oscar Wilde, but there was no escaping the Shavian inability to demonstrate The Importance of Being Unearnest.

Jollity that does not arise naturally from the soul is fortnightly demonstrated in *Read All About It* (BBC1) when Christopher Booker pops up at the end to introduce his bizarre little quiz. His opening 'Hello' is clearly such an uncomfortable aberration that it comes across as a most frightful grimace, the nearest thing this side of a Party Political Broadcast to the matey leer which makes one feel like a child being asked to run an unpleasant errand. A remark prompted by mirth, not malice. I think.

The highlight of last week's programme, however, was the appearance of Jilly Cooper in the guise of 'romantic novelist.' Either the reduced voltage of our present electrical supply is playing tricks with the colour of my set or I really did see something unprecedented on television. The lady *blushed*. And in these days of the Hite report,[345] the sight was more than disturbing, it was positively antique. She admitted to falling in love with her own hero. 'If you are married it's a lovely way not to skip around too much.' The panellists looked at each other furtively, imagining a jealous comma or a lustful apostrophe. And then, mercifully, the lights went out, though not all over Europe.

Similar random delights illuminating the non-stop comedy of the performing animal can sometimes be picked up in the drear afternoon programmes. The other day, for instance, Peregrine Worsthorne was sounding off on *After Noon* (Thames) about the young man who had secretly taped Dobson's 'bribing the wogs' remarks.[346] 'He shouldn't have dropped his father in the –' He paused, suddenly cautious. 'I can't say the word,' he said with a smirk. 'Go on! Say it!' urged his hostess, far too eagerly. 'Yes?' 'I think you should!' she bubbled. 'Dropped his father in the…um…in the *soup*,' concluded Worsthorne triumphantly. Ah well, that too can be very messy when it hits the fan.

Tonight
Interviewed by Ludovic Kennedy
BBC1, 7 November 1977[347]

KENNEDY: Dennis Potter, in your *Sunday Times* column this week, you quote an angry playwright who came up to you in a pub in Edinburgh and said, 'I think you should give up your column. […] Your reviews are mean-minded and malicious. You take your own pain seriously, but not that of others.' Was that a fair criticism, do you think?

POTTER: Erm, I think it was…it had some merit in drawing attention to some possibilities in my reviews, and I think critics are always likely to appear, to those criticized, as 'mean-minded and malicious' but I certainly don't set out to be mean-minded, and only occasionally do I set out to be malicious, and then I usually know when I'm doing it.

KENNEDY: What about your criticism of factual programmes? For instance, a little while ago you described Mr Michael Heseltine at the Conservative Party Conference as hilarious – 'A politician on the make […] a mad conductor on a broken podium'[348] – and then of Mrs Thatcher at last year's conference as someone who 'made small pawing gestures with her hands which reminded me of everyone's favourite celluloid bitch, Lassie.'[349] Now, was there not some malice there?

POTTER: Yes. *(Smiling.)* Yes.

KENNEDY: But are you happy with that?

POTTER: *(Giggling.)* Yes, very. I think if you're a politician, and I think if you're a performing animal as a politician, in the way that they were at the party conferences, then I think that's very fair game indeed.

KENNEDY: But, you see, you don't quite write about Labour politicians in quite the same way.

POTTER: I often have, but you probably haven't sussed out the quotes. I can't remember them. I can't even remember those, but I... Certainly the odium of a gangrenous politician upon the rostrum spilling out cliché after cliché, usually very consciously knowing that they're stroking the prejudices of that particular group, then I think there, when they're looming in close-up at you, I think your only defence is either to jeer if you don't share the prejudices, or possibly to applaud if you do.

KENNEDY: Well, you put your finger on it when you said, 'if you don't share the prejudices.' You see, in an interview with Joan Bakewell, you said, where 'there's a political point to be made, I make it emphatically on one side. The way I instinctively structure politics are all the rewards of a working-class environment.'[350] Would that be true?

POTTER: Yeah. That's basically true. And I think it's healthily true. I think that to reduce political debate to a contest between the two parties and just leave it at that, so that everyone else is an objective commentator upon what is going on, and sort of choosing rationally between the choices offered... A great deal of politics is not about *reason*, in that sense. It's partly prejudice, it's partly the exercising of your dream, your assumptions about the way society should be shaped, or might possibly go. And if you're a critic then you're dealing – or you should be drawing upon – your whole emotional structure, as you would as a viewer.

KENNEDY: And prejudices?

POTTER: And prejudices. And principles. And emotions. And feelings, in the widest possible sense. Otherwise, I don't know what you are. A computer or a robot or...

KENNEDY: No, I take the point. But isn't there another point, which is this: that you are writing for a national newspaper which has a very big readership, and you are writing for all shades of political opinion.

POTTER: Yes, of course, yes. But they don't merely read my column in the *Sunday Times*. I mean, the paper is dripping with other sorts of prejudice and the editorials are oozing a particular line a lot of the time. Any newspaper ought to be a federation of views. One of the troubles with the British press is the very predictability of the usual paper you pick up. I mean, you know what to expect half the time and that's…that's not a newspaper.

KENNEDY: Well, leaving the politicians aside, Mr Potter, you said recently of Angela Rippon that you thought her very funny, and of Malcolm Muggeridge –

POTTER: Well, I think her script is funny. Put it that way.

KENNEDY: Well, in the programme – which was *Any Questions?* – you said you thought she was funny.[351] But you meant that –

POTTER: I think the *Nine O'Clock News* is funny, on the whole, and she performs it with that cold-eyed… Particularly when she's bringing us news of the dear pound sterling, there is nothing to do but laugh.

KENNEDY: And is this particular to Angela Rippon, or do you find it hilarious when Richard Baker and Kenneth Kendall and the rest of them read the news?

POTTER: I enjoy the way Richard Baker wags his shoulders. It does tend to distract me somewhat from some of the gloomy news, but Angela Rippon has the icy cold This-Is-The-News, You-Will-Swallow-It, Take-It-Now-And-Go-To-Bed-Very-Gloomy-*Please* and I don't like that. Not very much.

KENNEDY: Well, lastly – I won't make this too long, Mr Potter – but of Malcolm Muggeridge you said, reviewing the film on Jesus of Nazareth, 'I would fall about with glee if I heard that he had slipped and broken his bones at Lourdes.'[352] Well, that wasn't a very Christian sentiment from a professed Christian.

POTTER: No, but you've obviously abstracted – and careful about that 'professed Christian' bit – but you've obviously abstracted just the sentence which was saying that charity is not the prime motive if you're a critic. And I was saying that the unctuous 'charity' of the film was something that I would resist because this sort of gooey Jesus-Christ-with-piles sort of thing, walking so tenderly on broken shells was something… Therefore I needed a counterbalancing thing to demonstrate my own lack of charity, which I think is the salt, perhaps, of a great deal of criticism and a great deal of life. As long as I don't actually mean it. I don't want the poor old soul to break his bones, but it's quite nice to put it down sometimes.

KENNEDY: Well now, turning to what the playwright I mentioned earlier on said about you – 'taking your own pain seriously, but not that of others' – you did suffer excruciatingly for years, didn't you, from an arthritic illness?

POTTER: Well, psoriasis and arthritis together: they're the two prongs. A sort of psoriatic arthropathy.

KENNEDY: And has the new drug now more or less completely cured you?

POTTER: Well, it's a control, not a cure. And it's a marvellous control to me. I mean, from March, when I came out of the hospital after the first administration of the dose, I thought that the whole world was washed clean, shining, bright. It was really a very marvellous feeling which I must never let go of, because the emancipation, the release, the sheer joy of, well…just sort of striding along, of not feeling sick – which the previous drug had made me feel – and of somehow, once again, being able to take and shape my life in the way that I wanted it to. All those things were such gifts, such a bonus, that I can't lose sight of that, the pleasure of that, which includes also of course the pleasure of 'malice'…that is, of simply being alive, of being…just like that. It's the only way I can put it.

KENNEDY: When you did have this lasting pain, how much did that affect your views and your writing?

POTTER: Well, it must have affected it, clearly, because the act of writing was physically very difficult and at times – there would be long months in hospital – at times I could only move my left arm, so I couldn't write at all. At least two days of the week I would vomit. My skin would crack and bleed and shed off wherever I was going. And that sense of isolation, reclusiveness, clearly shapes your responses to life – and makes you two things: more alert to the values of life and to what it is to be alive, and more conscious of the difficulties of reaching that golden pathway, if you like, which you wanted to follow.

KENNEDY: Did you ever ask yourself why, if there is a loving God – and you think there is – He should have allowed you to suffer such pain?

POTTER: Erm, I think there is… Yes, I did. Clearly I did at some stages, but the very formulation of the question is…releasing. It leads you to take certain things almost for granted – not in the sense of a passive acceptance, but in the sense of using that, because it also brought me many gifts. It made me write – I couldn't hold a job down; I was working on a newspaper – and it made me draw out of myself virtues and strengths which I didn't know I had. I think people – *everyone* – is heroic, when they're put to it. But most people don't get the chance of addressing themselves at their deepest level, and therefore they don't actually find out what it is like to be a free human being.

KENNEDY: You've said elsewhere that 'there is no access to God without pain.'[353] Is that rather a sweeping generalization?

POTTER: Well, I think Christianity asks us to concentrate our attention upon barbarism – upon a barbaric pain and a barbaric act. I mean, those neat crucifixes and crosses are symbols of horrendous cruelty and desolation and pain. And it is not possible to make a journey through this life without experiencing grief, pain, all sorts of anguish. It seems inseparable from our knowledge of what it is to be a human being. And that knowledge, in a sense, gives us freedom, but it enables us to actually shape our lives.

KENNEDY: Would you say that all your plays have been religious in the broadest sense of the word? And, if they have, what have you been exactly trying to say in them? What makes you different from other playwrights?

POTTER: I wouldn't say all of them had this impulse. But all of the recent ones have had this, I should say since *Son of Man*, which was written from an agnostic point of view but in the very writing of it I was suddenly aware that my attention was being fixed too strongly upon something which I could therefore not evade and would have to examine and pay attention to. I couldn't possibly say what it is that does or does not make my plays different from other playwrights, because I think the very act of writing is an affirmation of our distinctness as imaginative, fantasizing, and therefore *creating* human beings, which makes it the inheritor, I think, of religious acts.

KENNEDY: Do you feel, still, that bitterness that your play *Brimstone & Treacle* was banned by the BBC?

POTTER: I felt it at first. I feel more puzzled than anything now, because, of all my plays, it was made in a parable form, to demonstrate that – I can't go through the plot of it now, obviously – but to demonstrate that those whose conviction, that their faith...in this case, the mother of a girl who's brain damaged: she's the only one who wins in the play. Evil, I wish to demonstrate, often speaks in sentimental, religiose, sanctimonious terms. I think that is the characteristic religious approach of shallow-minded people of our time, so that religion is a yucky, unctuous thing which you don't actually want to know about. And I simply wanted to demonstrate that that was the way 'The Devil,' ie the sense of evil, would actually be addressing us.

KENNEDY: But you would agree, would you not – even though you contested the decision not to show it – that the BBC or any broadcasting organization has the ultimate right not to show any play that, for some reason or other, it doesn't wish to show? You don't challenge that right?

POTTER: I don't challenge the editorial rights. What I challenged was the process and the means by which it was done – when the whole Drama Group wanted to show it. And they, as it were, are the repositories of the genuine editorial right. And when it had been bought, rehearsed, filmed, made, scheduled – all that process, and all that money spent, and all those months had gone by and nothing was done, and then suddenly to take it off without any explanation or without me even being called in to say 'Would you cut this?', 'Would you consider this?', 'Could we put it out at a later time?' To simply receive a couple of paragraphs from Alasdair Milne saying he found it 'nauseating,' therefore it could not be shown, without giving the reasons why it was nauseating…

KENNEDY: Lastly, Mr Potter, you've spoken of what you call the 'downward drift of television standards generally.' As British television is generally admitted to be the best in the world, how do you justify that?

POTTER: Well, I don't see how those two sentences go together. There's the best in the world, and –

KENNEDY: I assume that you were talking about British television –

POTTER: Yes, but that doesn't mean that it can't be very bad, can it? Because the…

KENNEDY: …the rest of the world…

POTTER: …may be a great deal worse. I find it less courageous, less open, more… It's scheduled more now. It's tailored and cropped to fit some image of the viewer which doesn't make sense. 'Which programme follows which programme?' seems to be the thought behind the planners' minds – in other words, they are delivering something in the way that people who sell toothpaste, buttons and butter are: approaching a mass market. There's less excitement, less innovation, fewer live…not necessarily live television, but 'live' in the sense of an 'electric' addressing of the issues which concern most of us for a great deal of the time. It is its very predictability that I think is demeaning it.

KENNEDY: But you're still happy in your job?

POTTER: *(Giggling.)* I'm happy as long as I can say it, yes.

KENNEDY: Dennis Potter, thank you.

Pause.

The recording session continues. The camera is now pointed at POTTER and the back of KENNEDY's head is in foreground.

KENNEDY: Do you know this boring thing I have to do, which is for you not to speak? You know. They're doing an editing job, so it's just for me to speak at you. And it's a pity because I had to, even so, leave out a couple of questions. And one of the ones that I wanted to ask you was that you said of television plays that they have 'the short and uncelebrated life of a gnat.' And I was going to go on from there and ask you why, in that case, which I imagine is true, you didn't write for the theatre more?

The camera is now in reverse: favouring KENNEDY, with the back of POTTER'S head in the foreground.

KENNEDY: Now it's your turn, so you can answer.

POTTER: What, I can actually literally answer that question? Well, this is exactly what I'm going to do, after *Brimstone* and a few other things, I've accepted a couple – for the first time – to write original stage plays, which I'm now going to do.[354] So I am sort of partly disillusioned, yes. Inevitably. Also, I'm middle aged!

I accuse the inquisitors
Sunday Times, 4 December 1977

A producer at the BBC telephoned me the other day and asked whether I would consider 'writing a play about the Mary Bell case.' The violence of my reaction surprised both of us. He kindly waited for me to stop spluttering, and then observed, with an icily affronted clarity, that the extreme nature of my refusal was so 'implausible' that I ought to examine it. But this proved to be too difficult a task, for I was left with nothing more substantial than the conviction that to embark upon 'a play' about a little girl killing an even younger child would lead me straight into a depression so long and so black that life itself would be drained of colour.

The scenery changes so much when you reach the edge of a swamp, however, that you are compelled to look around and about with trembling caution. I became aware of certain deficiencies in my critical reactions to a whole new category of television programmes that ought, in fairness to those whom I have abused, to be brought out into the open. I am referring to the raw, 'real life' documentaries which prod and probe into human failure, weakness, and distress without in any way 'interfering' with the process being unravelled in front of the lens.

Michael Whyte's trilogy on violent youngsters is the current example of the type. It finished last Tuesday with a programme on *Aycliffe* (Thames) – a treatment and assessment centre for young delinquents

– which has received sufficient praise to make my own continued anxiety and revulsion of little account. A fortnight ago, his *Billy*, the first of the three, seemed to me to be an appalling exercise – not because of the casual brutalities it revealed, not because I wanted any sweet evasion or sticky euphemism, but simply and solely for the way in which it allowed, even encouraged, an already burdened youth to mutilate himself before the cameras.

The tyranny of the educated, the powerful, and the well-off can and does take many subtle and complicated forms. When you look at programmes from a decade or more ago, it can easily be picked up on the screen, but it is sometimes much more difficult to catch the shifts and switches of style that convey many of the same attitudes in today's documentaries. The rationale behind *Billy*, and many similar raids on the lower depths, has never been properly examined: a model, perhaps, being those wildlife programmes where the biped observer does not save the gazelle from being devoured because to do so would upset the very thing he had come to witness. And, yes, that *does* make sense. With animals.

We will not see fly-on-the-wall studies of the home life of our own dear bank manager or his cousin the television producer or his uncle the stockbroker. Why not? Because such people know how to protect themselves, know how to edit their responses, and would eke out their 'revelations' with a tight fist and a canny eye. *Billy* would never be, say, *Julian* of the Young Conservatives, for the techniques used to get at the scars and pains and anguish of the former would fail to breach the defensive walls already intact around the latter.

'Piss off with them cameras!'

The boy who cried out those words, not once but several times during Tuesday night's concluding film was breaking up his room with a hot and savage rage which (surely?) was being fuelled by the presence of the cameras in the doorway. His shame, his humiliation, and his palpable despair gave him no safety. It was his sixteenth birthday, and whatever cry it was that rose to choke him was reduced to this observable misery. 'Switch off them fucking cameras!' he shrieked. No, no. They wouldn't do that. The cameras stared and stared and stared, as they had done with others, relentless, unmerciful, unchallenged by no one except those already incarcerated. And they have no rights, have they?

Again, a disturbed girl, who was later transferred to a psychiatric hospital, was seen standing alone at a window in that peculiarly isolated, hunched stance which signals a special kind of alienation. She became aware that 'we' (the cameras) were watching her. She turned her back. The cameras crept sideways so that half her face, sullen and cramped, was again in shot. She turned again. And so did the camera, dutiful, fawning and undeniably oppressive.

Yet what did we learn from this? A vivid sense of lonely, sick withdrawal, certainly. We could see, if you like, how the gazelle is slaughtered. But who and what was the carnivorous predator was much more ambiguous. The image of a circling vulture fell across my mind.

But I cannot deny that by letting the cameras keep turning, Michael Whyte brought back a startlingly full account of what goes on at Aycliffe. I cannot impugn his professionalism, his skill, nor even his ethics. I am aware that the deficiency is almost wholly in myself. The nearly unbearable distress I felt when watching this programme, and what I now see to be my consistent yet often excessive opposition to the whole new range of television documentaries that it typifies, has roots which are tangled like nerves in the half-suppressed memory of my own experience of life. I cannot specify – except in fictional or dramatic form – the kind of assault which I endured in the summer between VE Day and VJ Day,[355] when I was 10 years old. But –

No. To hell with it. I should not review such programmes. I simply ask whether the questions I have put do not have *some* relevance. Cannot we be a little more careful when zooming in to map the shape of real life, real pain, and real indignity? Especially with those who are bereft of genuine protection.

'Not only will I not write a Mary Bell play,' I said to the producer, 'but I will make damn sure that I review it if anyone else does!'

The remark has clearly dishonourable intent, and it led both to the icy rebuke and to the content of this particular column. In which, of course, I have said too much and too little. But I believe that a critic who is not prepared to respond with his full emotions and failings, and who does not occasionally expose the darker workings of his own mind, is little more than an impertinent oik (sic).

Normal service (chuckles) will be resumed next week. I will not again lightly pass up the opportunity of reviewing Michael Heseltine performing in a Conservative *Party Political Broadcast*. 'I want to talk to you tonight about owning your own home,' he began. And a very good imitation of an estate agent it was, too. Especially if you want to sell a house with a gooseberry bush in the garden.

An innocent abroad
Sunday Times Magazine, 8 January 1978

A trip from Ross-on-Wye to New York City was always likely to be, for me, a far greater distance than any shown on the map.[356] Until last summer there seemed little prospect of ever going abroad. A long and irritating illness which needed a lot of attention meant that it would have been rather uncomfortable to spend more than, say, three nights away from home, and the temperamental affinity I had necessarily found to fit these circumstances persuaded me that I was in any case reluctant to squander money disturbing the relatively peaceful equilibrium of my English prejudices.

Why take in new sights and sounds when I had not used up anything like enough of the old ones? Work is the standard (or most socially acceptable) means of blanking out anxiety, and I imagined that holidays were an even more potent means of releasing it. Those who went in search of the sun often seemed to come back looking and sounding like people who had found only a paper moon. Mixing envy and contempt, I constructed a picture of them lying on the sand, staring with screwed-up eyes and mashed heads at the huge caverns of monotonous blue, and reduced to asking in their sweaty boredom *what-is-it-all-about?*

Sun-tanned limbs and laughter from the dunes would give some sort of answer, of course, but even then I imagined dread absurdity ready to pounce with the ominous chink of teeth on wine glasses, the chatter with strangers on the slowly mildewing terrace, and the spaces where the grinning band stops playing or (more likely) the muzak tapes rewind themselves on their bland spools.

Holidays? Thank you, no. Travel brochures and holiday-issue colour supplements seemed to be written by idiots soliciting the frivolous, and I found it quite impossible to read them without a protective sneer which was tempered only by an occasional yelp of derision.

And then – POW! ZAPP-P-P! – everything changed. The comic strip in which I sometimes like to think I star had a big cross-page frame with vivid new colours and torpedo-like exclamation marks. A new drug, administered in a clinical trial which is still continuing, suddenly and marvellously transformed every prospect. My hands are a bit too far gone with previous arthritic damage to open properly, so I could not clap them. Instead, one of the first and most bizarre things I did when I got out of the hospital on an appropriately sunlit morning last March was to lie down on the pavement and bang my feet together in the most exuberant applause possible. But it took my mind a bit longer to catch up.

'Now we can have a holiday,' said Margaret, my wife, still in tones closer to a question than an assertion.

I rehearsed once again what had become a meaningless incantation – my distaste for travel (travail), my dislike or even fear of strangers, my reclusiveness etc. etc. All the crabbed responses that I had claimed as virtues or elevated into what appeared to be an authentically stoical philosophy but which, when analysed with the aid of a new bio-chemical, turned out to be crudely simple rationalizations of what I could not have done or could not help being. It was weakness, not wisdom, which allowed me to say things like 'you only find *yourself* at the end of a journey' or to quote more or less accurately Pascal's observation that all troubles of the world stem from the fact that a man is unable to stay for very long in his own room.

Balderdash, every bit of it.

And as I dismantled this glum lattice, strange and alluring shapes began to form themselves in my mind. The Manhattan silhouette. Rearing skyscrapers. New York. *New York!*

Come on along and listen to
The lullaby of Broadway

A thousand celluloid images had always been waiting to dance back into my imagination, syncopated out of the smoke-wreathed beam of light which flickered above my head in the old Dean Cinema, Coleford, back in my childhood. The Empire State building, hugged by an ape. Yellow cabs with laconic drivers. A towering statue of a lady with a torch: the biggest usherette in the world, lighting the way to crackling B-movie dialogue, shiny dancing shoes, mysterious basement bars, glittering sidewalks, the Bowery Boys, the baseball park, snappy cross-talk over a counter at Macy's or wherever – *the hip-hooray and ballyhoo*, anyway.

All much less powerful, and much more ludicrous, than the opposing images of a bankrupt city seething with random violence and nameless tensions, source of that nightmare of urban chaos which provides the worst threat of the future. But either interpretation – magical or grotesque – acted as a magnet, and the iron filings of dream and anxiety, delight and foreboding, duly twitched into common alignment. If we could afford it, Margaret and I were going to go. I think the phrase, announced in nervous belligerence, was 'we'll damn well do it!'

The first difficulty to overcome was the inevitable bureaucracy attached to virtually every new thing that one wants to do. How and where did one get a passport? What about a visa? Incubations? I knew that there were Exchange Control Regulations, but not what they were. But these things, particularly daunting in prospect, were resolved with nothing more laborious than hunting for hours through drawers, cupboards, cases and trunks for birth and marriage certificates, swearing by signature that I was not a Communist on the United States visa application form, sitting with a controlled smirk in a railway station photography booth, collecting a dozen brochures and announcing daily in the words of the song – 'let's call the whole thing off!' The process for getting out of Great Britain, however, is in itself almost sufficient reason for *wanting* to get out of Great Britain.

The travel brochures all appeared to be uneasily torn between the need to offer adventure, excitement and novelty, and the subtler promise of reassurance and comfort. Words like 'luxury' had an even heavier load of ambiguity than usual. Silky blandishments and glossy photographs crinkled under the fingers, leaving not so much a sense of anticipation as a vague feeling of shame. I think I half-dreaded finding out things I did not want to know, for you cannot abruptly dismantle an elaborate citadel without letting in strange new fears and emotions. Ludicrously enough, reading through these brochures, I felt a bit like Dr Livingstone and haplessly recreated some of the anxiety I had experienced as a small child when dallying too long at a shop in Gloucester (an hour away on the bus) and finding that my parents had unknowingly walked on, leaving me utterly lost and terror-struck on a pavement crowded with indifferent giants. My wife, however, was sensible enough to be merely excited.

So we took a TWA 'Getaway America' holiday (chuckle, chuckle), 'the on-time airline,' at a price quoted in the brochure at £450 each, plus insurance, for the air-fare and 14 nights at the New York Hilton (room only, no meals). 'Luxuriously furnished rooms with air-conditioning, TV, radio, even an icemaker and electronic wakeup and message systems. The Old Bourbon Steak House, Place Lautrec Café, bars and cocktail lounges – all on the premises.' I read it out, loud, once in English and then again in an American accent. It sounded slightly more plausible on the second occasion.

There was some sort of surcharge by the time we came to pay the final account, so that the initial cost was a pound or two under £1,000. Add the two travel allowances (then £300 worth of dollars and £25 sterling for each person) and the cost of getting to Heathrow, and I thought we would 'getaway America' for about £1,700 all told. An expensive holiday, but not when averaged out over the years when we had not taken one. 'Today,' promised the TWA brochure, 'most things in America are surprisingly less expensive than in Britain. In New York, perhaps America's most exciting city, prices for most things are less than in London.' That's all right, then. I could not help wondering though, whether that floating 'perhaps' had drifted down to quite the right spot on the shiny page. Just in case it hadn't, I decided to do what the ad says and not leave home without my American Express card.

Heathrow was all crowded confusion, clicking boards, glum faces and occupied benches when we arrived on 9 September, a Friday, for our first-ever flight. I was quietly debating with myself whether I rated a single paragraph obituary in the *Times* or merely a full down-page column in both the *Ross Gazette* and the *Dean Forest Guardian*. That was before we actually saw the plane. When the gigantic 747 loomed into view I had no space left in my head or my stomach for such deplorable thoughts: there was just a solid lump of fear. I had never been so close to a modern airliner, and realized, with a sudden jump of incredulity, that I had vaguely imagined it to be something like a Spitfire, or a little bigger than the little wooden plane that had crashed into some trees near my primary school in 1942. The sensible thing would have been to turn back there and then, gibbering with relief, but I went on, and on, glumly recollecting a piece I had read which said that people would occasionally advance into extreme danger, or even face almost certain death, rather than cause a fuss or draw embarrassing attention to themselves. Besides, we had already handed over our cases to a TWA girl whose eyes remained distant and abstracted even while her shining lips stretched into a smile.

Perhaps she was clairvoyant. Perhaps she saw the ridiculously large plane crashing into the Atlantic. Perhaps – no, no, no. It was more than time to control my own floating 'perhaps.' 'I'm looking forward to flying,' Margaret said. And then, in a change of tone, 'What are you looking at me like that for?'

We walked about half a mile down the fuselage (is it?) to Row 40, and two seats which looked out on to an engine which was so fat and so obviously overweight that I had decided to close my eyes. But not before noticing that it was also black and scruffy with wear, tear and smoke. 'Good mo'nin ladies and genmen welcome on bah bah to TWA flahob wo conditions wboo good,' said the Captain, or somebody. Hostesses were moving up and down handing out menus and asking if we wanted 'a drink after take-off.' I wanted a drink *before* take-off.

And then several girls, in various parts of this cinema-sized monster, were demonstrating how to inflate what they called a 'life vest.' It was all so ridiculous I nearly screamed. 'She means life-jacket,' I said to Margaret with a quavering lip. And then, in a change of tone, 'What are you looking at me like that for?' Oddly enough, too, my knees were burning and aching in the nasty way they had done up until six months before. I think it was at this point that I realized that my old rationalizations about not travelling were indeed based upon profound wisdom rather than proud expediency.

Too late. Too late. The great fat roaring thing was thundering down the runway. Ourfatherwhichart – the sensation of speed was ghastly. Margaret held my hand, and I was man enough to notice that her palms were damp with sweat, and swine enough to leer back through a decomposing face, 'You're not frightened are you?' Ho! Ho! (I thought). I must remember this. I must write it down. Why do people never tell the truth about travel. *Oh God, the speed.* Why do people never tell the truth about *anything*?

'We have lift off,' said the Captain, in the only complete sentence I understood during the whole journey. The sensation of speed ceased. Everything-was-going-to-be-all-right. Flaps were moving up and down on the football pitch of a wing. The ground was falling away. Higher and higher. How strange. Look at the little cars, the little houses, little England. How peculiar. How – wait a minute, are you sure? Yes! – how *marvellous*. Drink? Certainly. What a nice girl. What a sensible fellow. 'Fancy you being scared!' I jeered at Margaret.

Come along and listen to
The lullaby of Broadway

Listen, they were playing my song again, that orchestra in my head. I was safely back in my own strip cartoon, practising how to say 'tomato' so that they would know I was English and therefore very bloody special, see. The 'see,' however, was pure Cagney. 'Thank you,' I said as the hostess brought me another Scotch. 'You're wel-come,' she responded, her lips and her eyes in the same contradictory position as the girl at the TWA desk. This was either unique to 'the on-time airline' or common to all American women. 'You're wel-come' was being chimed up and down the aisles in a way that made one feel distinctly unwanted. They were the two words (said as three) which will forever summon back New York to my mind, with a prickle on the back of my neck and a clenching in my gut.

Because here we were, waiting 'in line,' as they say over there, to hand over our landing cards to a customs officer in a glass booth before getting our bags and going through customs proper. USE CAPITAL LETTERS the card said. An Englishman in front of us, the picture of that polite diffidence which is supposed to mark the breed, handed it over. 'This is handwriting!' snarled the officer. 'Pardon?' said the Englishman. 'Sez here capitals!' the officer roared. 'S-sorry –' the other began to stutter.

The man in uniform hurled the card down and literally yelled, 'Next time fill it in in *capitals*!' then picked it up again, motioned the shaken Englishman on through, and muttered: 'Welcome to New York.'

I pushed Margaret on ahead of me. 'Whatdyado to your hands?' he said, looking hard at me. Was it all going to be like this? He didn't even appear to understand the word 'fortnight.' We struggled on through, my face as red as a tomayto. I didn't want to look or sound or behave like an Englishman. It clearly wasn't safe to do so.

An hour and a half later we had found our bags, but no porter, no trolley, so I had to push one of the cases towards the Customs desks with my feet. (I can't carry things.) Up ahead, an indignant Mediterranean was having a blazing row about a sausage which the customs officers wouldn't let him take through. Everybody seemed to be on the brink of anger. One of the officers emitted a hard, sharp laugh from time to time, and it sounded like a bark. This arrival point at Kennedy kept reminding me of a place long buried in the darkest part of my soul – and then, as we finally got past the desks, I realized what or where it was: the reception area at Blackdown Camp in Aldershot on the first day of my National Service way back in 1953.

Left-right, left-right, I instinctively straightened my shoulders. We were out of the hell-hole and searching for a taxi. There, in front of us, was one of the famous yellow cabs, with a squat, amiable looking driver who seemed more than capable of being laconic. The dream could start right now.

'New York Hilton, please. At the Rockefeller Center.'

Laconic he might yet be, but furtive he certainly was. 'Quick, quick,' he gabbled, thrusting one of the two cases into the boot. Dear God, is everybody mad here?

Yes. There was sudden pandemonium. A burly figure in a peaked cap hurled himself towards us, blowing a whistle.

'Did you say the Rockefeller Center!' he screamed at me. I honestly thought he was going to pull a gun or something. I nodded, as innocently as possible, quite prepared to put up my hands.

'I didn't hear him,' mumbled the driver.

'You fucking heard him!' shouted the man with the whistle. 'You know you're not supposed to take anybody there!' With which he seized hold of the case in the boot and strode away without so much as a further glance in our direction. Gulping with shock, we were forced to follow, past the hitherto obscured sign which said 'short haul taxis,' and on to the first of a long line of seemingly identical cabs to the one we had just left.

The new driver also looked exactly like the old driver, so much so that we were both prepared for the weird Lewis Carrollery to start over again. The two bags were placed in the boot, we dumped ourselves into the soft, low back seats, which smelt of something biological, and then – sure enough. The whistle was blowing shrill peep-peeps again, and an exceptionally sour face was being thrust towards the driver.

'Come on! Come on!' – whistle, whistle – 'Get your ass out a' here!'

'Fucking madhouse,' said the driver over his shoulder as we accelerated away in a manner which suggested that he intended to blank out the mysterious odours in his cab with the stronger stench of burning rubber. They were the only words he uttered during the entire journey. We didn't feel like talking either. By God, we didn't. Our eyes were full of the filth and rubbish to be seen on the way in, and our bodies were jerking up and down with the bumps and holes in the primitive, over-patched roads. Images of decay and poverty sped past, not even burnished into acceptability by the *Sun*. It was past teatime, and it was very hot.

Away to the left, the famous skyline at last zoomed into view. The streets smartened up a little. The taxi slowed into honking, hooting lines of traffic. Through the window, it looked like Soho, except here and there steam was coming up out of the road, between the patches. Tom-*ah*-to, tom-*ah*-to, to-*mah*-to: the word had lodged itself in my brain as though it were an irritating little tune. But any incantation would do so long as it took us safely to our hotel room, where we could fall on the beds and shout with laughter.

The New York Hilton slid up in concrete and glass over our heads. A man in a pretty uniform was taking our bags, and sticking something over the handles from a little machine. We went on through revolving doors into a cavernous lobby. And waited for the bags, and waited. I went back outside to see what had happened. A hand thumped down on my shoulder. 'I been looking for you!' snarled Pretty Uniform. 'I don't go in, see. I stay out here.' He shoved his hand out, palm upwards, demanding rather than asking for a tip. 'Thank you, sir,' he said. I gave him a dollar and pushed the cases through the doors, more hot and more bothered than ever. Oh, gracious town!

Our room was on the twentieth floor (that is, about half way up), looking over a tangle of lesser and equal buildings to the rocky scrub of Central Park. The air-conditioning hummed and fluttered. A little card on the table between the beds reminded us to *make sure* that we locked, bolted and chained the door at night 'for your security.' The chain and the peep-hole in the door had a forbidding eloquence. Way below, on West 54th Street, a mean sign flashed on and off, announcing Al & Dick's steak house, reminding us first of old films and secondly that we were hungry.

We went back down the high-speed lifts in search of the Place Lautrec Café. Security officers dressed like cops were prowling about the lobby with walkie-talkie sets. The Old Bourbon Steak House was there all right, but the Place Lautrec had changed into the Taveerne, a 'Dutch coffee house.' The waitresses had little Dutch hats, but no clogs. Hilarity was dangerously near the surface, and when I asked for a *carafe* of red to go with the Dutch liver and Dutch bacon and french fries the girl brought *coffee* instead. She couldn't understand my accent, rather as though I had a Dutch cap in my mouth. 'Thank you.' 'You're welcome.' Again, eyes and mouth belonged to different faces. Dutch muzak oozed out of hidden loudspeakers: Mantovani, I think.

The hum of air-conditioning and the treacle of muzak provide much of the interior landscape of New York. Outside, the clangour was deafening. Hooting cars, raised voices, jostle, jostle, whooping sirens. The time and the temperature flashed continually from dozens of buildings, and the effect was weirdly unsettling: time is running out, these are the last days, this is the end-of-the-world. Outside Carnegie Hall a man lay as still as death, a soiled windcheater pulled up over his head. Nobody took any notice. Nobody ever took any notice. New Yorkers have hard, snapping eyes and outta-my-way shoulder-thrusting walks because they dare not, must not, stop and look and think about what is going on all around them. Acres of burnt-out buildings. Drunks and junkies stretched out on the sidewalks. Palpably mad people gibbering and rolling their eyes at every fourth or fifth corner. Big stores that have the atmosphere of a doss-house. Perpetual arguments, scathing rudeness, endless garbage. And yet, too, an electric sense of personal freedom, a cordite smell of endeavour and enjoyment which both tightened the throat and relaxed the emotions. I was fascinated and appalled and totally disorientated. The murmuring, often hidden, deceptively subtle hierarchies of English life simply weren't there: the sound of English voices at a bar in the Barbizon Plaza, across the road from Central Park, made me realize that I had temporarily (and joyously) lost the swift sense of 'placing' people which is almost second nature in our own land. A few overheard sentences showed four Englishmen on bar stools who were in the dangerous state halfway between intimacy and being strangers which made it 'necessary' for them to dig and probe and place and judge each other by the most distant and arcane of social codes. I wanted to get away.

Overheard conversations in diners, restaurants, bars and hotel cocktail lounges were by far the most illuminating and startling moments in the fortnight. Thus, while eating crêpes at the Magic Pan on East 57th, two women on one side and two men on the other, talking without the slightest attempt to lower their voices, managed to convey inner and outer anxieties that seemed to incorporate every aspect of the entire city. On our left, a young woman with a shellacked face was telling an older woman about the skill with which 'my analyst' had made her acknowledge that she hated her bum of a husband because she had never fully realized how much she had hated her bum of a father. 'That's right,' nodded her companion. On our right, a young woman with green lids like painted doors on her eyes was talking about her new apartment. It had no fire-escape, but this was an asset. 'There's nobody climbing up it at night.' 'That's right,' nodded her companion. The risk of fire was much less terrible than the fear of murder, rape or robbery. Two sets of conversation mingled and fell across our plates, and the combination went deeper and deeper into the fear of one's self and the fear of others.

'You see that smile,' said a middle-aged man to his doddering father in an Italian restaurant. The old man trembled round to look at the grinning waiter, who was mixing an elaborate salad. 'Yes, I see it,' quavered the near-geriatric. 'Well – it's a *ven-eer*,' spat the son, with extraordinary venom. The waiter carried on smiling.

Behind us a Southern businessman was chewing jargon with his cutlets. 'No, no, no, this guy he said, shaking his head like you know – but I'm sure it wasn't a negative response.' Sometimes I couldn't eat for laughing.

There were cautious walks in the Park, boat-rides round Manhattan and down the Hudson, open-air meals (with Mexican musicians and a German band) in the Rockefeller Plaza, downstairs to strange and wonderful bars, movies (and a mouse) in our room, incredibly bad television, disturbing encounters with disturbed pedestrians, long strolls from safety to danger and (at quicker pace) back to safety again. American voices squawked, the air-conditioning became a sickening boom, the street noises more and more deafening. The best escape proved to be the Museum of Modern Art, virtually next door to the hotel.[357]

'Don't touch the paintings!' a father said as a small boy put up his hand to a Picasso. The attendant moved forward quickly.

'Why not?' asked the child. The characteristic American question.

'Because they are very, very expensive,' explained the father.

The presence of money and the lack of it are the two poles between which the city turns and preens and cowers. Swinging down Park or 5th or 6th (the Avenue of the Americas), the sun glinting on miles of plate glass, the high flags cracking and stretching in a maritime breeze, the shop windows like great cool caves full of wonder, it was impossible not to feel that this was an alluring, earthly version of Paradise – a mock semblance of heaven as distant from the real thing as the Hilton's tatty

Taveerne was from Holland. You felt both exhilarated and ashamed, free to be anything and yet trapped forever in a cornucopia of tinsel. A swanky, vulgar city of endless display and cruelty.

And then, a mere walk away, the dirt and the decay would be at your throat. Under a pier head a seven-foot (nearly) black man, eyes rolling white, was slicing through sack bags with a vicious cleaver, and trying the pieces on. As we sidled by, he stopped, stared and muttered. Time and again, we had these unexpected encounters, and gradually the spasmodic fears or shocks bumped together into a consistent anxiety which never quite went away.

WALK and DON'T WALK glowered at the junctions. 'Have a nice day!' and 'You're welcome!' glowered on a hundred thousand lips, the lights of Broadway and Times Square illuminated not a dream but a nightmare. I have never before witnessed such complete degradation. Several men were wearing T-shirts which asked, 'Where were you when the lights went out?' and the jeering question reformed itself regularly as the mind tried to make conjunction with the eyeballs. Pain, terror and hatred are waiting for the flicker, the dip and then the darkness.

The police whoop-whoop on television took up the same noise from the streets below so that when you switch the set off it is as though the sounds will not go away. I lay back on my bed with aching feet, and read an article about England in the *New Yorker*.[358] We are all washed up, apparently. We've lost the knack of looking after ourselves. *Whoop-whoop whoop.* I started to read it out loud to Margaret, but laughed so much that tears flowed down my cheeks. A couple of days later my eyes were still glistening when, three hours overdue by the 'on-time airline,' a wet, grey-green England greeted us.

I still haven't worked out what it was that 'happened' in New York, but certainly I – we – were changed by the experience. Travel may broaden the mind, but it shakes you up. If New York is the most likely vision of the future then we must learn to be more alone, more aggressive, more callous, more greedy and more vulgar than at any time since we were in the playpen. I must go back one day, if only to find out whether the lullaby really has turned into a prolonged, single note scream.

'Thank you,' the customs officer said at Kennedy as he handed back our passports, letting us out of the madhouse for the trip back home.

'You're welcome,' I said, at last, with all and proper English ambiguity.

Let the cry of rage be heard
Sunday Times, 29 January 1978

The reception area of the BBC Television Centre looks more and more like the foyer of a run-down hotel stranded in the middle of an inner-city slum. Ashtrays overflow, dirt smears the cold expanse of glass, furtive wheeler-dealers talk with their hands in the scatter of uncomfortable seating, and the lifts going monotonously in the background with the vague promise of escape, or tea in paper cups, or access to endlessly circulating passages where middle-aged tramps (presumably the producers) prowl about mumbling vacantly to themselves, but rolling their eyes and simpering dreadfully when they realize that you might have a kind word to say about their programmes. It is quite impossible to step into such a place without a droop of the shoulders and that dispiritingly insistent buzz in the mind which so often seems to be the major contribution 'media persons' make to the modern world.

Now and again it is good for a critic to spend some time knee-deep in the moral squalor on the other side of the screen. He picks up a few of the assumptions and a little of the rationale of the programme makers, though this may be too high a price to pay for such unnerving proximity to the paranoia, fear, demoralization and other lip-chewing psychoses which so manifestly disfigure the inhabitants of any dream factory.

Did you realize, for instance, that the brief title frame of Tuesday's *Play for Today, The Spongers* (BBC1) was added after the channel's Controller (Bill Cotton) had seen and passed the play? The frame showed gigantic portraits of the Queen and the Duke behind the emotive words of the title. Here, the pictures said, are the real spongers (simper, simper). The validity of the joke is not especially in question, but the manner of its insertion, and the furtiveness of its style, is a clear enough signal which a critic ought to attempt to elucidate.

Producer Tony Garnett is a past master at manoeuvring strong and challenging work of the highest quality through the muckily labyrinthine coils of the system. He is a brave, uncompromising, single-minded, incorruptible philistine, interested in only one kind of drama, and with enough conviction or fervour to make one speculate uneasily about what would happen on the third day after his eventual demise.

But he, and his writers, can never really say exactly what they want to say – and the disability shows.

In this case, *The Spongers* brilliantly gave the illusion of being more open-minded, or open-ended than is usual in a Garnett production. Jim Allen, the writer, has an altogether rare moral conviction that makes everything he constructs unusually vibrant and passionate. That is, he wants to use the box to argue about, to unsettle, to challenge what we think we already know. And we cannot or must not do without such figures.

But they know all too well that they have to operate with a Corporation which was not designed and is not capable of dealing with any 'propaganda,' except that which happens to be the current orthodoxy. *The Spongers was* political propaganda, directed from the leftist stance against the Labour Party and the bureaucratized mockery of social democracy it has called up from the depths of its long since compromised soul.

This propagandist zeal *cannot* be openly expressed. The ramshackle administration of the BBC, its lingering inheritance of concern for quality and 'public service,' and the hesitant goodwill of at least a few of its hierarchs, ensures that a fine and disturbing play like *The Spongers* does occasionally get on to our screens. It would have no chance of doing so on the commercial networks. And yet the very process of 'getting it on' seems to involve anxiety, deceit, and complicity with the conventions of 'balance' (the sacred yet ever untenable BBC concept) which give that persistent and uncomfortable apprehension of being 'got at,' that in my opinion mars the play.

The so-called naturalist mode of television drama works very well when the writer has nothing very contentious to say. It begins to crumble when too radical a conviction throbs at the heart of the drama. The sour little joke under the title is symptomatic not merely of childishness, or of a small triumph against dim superiors, but of the cry of rage locked up within the play itself and so movingly caught by Christine Hargreaves in the central role. Garnett and Allen have to endure the paradox of a commitment to a form of 'socialist realism' in drama which in its necessary styles cannot be transmitted without hints, nudges and almost expressionist devices that they are not particularly good at manipulating.

I realize now that at Controller level in the BBC, it is the surface images which cause concern. I am not being deliberately offensive when I tell you that the present hierarchy shows depressingly little gumption.

The former Head of Light Entertainment has already shown his small-minded mettle by refusing to allow Roy Minton's *Scum* to be transmitted, and Alasdair Milne, the Managing Director, has added his weight (to misuse a word) to the decision, thus spending another £120,609 of licence money. And sure enough, there are scenes in this play which undoubtedly shock and disgust. The Borstal in which the drama unfolds is a place for sadism, brutality, homosexual rape, an almost deranged Governor, and a suicide with a razor blade. I did not 'enjoy' it one little bit.

I am compelled to say that if I were reviewing it I would have many hostile things to say about the production. There is not one thing which tempers its argument, and scarcely a single alternative insight to modulate the shrill scream that rises in a sickening crescendo from the opening shots. But this is all the more reason why it should be shown. It is palpably *not* a documentary, and abuses no 'real' people.

It startles, and often in the best sense. You are forced to react, to think, to argue, to attack or to defend. And if drama is never allowed to do that, what on earth can we expect from the rest of television? Yet more and more pap, more sweeties, more evasions, more bland fillers to pass the time?

Milne gave a good account of himself in Monday's *Tonight* (BBC1) in argument about the play against insufficiently nimble Peter Fiddick, the *Guardian*'s TV correspondent. Characteristically, Minton himself was not asked to appear. Characteristically, too, he has not had personally a single word of explanation. Last night's *South Bank Show* (LWT) gave Minton his opportunity, his right, to answer back. Bragg's programme has thus already shown its immense value in keeping an alert eye on the surrounding bogs.[359]

A play astonishing in its excellence
Sunday Times, 5 February 1978

There was An Exchange of Dialogue at the controls of the spaceship in Monday's mildly diverting *Blake's Seven* (BBC1) which dropped down to planet Earth like a lump of radiating junk. 'We're too close to something we can't see!' exclaimed the captain of the ship. 'And we're not sure it's there!' added his co-pilot. The sense of proximity to danger, and yet the uneasy apprehension that what is feared may not be 'there' in quite the form expected – and could, indeed, be something totally unknown – is what makes the portable scanner bobbing along on top of the neck column send out such odd, such alarming bleeps of warning. Who does not watch the news night after night without feeling adrift in dark spaces, likely at any moment to collide with uncharted malignancies?

Later in the same evening Tom Mangold and John Penycate's *Terror International* (BBC1) sprawled upon either side of the dry gulch of the *Nine O'Clock News* with a portrait of political terrorism which had the numbing effect of reminding one that human life can be cheaper than videotape. Mangold tried to trace the web of conspiratorial violence which has its source in 'the desperation and hopelessness of Palestinians' but takes much of its tensility from the alienation of young revolutionaries far away from the muddy refugee camps or the legitimate nationalism of the dispossessed.

We have long since institutionalized our violence, and find it difficult to comprehend freelance versions that adapt the old use of war as an extension of diplomacy into war as a development of individual piracy and murder. 'Conscience' is stilled in the cockpits over Hiroshima or Dresden in the name of something presumed to be greater and even more noble than personal squeamishness, and on behalf of objectives wider and cleaner than present screams or immediate slaughter. Horror is born, as always, out of what we have already accepted.

Terror International was a serious and would-be comprehensive account of political terrorism that could not or would not – and, I suppose, dare not – analyse this obvious fact. Vaguely electronic music, as threatening as the whine of a dentist's drill, added to the sense of dislocation and random barbarism. A young Dutch revolutionary, questioned by a furrowed Mangold, spat back the orthodox response of her kind when she asked, rhetorically, 'What's murder?' Instead of an abstraction, however, she was given a flesh and blood answer. 'Murder is a dead German pilot at Mogadishu.'

And here we saw one of those pictures of the human face that stay and fester in the mind. She wanted to say so much, to turn from the individual image of a lone individual meaninglessly executed in the name of 'anti-imperialism,' to summon up the clotted evasions of ideology – all this and more. But the only thing she could do was to go utterly blank, look away, and momentarily puff air into her cheeks in what was either a gesture of disdain about bourgeois sentimentality or a muscular spasm caused by her own inconvenient humanity. There was a cut at this point, so we were left with no further elucidation, and no deeper access to her apparent dilemma.

'Murder is a napalmed baby.' 'Murder is –' Fill in the answers that were never thrown into the faces of the properly uniformed or the acceptably medalled and you can see why the young woman puffed out her pretty cheeks. Only pacifists can afford total indignation about this particular exchange, which is another way of saying that *only* pacifists can both put the question and answer it. Meanwhile, foulness continues to breed foulness, and what should be common humanity is checked and staunched by godless ignorance masquerading under the banners of politics – the politics we ratify as well as the politics we abhor.

In the end, therefore, the programme left us with no diagnosis of what is in the last resort a shared disease. It described, not analysed, pointing outwards and not inwards, leaving us not much wiser and scarcely any less puzzled. Political documentaries, after all, cannot have 'a point of view' unless it is that seen through the same old porthole. The present structure of our television permits (sometimes, that is) drama, only, to widen the focus, which is why the television play is so troublesome to the administrators.

The current exceptionally strong season of BBC drama reached its peak last week with David Edgar's *Destiny* (BBC1), a play which astonished me with its intelligence, density, sympathy and finely controlled anger. For once, too, the compassion was not withheld from those deemed beyond the pale. Here was an examination of the extreme right in British politics which caught up all the strands which make it function: the nostalgia, the disappointment, the dumbly aching resentments, as well as the psychotic anti-semitism and other such racism that traditionally disfigures these movements. At times, indeed, the play was so alert to the pain and, yes, grief which has drawn some people to the populist Right that it might even have persuaded a few, casual viewers that the National Front was worth supporting.

But this is praise, not criticism. Just as Koestler's *Darkness at Noon* was good enough to convert a few people to the Communism the novel was set on destroying, so *Destiny* carried within it the force and emotional appeal of what it, too, was concerned to eliminate. Mike Newell's wholly superb production, and the acting, without a single exception, served this tremendous play extremely well. I was so absorbed when watching it that I even lit up the filter end of a cigarette, and the nasty taste, the suddenly acrid smell, might well have come from the television set. The sight of Nigel Hawthorne weeping as he plucked at the folds of a Union Jack managed to be both disgusting and moving, thrilling and dangerous, an absolution and an accusation, at one and the same time. Great acting, great writing, great direction; among the very best I have ever seen. Malignancy charted.

The 'something' out there in *Blake's Seven* was a sort of huge spider's web. 'Every time I blast a hole in it, it knits up again!' Exactly so. Beware of metaphors – you never know where they've been.

The other side of the dark
All in the Waiting, BBC Radio 4, 23 February 1978

There can scarcely be one human being alive of even the greatest good fortune who has not experienced, or who in time will not fail to experience, the sudden and brutal intrusion of grief or pain or anguish in which that vital sense of one's self is all but extinguished. It is at these times, when the lucid grace of hope and joy seems to have been withdrawn, that we stumble up against what must surely be the oldest and strongest metaphor created by humankind, one born out of the turn of day and night, of light yielding to darkness, and the experience common to us all when everything is either bathed in brightness or thickly suffused in sightless gloom. We make it a metaphor by transposing this daily occurrence into the image, or the sense, the feeling, of good and evil, joy and pain or wholeness and distortion.

It seems so obvious as to be merely banal to say that it is difficult to see anything when you are in the dark. And yet this fact has wormed its way into the metaphor so that for many people it has become equally obvious to maintain that it is impossible to lay hold of the good, the bright and the joyful when forced to endure what certainly feels like the darkness of the soul, the night in one's head. At these times, we cannot or will not see. The world turns meaninglessly in a spiritless void, bearing without reason its wretched cargo of hungry, tortured and maimed creatures, inseparable in kind from the other animals only in their hapless and apparently absurd ability to recognize their plight and the certainty of their eventual death.

And, yes, there does seem to be something irremediably trivial and empty about too facile an optimism. The simpering fool who asserts that everything will turn out all right in the end is too often like a man who wants to sprinkle sugar on a festering wound or stuff his ears with cotton wool – or even candy floss – in order to block out the cries of the innocent.

There is in religion, or in the way that it often mediates with a secular society, quite a bit of this morally indefensible evasion, expressed in what might unfairly be called the Sunday School response to the world. The mind is coaxed into addressing itself to All Things Bright and Beautiful, as though to ignore – and by ignoring banish – all things dark and ugly. One of the funniest and, I suppose, saddest things I have seen is the young stand-in chaplain of a hospital doing a swift, head-bobbing round of the infirm: an amiable fellow with a pink countenance, his nerves nevertheless stretched to the full, scurrying up and down between the beds, nodding and grinning helplessly at each of his, ahem, denomination with a gobble-gobble that eventually articulated itself into 'Is everything all right?' An equal panic came back from the beds. 'Yes, yes,' we would say, terrified that he might linger, and perhaps even more alarmed about the prospect of answering honestly and thus giving too unguarded a voice to the anxiety or even despair kept for much later in the night.

What else, though, could the poor fellow do except make himself available to those who might wish to talk? His particular trade, so to speak, has retreated into the same residual service as the portable ward shop, the library trolley – or a bag of grapes. The analgesics and assorted biochemicals ticked off on the drug round seem to have demonstrably more useful application. Who, choking to death, would not rather have oxygen than a prayer? But then, who is *not* choking, the filth and cruelty and dead, suffocating materiality of the world clogging the throat, blanking out the cry, and filling the mouth with the bitter taste of pointlessness, of absurdity, and death?

Like you, perhaps, I have often stared thus into the enveloping darkness, trying almost at times against my will to discern whatever shapes or faint glimmers might yet take on lineaments of grace distinct from and yet indissolubly within the surrounding gloom. What, if anything, lies on the other side of the dark?

Our experience of life, our developing intelligence, our growing sense of loss and apprehension of mortality has the effect of both offering us the mature ability to recognise the human dilemma and of appearing to remove from us the instinctive trust or understanding of the answers that always lie in waiting. A classic double-bind. The better able we are to design, build, fit and work the tiller the more evident it becomes that the boat is going to fetch up on the self-same shore of whitened bones and lifeless ash no matter what we do.

Worse still, when we look back over the waves we recognize that we are, ourselves, compelled to enact the deepest and most poignant myth of Eden. We lose sight of the garden of peace and innocence in our own time, in our own lives. We expel ourselves by eating the fruits of our own knowledge – fruits we *must* and *should* eat. When we claim our maturity, and not before, we start to know death and to acknowledge darkness.

It has often been remarked that no child ever really believes that he or she will die. The idea of death is of course accepted, but not in terms of personal extinction. Things 'out there' in the world of teetering adults and random surprises may charm or puzzle or threaten, but they exist only because *we* exist. Their wonder, or so it seems, is solely dependent on our presence, and upon a sense of self, of 'me-ness,' which is unique and ineluctable. Think back. The trees, the sky, the stones, the whistle you can make with your own breath and lips, the crunch of gravel at your feet or the mushy pulp of a ripe plum in your mouth, the squeak of blackboard chalk, other children, animals, birds, people, all of it, all of them, are not *you*, but it is unimaginable that any of them should be what they are without your prior being. In what has been called 'the deathlessness of childhood,' everything is taken for granted and yet, in the most vital of paradoxes, everything is also especially itself because it is being seen or heard or tasted or felt for the first time ever.

And here, before habit corrodes or custom stales, and before the literally mundane necessities of workaday obligation clog the imagination, we can take back the gift offered up to our later selves by our own childhood.

As we grow older, we find it more and more difficult to step outside the rigidities of 'time.' Looking back with wry amusement, we recall the days when, say, a summer afternoon or an unpleasant school lesson, would appear to go on and on up unto the edge of forever. Because we once seemed to be 'making' things for the first time, or because what was in front of us and in our heads was not at once absorbed into the particular matrix of our adult social or political or habit-encrusted view of the world – because, in short, we were too new, too ignorant, too obviously 'unfinished' to slot every new thing too quickly into its appropriate category – we were able, once upon a time, to live out our days minute by minute. One of the strangest, most heartening, and indeed most irritatingly exhausting things about children, and therefore of what we ourselves once were, is their ability to live almost entirely in the present tense.

To do that, of course, presupposes an immense trust in the order of things. Apply it not to a child, but to an adult aware of the world and of his or her responsibilities, and the first thing you notice about such a mode of response is the immense degree of concentration and sustained *attention* that it implies.

Yet it is perhaps not quite so difficult. Whenever we play games, or act, or sing, or dance, or make love, we are outside 'normal' time, we are in the cauldron of the actual minute, and we have suspended or evaded the claims of any other moment except *this* one. When we are frightened, when we are in pain, when we are excited, and when we are greatly moved, the world stands still. Once again – to our delight or not – all things are as new.

It was from a starting point something like this, pieced together with an urgency rather too close to panic out of the need to do more than dumbly endure or complain about what I took to be a particularly humiliating illness, that I found that I was able, in time, to concentrate or pay attention to what was happening to me and in me and in front of me. I sought to inhabit the present, and the actual sting of the moment became a point of such unexpected clarity that I could use it, if not as a window, then certainly as a widening chink of light through which I could look. I was attempting simply to deal with the distortion of pain and what I admit to be a considerable amount of anger and fear – the predictable old 'Why me?' of the affronted – and I found instead that I was facing something other than my own beleaguered self, and gradually experiencing something other than an introverted locked-in anguish.

I understood then, and with such a feeling of emancipation that I will not or, rather, must not let this comprehension slip away out of my uncertain grasp – though, of course, it threatens to do so even as I try to formulate it in words which have been rubbed and chipped and sullied in their perpetual circulation as the coinage of our discourse – I understood that God (and, oh indeed, yes, put the embarrassing and abused word in quotes if necessary) is not an unctuous palliative, or a super-pill, or a sugary abstraction, but – and here the tension of the fact presses against my very ligaments – but someone present in the quick of being, one's own being, and in the present tense itself, in existence as it exists, in the fibre and the pulse of the world, and in the minute-by-minute drama of an ever-continuing, ever-poised, ever-accessible creation.

I understood that, because I paid attention. I do not yet understand, but can only describe in the most tentative way, something else which I know I feel. Which is that the world is being made right in front of us, and we stand always at the edge of this creation, and in living out our lives give back piece-by-piece what has been given to us to use and work with and wrestle with. We shape our own lives and find our own humanity in the long passage from premonitions of innocence through the darkness of mortal distress, carelessness and apparent absurdity into the light that we know is there if we have the patience and the courage to be still, to concentrate – to be alert.

'I am glad that I was here,' said George Fox at the end of his life. 'Now I am clear, I am fully clear... All is well.'[360]

All is well. Not by facile optimism, not in blinkered evasions, but in the richest and most active dimension of our humanity. It is the illumination we must and will ever seek on the other side of the dark.

Start the Week with Richard Baker
Interviewed by Joan Bakewell
BBC Radio 4, 13 March 1978

BAKEWELL: Popular songs have had an appeal for Dennis Potter for a long time. A list of his plays includes such titles as *Lay Down Your Arms*, *Angels are so Few*, *Follow the Yellow Brick Road* and *Only Make Believe*. Now, with *Pennies from Heaven*, he's gone a lot further. *Pennies from Heaven* is the overall title of the series but each of its six plays has a song title within that. Part One was "Down Sunnyside Lane", Part Two is "The Sweetest Thing". Dennis has been recognized as one of our most effective television writers for some 13 years now, ever since his *Stand Up, Nigel Barton* [sic] was postponed by the BBC because it was 'too strong' for a pre-Election period. That's in 1964 [sic]. Since then he's had, ooh, more than two dozen plays to his credit – his adaptation of Hardy's *Mayor of Casterbridge*[361] was the most recent and that left me in tears the other evening. He still had time, however, for his other career as a journalist and, particularly since his crippling illness first struck in 1962, as a television critic, first for the *Herald*, then the *Sun*, *New Statesman* and now of course, the *Sunday Times*. It's an unloved role, that of the television critic. It's too late for the public and too unsycophantic for the professionals, and Dennis Potter's certainly the latter! His articles reveal a fervent dislike and suspicion of, even despair about, most of what he sees on the box, expressed with a sort of biting contempt that makes you wince as you read it. Well, this double life has gone on long enough so, currently, he's yielded his regular column inches to someone else while this series runs.[362] 'Almost unanimous praise,' you said, Richard, I think, but these harsh words faced Dennis Potter yesterday morning from the column in the *Observer*: 'The central innovation of this series is that its characters repeatedly stop what they're doing and start miming to popular songs of the period instead. It's a daring and ambitious move and it doesn't seem to me to work at all.' Dennis, from one critic to another, how did you feel about that?

POTTER: I didn't feel like a critic at all when I read that. I felt like a writer who hates critics! And I think you just use different parts of your imagination when you're a critic and when you're a writer anyway, and when I'm reviewing a programme I don't think of the effect it would have upon the writer or the actor or the director, but simply does it represent what I felt about the programme, and can I put that down in a way that would communicate that feeling? But when I've written a programme, then that usual typical writer's paranoia about critics and about the reaction, whether they understand and all that, comes bobbing up to the surface, so when I open with trembling hands the *Observer*, and I knew that Martin Amis was going...and Martin Amis is a little dot-dot-dot. *(Laughs.)* I saw that phrase...

BAKEWELL: He says the same of you, I'm sure!

POTTER: Yes, quite! Yes. And I saw that and thought, oh well, critics, what do they know?

BAKEWELL: Yes, 'critics, what do they know?' I mean, they are a marvellous scapegoat for the failures of people in television to get across an idea.

POTTER: Yes, particularly because there's no audience. There's only an abstract audience, or there are a series of audiences of two or three or four people gathered round the set, so...in a sense a television critic is the only observable reaction apart from within the programme itself.

BAKEWELL: There's no applause, there's no long run in the theatre, there's no bestselling book, no, but from what you feel about that critic yesterday morning and 'what does he know, what do critics know?' – do you turn that round and point it at yourself?

POTTER: Yes, of course. I mean, I then imagine myself in the situation where I've been equally obtuse and stupid about a programme. There have been times when you later realise that you haven't picked up the thread of a programme properly, because if it ever comes back into your mind, you know that something about it must have been working, and if you've said it hasn't worked then you have committed an injustice. But that's part of being a critic. It takes a certain sardonic alertness and brutality and nerve and arrogance, to do...

BAKEWELL: Yes, you've done all of these things!

POTTER: No, it does demand those things if you're going to be responding with your full emotional energy to a programme that's in front of you.

BAKEWELL: I think what you have that a great many critics don't have to anything like the same degree, and that puts the fear of God into most television practitioners, is a command of language and indeed abuse that is so strong...

POTTER: I would have said polemic, not abuse!

BAKEWELL: *(Laughter.)* Well, polemical abuse!

POTTER: Yes, it's abuse if you disagree with it or are on the receiving end of it but I think you've got to be very careful not to abuse, you know, just to set out to pick someone to pieces, or put someone down. It's got to be triggered by something really genuinely felt watching a programme, I mean...and television does this all the time, of course, just as radio does!

BAKEWELL: Yes, you use sometimes the most banal contributions of television. In a sense, it looks like you riding your own hobby-horse, using television as an excuse.

POTTER: No, what I try to do is to watch the things that I would have watched if I wasn't a critic. Of course you can't do that all the time because sometimes you do stay with a programme which you would have switched off, but sometimes...across the whole range of television – from the guff to the, well, say heights for the sake of argument! – you are going to be picking up things which do offend and do, well...that are so bad that they become good, because they're part and parcel of this kind of ditchwater that's swirling around you, and you're part of it and you can dabble your feet in it and so you've got to react to it.

BAKEWELL: Dennis, can we pick up a few threads of your own *Pennies from Heaven* now. Do you regard popular song as part of the ditchwater of our lives, that swirls around us?

POTTER: No. I think – in some ways, yes – but I picked the Thirties in particular because the music at that time, the popular music, was perhaps at its most banal and its most sugary, least challenging, and yet it also encapsulates, somehow, some diminished image of the human desire for there to be a perfect and beautiful and just world, for the moon to rhyme with June and for love to be like this...for the sugar in the world to come, as a crust, to the surface. And I think it's…in Episode Two for example, it starts with…at school, with the teacher being called forward to read a psalm, and instead of reading a psalm she reads a psalm of King David and then starts to sing "You've Got Me Crying Again", which in fact is a straight translation of that particular psalm, and these songs pull together these dreams of, really, a kind of longing for Eden and for peace and for joy and for everyone to be flawless and perfect.

BAKEWELL: Dennis, your experience of these songs is not personal, in that you weren't an adult in the Thirties so you didn't experience them as your characters do, as the hope of utopia.

POTTER: Well, I don't know, because I was born in 1935, and in the summer of '35 – I'm putting it so I'm not 43 yet! – lying in bed, the wireless downstairs, and these songs drifting up the stairs, it must… It drops into that little hole that we all have about who and what we are, where we're going, and images, sounds that you can never quite place and locate because they kind of predate your full consciousness of yourself. So that I'm sure that Al Bowlly and Lew Stone and all these sounds were drifting up the stairs, and I must have…they do something to me, and it must be in that, that must be the reason.

BAKEWELL: They helped form you.

POTTER: *(Affirmative.)* Hmm.

BAKEWELL: Can I ask you about the production? Why do the people who mime the songs not mime songs that they might possibly be singing – when she mimes, a male voice comes.

POTTER: Well, because I wanted to make quite clear that it wasn't them, and that we're in another realm when this goes on. So the very first song that came on in the first episode was in fact Elsie Carlisle's voice-over, from a man's voice, so that no one was in any doubt about what I was trying to do and what territory I was attempting to claim.

RICHARD BAKER: Realism is not what you're doing, Dennis.

POTTER: Not with the songs, no, because I don't think that's how we receive the songs anyway. We can dismiss them out of hand. All popular culture we can dismiss out of hand, but what is amazing about popular culture – and which we can usually see in retrospect

– is how cleverly and commercially perhaps and, accidentally, often, it locates with our sense of ourselves and time and place. It's their very generality, their very banality that allows us to use our imaginations to take from them what we're sort of, really, about, what we're feeling. They're kinds of hymns, I think.

Bank holiday blues
Sunday Times, 3 September 1978

If you have ever fallen asleep in a deck chair and awakened with a start to discover the oily tide gurgling and sucking at your feet you will have sufficient idea of what it is like to open your eyes after a dangerously long break from the television screen and find yourself staring at the holiday weekend programmes. I had hoped to return to this space without rivulets of salty liquid scouring my cheeks, but when on Bank Holiday Monday ageless Cliff Richard turned to seasoned Val Doonican and simpered, 'Do you realize how long it is since I guested on your show?', it was time to acknowledge that the inexorable waters had already reached as far as my open mouth.

'Guest' is one of those warm and reassuring nouns which totally changes meaning when used as an adjective. 'Guest star' takes on the same connotation as 'guest house,' for example: something cold and cheerless and peculiarly threatening. Shades of interpretation more obviously manifest when Cliff and Val proceeded to make heavy going of "Travellin' Light", one of them standing as though the polished floor was bucking and heaving while the other sought to defend himself from that deadly old light-entertainment virus which both loosens and stiffens the larger muscles at the same time as it painfully elongates the lips into a cadaverous slobber.

The Val Doonican Show (BBC1) can be hailed as the archetypal holiday entertainment as dreamed down by those who plan the television schedules before departing for cowardly vacations to other shores. It had a toothily amiable compère perched on what even in hospitals is called a stool, a portable microphone used with the sort of oral intimacy which makes one hope that the props department sterilize it between numbers, a few songs, some interpolated seaside pictures, a couple of shots of the free-seat audience grinning happily at their own images in the overhead monitors, and an old joke or two. Plus the Nolan Sisters, a young joke or four.

I believe there used to be five girls in the family, but one of them has either become ambitious and 'gone solo' or become even more ambitious and given up altogether. Here, they belted out "Money, Money, Money" in blue suits with glitter jackets and fetching bow-ties, raising their left feet, then their right feet, then clicking their fingers, revolving once on the spot before returning to raise their left feet again.

Within the hour, the four gyrating colleens were again on show in *The Tommy Cooper Show* (Thames). This time, however, they wore satin blouses and black boots and held mikes which terminated in large red blobs perhaps meant to represent lollipops. I thought they were going to suck them to see. Variety is all, so this time they raised their right feet, then their left feet before revolving more than once on the gleaming stage. The song, too, was different. I think.

Cooper himself was the one act on the show which resists duplication – though not, alas, imitation from every mimic in the business. He is blessed with the face and demeanour of a lugubrious Cardinal who has discovered too late in life that he would rather have been a humble camel driver. An irritating little cough punctuates the irritatingly incomplete sentences he uses to talk us through satisfyingly incomplete bits of stage magicianship.

'Oh dear. What's gone wrong now?' A turn so well developed that it has by now reached the final consummation of total and complete boredom. A rose is a rose is a rose, and Tommy Cooper has collapsed into the essence of himself, sapped in his own endless repetition of one limited routine. Music hall would have cherished him as one of its greatest comedians, but television cannot bear the same thing done over and over in the same way. It wants the same thing done over and over in different ways.

Which is why, of course, one so often gets the feeling that one is watching something that has already been seen. The August holiday programme needs merely a sprig of holly and a decorated tree to become the Christmas holiday programme. The sets and the stars, the songs and the jokes and the studio audiences become more and rarely less interchangeable. The Nolan Sisters cross from one programme to another, meeting Peters and Lee, a singing duo, who in turn flip from

Tommy Cooper to Wednesday's *Tony Hatch and All Kinds of Music* (ATV). Hatch made a dreadful hash of all his 'introductions,' somehow managing to be both embarrassingly nervous and odiously self-congratulatory. Otherwise, the same old stuff.

Paul Daniels' Blackpool Bonanza (Granada) on Sunday night was neither better nor worse than the other half dozen variety shows of the holiday week. The freeloaders were told that they were 'a lovely audience,' exactly as though they were potentially troublesome children. Banks of yellow, blue and red lights gleamed into the shine of the stage, and long-legged girls pranced about in severely restricted choreography.

It seems that old and now used-up conceptions of 'glamour' drift out from these programmes like smoke curling under the doors of an abandoned and burning cinema or long-forgotten palais. All the more startling, therefore, to find in Eddie Flanagan a flinty Northern comedian who could resurrect harsh old images from the past and make them painfully funny.

Flanagan's monologue, about skipping ropes and cross-over pinnies and 'sharpening the knife on the step so that the woman next door would think you had meat,' was the one performance in all the holiday which forced me to work out connections between the tatty 'glamour' and the hunger that lies behind it in a perpetual yearning for life to gleam and glint and glitter like the coloured lights on the polished stage. Half close your eyes against a vermilion glare and the dancing girls, the magician's ruffled parrot, the burbled love-song and the plastic rose in the aerosoled hair speak of the ache to escape from the stolid intractability of things, and maybe turn real sorrow into the anodyne sobbing of a saxophone – blue ribbons of sound unravelling in that smallest space in our heads between the nerves and the memory.

Perhaps, then, it is not possible to do without at least some of these weary old variety shows. The Nolan Sisters would not be improved by standing still. The click, the stamp and the turn in the soft pool of overhead spots are like a faint imitation of what high camp itself imitates.

And *that*, in the end, is only one of the echoes by which we put down the absurdity of mortality by being even more absurd than we need. So, yes, click your fingers, clap your hands! No reason, though, to go as far as finding a kind word for last Saturday's *Seaside Special* (BBC1), the show in a rain-drenched marquee. It reminds me of one of President Johnson's more apt remarks, when he defended his choice of one particular colleague by claiming, 'It's better to have him inside the tent pissing out, than outside the tent pissing in.' *Seaside Special* made nonsense of the option by doing both at one and the same time.

The holiday programmes on commercial television were placed in a similar perspective by the constant interruption of an ad for something called 'That Stuff.' This slithery-looking goo apparently washes away virtually any sort of muck when squeezed over soiled hands. The BBC was unable to flourish the same antidote between holiday offerings, having to content itself with swift trailers for *Holocaust* in which it seems that Hitler's murdered Jews are to be rendered down into soap opera instead of just soap. No wonder we want a song and dance.

The lascivious leer of the senses
Sunday Times, 19 November 1978

The whiffling judges at a flower show do not forbear to sniff long and deep at the heart of a rose. The winner of the cake competition at the vicarage expects to have her triumphant walnut-layer well and truly masticated. Poodles at Cruft's must submit to being mauled and patted, and even dignified old shire horses at the county show allow their teeth to be examined. But the sickly male fantasy that, so not to speak, ejaculates the comical *Miss World 1978* (BBC1) contest into stained existence dare not, must not, could not put the so-called 'vital statistics' to the ultimate test. Suffice it to say, perhaps, that Miss Virgin Isles failed to live down the disappointment of her title on Thursday night, and was therefore eliminated in the first few minutes.

Narcissus and Echo might have understood the 'conversations' between the last seven finalists and Sacha Distel. The saddle-soaped French singer was hired to 'discover a little bit more about their personalities' by asking vapid questions mostly concerned with himself which elicited vapid answers as repetitive as though they had all come gurgling out of one and the same stretched and glistening gash of a mouth.

Miss Switzerland alone spoke intelligently. Her figure was as pneumatic as her rivals', but her tongue let out several words of at least three syllables each. Thirty seconds of such assertive loquacity is too big a threat to the paunchy old men in the audience who sniggered so lasciviously when giggly Miss Australia said, 'I've always loved old people.' The fantasy promise of sex, even of the oral varieties, precludes the use of a dictionary.

'Can you imagine, ladies and gentlemen! With a body like this, she imagines that the greatest thing on earth is the *spirit*!' Sacha turned to the audience in comic incredulity. Bodies 'like this,' the answering laughter conceded, are not meant for such wasteful speculation. Beauty equals desirability which is measured by desire which is best satisfied by what-must-never-be-said. Miss Austria loves to snorkel. Miss USA likes spaghetti. Miss Mexico is fond of fish and chips. But every ogle and leer and wink, every announcement about the size of the breasts and the narrowness of the waist is of course not designed to lay bare the hobbies and culinary tastes of the flesh in question. No, sir. No, ma'am. Yet nobody (and I won't write no one) was asked, 'What are you like in bed?'

The frantic scrabble of ageing and shapeless (and male) press photographers around the eventual winner was the nearest we got to the forbidden topic. It looked, momentarily, like a particularly nasty gang bang as they elbowed, shoved and jostled each other out of the way to get nearer and nearer to the lustrous but weeping lady. Impossible, in this collective gesture, to avoid a spasm of total shame. The elaborately corny staging, the dazzling lights, sugared music and odious pretence gave way to something equally unreal but more urgently unpleasant. Smile, dear. Cross your legs. Lean forward a bit...

Human gestures do indeed speak column-inches, if not volumes. The one I enjoyed most last week came at the beginning of Monday's *Royal Variety Performance* (BBC1). Bernard Delfont was leading the Queen Mother into the foyer of the Palladium, and he could not quite resist putting a proprietorial hand on her white fur wrap. It was a movement at once delicate and furtive, seemingly an acknowledgement both of illicit passion and commercial brutality – rather like a poacher tenderly fondling a trapped rabbit before removing it from the noose. 'I know *radiant* is a cliché' burbled Terry Wogan, a chandelier behind him and panic in his eyes. Knowledge of the law is even less a defence than ignorance of it, but this is one of those occasions when nobody is expected to behave, let alone speak, like a rational being.

Hospital patients are similarly supposed to abandon their reason when they lose their good health. The amusing dramatization of a consultant's discussion at the foot of a sick man's bed in Jonathan Miller's *The Body in Question* (BBC2) was painfully symptomatic not merely of the diagnostic skills being illustrated but also of the baby-talk indignities one is made to endure when unwell.

My absence from this spot during the past few weeks[363] has again been due to the treachery of my own ailing frame, so I am following this alarmingly entertaining series with literally ferocious concentration. 'Illness isn't something a person *has*. It's another way of being,' Dr Miller insists. A hint of wry melancholy, and some words released with the sharp intensity of the irregular peristaltic waves he was mentioning, temper the medical mechanism of his dissertation. An erudite and entertaining man talking to the point and without condescension, almost the complete opposite of James Burke and the wildly disconnected *Connections* (BBC1).

Miller drew our attention last week to the ways in which the ill use their hands to describe and locate the pain in their bodies. 'A pantomime of complaint.' The use of the index finger, or spreading palms, or a clenching fist, indicate the type and spread of the distress, and are valuable in diagnosis. Amusingly, his own hands scarcely once stayed still. Tempted by his graphic exposition of the relationship between the condition and the gesture, I tried out my own diagnostic abilities and decided that the mimetic dance of his upper limbs showed without doubt that here was a man casting his bread upon the waters.

The Body in Question, in consequence, is growing into a masterpiece of television exploration. Jonathan Miller's great skills as an entertainer, a writer and a scientist have for once joined together in common enterprise. We do not normally expect to hear the 'warm, damp monotony' of the intestine described as 'a sort of physiological Florida,' but in this series the wonder of our insides is celebrated with language of equally ordered grace. Miss Switzerland is, after all, a continent entire.

The *Fallen Hero* (Granada) of Brian Finch's new series is a rugby league professional with damaged ligaments. Del Henney played him with properly taciturn sullenness, exactly as though his knees really ached. Unfortunately, the rest of the cast seem to have been given infected gall bladders. The one moment of tenderness, adulterous though it would have been, came to an abrupt end when the telephone kept jangling. It was a reporter from the *Daily Express*. Coitus interruptus is unsatisfactory at any time, but this particular form of tabloid interference beggars all possible description. Dear Jean Rook, what *is* a poor girl to do?[364]

Goodbye to all that
Sunday Times, 26 November 1978

'See you next week!' announced a tanned but not beaten Jimmy Hill at the end of last Saturday's *Match of the Day* (BBC1). Everything above the otherwise waggish beard hurriedly composed itself into that peculiarly aggressive snarl known to the trade as a Front Man's Smile. '*And* next year!' he added, teeth almost slicing touchline markings deep into his lower lip. The threatened loss of 'Did you see that!' and 'Oh! What a save!' to LWT was sufficient explanation of the venomously cheerful facial spasm, but from where I was sitting in the dug-outs, the angry confidence seemed entirely enviable. Would that I could address you in similar terms!

Instead, I gloomily tuned in to Monday's *Panorama* (BBC1) to find out what is happening to this newspaper. As I was about to teeth-grind my way through this review, I was told that two other people would be writing here about last week's *Panorama*, so I cannot take up the kind of space which would permit apoplexy its due momentum.[365]

Two points, please, guv'nor: first, and public, how cruel of *Panorama* to demonstrate so conclusively that a pair of newspapers by no means free of the usual canting humbug about the plight of Britain or the woodrot of her industries should all the time have been pathetically worm-ridden examples of the very malaise they so ponderously curse in others. Secondly, and more personal, this will in the event of 'suspension' or closure (lock-out is the proper term) be my last column for this sadly embattled journal.

'Unless you have a date [for closure], you don't get anywhere,' piped 'Duke' Hussey, of Times Newspapers, my idea of a catastrophic manager, on *Panorama*. Quite so, old boy.[366]

But those who are most grievously affected by the astonishingly sordid manoeuvrings depicted in the programme cannot always afford my spittle-flecked bombast. They needs must comport themselves a little like the cautious Head Maltster in Václav Havel's *Audience*, the second of two plays by the Czech dissident in last Tuesday's fascinating *Play for Today* spot on BBC1.

This poor man, brilliantly played from burps to burps by Freddie Jones behind a giddy wall of beer bottles, was stung out of slobberingly drunken inanities into a bitter, although shamefaced, diatribe against all those who indulge in the luxury of 'principle' because their personal circumstance allows them to resist the suffocating collusions forced upon their colleagues. The irritating structure of the play, in which passages of dialogue were repeated again and again in an apparently trivial liturgy of the deliberately mundane, suddenly tightened into pain and pity.

The tipsy maltster was hectoring a diffident yet unyielding writer, who, like Havel himself, had been compelled to labour in a brewery because his actions had offended the authorities. Michael Crawford, as the harassed playwright, overcame lingering mannerisms from 'Frank Spencer' of Saturday's often hilarious *Some Mothers Do 'Ave 'Em* (BBC1), to reach for the type of passivity which mantles the most stubborn tenacity. He smiled, nodded, and twitched in near-parody of gutless politeness, as close to a cringe as it is possible to get without actually warping the spine.

Crawford, however, skilfully got beyond these surface weaknesses to scrape against the awkward integrity beneath. The mild eyes, the timid grin, the fawning shuffle of limb and muscle were shown not so much as a mask but as a nervously attenuated form of compassion. Scarcely nowhere do the meek inherit an inch of the earth, but when they know *why* they are meek, they can sometimes threaten where guns and clubs and rhetoric cannot reach. You cannot bargain with those who have nothing to lose.

Drama as obliquely understated as these two plays does not sit comfortably on a small screen which perpetually compensates for the domesticity of its diminished proportions by slam-bang excesses of presentation. In many of the popular series, so-called 'moral dilemmas' are given not just a passing nod but the breezy slap on the back – which knocks out their false teeth. Thus, last week's *Starsky & Hutch* (BBC1), a swiftly nasty tale of rape and murder, as wet-mouthed as a peeping tom, had one of its characters complaining that 'this country packages sex and violence like a breakfast cereal.' Right on, cornflake.

On the other channel, *The Incredible Hulk* used its strip-cartoon format for a story about a father who regularly beats his child very badly. 'No, daddy! No, daddy! No! No!' Then – zap! – the hero with the magical temper, the Hulk himself, turned his eyeballs milky white, his muscles dirty grey, and instantly puffed up into a roaring monster who then proceeded to thump the daylights out of the father. 'No, daddy! No! No!'

cried the child batterer before becoming – guess what? – overwhelmed with remorse.

The standard revelation that the father had himself been beaten as a child did not compensate for the use of the self-same mechanism within the 'play' itself. There is a perpetual swirl of this sort of morally ambivalent stuff across our screens, celebrating what it purports to condemn. Even with home-grown nasties such as ITV's *The Professionals* the routine cynicism about all political processes is not matched by any opposing system of belief. Last week's episode was content to assert that local and Parliamentary politicians are so totally without moral and financial scruple that only a dedicated secret service – answerable to none of them and none of us – keeps the muck from off our doorsteps. Ludicrous.

But it is the American imports which squelch most deeply into the bog. 'Our system is this – grab a piece of the pie for yourself!' insisted a character in a made-for-TV movie on BBC1 the other night. And at least one possible consequence of his pervasive attitude was chillingly shown on Thursday's *TV Eye* (Thames) by satellite from San Francisco. Sick religions, zany beliefs, warped ideologies, drugged passions – aerosol into the vacuum. The mass suicide of the People's Temple Californians can only be dimly 'understood' by looking, as this programme did, at the contaminated swamps which bred and nourished the movement.

Turn on, tune in, drop out…and farewell.

Theatre Call
Interviewed by Michael Billington
BBC World Service, 9 February 1979[367]

POTTER: I was conscious of wanting to write [with *Brimstone & Treacle*] a parable, exactly the kind of thing which in a sense is destroyed by simply reading a synopsis of what happens. In a sense, what happens is merely the structure to release preoccupations of my own about the relationship between good and evil, neither of which by definition one can understand without appreciating the other. We can obviously only define good by having a sense of evil. We can only define evil by having a sense of good. And I'm interested in the way the modern world has slid into the assumption that evil is an adjective and not a noun, and I wanted to personify it in perhaps its most obvious and cheap, easy manner, so there could be little doubt about what was supposed to be going on.

BILLINGTON: There are difficulties attached to the meaning of the play even now, it seems to me, because the character who is ostensibly evil – Martin – and who in this production is clearly identified with the Devil – is the one person who does good, isn't he? To the girl, to the vegetable girl.

POTTER: Yes, well, I think that there is a continual interaction between these two – I'm tempted to say 'forces'...and that's a way that I personally conceive them and react to them – and that no human motive is not mixed. Even if you set out to do an evil act, or if you set out to do a good one, you cannot predict with certainty the consequences of such action, but more interesting than the fact that it's because of his diabolical actions that good results, there is another force going on which is the very laughably 'simple' faith of the mother, and of the characters on stage it's the mother who wins. It's the mother who asks for the prayer. It's the devil who mocks the act of prayer, the prayer itself is mocked, the act of praying is mocked, and yet the prayer is answered.

BILLINGTON: This to me does indicate your own division about formal religion. Am I right in this? That it does seem to me that you are saying in several instances that prayer is often ineffectual, that there is a kind of self-induced religious ecstasy, *but* there are moments when the religious force in people's lives does change things.

POTTER: Yes. I'm not conscious now of any particularly sharp division in myself about these things. Prayer is obviously a human difficulty. If you believe that somehow, against all the odds, in the teeth of the apparent total absurdity of existence, that there is a loving God, and that creation itself is the consequence, that the world around us is a consequence of the reaction between human motive, human will and perhaps human perversity and the given fact of creation, then prayer – which is allegedly the dialogue between the given and the creator – is always tainted, contaminated, by a human impulse of... you know, when a bishop comes on during the drought and prays for rain, I just feel like laughing. I feel, right, if you want to look for blasphemy, where's the obvious place to look for it? In the church. And it's that mock religiosity, the fact that religion now is merely a piece of drivelling sanctimony in the mouths of rather dreary priests, that I'm getting at. Because religion to me is much more vital and much more creative an impulse – it's a minute-by-minute thing that we make as we go along, and religion that is simply...that has degenerated into this sort of sentimental drivel was what I was also getting at in this parable.

BILLINGTON: Can I bring you on to the political aspects of the play, because those intrigue me honestly as much as the religious ones. The head of the house, Mr Bates, Tom, does in fact lean towards the British fascist organization the National Front, yet you also give him a speech in which he laments the England that once was, and in which he foreswears racial violence, and I wonder, do you feel that in England today there is a sort of sour middle-class discontent, but one that stops well short of fascism and well short of physical violence?

POTTER: Yes, I think in England it will take something utterly exceptional to produce a genuinely dangerous, fascist party. On the other hand, there is in England – and quite understandably – a yearning, a nostalgia, a basically right-wing impulse which is simple in the sense that it wishes things to be as they were: that is, socially, politically impossible. When the consequences of that 'dream' are pointed out to people, I think they recoil from them. I also wanted to show in that sequence that when people are genuinely presented with evil as a positive alternative, they do recoil from it. They do not actively wish it. So when Tom, at the end – obviously his anxiety is linked with a desire that the accident shouldn't have happened, that his fear and his guilt shouldn't be swirling around him and oppressing him in the way that it does, and right-wing thought in general – which has many noble and dignified strands in it: its desire for order, for peace, for things to be changed only if they have to be changed, all that, which one instinctively, whether one is on the Left or not, ought to be able to appreciate as a force in human society – but nostalgia... I wanted him to have a speech of some dignity which would reflect either the openly acknowledged or the hidden and unacknowledged tensions in some of the audience, which is that, yes, old ladies ought to be able to walk safely in the street, yes it was nicer once, yes, the past – when we look at it through whatever lenses we look at it – always does take upon this shimmer which nostalgia gives to things, which makes one think it is better. Of course, it isn't and the temptations that the Devil figure offers to the father is to recreate the past by violently contaminating the present.

BILLINGTON: I also sense in the play something else, a feeling of what attitude one adopts towards people who are – in this case, the girl is a virtual vegetable in this bed – but towards people who are severely afflicted, and I sense you're saying that compassion isn't enough and patience isn't enough. Something more is required. I wondered if that was true and if it springs from the fact that you yourself have been through a good deal of physical suffering in your life?

POTTER: It's very difficult to know how to react to pain, anguish, suffering, degradation…any extremity that takes the subject of that extremity either further and further away from humanity or beyond our ken altogether. And it seems to me that the totally rational approach or a cynical one or a merely…you know, dropping a coin in a collecting box, or pious affirmation of the humanity of the wretched subject, just simply leaves one with an absurd taste in one's mouth. And the final affirmation of trust in some order that human language and society has always sought to comprehend seems to me the only affirmation left to human beings in the end, that in the end things are either absurd or there is an order to which we can appeal, and I've found [myself] over the years being pulled towards the affirmation of an order in which one can ultimately, no matter what buffets one, actually trust.

BILLINGTON: Well, out of that tension that you're talking about, between the sense of the absurd and the desire for order, there seems to come good drama, and your good drama specifically. One thing that puzzles me about your work, though, is that it has been almost entirely for television. Why have you never written for the theatre?

POTTER: I don't know. This may be a sort of inverted snobbery on my part or maybe due to my…if I was using a grand word, I'd say my democratic instinct but it must be more complicated than that. I just believe that television…could be, potentially ought to be the national theatre of our country, and that it aspires and is capable, technically – because of technological development – of reaching the sort of audiences that the theatre always sought; that is, all types and conditions of men and women across whatever lines may be dividing them, so that in the cant phrase you have a don and a coal miner watching the same programme. You don't see that, have that in the theatre, alas. If the theatre opened out a bit more I would be more eager to respond to it.

Anteroom to purgatory
Tatler, November 1979

On this side of the rainbow there are few more exhilarating sights than that of an otherwise mediocre man in the throes of a Vision. Indeed, only the spectacle of a pair of butterflies copulating in mid-air above a flowering gorse bush can even begin to measure up to the electronic image of Sir Keith Joseph simpering and throbbing and crinkling up his dark, hot eyes when, after years in the wilderness, he at last hears the pathetic whimpers of those stunted miscreants who have wasted their inglorious little lives at something so utterly, wickedly perverse as making steel or building ships.

A similar white-hot light has fallen upon my own formerly humble visage. My many dependents and fewer friends have commented behind their hands in furtive tones of envy, fear and contempt about the formidable new thrust to my once quivering jaw, the confident swagger of my hitherto sloping shoulders, and the faraway gleam inches deep behind my old fashioned spectacles. Hints which, taken together, unmistakably signify the awesome presence of a man who has suddenly found a new path to personal salvation.

The truth is that I have been to Eastbourne, and I no longer fear death.

Better still, I can now peer ahead through the murk of these Thatcher-ridden days and see the ultimate flowering of my destiny as the fourteenth most gifted man of letters in the kingdom. In the squashy ripeness of time, that is, I shall mature into a seemingly contented and continent old man who has outlived all his despicable contemporaries and anyone else he has ever pretended to love. And then, oh then, I shall expend the last of my spirit and the remainder of my money in an ample suite with a fat stone balcony at a sumptuous Victorian wedding-cake of an hotel which looks out in suitably emphatic disdain upon a pewter English sea. At Eastbourne, of course. At Eastbourne.[368]

The picture forms itself for me with perfect clarity. I see myself creaking down the wide sweep of staircase to the dustily chandeliered lounges for a tepid pot of teabags and a couple of stale macaroons. But I will undoubtedly spend most of my declining hours at the reproduction writing-desk in my slightly damp sitting room, cackling and dribbling over the kind of scabrous autobiography which could only be published (if at all) long after an almost equally elderly porter in faded livery had failed to get any sort of answer to his feeble but prolonged knocking on my door.

Not even the plangent cries of the seagulls outside the smeared window panes can give this image the slightest trace of sadness or regret. I repeat, I have *already been* to Eastbourne, and am thus fully prepared for every eventuality up to and including senility itself.

What great good fortune it is to have stumbled upon a sense of calm ease so honourable, so deep and so sustaining when I might otherwise, like Peter Jay, have lost my way in the dark wood which gloomily presses in upon every soul during the middle passage of life. And the gift which came to me in the middle of a bad summer had yet more layers of richness to come. What had appeared at the time to be an inexplicable, indeed horrifying, impulse to waste a few days in July at an expensive mausoleum of an hotel in Eastbourne was followed shortly afterwards by an even more inexplicable, indeed horrifying, invitation to write for the *Tatler*. The two mysteries have since marinated in my own alcohol to yield up the entirely new and completely wholesome perspective I am trying so joyously to describe.

I realized in a shell-burst of brightest revelation that nobody I have ever known has gone quite so far as actually to read, let alone contribute to, the *Tatler*. At least, not until this issue. Thus, I have now obtained more than an inkling of what it will be like to construct what I hope will be an entirely shocking autobiography in the days yet to come at Eastbourne. In this magazine I will have my first taste of what Auberon Waugh obviously swallows down whole every day of his life – that is, the emancipation and refreshment of writing as though everyone else of any shared sensibility whatsoever has totally disappeared from the face of the earth altogether. In space no one can hear you scream. Mr Waugh seems to have to face the same predicament down there in the black holes of Somerset.

Dear, sweet Eastbourne, too, gives its unsuspecting visitors the vertiginous feeling of being lost in time and space. A sense of dislocation made even more disconcerting by the not-quite-believable echoes of *I-have-been-here-before* which drift hauntingly into the mind rather after the fashion that an evocative taste or smell or sound faintly remembered from childhood can again at an unexpected angle fleetingly touch the membranes and leave a sting at the back of the eyes.

Walking between immaculate flower beds spaced in decorative clumps at the properly swept edges of long, clean promenades where wrapped and muffled old people slump on unvandalized benches staring vacantly at the grey wash of the incoming tide, I was unable to resist the feeling that I was on an impossible voyage into two strange harbours: the make-believe, inexorably doomed world of England as it used to be, and the quiet pool of one's own eventual old age and inevitable death. The sky above the Channel was the colour of pale Camp coffee, as neutral as a gallery wall. A constant invitation to make your own pictures in your own head and hang them wherever you want.

As soon as I arrived all agog at the wedding-cake hotel – described in the guide as 'one of Europe's great hotels' in unnecessary obeisance to the political absurdity of a Common Market which would have us ignore the demonstrable facts of geography – I sniffed and crept my way along vast corridors towards a cavernous lounge where I expected to be served my tea. I had been attracted to the place in the first instance by a tariff which, to my whooping incredulity, offered marginally reduced rates in back rooms not overlooking the sea to nannies accompanying families with children.

The eager pulse of expectation was thus fluttering strongly in my imagination as I entered the Lounge. Would there be rustlingly stiff nannies sitting bolt upright at the tables administering modest proportions of cream bun and assisted sips of milky tea to smirking little beasts in much the same cravenly poignant manner that Norman St. John-Stevas attends so diligently to the similarly petulant needs of the grocer's bullying daughter? And would pretty little maids wearing frilly little caps and crisp white aprons nod and smile at me as they bustled about carrying plates of shaving-cream cakes and steaming brown pots of the better brews?

Well, no. Eastbourne does not present its anachronisms quite so crudely. It is not yet a museum. More a sequence of hypnagogic images where a gently drugged mind can mix together both recollection and premonition, both VAT and an old song.

There seemed at first to be no one in sight at all. I sank into a deep armchair by the high windows, listened to the quiet drone of a geriatric fly, stretched out my legs, and waited. And waited.

Gradually, as though in a slow dream, I became aware of the ghostly presence of a few other patient residents. A grey and knobbled head just discernible behind the protruding wing of a chair jerked forward in a sudden paroxysm of coughs and splutters. The elderly bluebottle buzzed and bumped towards the shadows of the far wall where a cashmere dowager with a straggling moustache and the beginnings of a wispy beard was complaining softly to herself about the iniquity of estate agents and the longevity of stray cats: two unarguable propositions which I had not until then been able to coax into an even halfway successful conjunction. A waitress wearing neither cap nor apron appeared, looked about with a curling lip, haughtily ignored my admittedly less than forthright gesture, and went out again, bearing neither cakes nor little brown teapots. The fly buzzed. The gulls cried.

I must have slipped into a delicate reverie barely this side of sleep. Not since I stumbled on a pavement in Cheltenham and fell headlong in front of a broken and abandoned building called The Empire Hall have I experienced so graphic a sense of the changes which have both afflicted and liberated my country. Insubstantial shapes drifted across the lattice of my unconsciously clenching eyelids. Sleep was gently beckoning to a strange distant tinkle of a lift bell somewhere deep in a big old hotel that was floating off unanchored into the past. I think I heard again a plummy voice on a scratchy wireless set announcing that 'we are now taking you over to the Palm Court of the Grand Hotel.' Five minutes of Waldteufel. Three minutes "In a Persian Market Place"...

The voice of modern England pulled me up with a guilty start. 'Did you want something?' asked a waitress with a properly democratic disdain. 'Or are you just sitting there?'

All along the front, too, people with glazed expressions were 'just sitting there.' There were, of course, brash young families and boisterous children romping among the incipient corpses. And on the shingle, the usual sensual spangles of luscious off-white bodies gleaming with hopeful lotions. But the dominant impression was of an infinitely extended old people's home with the roof off. Elderly ladies with blue rinses walked placid old dogs on long leads. Elderly ladies with bluer rinses walked placid old gentlemen on rather shorter leads. At the tawdry pier entrance, ambulances from Lambeth had brought a score or more of the old and infirm to sit in huddled clumps along the girdered and decaying bridge that leads nowhere except out into the choppy sea. They sat and sat and sat by the rails as though patiently waiting for a boat. Perhaps, indeed, they were: the dark freighter which will one day carry us all to another shore uncharted on any map.

Melancholy, unlike depression or grief, is a valuable experience. It is the nearest some of us ever get to the longer perspective wherein we can momentarily glimpse and even hold the shape of our own lives and what used to be called our destinies.

Our secular age has long since downgraded rational approaches to the ancient need for pilgrimage and penance. The fear of death is now so universal that even those who are closest in time to it are called 'senior citizens' instead of 'old people.' Believing neither in heaven nor in hell we are compelled for want of else to live out the grand old cosmic drama on a few polluted acres of here and now. Solacing ourselves with euphemism and monosodium glutamate. Cheers.

Theologians at a dull-witted loss to invent sustaining new metaphors might do better to abandon a few of their old playthings and dream up more fitting constructs. Let them go to the seaside. Not to dirty old Brighton, windy Yarmouth, raucous Blackpool. Much of what they seek can be found in comical Bournemouth or even funnier Torquay.

But it is only in the ultimate hilarity of Eastbourne that the old cosmologies flicker in full, purging glow. Only in Eastbourne that one can decently rehearse death. Only in Eastbourne find any sort of semblance to purgatory itself.

'Did you want something? Or are you just sitting there?'

I asked for a macaroon and a nice cup of tea.

Cheryl Campbell – An appreciation by Dennis Potter
Over 21, March 1980

The first time I saw Cheryl Campbell I had to work hard to swallow my disappointment. It was at one of the barrack rooms which BBC planners, in their abiding fear and hatred of all so-called 'creative people,' deem fit to be a drama rehearsal block. The occasion was the read-through of my six-part play *Pennies from Heaven*,[369] and in my mildly paranoid anxiety about this new project I could see that some of the cast-to-be had already made up their minds that small change was indeed all they were likely to get from such a potentially disastrous set of scripts.

Cheryl, however, was not one of those. Enthusiasm and nervousness contended with each other on her expression. But was this supposed to be *my* Eileen – the demure school-teacher who turns into an accomplished whore?

I had imagined, months before, in the privacy of that little theatre between the bones of the head, an Eileen who was small, dark, palpably erotic and with eyes as big and bright as costume jewellery. But Cheryl Campbell did not seem to be any of these things. Her complexion is so classically English that she might well have been left out in the damp and the mist through her entire childhood. Her long tumble of hair – not yet able to decide whether to be blonde or copper – came straight out of a forgotten Amami Friday Night.[370] And she had, God forbid, what even other women readily call 'a sweet face.'

Good fortune has left me far too shy and awkward to enjoy what I rather wistfully assume to be the traditional relationship between successful playwrights and up-and-coming young actresses. I therefore gave this, to me, new young woman, what I took to be an amiable greeting, which I was later told turned out as nothing more warming than a curt nod.

Everybody sat down in tubular-steel chairs, like out-patients in a particularly badly organized hospital, opened their hundreds of pages, and started to read out loud. From the beginning of Part One to the end of Part Six – almost eight hours of it, cold, apparently listless and with the 1930s songs punctuating the reading from a very bad tape-machine. I have rarely felt so depressed.

The convention among actors nowadays is not to do anything so disgusting as 'to project' or 'emote' (in other words *act*) at a read-through. Instead they drone and mumble through the lines like a group of geriatric clergymen at an Anglican rest home. Any sort of facial expression, any kind of vocal inflexion, are alleged to put at risk the later application of intelligence, emotion and conviction, which rehearsal is supposed to bring to the part. The result is that read-throughs are a dread to the author and a painful bore to everyone else.

And then, as the torpor thickened, Cheryl started to read. She tried to follow the convention, I'll allow her that. But it is her strength – and her possible weakness – as an actress, not to be able to suppress an emotion. Even here, sitting on a stackable chair in a drab cavern, without rehearsal, and under the cold eyes of producer, director, writer and whoever, she could not altogether avoid making her voice tighten and loosen, her eyes moisten, her head bob and tilt.

These little dabs of feeling were like the first blotches of colour on a featureless canvas. I could feel my own anxiety and disappointment trickling away. Here was an Eileen without costume jewellery but made of real flesh and bone. It is always difficult when a playwright sees the first sketchy performance of an actor in a part which until then consists only of the loops and whirls of words on a page. Sometimes you can be appalled, but more often – thanks to the extremely high standards of acting in this country – you feel relief. But rarely does a writer feel, at once, and with certainty, that the lines he has sweated over have met their ideal configuration.

Cheryl Campbell has since shown in the central role of Vera in *Testament of Youth* (BBC2) that she is able to take the strain in a very different sort of part. She was on the screen a great deal of the time, but oddly enough, she was, for the greater slice of the action, reacting to other people and other events: a difficult and potentially thankless task. It is a rough and ready guide in the judgment of good acting to see the way a person *listens* rather than speaks. Bluestocking Vera had a lot to say – much of it smug and some of it very wet – but the most vital thing about her was the capacity to grow and widen her sensibilities.

It was this test which Cheryl Campbell passed triumphantly. I especially liked the scene of the women's debating society at Oxford, not just for the fine passion of the words she had to speak but also for the disappointment, arrogance and unwisely contemptuous superiority the character had to show when listening to others. Cheryl apparently played this scene when heavy with flu, but it was a much stronger virus that she was able to pass on: the sniffy bug called 'intellectualism.' The most noticeable thing about very clever people, after all, is *not* their wisdom.

I learnt about the flu when lunching with Cheryl a few days before Christmas.[371] A large party of people at the next table recognized her. They were coming to the end of their meal while we were still spooning out our avocados. I had met her for the purposes of this article, and in throwing out the usual who, what, where, when and hows of the crass interviewer type, I had inadvertently touched on some half-buried ganglion of pain in her. Instantly she showed distress, and I realized that she lives and works on that sharp and dangerous line between real personal feelings and the simulated passions of performance. She uses herself up in the way that many of the greatest artists in all the creative professions do.

For the moment, a few seconds only, the well of feeling in her threatened to break surface. Her eyes glittered with pain. The people at the adjoining table trooped out and one by one they stooped to congratulate her on 'your performance.'

'Thank you very much,' she said, like a little girl taking a prize.

It gave me time to return to less personal generalities. Cheryl Campbell is the least actressy actress I know, but there is something about her which makes you aware that feelings and emotions are more to her than mere projections and games in front of the lens. They are the stuff of more than dreams. Some actors suffer from the grievous fault of letting you know they *are* acting. Cheryl Campbell has the enormous virtue of making you think that she does not know the difference.

Potter rights
Broadcast, 6 October 1980

Sir,

What you call my 'passionate and hitherto unquestionable integrity' (*Broadcast*, 15 September)[372] is presented in the last paragraph of your article "What price Pennies from Hollywood?" rather in the manner of a poisoned apple. I think, however, that I must reject it. A single telephone call to me could easily have established the facts about *Pennies From Heaven*, MGM, BBC, NFT, and my own alleged collusion with the possibility that the six-part TV show might not be shown at the National Film Theatre retrospective of my television plays.

It is a possible argument to say that the author of something that has been shown on television should not then be allowed to sell the work to a film studio, whether here or in Hollywood. But as a professional writer with legitimate ambitions, inevitable anxieties, and a fair measure of what used to be called avarice, I'm afraid I do not find that line of reasoning particularly appealing.

Indeed, an option on the film rights was first acquired by a British film producer, who was instantly turned down by, apparently, everyone of consequence in the remaining segments of the British film industry. This was the first time I gained any real insight into what goes on over here when someone hopes to make a movie, and I vowed to do something about it.

I coaxed myself onto the Los Angeles plane, chain-smoked my way into whatever gilded sanctum I could get into, and eventually managed to sell the film rights to MGM. This is shorthand, of course, for a series of not always dignified adventures which, with suitable adjustments for a gender, might rival those of *Alice in Wonderland*. But I *did* emerge clutching something like a quarter of a million dollars and the outline of a contract – or, rather, my agent Judy Daish did, with an aplomb that did not fail to match my own, shall we say, hitherto innocent bravado.

As a result, MGM were to buy all the rights that were not already reserved, except the book rights that we were able to retain. Since the reserved rights obviously include the BBC's rights – which have not been sold, either to me or anyone else – there could be no interference with the television life of *Pennies* over here (and hence its repeat), or of the sales already made by BBC Enterprises and Time/Life anywhere else. As a TV series, indeed, the plays had been sold all around the world, and in America, and had already received as much exposure as I could have dared to hope. Incidentally, the BBC's licence in this country has already exhausted.

But MGM *insisted* that they would not complete the deal if any *further* sales were made. They did not want TV stations in America to buy and show the TV version on the wings of, and at the same time as, their own movie was being released. Such stations, after all, had *already* been offered the chance to buy the series. We checked directly with Time/Life in New York and were told, emphatically, that in the US 'the sales have peaked.' It has now been shown twice in Los Angeles, for example, and twice in New York.

Armed with this information, and conscious that the MGM deal was a nonstarter if no agreement with the BBC could be obtained, my agent went to BBC Enterprises with the plea to stop any further sales effort so that a British writer could take the chance of being hired to write a major Hollywood film. The BBC, after all, had got its full value out of the work. But someone at BBC Enterprises realized that I was in a corner. Yes, they said, we won't make any more foreign sales (knowing full well they weren't likely to anyway), so please give us $100,000 and half your further profits on the film. They actually asked for more, but this was their final demand.

Thus, contrary to your story, I have not bought any rights from the BBC, nor sought to limit their rights in this country. I have simply been forced to pay them what I think is something extortionate but which they consider to be fair compensation. Certainly, they have done well out of a set of scripts they were worried about in the first place.

MGM, as the purchaser of rights not already reserved, thus automatically has claims on the showing of the TV version in any *new* venue. I have no control in this matter, and I am not 'conniving' in anything. In my opinion, MGM should allow the NFT to show the series, and I have told them so. At this moment, the matter has not been settled, and I hope and trust that *Pennies* will be part of the retrospective. Herbert Ross, the director of the MGM film has also said that he has no objections to it being shown. The NFT, incidentally, has not once talked to me about the matter.

A final point: the MGM deal, and other scripts I have written for Hollywood this year, and the LWT deal which is in the process of being resuscitated, are part of what is turning out to be an exhausting strategy. The money gained is not going into my own pocket. I have ceased to be self-employed so that these sums go to PFH Ltd, which pays me a monthly salary. Partly as a result, and with the energy and commitment of my three other colleagues in the company, and because we are set upon changing what now happens within the British film and television industries, we plan to make the banned *Brimstone & Treacle* into a movie here in England in the spring. We are putting our money and our skills where our mouths are, and will work on this, the first of what will be an annual British movie, without fees or commissions.

You can question my integrity if you like, and you may even seek to tell me whether or not I am allowed to sell my own work, and I shall not be looking to swell a tight budget with money gained in the Courts. But no one who stands on the sideline is entitled to doubt the commitment of myself or my colleagues towards the British television or, now, film industries.

Yours faithfully,
Dennis Potter
Ross-on-Wyc

Writers' reading in 1981
Guardian, 10 December 1981

I have not been paid to review books, Clive James or television programmes this year, which has meant that I've enjoyed the first two industries much more, and the latter a great deal less. The book pleasing and troubling me most is the fat paperback edition of Ronald Hayman's *Nietzsche* (Quartet). A marvel of sympathetic exposition and quotation-larded richness, in which a life so full of suffering and a head so full of torment are scraped on to the pages according to the dangerous old philosopher's own formula: 'I have gradually come to understand what every great philosophy until now has been: the confession of its author and a kind of involuntary, unconscious memoir.'

Nothing involuntary and little unconscious about John Osborne's *A Better Class of Person* (Faber and Faber). An exhilaratingly nasty little fillet from his own crepitating shanks, where one discovers how to recycle used contraceptives and old malice. As H.G. Wells asked, 'Who would read novels if we could write autobiography flat out?'

I've also bought books by D. Owen and S. Williams of the helium-filled SDP (on my Access card, of course), but am half-afraid to open the glossy covers in case the pages are blank.

Pruning dead wood in *Gorky Park*
Sunday Times Magazine, 18 December 1983

The second thing which attracted me to *Gorky Park*[373] was that the smoothly unscrupulous and appallingly sadistic villain is graced with the name of John Osborne. More, and perhaps even better, the unwholesome little pathologist in the tale who so diligently hacksaws his way into the pickled flesh of long-dead bodies in order to discover only that which is already obvious is a man who is called Bernard Levin. Well, just Levin, to be honest; but a redundant forename could not chase away an image already so pleasingly lodged in my mind along with the congealed blood, crusted snow, pendulous icicles and wearily rhetorical slogans which characterize the prose styles of both those real-life luminaries, as well as the mood of the make-believe yarn.

As I trust I have already demonstrated, it is important for the hired writer to get purchase on as much totally irrelevant ill-will as possible when trying to operate from within the glittering coffins of the film business. There is no more potent aid to one's concentration and stubbornness than a little festering malice, decently obscured. All screenwriters bought by a Hollywood studio, especially if they are British, need to know from the very moment of signing their 60-page contracts how to make a nasty or subversive smirk appear as a smile of humble consent. I have noticed before that such moral and facial contortions are a trick of the colonialized, by no means confined to BBC newsreaders.

But the main reason why I wanted to write the film of *Gorky Park* was not the accidental delights of nomenclature.

The fat book had waddled its way into the bestseller lists with something much sleeker and faster locked inside it. The story seemed to me to have hit smack in the middle of a familiar, much loved, and cinematically very useful *genre*: the steadfastly incorruptible detective unravelling apparently complex homicides against all the odds, while at the same time successfully pretending to be something much more exotic, even to the extent of political and psychological profundity. It was the sort of book, in other words, in which the scalpel that has to be used in any movie adaptation of a prose original could for once be employed to get down to real bone and healthy marrow at the expense of the flaccidly obese. On much the same principle, for instance, you could lay hold of a good 10-minute cartoon from any of the fictions of the late Professor Tolkien – whereas *The Pilgrim's Progress* would surely need at least six episodes. And, even then, the advertisements in between would have to do some of the work.

The story begins with the fortuitous discovery of three rock-hard bodies embedded in the snow and ice of Moscow's Gorky Park. Their faces and finger-tips have been sliced away, thus removing what appear to be the only remaining points of identification. Enter brooding Arkady Renko, the splendidly old-fashioned hero, a brave and sometimes properly sardonic Soviet Militia officer who has preserved the stars of high rank on his shoulder-boards despite an unwise indifference to official ideology and a previous near-lethal entanglement with his sartorially smarter rivals in the KGB.

He then unravels the homicidal puzzles at great danger to himself (though, as is usual in these stories, even more to his friends) by means of unpicking a few of the seams which hold the red tarpaulin down over the higher reaches of Moscow society. And in the process, of course, he meets, falls in love, contends with, and, as surely as Lenin did not make little apples, duly beds the most ravishingly beautiful girl to be found on either side of the Urals.

Play "Lover Come Back To Me" on a smokey piano instead of "Black Eyes" on a plangent balalaika; shift 'The Soviet Union – The Hope of the World' off its block-long banner and replace it with on-off neon and an equally excessive claim on behalf of, say, Lucky Strike cigarettes; let a few Russian syllables squeeze out of the side of a tightening mouth, and the lineage of the hero becomes even more obvious. 'It's Philip Marlowe in Moscow,' I said, almost succeeding in striking a match against my thumbnail, 'and down those mean streets I must go.'

A few glasses of wine can turn a man into a posturing fool quicker than the deliberate wiggle of an accidentally pretty girl. But it was not raining in the foothills and the Californian sun was beating down on the billboards under the rat-infested palm trees: 'Groman's Mortuaries: One Call Takes Care of All Your Needs,' and other things just as nice to know. I was lunching at the Country Club with a producer who was propositioning me, trying to hold on to my wits while forking some rubble out of an omelette that was endeavouring to be an egg pudding.

Howard Koch Jr. and his then partner Gene Kirkwood had apparently put down a huge amount of their money to acquire the screen 'and ancillary' rights of a book that had sat as emphatically on the top of the bestseller lists as Cyril Smith would have to on a bidet. The fact that they *said* they had mortgaged their own substantial homes to make possible the purchase did not necessarily mean this was not true. Either way, they were for the while marooned on that narrow strand in the pre-production of 'a property' where 'the writer' of the potential screenplay has maximum power. That is, there was as yet no studio putting its wide outta-my-way shoulders and its wet mouth where its money was. There was no twitchy director on board. No star actor to be coddled. No pages to maul.

It was time for me to start snapping hard eyes behind my mild spectacles, right here and now, right across the table. I demanded an armagnac. And then a whole series of major changes in both the narrative and the emotional textures of the proposed film as compared with the book, trying to tip a shaggy borsalino hat, Chandleresque, at a pair of snappy alligator shoes under the table which could all too easily have turned back into the bloodied jaws of the original beast.

The tone of voice I am using here is not, perhaps, quite so irritatingly trivial as its haplessly derivative style might suggest. For the style I am both mocking and celebrating is being called up to represent what I considered to be the most crucial decisions that ought to be taken about the film before a word of dialogue got on to the page. Get the floor plans all askew, and the building will always be the wrong shape. I was at that time (the summer of 1981) seeing what was happening to *Pennies from Heaven* at MGM, a film of considerable virtues and some courage which was nevertheless diligently subverting itself on just those basic questions of style or inner coherence.

I have always loved working within the shell of familiar conventions (fairy tale, detective story, spy drama, musical romance) and then seeing whether it was possible to punch a few holes in the carapace. There are many advantages to be gained by a play or a film which first of all concentrates itself on being one thing in particular, and then discovers, almost to its surprise, that the irony, grace and metaphors of something wider have smuggled themselves back into the frame. Thus, the purpose of my so quickly bandying the name of Philip Marlowe around as though I had put my legs up on his desk was to give point to the conditions I somehow contrived to lay before accepting the commission. I was very anxious to get the job, but I made it 'break point' if the producers would not agree to let me leave out all the New York stuff, and that which immediately precedes it in the book.

For it was here – in the last third of the novel – that a crackingly good yarn tried and, in my opinion failed, to inflate itself up into another category of fiction. What looked to be in sharp focus in Moscow suddenly blurred into a babble in New York. Worse, the film would have stopped, and then started all over again, breaking its own back in what in any case would be a foredoomed attempt to make cinematic sense of the mash of prose the novel had suddenly become.

What we surely needed was a city-in-the-head. A mythic Moscow, shorn of onion-domes, Kremlin, and all those things which make films of a certain kind show the Eiffel Tower to mean 'we are in Paris now.' A paranoid Moscow, with lethal mysteries eddying down long grey streets, and the cold breath of shuttered or frightened souls hanging against the cold glass of the air. Not Reagan's capital of all the evil in the world, not a political parable from an American angle, but a city for a classic detective. A Soviet Marlowe or Spade or Archer, but aware of none of them... I got my way: I was hired. And delivered a script within a month.

A year later, after two potential directors had come and gone, and after Koch and Kirkwood had been turned down by studio after studio (without once abandoning me, even when invited to do so), I heard from Howard Koch that we had at last got a green light from Orion. And that my compatriot Michael Apted was to be the director.

Second Draft. Third Draft. Revised Third Draft. Revised Revised Third Draft. Revised Revised Revised Third Draft. Final Draft...Revised Final. The Americans, who are bloody ignorant in matters of spelling, use the same letters for this giddy process as (perhaps appropriately) they do for a wayward eddy of air coming through the cracks in the walls. I felt I was in the middle of more of these so-called 'drafts' than there are in an abandoned cowshed in a blustery March. Naturally, I was sufficiently churlish to think degeneration rather than improvement was taking place.

Meanwhile, Dustin Hoffman was passed over for the lead, apparently because he had held out for too much money: probably about enough to keep the National Health Service afloat for another month or so. And I didn't like the way Michael Apted pointedly did not look at me when more than once using the term 'arty-farty' about certain sorts of stage direction. But he was more often right than not, even when he was, so to speak, wrong. Apted does not come across upon first acquaintance as an assertive man – at least not in the way the term is used as an euphemism for downright bullying. Yet he refused to allow the basic structure to buckle, occasionally stood between me and assorted muggers, and got much of his own way by a curiously languid mixture of politeness, diffidence, convoluted persistence and a pretended and strategic 'bewilderment' when under pressure which at first irritated, then amused, and finally impressed.

Six months later, with odd 'drafts' still rustling a page here and there, camp had been established in Helsinki, the cold and melancholy substitute for a forbidden Moscow. January had come in wet and dank, and Howard Koch paddled about the *ersatz* city in a beard, a snuffle of a head cold, and moon-boots, rather like a distraught astronaut. It looked as though the three bodies at the start of the story would have to be dug out of mud rather than snow and ice.

I am always secretly a little pleased when the guns of heaven are suddenly trained on all our scrabbling enterprises, but even this degree of perversity had to give way to a more wholesome relief when the skies turned white. By the time I arrived for the rehearsals, every vista was a Christmas card, and the air was so cold it cut off your face.

A frozen zygomaticus is no bad thing, when making first acquaintance with *some* actors. It is easier to suppress incredulity and amusement when your cheeks have just been flayed by a bitter wind: but no power on earth will stop my eyes taking on a Wedgwood glaze when I am forced to listen to the anxious monologues of the New York school of acting, which are mostly about 'motivation' and 'space' and what the character's grandfather's second cousin was likely to have eaten for breakfast. 'Christ Almighty,' said one of the British crew about one of our stars, 'if you had to live with him you'd lock yourself in the bleedin' khazi.' When a film unit is on location for a long time in foreign parts it tends to resemble too many of one's memories of National Service. In wintering Finland there were shoe-leather reindeer steaks on the menu, live bears in the rehearsal rooms pretending to be human beings, and (most intolerable of all) every other person in the frozen streets looked exactly like David Hare.

Unthawed, unentertained, and simmering with obscure rages, I decided that I needed actual fisticuffs, and cravenly picked on an elderly little Finn with a withered arm who was quietly singing what sounded like a Wesleyan hymn[374] to himself in the far corner of a swanky glass and chrome bar. But he insisted on being friendly. 'I swear to God you must be Irish,' reiterated the huge and amiable Irish-American actor Brian Dennehy, mistaking occasional rhetoric and frequent booze for

293

the bloodline of his own miserable tribe. I simply could not make him understand that he was insulting me. 'No, no,' he would repeat, as one cold day cracked against another, 'they must have swapped you in your cradle.' I like it when people like me.

Americans tell jokes about the Poles in the same wretched way that we do about the Irish. A film business quip, which says a lot about the status of screenwriters over there, asks, 'Have you heard about the actress who wanted to use her bed to further her career? She slept with a writer.' Ho ho. And the hollow laugh stayed rather speculatively in my mind as I cast a gleaming eye across the dinner table at the beautiful Polish actress Joanna Pacula, who was playing The Girl in the picture. But no, she'd heard the joke too.

The cast of *Gorky Park* are not in every case the kind of people you would want to share a rowing boat with; and at least one of them has his paddles almost permanently out of the water. (I also like it when people don't like me.) But in performance there is not one weak link. Whatever else may be said by others about the film, I do not think that anyone can seriously argue that its tone, its style is inconsistent. It has the drive and the energy and the confidence of an earlier Hollywood, and I am grateful that Howard Koch and Michael Apted protected as much of the script (and all of the original design) as they did.

Lee Marvin and Brian Dennehy turn in the kind of performances that used to make one want to queue up on a Monday night outside some great cavern of a cinema; Joanna duly sizzles even with her clothes on, and a host of British character actors again show that easy skill which is one of the glories of our nation. 'Is this what you want? Or this? Or *this*?' they say, without once talking about 'the space around me.'

William Hurt, as Arkady, was always doomed to be a star because the cameras love him so. He gets to where he wants to be by the most circuitous route it is possible to imagine. And just as some stars are obscured by the dust veils of outer space, and are traced only by an infrared detector picking out the radiation from the cold masses of gas, so I lacked the right sort of equipment to penetrate what seemed to be the similar aura around Hurt. On the screen, though, my obtuseness does not matter: he is the bone and blood of the part, which for my purposes is all that counts.

'I like your performance, Bill,' I unctioned as I left Helsinki, aware that a sort of pillar in the lobby of the hotel was not quite hiding me after all. It was necessary to say something, and it helped to be able to tell the absolute truth.

'Yes,' he said, his pale eye switching about, 'but what is your motive?'

In the slithering taxi on the way to the airport, snow pressing softly against the windows, the inevitable *esprit d'escalier* provided my response. But I swallowed it down, for the entire phrase consisted only of two monosyllabic words.

Two other words, equally abrupt, summon up for me the last injunction out of the process that had begun with Philip Marlowe bending my inner ear across a Los Angeles lunch-table: see it. The only thing about the film which I truly regret is that I changed the wicked Osborne's first name from John to Jack.

Introduction
Tender is the Night by F. Scott Fitzgerald
The Folio Society, 1987

There are some, and few, moments in one's life which stand out so clearly from the surrounding murmurs of the ordinary that they throw back light on all that has gone before and cast forward a glow upon everything which is yet to come. The illumination may become faint as the years pass, sinking down like a guttering candle into little more than a fugitive burnish occasionally gleaming on the dustier surfaces of memory, but it is still there, still capable of unexpected rescue.

An old song tinkling out of the heavily draped recesses of the mind, or a sudden glimpse of the way a stranger threads a passage through the traffic, or the wayward drift across the senses of the transient odours released in the silent cry of a crushed flower, can retrieve or revivify the apparently lost moment. And so, too, by diligence and talent, by holding steady as the words break on the rim of discovery, does good writing reach back and stretch forward into those especial resonances or particular epiphanies. The lattice of words, spiked and dotted in a fence of letters, seems then to dissolve into the very substance of what is being described: to become the emotion itself, and to be the light, catching at the skeeter, and grasping it forever.

Tender is the Night has its share of flaws and irritations but it is marvellously full of just such moments. The book is, of course, entire to itself, making its own spangle across the chapters of invented lives. Behind it, though, burns another set of images, a great banked-down fire upon which a blue flame intermittently curls and flickers, ready to burst into more vigorous tongues. The crackle and the fizz, the blaze and the ash, of F. Scott Fitzgerald's own career.

The moon shines over Alabama much as it does anywhere else on the slumbering globe, but whether it is made of antique silver or of mouldering cheese depends less upon where you are standing than on what is whispering in your head. The heavens themselves were a projection of his own self-conscious apprehensions of glory when Scott Fitzgerald first set eyes on 18-year-old Zelda Sayre at the country club dance in Montgomery. A lovely girl with grey-blue eyes and a glint of devilment on her. He, too, was as fresh as paint in his spankingly new American officer's uniform. It was the long, late summer of 1918. She smiled and she sparkled and he danced inside. A literary legend was already in the making.

'Every emotion and any life work decided,' he wrote for himself, pinioning butterflies into the reflecting glass case of his imagination. 'Miserable and ecstatic, but a great success.'

Fame and fortune had begun to play their seductive tunes in silken chords. Zelda was going to be light and joyous on the bone of his arm, and the injured old world shone once again to every horizon. The ingredients are all there, in a heady mix, for the Life and Times of a leading character in a Hollywood biopic, with ragtime accompaniments.

But one of the many bad things they do not tell you about the citadel of tinsel, where much later a by now frightened F. Scott Fitzgerald dowsed his talent in the bottom of a highball, is that the peculiar rustling noise occasionally to be heard in the raggedy palm trees of Hollywood (even on a blue night with no whisper of wind) is actually the sound of long-tailed rats crunching up their food, or each other, while perched safely high above the untrodden sidewalks: not all rodents, it seems, are to be found moistening their pink eyes in a scrabble of false sentiment behind walnut desks in the head offices of the film studios.

Similarly, if one were to force a queasy connection, the tantalizing scatter of jewelled reflections on the sun-soaked waters off Fitzgerald's earlier and happier Cap d'Antibes owes at least a little to the beckoning glint of light refracting back from unbiodegradable specks of nastier matter, disgorged by means of pipes too old and, alas, too short, from kitchens and bathrooms further along the mimosa-clad coast.

Glamour, so-called, rarely stands up to any such hard-eyed inspection. Those who come to seek the high polish of it above all else should not be too surprised to discover that the winking bubbles at the brim eventually burst at the back of the throat with the taste of some much more bitter juice. Scott Fitzgerald usually knew this when he was holding a skein of words, but often went and forgot it when he was holding a glass in his hand. It made him – 'the chronicler of the Jazz Age' – the witness, the recorder, of waste.

Half accidentally, half in dread premonition, and yet with a limpid grace, *Tender is the Night* shadows, duplicates, comments upon, approaches, evades, his own avid search for glory, his own confidences and despairs, his own closeness as a witness to the fractures of madness, and his own seemingly inexorable collapse into driblets of remorse and torrents of an even harder stuff: the kind you empty down your throat.

'Everything I have ever done or written is me...' Fitzgerald once insisted in a letter to his increasingly fretful agent. There is a slightly suspicious bravado to the claim, which also manages to edge towards the plaintive. Both are needed, perhaps, when you are standing with a giddy swirl of yearning on a perilously tilting crate of emptying hopes in order to reach for, and reach and reach for, the golden apples on the overspreading bough. The trembling fingers and the unsustainable posture, so to speak, of a brilliant man who was able to keep his eyes open in the middle of his own slow nightmare, but who upon waking into the swifter clamour of morning imagines the receding dream to have been so much sweeter than it really was. As sweet, maybe, as the silver of moonlight on the inviting lips of the upturned face of the loved one. The dance band plays its muffled syncopations in the distant ballroom. Echoes bounce off the polished floor. Tunes die in the silky air. And then the words, trying to gather up what has already gone, take on unexpected tensions. The bad dream insists upon its reality...

Fitzgerald was puzzled, hurt, and scared to the bone by the relative commercial failure of *Tender is the Night* in America, where stories about failure always threaten to taint the native dream of the proper order of things. He did not try to apportion any blame, but he might well have wondered what had happened to the once so eager throngs of admiring readers. *Tender is the Night*, after all, was the novel which had come the hardest to him, bearing his most vivid hopes, and which, in shape and detail, had been the closest to his own marrow.

He had worked and picked at it, on and off, for a considerable part of his maturity. Piling up the words, cutting them, adding, cutting again. Shifting and sifting, putting aside, and going back to with differing resolves, and perpetually brooding upon it as the events and people around him seemed to partake of the stuff of his own text. When Fitzgerald at last delivered it up – perhaps better say, let it go – he demonstrated the sort of exhaustion which has the disconcerting habit of masquerading as triumph.

One particular image for all this can be excavated from a few sentences in the book. Dick Diver, the spiritually doomed hero of the novel, is shown to us – and to the watching eyes of a beautiful young film actress – raking the sand on the exclusive stretch of beach in front of the basking, suitably rose-coloured hotel where money speaks to money across the marbled spaces. He is wearing a jockey cap, and moving the rake gravely, up and down, 'ostensibly removing gravel and meanwhile developing some esoteric burlesque held in suspension by his grave face.'

The manner, the action, for me irresistibly suggest the picture of Fitzgerald himself, raking over his own prose. Rills and ridges on both the white page and tan-coloured beach, waiting to take the imprint of golden bodies, languorous and indolent, but calling across to each other. And then, when the sun has gone down in the tide of its own vermilion, or inspiration has momentarily withdrawn, and a wind stirs and frets from across the now darkening sea, the obdurate sand of grainy imagining needs to be raked all over again.

Years he worked upon it, this stretch at the rim of his talent, until the words heaped themselves up against the breakwater in almost unmanageable drifts. Long after it was supposedly finished, by now half-submerged in the tepid channels of its initial reception, Fitzgerald continued to nag himself about the novel's structure.

As first published (and in this edition), *Tender is the Night* opens on that dazzling strand between the rose-coloured hotel and Cannes, five swanking miles away. 'Now, many bungalows cluster near it, but when this story begins only the cupolas of a dozen old villas rotted like water lilies among the massed pines...' The cork is pulled on a richly seductive vintage, and the senses cannot but respond at once to the especial bouquet. But there is also something else at work, drawn from deeper down, mingling with that first fine savour, threatening the taste of dankness, and redolent of that which has already faded. You are gradually made aware of premonitions and echoes, or, rather, of a sort of stealthy tension silkily stretching between the two. A sense of mystery is gathering itself together like mere wisps and tatters of cloud far out over the glistening bay, by no means certain to move inland, and not yet much of a threat to these first few figures disporting themselves on the fringe of the golden land.

Dick and Nicole Diver – the one to fall, the other to rise – are glimpsed at an angle and at one remove in the full flush of their strangely hypnotic charm. A happy and entrancing couple, it seems, with their due retinue of admirers and the excluded outer-ring of the fascinated and envious. The witness – soon to be drawn in – is the newcomer to the beach, the young actress Rosemary Hoyt.

Rosemary falls asleep in the sun, and her valuable young skin begins to broil. When she awakes – and it happens in at least one fairy tale – the beach is deserted, except for Dick Diver. Everyone has gone in to luncheon, with its blaze of silver and flashes of white linen, and even the rake has been stowed away in a rock crevice. 'It's not a bad time,' he says to her. 'It's not one of the worst times of the day.' The phrasing, the style, not much to go on, are nevertheless instantly the man. Dick Diver has stepped out of the haze – and she falls for 'the bright blue worlds' of his eyes as quickly as she would in one of the plots of her silly films. Indeed, there are always disconcerting moments in any Fitzgerald story which seem to belong in a bad movie: one of the reasons why other writers feel so fondly about his work.

When people call into question the true quality of Fitzgerald as a writer, and falter upon this or that reservation before venturing any genuinely confident measure of his stature, I would point to an ample number of exceptionally compelling or at times almost magically luminous passages in *The Great Gatsby* and *Tender is the Night*. Sumptuous prose not quite holding back more febrile anxieties. One such passage is this opening sequence on the beach, which so deftly uses a predilection for the baroque and the romantic to do and to reveal so many more things than the purely functional one of setting the time and place.

'– when this story begins…' chimes the cadence in the first few lines, an old manner of implying a properly chronological narrative. Years later, though, Fitzgerald was at pains to persuade himself that he had put this opening paragraph in the wrong place. The *true* beginning – to use his own emphasis – sits much further on in the novel: Book Two, in fact, at the psychiatric clinic near Zurich, where young Doctor Richard Diver meets impossibly rich Nicole Warren for the first time.

We already know when we reach this place, going forward in pagination but backward on the calendar, that there is something wrong with the magical couple. The high-gloss glamour of the Divers and the charm of their company, their good looks and money and grace and magnetism, are threaded with other things, and threatened. An unknown or undefined darkness, even an evil, lies coiled in waiting, ready to seep into all the crystalline spaces between the laughter, the brittle chatter, the tinkling tunes and the chink of the glasses. Certain warning asides and a few bizarre incidents, graphic but nevertheless puzzling and ominously incomplete, have opened up alarming fissures in the glittering surfaces. Unease is quickening the nerve of the story. The innocent eyes of the first observers cannot remain the dominant perspective. We are to be pulled back to the source of the mystery, to probe at last at the suppurating root of the ache.

It is 1917: a wise time to be in Switzerland. The world beyond the clean mountains is bloodily engulfed by more than the usual quota of madness. The young doctor, who has a different sort of glory in his sights, laughs off the idea that the carnage is a threat to him. He enjoys 'the illusion of eternal strength and health, and of the essential goodness of people.' The muffled note of bitterness is a later comment, an 'editorial' interjection. Such overt interventions are rare, and oddly unsettling. Whenever they occur, the portrait of Dick Diver momentarily blurs then reforms as a reflection of Scott Fitzgerald at one of the times when he was awash with depression, anxiety, or weariness.

Dick goes off to the war, clad in a spankingly new American uniform that makes him feel like a fraud. As he leaves the haven of the clinic, there is a chance encounter with a young girl who is 'about the prettiest thing I ever saw.' And yet this crucial first encounter between Dick Diver and Nicole Warren virtually takes place in a gap between paragraphs, so to speak. It is all but thrown away in the form of later and reported speech. The echoes of the way Scott Fitzgerald met Zelda in the country club are deadened a little: but the prettiest thing he ever saw, author and fictional creation both, flitting so briefly across a few spikes of conversation on the page, is a wounded creature, wife and fictional creation both. "Poor Butterfly", as the song has it, with a blue sob on the saxophone. We are tipped, then, into the notes for a psychiatric case study: a shift in style which can hardly be accidental.

The perpetual reworkings of the novel, as well as the many opposing moods or ambitions which prevailed during the separated bursts and crawls of its composition, have undoubtedly left their scars. Even the most generous critic, to say nothing of the patient reader, would have to concede that there is upon occasion a feeling of incompleteness about particular scenes. A doubt which hangs over more than just the chronological structure of the book.

So marked a characteristic is this, indeed, that one is perversely tempted into the fond exasperation of asserting that *Tender is the Night* is a great novel because rather than in spite of such an apparent failing. You get the sense, while reading it, that there are cupboards or even rooms in the edifice, or places just off the page, into which you are invited to look and then almost absent-mindedly not shown. The decorators are still around, the pastel-dipped brushes are still soaking in the pot, and the plaster needs to be replaced in that far, dark corner.

Far from being damaging, the effect is to draw us into the feelings of ambivalence and tension in a way that stays open and unresolved in the mind. As Dick Diver loses his glory, he appears to recede from the centre of the narrative. Nicole's growing strength is taken directly from him, it seems: and yet this is also shown not to be the case. The romantic prose, brilliant in its evocations, bumps against hidden reefs. It almost flounders. The struggle and the sadness reach out beyond the style and the structure of the narrative. The reader who is prepared to acknowledge this, and to use a responding concern or imagination, will be rewarded at deeper levels than is usual in the literature of our times.

Such a response, if given, will also allow a more direct access to the author himself, who in later years was reduced to insisting in a humiliating emphasis to a Hollywood director that he was, really was, a good writer. *Tender is the Night* is about waste, but never about indignity of this order. A wise reader, perhaps, will permit himself at least one small shudder of recognition to temper the many beauties offered by the flowing sentences.

It would not only be vulgar in the bad, wet-mouthed way, but also factually incorrect to draw out too close a symmetry between F. Scott Fitzgerald and the subsequently troubled Zelda, and Dick Diver with the dazzling young schizophrenic, Nicole. But such proper scruples cannot allow one to deny that *Tender is the Night* takes on an extra poignancy when laid against the turmoils of Fitzgerald's own life. The man himself casts first a long, then a shortening, and then once again a lengthening shadow across the page. The reader comes to feel like a solitary walker whose shoes ring on the stones as he approaches, comes alongside, and then passes the fluttering glow of a single street lamp. But shine it does. Oh, yes, it shines.

Writers' attitudes to wealth creation
Independent, 17 June 1987

Sir,

In jerry-building his conjecture on Friday about 'why' some writers abhor Thatcherism,[375] Stephen Glover may perhaps have been right to cast me as a peripheral and alienated figure with a twisted morality. Even so, it seems unduly impertinent of him to demand that I should keep my mouth shut until my observations more closely coincide with his own.[376]

The *Observer* had asked me to say in about a hundred words how I would vote, and why. I said I would choose Labour, but 'without a song in my heart or a plastic rose in my lapel.' A relative lack of enthusiasm because the party still has much to do to move to one-member-one-vote, cleanse the London Labour Party, and drive off or at least diminish the worst of its hard-left boneheads.

I love my country dearly, and the poll has been a tragedy for it, as I think events will gradually reveal. I hope that I am wrong. Glover is under the impression that such painful opinions are casually thrown off, and that writers like myself do not have much knowledge of how people create wealth, 'or much interest in that process.'[377] How does he know this? 'Money,' he says in a gross and foolish parody, 'is something which is given to the poor, or earned in large quantities, but it should not be much talked about.'

I *have* earned a lot from around the world, by working exceptionally hard in the teeth of a chronic and frequently disabling illness. My talent has been my privilege. Out of my work, I pay myself a high salary. The majority of what I earn is put to other uses, employing other people. Perhaps your Mr Glover would care to find out what goes on under my other hat?

It is true, though, that up until 1964, I *was* engaged in a frivolous, unproductive trade, spun of casual opinions and glib assumptions, ignorant of the real world and its travails; I was a journalist.

Yours faithfully,
Dennis Potter
Ross-on-Wye
Herefordshire

The John Dunn Show
Interviewed by John Dunn
BBC Radio 2, 13 December 1989

DUNN: Well, the first programme [of *Blackeyes*],[378] I think, had the largest BBC2 audience of any programme except Wimbledon this year.[379]

POTTER: Really? Oh, I didn't know that.

DUNN: Are you gratified about that?

POTTER: Yes and no. I wonder what some of them…the reasons why the audience was large. It may well have been due to some of the tabloid publicity beforehand, and that eager, wet-mouthed salacious way in which they latch on to what they think is a play about sex or 'bonking' – in the words of the *Sun*[380] – may well have induced people to come to it and then recoil from it. But *Blackeyes needs* its reaction, like a buckle on a belt. Because if I'm dealing with male sexuality, the way men, even decent men, are colluding with the commerciality of sexuality, every poster, every image… If a woman undressing is used to sell a mortgage or a piece of cheese or goodness knows what, these vibrating, whispering, susurrating, sensual images which come at us, come at us for a reason which is, alas, what the male mind is more like than people acknowledge. And what I wanted people to do was enter, even complicitly, into that, even to share in that, in order to show what it is like, what happens.

DUNN: What sort of reaction have you had? OK, a lot has been written about it and you say the tabloids may not have got the right end of the stick.

POTTER: Well, not just the tabloids. I feel as though I've just pushed a stick into a hornets' nest, you know, and you suddenly...clench against the action. What disturbs me and what is odd about it, to me, is the intensely personal reaction, as though it's me, me, me.

DUNN: Mmm. Well, it is very largely, isn't it?

POTTER: No...but I don't know – isn't a piece of work to be judged on its own terms? I mean, I've even had people like *Time Out* making a delicate reference to my physical condition, but then said he can't hide the fact that he's 'crippled inside.'[381] And then, *City Limits* said, he deals with very unpleasant themes because he's got a very 'unpleasant personality.'[382] People are suddenly showing their reaction, which shows that they're agitated by it. That agitation is what it's about. What depresses me is that the odd good review isn't actually dealing with what, I think, [*Blackeyes*] is dealing with.

DUNN: But are you concerned that people are confused about it? I have to admit that I am confused about it, and if I hadn't read about it...

POTTER: Yes, it depends on the nature of the confusion. It depends on whether the confusion is just that of irritation and washing your hands of it and saying, 'Oh God, this is too difficult and I won't deal with it,' or whether that... People say two things, don't they, normally: they say, 'No, I don't watch much television, it's anodyne, it's pap, it doesn't ask anything of you, it's wallpaper,' all that; and then there are the other ones who say, 'Oh, it's confusing, it's difficult,' where all that goes on. Well, I know that the people who run television, in general, tend by exactly this lifetime's habit, of assuming that people are...I'm not talking about IQs. I'm not talking about education, or anything. I believe that people work things out. I mean, there's nothing more complex than living a life, and we do that. We have all sorts of series of images bombarding us about our memories of our past, about our sexual desires, about our fears of death, illness, bereavement, whatever it is. We've got this huge *thing* going on that we deal with by a series of images, memories, recollections, hopes, what have you. And I have always believed that that screen in most living rooms could reflect some of that.

DUNN: But do you think you were wise, honestly (*POTTER laughs*) because you've written it, you've narrated it, you've directed it – which is the most important probably of those three, in this context. Do you not think it would have been a good idea if somebody else had directed it, because then they would have come to it freshly, because you're so close to it?

POTTER: It might have been, it's not for me to say that it wouldn't be a good idea, but I couldn't have asked another director to take on the risks that I was taking, where you've got all four main characters [who] are alone. Nobody relates to anyone except physically and commercially. There are no feelings except those which the world gives us: so that the old man in his loft, the supposed writer of the novel...the niece Jessica in her mews flat, alone; the man watching her across the way, alone; Blackeyes, alone in every sense of the word. So, that alienation, that emptiness, that 3am feeling, you know...most people at some time will wake and feel, 'What is it all about? Nobody gets me. Nobody understands.' And you deliver these little pellets of conversation to each other and yet under it who knows what sort of aches and anguishes, what sort of pictures you have in your head.

DUNN: Can you be objective about it? Can you look at it now?

POTTER: I don't know. Can you be objective about any 'work...I daren't... use the word...I'll put quotes around it – any 'work of art'? Is one meant to be objective? Has television so corrupted us in its saying, 'That is the world out there. That is the sort of documentary realistic style. Looking through your window is like looking into the set.' That used to be the old phrase: 'Television is the window on the world.' What has objectivity got to do with it? If something is about feeling emotion, alienation, that emptiness of the spirit – which is a very difficult thing to try to do – in the end, one will have an objective judgment. When all four [episodes] have done and you can look at them, maybe...if it has any effect on anyone at all, and you think about it or digest it or react to it, then maybe that is a sort of objectivity. But the claim that it's like a documentary in any sort of way, or naturalistic, or 'realistic' in any sort of way, is not one that I ever want to entertain.

DUNN: You sound depressed about it.

POTTER: I'm probably in an almost terminal state of depression! First of all, in a few weeks time it will be 25 years since my first television play, film, call it what you will. And there's been something about the level of reaction to this [*Blackeyes*], which is making me feel... They wouldn't say it about a film. They wouldn't say it about a stage play. The very people who are crying and shouting and shrieking about how much pap there is on television, turn with an extraordinary degree of venom – as it seems to me, in my down state, receiving it – upon a piece that is asking something of the viewer, to give back to it and to say, 'Is that true of you? Are you like that? Do you have any of those feelings in your head?' And for the first time in that 25 years, I have to honestly admit that this is probably the end of my television career...

DUNN: Really?

POTTER: Because I do feel extraordinarily...not affronted, but a sense of weariness about... If that is the case, [television] is not any longer my medium.

DUNN: I think, apart from your depressions of the moment – and one hopes that they will pass, obviously, because I'm a fervent admirer of yours – when it's reshown, and I only hope it's reshown fairly soon...

POTTER: Well I wish it could be shown a night...each episode...

DUNN: Yes, that would be good. But without the ballyhoo beforehand, because everybody was told what a sexy show it was going to be and everything, before it actually hit the screen. I think, if it can be shown again, when all that's died down and you can actually see it and perhaps having had the advantage of having seen it once before, I think it will have a totally different reaction.

POTTER: Well, I hope you're right, obviously. I'm half grinning and half weeping! I don't know how to react, you know. Maybe it's the fact that I've had a couple of drinks (*Laughter.*) but I've had this feeling. It comes like a mist. It comes out. If you have spent what is such a long time believing in the possibilities of a common culture on the TV screen, believing that you could actually get over the heads of people who say, 'Oh, people are stupid, people are this, that and the other,' when I *know* they're not…and then you get that shrieking of 'Dirty Den'…[383] I feel as though I'm covered in pubic hair or something. I feel that people are not dealing with the essential loneliness, alienation, sexual imperiousness, the maleness of manipulation, and of commercial manipulation of our sexual feelings.

DUNN: I wonder if you can put those images on the screen and then expect people to react to them in a way differently to…

POTTER: Well, it appears that I can't but I thought that I could. I wanted to. I hoped to.

DUNN: But what about the directing side of it? Because this is also your debut as a director. Did you enjoy that? Was that something you'd wanted to do for some time?

POTTER: I had wanted to, but variously – partly fear, mostly health… I started shooting on February 6th and I finished in the last week of July, and I've been editing since. I had been a recluse. I'd been hidden – unnecessarily, perhaps – in myself, away, and then suddenly I had to deal with this enormous swamp of people, and colleagues' demands, questions…and when, on the very first day in the studio, when I first shouted…whispered…croaked 'Action!' and every face turned and nobody did anything, I thought, well… In fact I'd actually shouted at the wrong time! But from then on, as the fear began to slightly fall away, I found it exhilarating and emancipating. I felt I was directly plugging into my own imagination, and I was dealing with more people in, say, a two week period, than I'd dealt with in a 20 year period. And it was exhilarating to me.

DUNN: You'd worked, obviously, with directors, as a writer, so you knew everything that they did, in theory…

POTTER: Sure, but…

DUNN: …but what were the things that surprised you when you actually got the job?

POTTER: Well, partly the physical energy needed. The decision-making on every tiny thing. I had reacted against the normal way of shooting – the barbed wire fence of medium shot, close shot, two shot, reverse shot – which I hated, because everything looks the same, whether it's *Dallas* or the latest movie. And I'm interested in the relationship between the form of a thing and the way it looks and what it is trying to say, so I was trying to get an alienating effect. In Episode Two last week, for example, there was one shot that was nine-and-a-half minutes long, unedited.

DUNN: Really?

POTTER: That needs an immense choreography of camera and lighting, but rightly or wrongly, that's what I... There was no point in me doing it unless it was in the way I wanted to do it, and having waited so long and watched so much and thought about it so much, I wanted to show the relationship between the way we see things and the way we think.

DUNN: Nine-and-a-half minutes.

POTTER: Yes.

DUNN: Gosh. That's a huge demand.

POTTER: Well, a magazine of film only lasts ten minutes. It wasn't an attempt to make that length. It happened to be that length, at the end of the shot in the mortuary between the policeman and the advertising owner...

DUNN: Colin Jeavons.

POTTER: Colin Jeavons, playing Jamieson... It just happened to last that length of time. There was no cut in it, because I wanted to go from that claustrophobic, horrible feeling – you know, 'There is death... there is a young woman...she's dead'...and it's a familiar headline, 'Young model kills herself' – on one side of it death and the other sweet music, with a near-pornographic copulation in between to place exactly those images in their contexts. You see lots of simulated lovemaking on films and TV and I just wanted to put it into its context, to make one recoil in exactly the way that some people did, but they then go on to editorialize about it. In other words they won't wait 10 seconds to deliver their little pellet of opinion.

DUNN: What about the illness? You said that was in a way what had stopped you from directing in the past...

POTTER: Well, simply as a matter of physical facts it stops...

DUNN: So how have you managed to conquer it now?

POTTER: By taking methotrexate every weekend, which is a cytotoxic drug. I'd been on another drug, a so called 'miracle drug' that was then withdrawn. I then had to wait for my bone marrow to recover. It's not an easy thing to take. But I yearned and wanted to do this, and there are some prices – if you want to do something badly enough – there are some prices you're prepared to pay.

DUNN: So are you now through it?

POTTER: No, I'm about two thirds covered in psoriasis and I take methotrexate every weekend and I take etretinate every day. It means that I vomit at the weekends. If you take cytotoxic drugs, as anyone who does take them will know, you have to deal with certain physical difficulties, but the [filming] schedule therefore was longer because I didn't shoot at weekends. I shot Monday to Friday and used the extra hours where they could be used.

DUNN: So you were working on the film Monday to Friday and then Saturdays and Sundays you were working on the illness?

POTTER: On Friday night I would take the drug and by Monday morning I was able to face all those shining faces again! Yes.

DUNN: Are there a sort of collection of you people in this country who have this condition? Can you form a sort of mutual support society?

POTTER: Well I believe there is. I'm terrified of making my illness my hobby, but I know that there are such societies. But it's not actually for me.

DUNN: You're not in touch with them, obviously.

POTTER: No. I'm not in touch with them.

DUNN: Because it came at a time when your career looked like going in an entirely different direction. You were standing as a Labour parliamentarian!

POTTER: Yes, thank God for that. There are some good things about even visitations! Yes, the idea that I might now be a politician is even more appalling than what it is, apparently, that I am doing, yes.

DUNN: Why? What's changed so dramatically about your views?

POTTER: *Many* things have changed about my views, but they would still be, I suspect, recognizably on the same shelf. But the political necessities of expressing those views in an adversarial political House of Commons, and collecting and garnering votes and so on, leads to a certain kind of personality development which is probably more akin to leprosy than what I have!

Laughter.

DUNN: But was that really why you started writing plays? I know you did start after that, you'd left the journalism and that sort of thing.

POTTER: Yes, well...my first two books were political books. The first I'd written in my last year at Oxford, and then within 18 months of leaving Oxford, the illness struck. And although politics was my chosen path, there was something about it even then which I was half recoiling from. I can hardly remember the self that was not ill, you know. I can hardly remember myself playing rugby or running, all those things which I used to do. So there is some part of my mind, therefore, that I can hardly remember. Illness that is prolonged and difficult and painful pulls you into yourself and makes you think about what the hell it is you're supposed to be doing and why and what for.

DUNN: Right from the very beginning, though, when you started to write...I mean, all your plays nowadays are about what goes on inside people's heads. Is that really what has always intrigued you, rather than action pieces?

POTTER: Well, some action. I mean, we talk about copulation (*Laughter.*), rape...goodness, some action, yes, but what goes on in people's heads is not what is usually reachable by naturalistic means. This is obviously what interests me because I've been interested in turning into myself perhaps too much, which is why the directing was... Even if I have not done it properly, or done it badly, the experience of *doing* it, of stepping back into my old self in a way, was a wonderful one to me. But there are enough films, enough plays, enough programmes, enough television dealing with 'reality' naturalistically for there to be a small space to deal with this 'other.' Well, that's what I've always thought anyway!

DUNN: A large space, I think. All right, so at this moment you're feeling that you're not going to write for television again. How serious are you about that?

POTTER: I'm very serious. I've said it to my producer Rick McCallum and to my agent and closest friend Judy Daish. They said, 'Don't decide until Christmas,' ie 'Let these feelings pass.' They may be right.[384] This may be very childish of me, except you finally reach the stage where you think, never get locked into a situation where you can't turn on your heel. Never say 'I can't do something else.' Never, never accept what seems to be implacably opposed to what you do. Every writer, every actor, every director feels stung by criticism. That's a normal human thing. But I'm talking about the general tone, level, *perception* of something. This feeling that maybe this isn't the medium to do it on.

DUNN: I was going to say, *Blackeyes* was originally a novel. Would you perhaps be turning more towards novels?

POTTER: Well, whatever. I have to earn my living, whatever I do! So yeah, even – God knows – novels, stage, or just, as I did, when you break your heart by writing Hollywood screenplays…

DUNN: Well the last one you wrote, *Christabel…* that was not Dennis Potter really at all. That was real life.

POTTER: Well, you know how you sometimes want to go on a jog? It was almost an act of hygiene for me, to write a piece of naturalistic drama. To say, here's this life. Here's this person, still alive. I can't play tricks. I have to deal with the surface and the reality, over those years, of that one woman's life. And a remarkable woman. And it was like washing your brain under a tap. It was a good thing to do as more than an exercise, but as a way of disciplining oneself to write in a naturalistic way. And then of course they said, 'Why doesn't he do his usual mix of fantasy…'

DUNN: Did they really? I never saw that!

Laughter.

POTTER: Yes, of course they did! But that's a perfectly right and proper reaction.

Sincerely theirs: letters as literature
New York Times, 27 May 1990

François Truffaut: Correspondence 1945–1984 edited by Gilles Jacob and Claude de Givray, translated by Gilbert Adair (The Noonday Press/ Farrar, Straus & Giroux)

'It's one of those days, more and more frequent, when I feel like ending it all.' François Truffaut, barely past his twentieth birthday but already on the far side of delinquency, petty theft and army desertion, is moaning in the mail to his best friend, Robert Lachenay. Robert is by now well used to receiving a Gallic shrug in an envelope. 'It won't happen this time, but I am more or less convinced that I won't be capable of holding out till the end of the year and what makes me think so is that I contemplate suicide with an extraordinary serenity – I will kill myself out of nonchalance, just letting myself go, the way I let myself go to sleep in the cinema with the great satisfaction of knowing that one could rouse oneself if "one wished," but that one might just as well not.'

The sweet perils of self-invention are almost as tenderly on display in this hefty, well-annotated collection of the great French director's letters as they are in the shining ironies of his much-loved films. Already, in the apparent despair but evident mockery of the remarks to his friend, the dreamlike seductions of the movie theatre are called up to illustrate and yet somehow temper the depression. Right from the beginning, one glimpses a small and intense youth sitting sometimes in a concentrated hunch and occasionally in a dolorous slump beneath the switching, flickering beams of light in which blue cigarette smoke drifts and curls and stories blaze out of an expectant darkness. Movies, movies, movies: luminous deceits beckoning urgently to the boy and then so flooding his mind that he could scarcely separate himself from their processes and demands.

The letters are often attempts to pass on this obsession, although sometimes as inadvertently as one might a cold in the head. Friends, other directors, actors, writers, business acquaintances surface out of a litter of film quotations, direct or oblique. Louis Malle, Eric Rohmer, his adored Hitchcock. An occasional critic, too, for those who like bloodier sports. Even the most casual reader of this book, dipping here and there into the inky depths of almost 40 years of compulsive correspondence, cannot fail to trawl up the true nature of Truffaut's ruling passion. There is a sadly beautiful mermaid glistening in the net, where human life and its imagined creations become one and the same. But, ah, those melancholy eyes…

The relationships between 'art' (even, or is it especially, popular art?) and 'life' are many and complex, skin and scale, in ways that are often demeaning in their shallowness and yet profound as a startling or revelatory analogue for the most elusive and fugitive workings of the soul.

In his justly celebrated 1973 film *Day for Night*, Truffaut hid behind an almost fawning charm (an undoubted flaw in some of his work) in order to release his feelings about the importance of the cinema to his own life. He was to describe the film's subject, in a letter written a year later, as 'quite simply, my own reason for living.' The worryingly unadorned baldness of the statement is the precise opposite of arty self-entrancement. Truffaut, in *Day for Night*, half joking and half revealing, allowed himself to play a movie director in front of as well as behind the camera in a deftly amusing tale of a film crew between takes and between bedsheets. 'Films are smoother than life,' he points out as the fictive director to an emotionally troubled actor. 'They just don't grind to a halt. They glide on like trains in the night. For people like you and me, our happiness lies in the cinema.'

Again and again, the letters in *François Truffaut: Correspondence 1945–1984*, capably translated by Gilbert Adair, show that he means this in an absolutely literal sense. Film is both the moral centre of his being and a continuing source of what can only be a legitimate anxiety. Even the collapse of his marriage is seen in terms of his most recent shoot: '*La Peau Douce* [*The Soft Skin*] was painful to make and, because of the story, I now have a loathing of marital hypocrisy; on that point I feel total revulsion at present.' Because of the story. These few words are like tiny

313

splinters that work their way beneath the skin and then gradually fester. What we love too much can certainly injure us, and if art really is the sole inheritor of religion in our secular age, then those who seek to practice it must perhaps become aware that what they take to be, and represent as, the bandage is in fact the wound. I don't quite know why I shudder and look around to see if there is anyone else in this otherwise empty room.

Maybe you do not need to seek much farther, though, for some kind of explanation for the swings between a disgusted melancholy and a chirpy grace that the letters evince. But what they also show, without any semblance of doubt, is that François Truffaut – whether or not prowling along the perilous edge of obsession – was a decent, generous and caring man in a working world too often peopled by slavering monsters.

And this essential humanity is, at heart, the reason why we love so many of his films. Not 'because of the story,' but because of the way it is told, the confident switches of tone and the deceptively casual ease in which great effort is subsumed within the dancing glow of the screen. The restlessness of *The 400 Blows*, raw at the edges, or *Jules and Jim*, melancholy at its heart, became in later movies more settled, more aesthetically demanding – for example, in the darker tones of *The Story of Adele H* and its portrayal of a woman's desperate love. An ache in the dusk, rather than a train in the night. Nervy energies gradually softened into a certain reserve, while initial exuberance flipped itself over, blinked and found anxiety whispering it to be still. Such is the way we grow.

The man is the work, and then the work becomes the man. 'It is impossible to create something – a film, a novel, etc – that does not absolutely resemble oneself,' he insisted in a 1957 letter, the first of many similar claims in these pages. Nowadays, of course, the very idea that a movie could be such a strange thing as a personal creation is even harder to hold. Film companies are like the back-end afterthoughts of larger 'leisure' corporations, run by people who are not so much puzzled as genuinely offended by idiosyncrasies of content or style. The independents (so-called) are cut down in swathes like already half-dead daisies on a uniformly cropped lawn; the accountants do not need to look for partners in their routine thuggeries when almost everyone discusses a film in terms of its box-office returns.

Truffaut had his share of trips and stumbles on 'that tortuous path that leads from the editing-room to the cinema auditorium,' but the letters show amazingly few signs of serious compromise *en route*. 'I may be a whore, but I'm the coquettish, crafty, subtle type who keeps his hat and shoes on.' Bet he could spit out of the side of his mouth as well, and pretend it was a smile.

The director general of the Cannes Film Festival, Gilles Jacob (who edited this collection with the director Claude de Givray), explains in his introduction that some of Truffaut's letters 'were, rightly or wrongly, judged too intimate for publication.' So it is, alas, that there are no love letters from a man whose films are graced with lovely women and whose sympathies usually remained alert to their exploitations. The style of the correspondence escaping this protective sieve is so exuberant, so keen and so freshly individual that it is not mere prurience that makes one regret the letters remaining in the mesh. The director of *The Man Who Loved Women* is left dry at the loins.

It took the venomous accuracies of Truffaut's old colleague Jean-Luc Godard to put into the frame the question of why the director is the only one who does not make love in *Day for Night*. 'Probably no one else will call you a liar, so I will.' Truffaut's style, Mr Godard meant. His way of seeing, of telling, of showing. The Godardian knife slid between the ribs with the smirking aplomb of a professional killer.

Previous hints and gleams of Truffaut's power of invective, fragments of broken glass in a sugar bowl, are as nothing when injured François plucks out the blade, hones it to a new edge on the ganglia of his exposed nerves and plunges it back whence it came with all the jaunty slaughterhouse brutality French artists especially relish when they fall out with each other.

Mr Godard is dismissed as a mere lump of ordure 'on a pedestal,' a poseur and a political hypocrite. 'You need to play a role and the role needs to be a prestigious one; I've always had the impression that real militants are like cleaning women, doing a thankless, daily but necessary job. But you, you're the Ursula Andress of militancy.' On and on, biff and bam, in a way that gives an unintentionally comical gloss to the last, irritating sentence of Mr Godard's brief but not unpoignant foreword to this collection. 'François is perhaps dead,' he concludes. 'I am perhaps alive. But then, is there a difference?'

Let us presume that this is not exactly a theological question, and ignore the disturbing odours that drift from the remains of the pedestal. In truth François Truffaut will remain vividly alive for those who love films and their possibilities. This delightful book conjures up again so many of those peculiar yet enhancing resonances between 'art' and 'life' that whirr like a projector within the soft spaces of the theatre that we all carry, bob-bob, upon our own shoulders.

Pride

Introduction to *'Breathe on 'um Berry!': 100 Years of Achievement by Berry Hill Rugby Football Club* (Commemorative book, 1992)

One hundred years! And that is what it must have felt like during a sodden November afternoon if you had been one of the backs waiting for the slithering ball to be released by your own forwards in the kind of long-gone Berry Hill teams I once so briefly adorned.

We in the grunting pack, greased, bristled and toothless, had little regard for the allegedly more elegant creatures behind us. A rolling, steaming, trampling maul was the veriest heaven. On the touchline, a little man with fierce eyes used to run alongside the advancing eight shouting 'Up! Up! Upupupup!' with the rapidity and the menace of a machine-gun. His other claim to fame was that he had once written a letter to the King. It could not have been about the perfidity of the second-row forward on our own side (rest in peace!) who specialized in breaking wind in the scrum. No fun at all for Number Eight.

Black-and-amber jerseys, fare thee well. Black and amber bruises, too, for distant memories of my own youth and 'fitness' certainly include aching ribs, Saturday night limps, and Sunday morning doubts about the probity of the referee.

And also *pride*, of course.

The kind of pride which is always so difficult to put into words. It is part of sport, yes, the pleasure in pulling on the jersey, the relish in the huggermugger continuous present-tense of the field of play, the breathless black-and-amber fellowship. But the pride was – and is – so much more than any of these things, for it reaches back in the heart of the sprawling village and the grey-and-green Forest of Dean around it.

A forest which has changed so completely – gaining much, losing much – that it is becoming harder to recall how close, how tightly knit, how self-absorbed so much of its culture really was. The chapel, the Silver Prize Band, the pub, the pit, *the rugby team*. Generations of us

316

knew this, occasionally chafing at the suffocating tightness but more often celebrating its distinct rhythms and its deep, old feelings.

The Berry Hill fifteens of recent years are far more skilled and infinitely more sophisticated than most of the sides which preceded them. Indeed, their name has resounded far beyond the land between the two rivers. But whatever they achieve and whatever glories are yet to come are also in some measure a tribute to all those who have gone before. The dead ones, the old ones, half-lost in memory like phantoms in the second-half fog. Perhaps those cauliflower ears are listening to something other than celestial strains, and maybe at the far edge of the fading harp they can again pick up the faint 'Up! Up! Up!' of long ago, or the still reverberating 'Come on, Berry!' which we proudly toast today.

Downloading
New York Festival Programme, January 1992

I am almost as reluctant to write this shifty little piece as I am astonished by the occasion for it.[385] Embarrassment is no longer a particularly obvious sign when seeking to identify a liar (or else nobody could bear to vote) but it certainly does strange things to the nib of a pen. The slow pink flush you can almost see between the lines is because I am edgy about this 'retrospective.' My previous television work is unlikely to travel well, not across the long years nor over the great distances – in so many senses – between my musty homeland and murderous New York. Downloading old pictures from dead brain cells ought better to take place in the cephalarium of a cryonic chamber. Watch out for frostbite, please.

Part of me is flattered, of course, that someone is trying to reanimate the long-stored molecules of my former passions, but it would surprise and maybe short-circuit the remainder of my head if this odd attempt were to succeed in any other way than as a mildly amused and antiquarian condescension of the kind that a middle-aged Englishman has already taken in with his mother's milk. If you see some of the scenery tremble on the verge of collapse, pay attention to the dialogue. And vice versa.

Television is such an ephemeral medium that holding up any elderly bits of it for too long, as an examination, is like drawing outlines around the flickering shadows cast by a blazing coal fire in an otherwise unlit room.

An ordinary enough simile, for sure, but it sprang from somewhere unbidden. This room, wherever it was or whenever it will be, comes again and again to the far edges of my mind when I am purportedly thinking about other things, but I did not expect to glimpse it so soon in the consecutive prose of this self-exculpating chore. Were I adept enough or lazy enough to use a word processor I would probably delete the small paragraph in question and start again: but now that the words are looped and thorned in real ink on a more intractable page I will let the image waylay me, as has become my habit.

A blazing coal fire in an otherwise unlit room. Where is it? A man and a woman are there. Who are they? Their humped shapes in the hard-backed chairs on either side of the grate are tantalizingly ill-defined, and half of each face is all but masked by the unsteady darkness. One of them is laughing, the other is crying, but the bouncing shadows make it difficult to distinguish between two such similar contortions.

They are not looking at each other, nor slanting a sunken eye socket at anything else in particular in the small and apparently still narrowing space. A clock on the wall ticks, as though something bad got caught in its pendulous throat when it tried to eat up the hours which once belonged to me. Tick-h tock-h tick-h tock-h. The fire loses conviction and eventually goes out, becoming ash and clinker. And then the one who was laughing begins to cry and the one who was weeping starts to laugh. Perhaps now, though, they will look at each other, or even say something. I wait, and wait, to see if this will happen, crunching up smaller and smaller with tension until I am again as a child.

But where am I hiding? It can only be under the table, whose roof is so much nearer to a prickling scalp than is the ceiling. There is no longer enough light to find out, and when dawn pearls at the single window (as though serenely indifferent to cliché) it is only to illuminate another room altogether. One with a littered desk, a bottle of red wine, lots of cigarettes, and all the pens, pencils, and paper anyone could need to build a shelter or a palace, or a cryptic evasion. Now, there is only one person between the walls, but millions of other eyes. Bugger off, I say. Bugger off!

I know of old that I cannot nudge into shape half a paragraph or knock up a single exchange of dialogue if anyone else is in the room. That room, this room, any room. Not simply because an intruder might breathe in a way I could overhear, or rustle cloth against flesh, or look out of one of the other windows and see things which are not on the page. No: it's most of all because another presence would inevitably break into the fugitive yet very precisely delineated cusp that makes its delicate, seagull-winged shape between the public manifestations of writing and the utterly private maelstroms of being able to do it at all.

Say all that out loud and you will realize that I am up to mischief. Irony is the stench of modern prose, but it's better than the gastroenteritis which causes it. I can no more hold back a satiric excursion of this order than I could exchange a merry quip with Dan Quayle. But the lengthening syllables should tell you that rather than further expose what should remain hidden I am backing off toward the pretentious impotence of some wretched academic in a polystyrene tower. Philistinism may yet turn out to be the last defence of the reasonably honourable, assailed as we are on all sides by collapsed theories, suddenly furtive theoreticians, and (as ever) by learned people who hate literature so much that they cannot even bring themselves to acknowledge that someone actually writes it.

Put it another, politer way: some form of yearning or (pardon me) idealism, with all its related fervours, is often the one and only genuinely tender offshoot of ignorance or fear, so I am glad that I did not know this when I first began to write. I would not have been able to fill a single page if I had had the misfortune to begin my career in the midst of our present contaminations, and I am grateful that it took nearly a decade before someone scarcely able to rub two ideas together (in what must have been a back pocket) had the temerity to demand a so-called 'second draft.'[386]

OK. Out of order. I am swinging now in a funfair bate of breath between the apparently opposing need to be alone with my own being and the equally urgent desire to address what used to be called the public at large. The dream or fantasy of a common culture was once as real to me as the tongue in my mouth – and television (one national channel) came to me at virtually the same time, salted with the guilt of rising through all the suffocating layers of the English class system, just when I was first able to measure what I had lost and what I had gained. I chose this new medium with the myopic precision of a watchmaker who was blissfully unaware that quartz crystals would soon be able to take over the job, and it is now too late for me to think otherwise.

Americans would probably be too astounded to give credence to the idea that anyone could think such things about a medium which in their land has so long since been handed over lock, stock and shampoo-sachet to the hucksters. A present-day BBC executive will soon be just as surprised, though in this case the necessary rictus will be tempered by one of those mannered English lifts of a single eyebrow, or a similarly would-be exquisite swoop of the blade of an extended palm. Two related gestures which always invite me to believe that Pontius Pilate must have finished his education at Oxford.

'As you did,' said an indignant someone at the decaying Corporation when the thought, less judiciously expressed, last came to the brink of my lips. A long pause followed. A throat cleared. 'Why,' came the voice again, 'why do you constantly try to bite the hand that feeds you?'

Stumble, yawn, and occasionally blink your passage through a good slice of my life's work in the days ahead and, perhaps, you will be able to answer that on my behalf. If you ignore the teeth marks, I have already said that any such response would be distinctly unsettling. Worse still, it would move me. Is that a happy ending?

Smoke screen
Guardian, 28 March 1994

Sir,

It would, of course, be the dear old *Guardian* who, in telling of my terminal cancer, smuggles in a reference to my heavy smoking (March 25).[387] I have cancer of the pancreas with secondaries in the liver, and my beloved cigarettes have nothing to do with it: much less, for sure, than decades of cytotoxic drugs used to contain my other illness. You should amend what you said from 'Mr Potter, who is 58, and is a heavy smoker...' to 'Mr Potter, who is 58, and regularly eats fresh fruit and vegetables...'

Dennis Potter
London W2

Introduction
Karaoke and Cold Lazarus
Completed: 28 April 1994[388]

We all know that we are going to die, and so the bleak clinical statement that the event is indeed about to happen to me in rather shorter order than I might have expected should not in itself make all that difference to the way I live, work and feel: that is, the way I *write*. But let me rush to assure you, in what may turn out to be an importunate gabble, that *everything* feels different. Sometimes, too, in modes that are almost perversely serene or emancipating, thus making the whole experience far less dread-filled and ceiling-contemplative than I could ever have dared to imagine.

Every word written by me in this book has been composed under the matter-of-fact death sentence given to me in the middle of 'February, fill ditch black or white.' Let this go some way, therefore, to excusing the odd shape of this little piece I am now writing to serve duty both as an introduction to my last two productions for television, as well as a glancing valediction to all the previous works as well.

The prognoses have jumped about a little disconcertingly, varying in these last couple of months between 'certainly a few weeks more' to 'three to five months,' and one passing, pinky-blue sort of haze that implied life deep into high summer and the first tinges of the leaves beyond. These variants appear to have as much to do with the temperament of the doctor in question as with the well-charted histology of the disease.

But perhaps (and importantly) it is the other way around, and they are reacting to the manner of my own assertions. It almost seems to me as though it is *me* who has to make up his own mind about how and where and when on the limited scale I should pack up my bags and go. It depends, so to speak, on the pen in my hands.

My first thoughts upon hearing that I had cancer of the pancreas, with secondaries already on the liver, were that 'my affairs' were in one hell of a muddle – and I'm not just talking about a lost premium bond. No, they'd been worsened by recent and seemingly endless pain which had made me push things aside or abandon them altogether, by my wife Margaret's illness, and further jammed up by some bad risks I had taken with the business side of my working life.

Like most husbands and fathers I had assumed it to be a paramount duty of mine to leave my family as much as I fairly could in terms of their financial security, and with as few tangled-up administrative problems regarding my by now quite sizeable assets and their future earning powers.

I totted up all I *thought* I had, and began the coldly fascinating process of 'the time he has to put his affairs in order,' a phrase which had always intrigued me since I first read it as a child in, I think, a Biggles book. In other words, I had to concoct some sort of family trust to take care of all my works and their licences, and I had to make a will, the one document in which one cannot literally afford to be pusillanimous.

This took me several long days of mind-crunching paperwork. The great complication was the fact that I had not long before badly broken one of the cardinal rules of the biz there's no other biz like (or the biz all other businesses are getting to be like) by investing fat sums of my own present and presumed future resources in my own work – only to find it not very well received.

A year before, thanks in part to my legally permissible borrowing powers over my own self-regulated pension fund (started off by MGM money, and swiftly swollen by decades of other ready American booty for projects that rarely passed the start line, as well as all the others which, mostly elsewhere, did), I was able to put in more than half a million pounds of my 'own' money into the ailing budget of a BBC film I had called *Midnight Movie*[389] without any intention of ironic foreboding. By becoming the Corporation's sole if minority partner, the movie was able to begin shooting.

'The film has been completed but has not yet found a distributor': the most common epitaph in the sprawl of chipped, tarnished, sloping memorial slabs to an independent British film industry which by now must be as big as that enormous sprawl of the dead at Kensal Green Cemetery.

Writing, producing and hustling for the as yet still unseen *Midnight Movie* had already wrenched out large chunks of my working year. I'd not taken any fees for these combined full-time jobs (not even, oh whisper it low, for the script itself). Worse, I had helped finance our normal and by no means spartan living standards by airily taking on two rich commissions that had been dangling so sweetly in front of me for some time. These were for a six-part original series for the BBC,

322

and another six-parter for Channel 4, the latter spun out on nothing much more than what had felt like an inspired lunchtime burble where I thought I suddenly saw the myriad glistenings of a 'great story' about halfway down my wine glass.

The common perception behind all this, of course, was that *time* was not at issue. Time was something one had, a physicist's T, in plenty, ever available, waiting for use. And it was the great shock of finding out that this was not the case which has provided me with the only genuine moment of panic about my imminent death I have so far experienced: a feeling as swiftly and brutally done with by the time it takes to fall down a flight of stairs.

My account books were so much less healthy than I had been blithely assuming. I had a four-to-five year overhang of debts-plus-interest to my own pension fund, and – if this were indeed to be the point of crumble and collapse – I would have to pay back £60,000 in upfront advances to the BBC and £100,000 to Channel 4 – as well as forego all the delivery-and-acceptance payments, production fees, sales and 'associated residual rights' connected with the original commissions.

I have for a long period now been exceptionally fortunate with my earning powers in what is a very frail trade, so much so that I tended to walk along certain circular corridors at, say, Shepherd's Bush with something of the exaggeratedly furtive air taken by a pantomime villain tiptoeing away from a scene of his own particular dastardy. Now, maybe, the game was up at last.

When the cancer was so belatedly diagnosed, and thereupon found too advanced to be treated either by surgery or by chemotherapy, I was led deep into the drowsing valleys of morphine and heroin where hobgoblins wait to chatter. This had to be the landscape of *What-am-I-going-to-do?*, where the first signposts indicate how to curl yourself up into a ball and weep away what is left.

Journey past those, though, and the choices soon became very simple for me, especially as the truly ravaging pain became more under control.

By chance, I had also just been offered a first stab at a remake of an old but not very good movie, and the whacking great upfront fee the Americans guaranteed would soon take the sting out of those pay-the-money-back issues at the two British television stations. Did I therefore go flat out at my most now-hear-*this* pitch for the Hollywood number, and duly deliver the first draft of whatever quality they would have guaranteed to buy, so long as I hid the news of the lethal diagnosis until the contract had been signed? Worse things have happened, after all. But no, I didn't want to squander my last energies on work of this nature, where the better you make it the less chance there is of the film actually being shot. 'No' went back down the transatlantic telephone line, and with it a few shards of saved dignity as well.

The issue was, then, did I work on and on with the muddle *Karaoke* had become through the months of pain that had followed the earlier neglect, trying to rescue a complicated play and its central metaphors from the disaster I think I had made of it? Or did I dive in, hell or glory, and find in *Cold Lazarus* something like 'the story' I had glimpsed deep down in the Gevrey-Chambertin?

Time was again the leading question, followed hard upon by some doubt about what making words would be *like* when making them under such duress. Would they become too careless without the restraints of their future reception, critical or otherwise, being of little or no consequence? Or would they warp and buckle, would I lose control of them, so that things yukky, maudlin and sanctimonious could come slinking and nudging across the ready-laid duckboards?

In the end – it was the struggle of just one day and one night – I decided that I would cast adrift all I had so far written of *Karaoke*, and start as from new, scene one, page one. And that then, oh, if there were time, that then I would plunge headlong into *Cold Lazarus*. Even if strength and spirit gave out during the progressive degradations of the growing tumours, and even if I ran smack into the most blank-eyed of writers' blocks, there would surely be enough pages of any kind of quality – gibberish, even – for my redoubtable literary executor, my agent Judy Daish, to resist any 'please pay back' affronts or solicitations.

'Putting my affairs in order,' plus some hospital business and a few other attendant nasties, meant that I could take the first day of March as my start-up day. 'A pinch and a punch, the first of the month!' There was a pleasing symmetry to that, of the same nice kind I used to get when starting a shiny new exercise book at school.

When writing flat-out, seriously no-nonsensing with anything else whatsoever, I always set myself certain targets per day in terms of page numbers, and if a page or two are lost in one day's difficulties or interruptions, they have to be made up during the next 12-or-so-hour session. I also reckon on the basis of a minute a page when calculating the length of a script, and lay the work out accordingly in longhand on an A4 writing book. In a sort of print costive enough to drive its first reader (my daughter Sarah) mad, not on the basis of illegibility but in anxieties about the true nature of the person who has composed it in so appallingly neat, clear and orderly a fashion.

The combination of 10 pages a day, every day, to make from the first day of the month also had its charms in terms of simple mental arithmetic. I realized from the beginning that the 360-pages a six-hour serial needed would be too much to leave space for the other 360 pages that the waiting *Cold Lazarus* would also need – especially if there were to be no gap in between to catch a new breath let alone a violently new subject. Such a schedule demanded 72 days without break from 1 March, and that would take me to close of play on the evening of 11 May.

Mind you, this date was on the right side of the fifty-ninth birthday (17 May) I had somehow privately resolved to reach in the midst of all the prognoses. A draconian stint in further deliberations might not yet be totally out of the question after all. So I mentioned the 11 May target-for-work to one of the more tacit of the doctors who were suddenly drifting in and out of my attention, and asked whether it was likely that I could work properly for such a span. A sharp intake of incredulity was sufficient answer. I then enquired of another in the deliberately more sardonic terms I was ready to use in my own dialogue. 'Tick one box,' I invited. 'Possible, Probable.' The hesitation was long enough to make the answer real enough, and it wasn't the gentler of the two.

But...*if* I tried *two four-parters*...?

Well, this still kept the kind of lengths each of the two themes needed in a form natural to the television schedules. I could think, then, in terms of 480 pages in fifty days, allowing at least a full day for the turn-around of mood, theme and subject. I would have until the end of the working day on 15 April, which was far more safely tucked into the stretches I had been given. All I wanted was a path through all the opiates and analgesics, all the clutches and the humiliations, that would show up sufficient patches of calm or clear landscape where I could genuinely 'write my all.'

I made myself sit at my desk at five o'clock in the morning of Tuesday, 1 March, 12 hours before I was due to see my accountant, Stanley Rosenthal, a co-trustee of the family trust for my work. I sat down and wrote the word KARAOKE in big bright capitals, and almost immediately ignited. As soon as I began to write I began to live again. Within hours I knew I was writing freely, within days I felt I was writing well, and I knew by the time the week was out that I was writing truthfully.

Already, as I sat down on that first darkly early hour of the first morning, I had been unable to avoid the strange and rather disturbing feeling that things directly in front of me were somehow *presenting* themselves to me. Everything was demanding look, look, look at me; and all the dignity of everything was in the present tense, the one that breaks at the tip of your tongue or your pen, the tense that is itself a sense, like a taste. On that morning, as in some wholly new experience not at all mystical or dream-like but flint-hard and clean, I submerged a great part of myself to the nowness of that self, where everything was both trivial and significant, including the differences between the two.

The rim of the coffee cup, the faint seagull-wing cusp made by a slant of light on top of the coffee, and the pleasurable surprise in finding the fold of the bedsheet should be just like that. The hard edge of the continent that was my desk, the emptiness of the paper, the wonderful slithers and curls to make with the ups and downs of letters and punctuation marks, and, above all, the curious little bite as the fine-tipped pen I work with made contact with the crisply waiting paper! I could of course go on and on, multiplying to distraction, but it didn't come out as promiscuous multiplication at all, rather as division. A paring down to what was precisely here precisely now in the very present tense itself full stop.

Present tense. First person. I decided, as I have often in the past, to use the outward *forms* of autobiography to give the engine-power *Karaoke* needed. My man had to walk alongside me in this adventure. He had to be ill, and in pain, and with an impending and intractable death sentence. He had to be more than a little withdrawn, a little sardonic and a little lost. And he had to be a proud writer. None of which, I hope it goes without further saying, means that he had to be *me*. Indeed, in many crucial ways (especially in terms of his isolation) precisely the opposite. No more like me, in fact, than the singing detective who had shared my natal patch and peeling skin. But like me enough to understand one of the minor aberrations I sometimes have felt about the scenes going on in front of me.

I have sometimes caught myself thinking, or half-thinking, that the world going on out there right at the brink of one's self has somehow been momentarily prearranged so that even the present tense has been turned in upon itself and there is no point of equilibrium to be found anywhere in anything. A sort of horizontal vertigo. It is only a passing fancy, or the mildest form of lunacy, easily understandable as one of a writer's plausible derangements as he so regularly patterns his thoughts and emotions into acceptable shapes and forms. I simply wanted to make the gap widen, or the unease spread and spread until, under the force of purely physical pain and sickness, plus plenty of alcohol, that old whole background murmur of writerly anxiety could become the long tunnel through which My Hero would have to crawl.

Daniel Feeld, the central character, is already in physical crisis at the start, and he begins by more than half-imagining that something he has recently written has *escaped* into the world outside, almost as a contagion might. He thinks he is being fed back bits of his old dialogue. Things keep arranging themselves to fit an old storyline. He keeps stumbling into the debris of styles and contents that belong on other pages, pages that should have been abandoned and are dangerous to use.

In this extremity, he has to struggle back towards relationships and understandings he thought he had managed to do without. He has to find out about his own work, and so he has, without knowing it or without consciously going through the experience of it, to *find out* about *himself* and thereby expose himself to himself in order to discover where the constant pre-written *Karaoke* stops and his own song might survive a line or two.

Such a process means, I hope, that you will not be too surprised to come across many a sly nod back to my own working styles, as well as a few deft gleanings from some of my other pieces; not remotely in any sense of self-plagiarism or self-pleading, but as the one genuinely autobiographical strand in the piece, part of the truth of Daniel's own present-tense experiences and the physical burdens which go with them.

I had no idea how the story was going to unfold, nor whom he would meet along the way, except that I was sure the use of pictures in a cutting room was going to be something that both reverberated and explained, threatened and unravelled. I also had no idea how it would all end, except that he had to know that he was going to die and had to make appropriate arrangements with his affairs and himself.

Getting to know Daniel Feeld made me wonder a lot about what kind of thing he was now writing, because he was obviously the sort to have something on the boil. And during this time, of course, in the physical effort and sheer joy of writing the eccentricities and styles of *Karaoke*, I too had lurking somewhere the original thoughts about *Cold Lazarus* which had made me put it up so eagerly to Channel 4 in the first place.

It came to me as strongly as the taste of the moistly raw shallot dipped in salt that Daniel was writing *Cold Lazarus* partly out of fear of death, partly as a way of pushing the world back into an utter otherly place, and partly as a means of smuggling in a few memories or events or patterns that he needed to face down once more in his remaining, guttering-candle stump of life.

Once that link had been made in my own head, I had no fear of the transition between the two plays. Daniel and I could jump across from one heaving boat to the other. Moreover, by knowing this, I had a richness of emotional detail denied to everyone but myself until the time came to let it explode. The two works, so called, were actually *one*. The reverberations or even merely the syncopations between the two would also be far more than retrospective; they would cast forward too, and be there under the surface, all the time, and growing.

Twice I severely had to resist the almost overwhelming temptation to break into the latter part of *Cold Lazarus* with a scene of Daniel Feeld actually writing it at his own cluttered desk in the time between his murder of 'Pig' Mailion and his own death, which would have meant that he would have to have written his own deathbed scene at the start of *Cold Lazarus*, something not too far removed from what I was actually doing myself.

Fortunately, the temptations were finally scourged and driven off, otherwise the whole edifice would have been twisted into the kind of game, or cheat, that it had so far resisted becoming. Certainly, it is in ludic mode, and walks along that perilous line all the time, for it has to if it is to work at all.

Whether or not the two – or the one, as I now see it – 'work at all' is not, of course, something for me to decide. You will understand that there are now ways in which in my present situation that cannot be of the slightest consequence to me. You will also understand that, again in my present situation, there are now ways in which on this matter *only* my opinion has consequence. As for that I simply wish to say that *Karaoke* and *Cold Lazarus* are as fitting a summation as they are a testament both to my character and my career as I should ever want.

There is one other thing that must be said. Throughout this hurried description of work, of page numbers, day numbers and draconian schedules, there had to be an answering measure of great emotional and physical effort as my condition necessarily deteriorated. All of which means that, almost exhausted now, almost extinct, I had to that self-same degree to neglect those in front of me who were suffering as well, particularly my own sick and struggling wife, Margaret, the steadfast green-eyed one ever.

All vocations tend towards the self-mutilating as well as the cannibalistic of the nearest and dearest, but I don't think I would have had the stomach for the possible brutality if Margaret and all the others so close to me had not all immediately seen that doing what I did in the way that I did meant that I was able to live by the means of this work – and to live with the dignity they too needed for me and from me. I offer up the pieces in my love and my life.

The Artist
The Dane, July 1953

Beauty is like the transcendent God
whom earthly pilgrims never attain;
for as in the cradle man seems to lurk
behind the facade of infancy,
the greatest beauty ever gained
hints at a glory yet to be,
however wondrous the artist's work.

But in recompense for transcendence
we have the idea of immanence:
even if beauty shines afar
its bright beam sparkles within us all
like a slanting dusty ray of light
sliding through the dark caverns
of some great Gothic cathedral.

There lies the purpose and the tragedy
of the artist who seeks mastery.
Pity him walking an endless road
like a pilgrim to a holy city,
every other objective lost before
the power of one Jerusalem.
But unlike the pilgrim he will not
reach the towers of the city walls.
On he may travel through the valleys
and over the hills, the hard-won slopes,
eager with false hopes, as futile
as a dirty city cock's crow;
but always the spires will be distant,
further in the imagination, beyond expectancy.

Yet sometimes when he stands on a hill,
after a particular piece of work,
the mind clears suddenly before the sun
and tall towers of beauty are bared
into naked actuality.
That moment is all, the time for which
he lives: eternity.

NOTES

INTRODUCTION TO PART ONE: THE CONFIDENCE COURSE

1   Graham Fuller (ed.), *Potter on Potter* (London: Faber and Faber, 1993), p.122.

2   "XL", A.E. Housman, *A Shropshire Lad* (London: Kegan Paul, Trench, Trübner and Co Ltd., 1896), p.57.

3   Humphrey Carpenter, *Dennis Potter: A Biography* (London: Faber and Faber, 1998), p.40.

4   The Eleven Plus was an examination taken by children in the final year of primary school. It determined the nature of secondary education that children would receive, generally either grammar, technical or secondary modern school.

5   Potter first travelled to Hammersmith in May 1945, when the cramped living arrangements with Potter's paternal grandparents in the Forest of Dean had forced his parents to partially relocate to London with his maternal grandparents. Potter's father remained behind on that occasion, and Potter himself went back to the Forest of Dean without his mother and sister around seven months later. For the reasons behind this, see p.368 endnote 355 of this volume. In June 1949, Potter returned to Hammersmith. See Carpenter, pp.27-32.

6   Joan Bakewell, "Wrestling with a vision", *Sunday Times Magazine*, 14 November 1976, p.66.

7   Potter, "Ashridge, 1952", *The Dane*, July 1952, p.352.

8   The supplement was entitled *Verse and Prose*, and part of *The Dane*, July 1953, pp.432-441. Potter's own poem "The Artist" appeared on the final page and closes this present volume on p.330.

9   As Potter did not have Latin O-level, he was required to pass the Latin part of the Oxford University entrance exam (otherwise known as Responsions) before he could be admitted.

10 Kenneth Trodd (1935–) changed his name to Kenith in early 1966.

11 Potter was editor of *Isis* – the long-established Oxford undergraduate magazine – from 30 April–11 June 1958.

12 *Clarion* was a periodical published by both the National Association of Labour Student Organizations and the Oxford University Labour Club which Potter edited during

October and November 1958. This was a relaunched version of *Oxford Clarion* which Potter also edited alongside Natasha Edelman during Michaelmas term 1957.

13 On 21 November 1957, during a Union meeting, it was alleged that Potter had written an unpublished article for the *Isis* which claimed that at a private meeting on 12 November, Brian Walden – the President of the Oxford Union – tried to persuade Potter to carry out an attack on one of Walden's electoral opponents. This caused a sensation, and the national press avidly covered the resulting story. Walden fiercely denied any wrongdoing, and eventually an independent inquiry commission was established. The commission delivered its report on 18 January 1958, but it was inconclusive, finding fault on both sides, and ultimately the controversy fizzled out. For further details of the report see "Tribunal report: Text of Union Society findings", *Cherwell*, 18 January 1958, p.10, and also Carpenter, pp.69-71.

14 Potter was sacked a week before he could edit his final issue (which should have been 18 June 1958), and along with the rest of his editorial team was locked out of the *Isis* offices by Holywell Press, the proprietor. The dispute concerned the nomination of the magazine's next editor. Traditionally, the outgoing editor made the selection, but Potter's term of office had led the proprietor to believe that his choice would be too left wing. Ultimately, Potter's proposed editor, Nicholas Deakin, was appointed.

15 The 26 February 1958 edition of *Isis*, edited by Lewis Rudd, published an article about cold war strategy written by Paul Thompson and William Miller. On 2 May 1958, shortly after Potter became *Isis* editor, Thompson and Miller were arrested and charged by Special Branch for a breach of the Official Secrets Act. Potter used *Isis* to launch a defence fund which reached £541. Thompson and Miller eventually received three-month prison sentences. For more details see Carpenter, pp.75-76.

16 Richard Hoggart, *The Uses of Literacy* (London: Chatto and Windus, 1957).

17 J.B. Priestley and Jacquetta Hawkes, *Journey Down a Rainbow* (London: Heinemann-Cresset, 1955), p.51.

18 Potter, "Base ingratitude", *New Statesman*, 3 May 1958, pp.560,562, and on pp.17-21 of this volume.

19 *Does Class Matter?* Episode Two: "Class in Private Life", BBC-TV, 25 August 1958. Potter's interview was recorded in Oxford on 16 May 1958, for which he was paid three guineas (Carpenter, pp.79-80). The programme ended with a studio discussion, led by Christopher Mayhew whose guests were Canon Ronald Preston and Richard Hoggart.

20 Potter, *Seeing the Blossom: Two Interviews and a Lecture* (London: Faber and Faber, 1994), p.63. Potter also expressed his guilt in *Stand Up, Nigel Barton* when the eponymous hero confesses, 'I talked about my own father and mother! I *used* them, Jill. I damn well, bloody well, *used* them!' – Potter, *The Nigel Barton Plays: Two Television Plays* (Harmondsworth: Penguin, 1967), p.66.

21 Potter, "I'm proud of my home and family…no obsession", *Dean Forest Guardian*, 5 September 1958, p.7, and on pp.24-26 of this volume.

22 Ialdabaoth, "The Forest decides that Dennis is a menace", *Cherwell*, 11 October 1958, p.4.

23 The publishers Gollancz had been courting Potter through the summer of 1958. On 21 August, Potter sent them a sample chapter of his proposed book – *The Glittering Coffin* – and he was formally commissioned, with an advance of £100, just over a week later. The book's publication was delayed by a one-year printers' strike, but eventually emerged in February 1960, and was greeted with a large amount of press coverage.

24 On 14 October 1958, Christopher Mayhew wrote to Potter, 'If you have not already heard – the Director-General [Sir Ian Jacob] rang up himself immediately after your interview with me was broadcast and made the suggestion that you might be taken on the staff!' See Carpenter, p.84.

25 Potter's time at *Panorama* is well documented, but his other BBC attachments are subject to a certain amount of anecdotal evidence. In his appearance on *Desert Island Discs* (BBC Radio 4, 17 December 1977) Potter mentions working at Bush House and then on *Tonight* (BBC 1957–65), but in the latter case it is likely he was recalling later freelance work. For further details see Carpenter, pp.98-100 and W. Stephen Gilbert, *Fight and Kick and Bite: The Life and Work of Dennis Potter* (London: Hodder and Stoughton, 1995), pp.75-76.

26 Potter, *The Glittering Coffin* (London: Gollancz, 1960).

27 Kenneth Allsop, "The Angriest Young Man of all…", *Daily Mail*, 8 February 1960, p.6.

28 *The Glittering Coffin* was serialised over three days in the *Daily Sketch*: "What's eating Dennis Potter?", 16 February 1960, p.7; "A land divided – by humbug", 17 February 1960, p.7; and "Pay and Dennis Potter", 18 February 1960, p.15.

29 *Panorama*, BBC-TV, 30 November 1959. The film item "Closing of Pits in the Forest of Dean" was presented by James Mossman. Potter worked on this as assistant to producer David Wheeler. The film caused controversy in the Forest of Dean, and was covered in the pages of the *Dean Forest Guardian* including "Forest protest to BBC's *Panorama*", 11 December 1959, p.3, and "Readers' Views: What of the next 20 years in the Forest", 18 December 1959, p.6.

30 Denis Mitchell (1911–90) was an award-winning and highly regarded documentary filmmaker. When Potter arrived on attachment, Mitchell was finalising a trilogy of films about Africa called *The Wind of Change* (BBC-TV, 10–12 April 1960), and Potter worked on the final episode "Between Two Worlds", although he received no on-screen credit (Carpenter, p.99).

31 *Between Two Rivers*, BBC-TV, 3 June 1960.

32 "Readers' Views: Dennis Potter gets a rough handling for his TV piece", *Dean Forest Guardian*, 10 June 1960, p.7. Potter replied to his critics in the following week's letters page, the gist of which can be gathered from its opening paragraph: 'Perhaps I could try to answer some of the extraordinary abuse of Mr Ron Nelson as well as the more moderate irritation of the others. "This Angry Young Man with the inferiority complex

should be ashamed to come home," says the delightful Nelson, dreaming of his salmon bar and continental beer garden. Why ever should I be "ashamed to come home"?'

33   On 22 August 1960, the BBC were given notice that Potter intended to resign his traineeship. His contract formally ended on 30 September 1960 (Carpenter, p.108).

34   Potter, *The Changing Forest* (London: Secker and Warburg, 1962). See Carpenter, p.108, which cites information from Potter's BBC file to support this interpretation of the reason behind his departure from the Corporation. It seems unlikely to be the only significant factor contributing to his decision to leave.

35   *Bookstand* (BBC-TV, 1960–1963). Potter was credited as script associate on Series One (16 October 1960–25 June 1961), which was produced by Stephen Hearst and directed by Christopher Burstall. The dramatic sequences were most often directed by John McGrath, but occasionally handled by David Willmott or Peter Hammond.

36   On 17 February 1961, Kenneth Adam (Controller of Programmes, Television) wrote to Leonard Miall (Head of Talks, Television) to pass on the view of the Director-General, Sir Hugh Carleton Greene, that the recent adaptation of Albert Camus' *The Outsider* on *Bookstand* was 'quite unworthy' of the book, and that 'it reinforced his dislike of this method of treatment.' (T32/1,579/1, *Bookstand* General, BBC Written Archives Centre.)

37   See Carpenter, p.110.

38   Raymond Williams, *Culture and Society 1780–1950* (London: Chatto and Windus, 1958).

39   Potter, "Unknown territory", *New Left Review*, January/February 1961, pp.63-65. Williams's novel *Border Country* had recently featured on *Bookstand* (BBC-TV, 11 December 1960). In 1970, Potter took part in Williams's contribution to the documentary strand *One Pair of Eyes*, which was also called *Border Country* (BBC2, 1 August 1970).

40   The *Daily Herald* was founded in 1911 and went through various upheavals, liquidations and changes of ownership over the years while still remaining close to its roots in the Labour movement, particularly the Trades Union Congress, until it eventually came under the same ownership as the *Daily Mirror*. Finally, with sales falling, on 15 September 1964, the *Daily Herald* mutated into a new newspaper called the *Sun*. For further reading, see Huw Richards, *The Bloody Circus: The Daily Herald and the Left* (London: Pluto Press, 1997).

41   Potter first had symptoms of what was later diagnosed as psoriatic arthropathy during Christmas 1961. Later, on 24 February 1962, he attended the Young Conservative and Union Organization's annual conference held in Euston. In many interviews Potter referred to this miserable occasion as the point where his knee ballooned to the size of a football and he first fell ill, totally unable to work. This is partially contradicted by the fact he wrote a number of articles for the *Herald* immediately after this date, but whatever the exact truth, Potter was certainly admitted to hospital in June 1962 for almost a month, and from that point on his health was permanently compromised.

42   Potter took over the permanent position of television critic on 23 July 1962, and he remained there until 29 August 1964. In a 1973 interview he commented that 'in those

days, the cripples, the has-beens, the deadbeats, and those due for retirement were allowed to be television critics.' – *The Hart Interview*, BBC1 (West), 14 August 1973, and on p.140 of this volume. See also his reminiscences about this period in Potter, "Various kinds of scavenger", *Sunday Times*, 24 July 1977, p.38, and on pp.201-202 of this volume.

43   For more on the 'flow' of television, see Raymond Williams, *Television: Technology and Cultural Form* (London: Fontana, 1974).

44   *Compact* (BBC, 1962–65) was a moderately successful soap opera set in the editorial offices of a woman's lifestyle magazine.

45   *Emergency – Ward 10* (ITV, 1957–67) was a smash hit soap opera set in a hospital.

46   *Sportsview* (BBC, 1954–68) was a midweek sports highlights show. It was later replaced by *Sportsnight* (BBC1, 1968–97).

47   Hughie Green was an irrepressible game show host who first came to fame with *Double Your Money* (ITV, 1955–68), and later achieved immortality as the compere for the talent show *Opportunity Knocks* (ITV, 1956; 1964–78).

48   Potter (1994), p.55.

49   Potter, "This TV newcomer smiles as she bites", *Daily Herald*, 26 November 1962, p.3, and on pp.40-41 of this volume.

50   Potter and Nathan's piece "Shakespeare Sketch" was rejected for *TW3*, but reworked for *Dear Sir, Stroke Madam*, the first show at The Poor Millionaire. For further details about The Poor Millionaire, see p.344 endnote 121 of this volume.

51   The *Sun* replaced the *Daily Herald* on 15 September, 1964. After an initial increase in circulation, its fortunes declined sharply, and by 1969 the parent company IPC was keen to offload the ailing newspaper. Australian businessman Rupert Murdoch stepped in, and on 17 November 1969, the *Sun* was relaunched as a tabloid.

52   Potter lost his deposit. The incumbent Sir Derek Walker-Smith won a majority of 8,000 in East Hertfordshire, down from 10,181 in 1959. – Anonymous, "Verdict of the voters", *Sun*, 17 October 1964, pp.4-6.

53   *The Wednesday Play: The Confidence Course*, BBC1, 24 February 1965. It was directed by Gilchrist Calder and produced by James MacTaggart. Roger Smith – the best man at Potter's wedding – commissioned the play on 18 February 1964, and it was delivered by June. Its theme derived from a report Potter was asked to prepare for BBC Radio's *Ten O'Clock* (1960–70) but which was ultimately not transmitted. It then became the basis of a novel, but this was abandoned at Smith's suggestion. David Nathan recalls a brief attempt to script it together, although this too was dropped. The studio recording for the finished play was 9–10 February 1965. The telerecording was sold abroad until 1972, after which point the master recording was destroyed as a consequence of general BBC archive policy. At time of writing, *The Confidence Course* is one of two missing Potter plays.

54   Potter, "This was a glorious wallop", *Daily Herald*, 30 March 1963, p.8, and on pp.49-50 of this volume.

55 Troy Kennedy Martin, "nats go home: First statement of a new drama for television", *Encore*, 11:2, March–April 1964, pp.21-33. The article was also reprinted in the Spring 1964 edition of *Screenwriter*.

Kennedy Martin's 'manifesto' became such a huge talking point that *Encore* devoted a section in the following issue to the reaction, which featured contributions from Potter, Sydney Newman, Michael Barry, Ken Taylor, Philip Mackie, Tony Garnett, and a concluding response from Troy Kennedy Martin. Potter's views were enthusiastic, opening with references to a script extract featured in the original piece:

> The example almost clinched it, of course. And on both sides of the dramatic excerpt, Troy Kennedy Martin's case was pushed with such vigour that doubts were bashed and bruised almost before they had the wit to parade in snide sequence behind that miserable little word 'but.'
>
> *But*...even granted almost all the vices and irrelevancies of stodgy old naturalism, Kennedy Martin's conception of the "enslavement" produced by talking faces is still too brusque a dismissal of the kinds of experience which can be well conveyed by this means, providing the dialogue is good enough and the writer genuinely has something to *say*. After all, *Z Cars* is not the yardstick.
>
> What you want to say still comes first...and you can say nothing in all sorts of ways.
>
> Splendid, the narrative method opens up new perspectives. The writer can begin to pick out a priority among objects and feelings and human speech. But this way, too, people can get so entangled with things and bits of things that we get utterly dehumanised art.
>
> For if, as Kennedy Martin suggests, even "wild editing of random objects" can give us those "pictures in the fire" (alarming phrase), the temptation to say nothing elaborately becomes overwhelming. It might be a perfect formula for decadent art...and there are enough people looking for it.
>
> But even the mildest sort of revolution produces its traitors, and no one can formulate a technique which beats the dishonest for good and all.
>
> One final thought: Kennedy Martin suggests that his ideas will "not suffer the didactic gladly." If by this, he means the great wodges of propaganda, he's right, thank God. But the sort of didacticism we need, passionately concerned to present all sorts of evidence, constantly infiltrating all our defences, is ideally suited to the narrative method. The writer can attack from all sides at once, out of a mosaic of objects, details, moods, memories and conversations. Pictures in a real fire, pictures ablaze.

– Contribution to "Reaction", *Encore*, 11:3, May–June 1964, p.40.

The reprint of the article in *Screenwriter* featured responses from Arden Winch, Jack Pulman, Allan Prior and Peter Yeldham. For a later continuation of these debates, see Potter, "Realism and non-naturalism", *The Official Programme of the Edinburgh International Television Festival 1977*, p.34-37, and on pp.203-213 of this volume.

56   *Diary of a Young Man*, BBC1, 8 August–12 September 1964.

57   On 23 June 1965, Potter appeared on BBC Light Programme's *Woman's Hour* to discuss 'Ideas in the Air.' Then, just after 2.30pm Kenith Trodd called Potter at Broadcasting House, leaving a message that the broadcast of *Vote, Vote, Vote for Nigel Barton* had been cancelled, and Potter returned the call at 3.00pm once *Woman's Hour* had finished.

The BBC's files reveal the thinking behind the cancellation. Paul Fox (Head of Current Affairs Group, Television) offered his thoughts to Huw Wheldon and Sydney Newman in a memo that same day. He opened by saying that 'the play is very nearly a documentary. It says this in almost its final line.' Newsreel footage and authentic use of Labour posters were also used to bolster his argument. Potter's closeness to the material was seen as an issue, with Fox touching on elements of autobiography in the play. He predicted that offence would be caused to both of the leading political parties, applying an idea of balance to a drama that would more appropriately be aimed at news programmes: 'Furthermore, on a time basis, the Tory is on for about seven minutes – looking a buffoon – the Labour man is on for nearly 60 minutes: a bit starry-eyed, but basically the good guy.' (T5/691/1, *Vote, Vote, Vote for Nigel Barton/Stand Up, Nigel Barton*, BBC Written Archives Centre.)

58   Potter mentioned this on a number of occasions, firstly in an interview with Paul Madden where he said that Newman commented 'You don't want to shit on the Queen.' (*Complete Programme Notes for a Season of British Television Drama 1959–1973, Held at the National Film Theatre, 11–24 October 1976*, London: British Film Institute, 1976.) A year later Potter mentioned the encounter again, only this time it had been subtly changed so that Newman was questioning 'Do you want to shit on the Queen?' to which Potter apparently replied 'Not particularly.' – *Festival 77: Late Night Line-Up*, BBC2, 1 August 1977.

59   *The Wednesday Play: Vote, Vote, Vote for Nigel Barton*, BBC1, 15 December 1965. It was directed by Gareth Davies and produced by James MacTaggart. Commissioned on 23 June 1964 and delivered by December, the play was plagued with production problems even leaving aside the controversy over being pulled from the schedules. The original recording on 12–14 April 1965 suffered from a fault due to the mis-registration of the film in the camera gate and this necessitated a remount which took place on 7–8 June. When Potter agreed to rewrite a fifth of the play after the cancellation, a third recording session took place on 6–7 October to mop up these final changes. In the end, the total recording cost of the play was £12,326 19s 11d, almost twice its original budget.

The script's first publication was in issue 10 of *Views* in Spring 1966, and then as part of *The Nigel Barton Plays: Two Television Plays*, a Penguin collection which appeared in 1967. The Old Vic Company produced a stage version at the Theatre Royal Bristol, opening 27 November 1968. The original production was released on Region 2 DVD by 2Entertain on 26 September 2005.

60 *The Wednesday Play: Alice*, BBC1, 13 October 1965. It was directed by Gareth Davies and produced by James MacTaggart. Location material was shot from 21–28 August 1965, with studio dates falling on 14–16 September 1965. The play was later adapted for radio by Derek Hoddinott and transmitted on the BBC World Service on 17 June 1979, and later as part of *Afternoon Theatre* on BBC Radio 4, 28 November 1979. The original production was released on Region 1 DVD by BBC Home Entertainment on 2 March 2010, as an 'extra' feature to accompany Jonathan Miller's *Alice in Wonderland* (BBC1, 28 December 1966). *Dreamchild*, a film released in 1985 and written by Potter, reworked sections of *Alice*. See p.364 endnote 307 for further information

61 *The Wednesday Play: Message for Posterity*, BBC1, 3 March 1967. It was directed by Gareth Davies and produced by Lionel Harris, but was at one time under Michael Bakewell's wing for *Theatre 625* (BBC2, 1964–68). Production clashes and casting difficulties ensured that the play did not enter the studio for some time. It was commissioned on 28 June 1965 and delivered in January 1966. Filming did not take place until 30 March–5 April 1967, with studio dates following on 13–15 April 1967. Sadly, this is one of two Potter plays missing from the archives at time of writing, although it was remounted for *Performance* (BBC2, 1991-98) on 29 October 1994. This production restored material cut for time in 1967, and was introduced by Brian Walden.

62 *The Wednesday Play: Stand Up, Nigel Barton*, BBC1, 8 December 1965. It was directed by Gareth Davies and produced by James MacTaggart. The commission came from Tony Garnett on 20 April 1965, with the script delivered on 19 August. Location filming was from 2–3 November and studio from 16–18 November. The script was published by Penguin in 1967 as part of *The Nigel Barton Plays: Two Television Plays*. Parts of the play also featured in the 1968 stage version of *Vote, Vote, Vote for Nigel Barton*. The original production was released on Region 2 DVD by 2Entertain on 26 September 2005 with music changes for rights reasons.

63 *The Wednesday Play: Where the Buffalo Roam*, BBC1, 2 November 1966. It was directed by Gareth Davies, produced by Lionel Harris and was the product of another Tony Garnett commission on 6 October 1965. It was delivered by Potter on 2 June 1966. Shot entirely in Wales, the studio dates came first on 24–25 September 1966 in Cardiff, with location filming continuing until 4 October. The production was shortened by almost three minutes for its repeat on 2 August 1967, and it is this version which is held at the BBC archive. The play was later adapted for radio by Derek Hoddinott and transmitted on the BBC World Service on 4 May 1980.

64 *Thirty-Minute Theatre: Emergency – Ward 9*, BBC2, 11 April 1966. It was directed by Gareth Davies and produced by Harry Moore. Originally commissioned as *Emergency Ward 11* by Kenneth Trodd on 11 January 1966, it was delivered on 24 February under its new name. Unique amongst Potter plays as a live transmission, it was long thought lost until a film recording was recovered by collector Ian Beard in 2011.

65 Potter's first article for *New Society* appeared on 8 July 1965 and he regularly appeared in its pages until 20 June 1968, at which point illness caused Potter to withdraw from a great deal of his journalistic commitments. He later returned to *New Society* for a six month spell in 1975.

66   Potter, "Aberfan", *New Society*, 27 October 1966, pp.638-639, and on pp.71-76 of this volume. As well as having a profound impact on Potter personally, the tragedy had a more trivial consequence. On 24 October 1966, Gerald Savory (Head of Plays), wrote to the Controller of BBC1 (Michael Peacock) proposing a postponement of *Where the Buffalo Roam* owing to the coincidental echoes in the play's Welsh setting and the recent Aberfan disaster. In the end, the play was not postponed, but it was decided that the scene using newscaster Ronnie Williams, who had brought news of the Aberfan disaster to television audiences at the weekend, should be reshot with newscaster Michael Griffiths. (T5/698/1, *Where the Buffalo Roam*, BBC Written Archives Centre.)

67   Potter was television critic at the *New Statesman* from 17 February–1 September 1967. He was engaged by the Arts Editor Nick Tomalin who rapidly cooled on Potter and exhorted him to 'be a proper television critic instead of someone who apparently just doesn't like television, and keeps on smashing a wordy fist into it.' Potter did not change his attitude, and eventually Tomalin relieved him of his post. Despite this, he returned to the *New Statesman* as television critic in the following decade, this time for a much longer period (Carpenter, pp.195, 205).

68   Potter wrote for the *Times* between 21 October 1967–29 November 1973.

69   Potter won the award in the best original television play category for *Vote, Vote, Vote for Nigel Barton*. *Stand Up, Nigel Barton* was the runner-up. The Writers' Guild of Great Britain hosted the ceremony at the Dorchester Hotel on 10 March 1966. – Anonymous, "Dud and Pete win Best Comedy Series award", *Daily Express*, 11 March 1966, p.10.

70   The production file held at the BBC Written Archives Centre (T5/994/1) is called *Cinderella*, but the title of the play alternates between *Cinderella* and *Almost Cinderella*.

71   For more detail on the *Cinderella* controversy, see Carpenter, pp.191-193 and Gilbert, pp.146-149.

72   Hunter Davies, "Atticus: Trial of a TV Man", *Sunday Times*, 30 October 1966, p.13.

73   Gerald Savory, 9 November 1966. (T5/994/1, *Cinderella*, BBC Written Archives Centre.)

74   *Playhouse: The Bone-grinder*, Rediffusion, 13 May 1968. It was produced and directed by Joan Kemp-Welch.

75   *Company of Five: Shaggy Dog*, London Weekend Television, 10 November 1968. It was directed by Gareth Davies and produced by Stella Richman. *Company of Five* was, as its title suggests, a series of plays featuring the same five actors. A similar format was used for BBC2's *The Sextet* (1972) which housed Potter's *Follow the Yellow Brick Road*. Lost for many years, a film recording of *Shaggy Dog* was recovered in 2005 and released on Region 2 DVD by Network as part of *Dennis Potter at London Weekend Television, Volume 2*, on 24 September 2007.

76   See p.345 endnote 131 of this volume.

77   On 16 January 1968 Potter returned to the newspaper until 23 February, when Nancy Banks-Smith's maternity leave ended. He was brought back as a general columnist on 11 March, before finally leaving the newspaper on 21 October 1968.

78   Potter, "Dennis Potter exposed", *Sun*, 20 May 1968, p.12, and on pp.88-90 of this volume.

79 Potter was admitted to Birmingham Skin Hospital at the beginning of September 1968 and eventually discharged towards the end of October.

80 *The Wednesday Play: Son of Man*, BBC1, 16 April 1969. It was directed by Gareth Davies and produced by Graeme McDonald. The play was commissioned by Kenith Trodd on 10 November 1967 under the title *Take This Water*, and delivered by October 1968, much delayed due to Potter's ill health. It entered the studio from 15–17 November 1968. A stage production quickly followed, with Frank Finlay starring as Christ at the Phoenix Centre, Leicester from 22 October 1969, under Robin Midgley's direction. It transferred to the Roundhouse, London on 12 November 1969. The script was published by both Andre Deutsch and Samuel French in 1970, and then by Penguin in 1971. On 20 April, four days after the play's transmission, the BBC showed *Son of Man Reviewed*, a half-hour discussion programme chaired by Robert Robinson. The play was also discussed on *Talkback*, BBC1, 22 April 1969.

81 *Saturday Night Theatre: Moonlight on the Highway*, London Weekend Television, 12 April 1969. It was directed by James MacTaggart and produced by Kenith Trodd on behalf of Kestrel Productions. The play was later adapted for radio by Derek Hoddinott and transmitted on the BBC World Service on 11 May 1980. The original production was released on Region 2 DVD by Network as part of *Dennis Potter at London Weekend Television, Volume 2*, on 24 September 2007.

82 John McGrath commented, 'I always felt Dennis had a cunning awareness of what was newsworthy, like doing the life of Christ. He was very good at knowing what would make the hard news rather than just the review columns. I didn't trust that' (Carpenter, p.245).

83 *The Wednesday Play: A Beast with Two Backs*, BBC1, 20 November 1968. It was directed by Lionel Harris and produced by Graeme McDonald. The play was commissioned on 16 June 1967 as an entirely different piece, *Tell Me Not Here*. The substitute *Beast* was delivered on 6 September, with location filming from 29 February–13 March 1968 and studio on 23–24 March. The original production was lost for many years, but a work print minus sound effects was kept by the director and restored by the National Film Theatre for screening on 15 October 1980.

84 Maurice Wiggin, "Choppy across the Channel", *Sunday Times*, 24 November 1968, p.59.

PART ONE: THE CONFIDENCE COURSE

85 Peter Simple was a pseudonymous author who made regular contributions to both the *Daily Telegraph* and *Sunday Telegraph*. Colin Welch (1924–97) was the original Peter in 1955, but after a couple of years Michael Wharton (1913–2006) took over, and didn't stop until his death five decades later.

86 The National Coal Board was a corporation founded in 1946 to run the newly nationalized mining industry in the United Kingdom. It managed the mines until 1987 when it was renamed the British Coal Corporation and subsequently privatized.

87 The Left Book Club was active from 1936–48 and supplied socialist literature to its members. At its peak, the Club attracted 57,000 members, and it is generally thought

to have raised the political consciousness of a generation. For a short introduction, see Paul Foot's *The Vote* (London: Viking, 2005), pp.298-300,302.

88 Bedwas is shorthand for the Bedwas Navigation Colliery in the South Wales coalfield. It did not reopen after the Miners' Strike of 6 March 1984–3 March 1985.

89 The *Report of the Advisory Committee on Organization* was delivered by the Fleck Committee in 1955. The Committee was specifically tasked with assessing management structures within the National Coal Board.

90 Frederick William Harvey (1888–1957) was an English poet and broadcaster.

91 This piece was reproduced in Julian Mitchell, John Fuller, William Donaldson and Robin McLaren (eds.), *Light Blue Dark Blue: An anthology of recent writing from Oxford and Cambridge Universities* (London: Macdonald, 1960), pp.88-93.

92 A British Warm is a double-breasted, short, thick overcoat of military cut.

93 Potter was voted by a landslide to the Chair of the Oxford University Labour Club in November 1958. He stood down as *Clarion* editor as a result of this win.

94 *The Uses of Literacy* by Richard Hoggart was published by Chatto and Windus in 1957.

95 The girl was Margaret Morgan (1933–94), whom Potter married on 10 January 1959 at Christchurch Parish Church, Berry Hill. The wedding featured on the front page of the couple's local newspaper. – Anonymous, "Mr Dennis Potter Married", *Dean Forest Guardian*, 16 January 1959, p.1.

96 Guy Mollet (1905–75) was Prime Minister of France during the Suez Crisis.

97 John Sparrow (1906–92) was Warden of All Souls College, Oxford from 1952–77. Sir John Cecil Masterman (1891–1977) was Vice-Chancellor of Oxford University from 1957–58. He later became famous for his role during World War II as Chair of the Twenty Committee, a group within MI5 that managed German double agents.

98 The interview with Potter was transmitted during the second part of BBC-TV's *Does Class Matter?* on 25 August 1958.

99 Potter was responding to the short, unsigned article "Class", *Dean Forest Guardian*, 29 August 1958, p.7:

> When I heard that Mr Christopher Mayhew, MP, was to be responsible for a series about "Class" on BBC Television, I thought that sooner or later Mr Dennis Potter, the Oxford undergraduate who is a native of Joyford, would appear on it. And sure enough, in the second programme on Monday evening there he was.
>
> Mr Potter, as can be gathered both from this programme and from an article he wrote a few weeks ago for the *New Statesman*, is obsessed with class. In this respect I very much doubt whether he is typical of Foresters from working class homes who have secured admission to our older Universities.

Potter's retaliatory letter of 5 September 1958 received the following response from the editor: 'We feel that an apology is due to Mr Potter. The short item he mentions was written with the intention of including it in "Forest Topics", where the expression of personal opinion it contained would have been quite permissible. It is unfortunate that when, owing to the shortage of topical items last week, it was transferred to the ordinary news columns, it was not noticed that it contained this expression of opinion which was quite out of place in a news item. Further reference to this letter is contained in our leading article.'

The lead article (p.6) was less conciliatory and apologetic, claiming that some working-class students – though not necessarily Potter – are 'intensely class conscious, even [...] to the extent of flaunting their working-class origin, habits and opinions before upper- and middle-class undergraduates and so start a very promising class cold war.' This did not close the debate, and the letters page remained lively over the next two issues.

100 Fred Cooke, "Miner's son at Oxford felt ashamed of home: The boy who kept his father secret", *Reynolds News*, 3 August 1958, p.7.

101 Strix was the *nom de plume* of Peter Fleming (1907–71), brother of James Bond creator Ian Fleming, who wrote a column in the *Spectator* for several decades after World War II.

102 Operation Britain was a scheme that notionally began in 1956 and was 'sponsored by a number of advertising firms [...] to tell the story of Britain's achievements at home and abroad.' The advertising controller of the scheme, Mr W.C. Thiele intended that Operation Britain should counter 'the astonishingly widely held belief [...] that Britain is finished.' (Anonymous, "Progress of Operation Britain", *Times*, 29 October 1957, p.12.) The company itself was formally established and announced in June 1957, and the name Operation Britain was regularly seen in newspaper advertisements – alongside the slogan 'British Achievements Speak for Britain' – but by the start of the 1960s, it had faded into obscurity. The president of the company, Lord Luke of Pavenham, was the grandson of John Lawson Johnston, the man who invented Bovril.

103 John Austin (1911–60) was a British philosopher of language, and the White's Professor of Moral Philosophy at Oxford University. He died a fortnight after this article was published.

104 The Senior Common Room, or SCR, is a common room for the use of academic staff, and generally a hotbed of gossip, feuds and malice.

105 Stuart Petre Brodie Mais (1885–1975) was a British author, broadcaster and the original host of BBC Radio's *Letter from America*.

106 The Establishment was a nightclub founded by comedian Peter Cook and the writer Nicholas Luard. Based in 18 Greek Street in Soho, London, it opened for business on 5 October 1961 and ran under their ownership until Cook & Luard Productions were put into liquidation on 23 September 1963. From that point on, the club was run by a number of owners until the Establishment name finally disappeared when a new venue, the Zebra Club, opened at 18 Greek Street in August 1966.

107 Potter had three children: Jane (born January 1960), Sarah (born July 1961) and Robert (born March 1965).

108 Potter himself had been selected as Labour parliamentary candidate for East Hertfordshire in early 1962, and, despite being hospitalised with arthritis in June of the same year, had agreed to continue with his candidacy.

109 Television Audience Measurement (TAM) represented the ITV franchise holders and measured ratings via meters installed in a sample of roughly 2,000 homes. The BBC used its own method of calculating audience figures. For further reading see Robert Silvey, *Who's Listening?: The Story of BBC Audience Research* (London: George Allen and Unwin, 1974), pp.176-186.

110 This production of *War and Peace*, which occupied a three-hour timeslot on ITV (including a break for the news), was translated by Robert David MacDonald, from an adaptation by Erwin Piscator, Alfred Neumann and Guntram Prüfer. It was directed by Silvio Narizzano and transmitted on 26 March 1963.

111 It seems likely that the 'sticky pile of plays' referred to was ATV Television's *Drama '63*, a series of single plays that ran from 13 January–22 December 1963.

112 Potter was reporting from the set of *Dixon of Dock Green* (BBC, 1955–76).

113 Potter had an interest in science fiction, and in 1965 he was commissioned by his old *Bookstand* colleague Stephen Hearst to write a 45-minute programme on the subject for *Sunday Night* (BBC1, 1965–66), the successor to *Monitor* (BBC, 1958–65). Potter's burgeoning career as a dramatist caused the commission to fall through, much to the anger of Hearst who wrote to Potter on 5 October 1965 stating, 'I realise that writing an arts documentary is chicken feed in terms of money compared with writing a play but you ought not to treat me as if it were.' (T48/476/1, TV Scriptwriter, Potter, Dennis, 1964–1987, BBC Written Archives Centre.)

During an interview to promote *Secret Friends*, Potter revealed that he had once pitched an idea to *Doctor Who* producer Verity Lambert. Recalling the storyline rather hazily, he added that 'it was probably about a schizophrenic who only thought he was a time traveller' (Ginny Dougary, "Potter's weal", *Times*, 27 September 1992, Saturday Review, p.10). Lambert was producer on the first two series of *Doctor Who*, departing in the summer of 1965. Potter at this time shared an agent – Roger Hancock – with *Doctor Who* writer Terry Nation, whose Dalek creations had boosted the series' ratings upon their debut in December 1963.

114 *A for Andromeda* was a seven-part BBC-TV series transmitted from 3 October–14 November 1961. A sequel, *The Andromeda Breakthrough* followed in 1962. The original series featured Julie Christie in her breakthrough role as Andromeda.

115 Potter is probably referring to *Out of This World*, a science fiction anthology series produced by ABC Television which was transmitted from 3 June–22 September 1962. This highly regarded series was produced by Leonard White, alongside Irene Shubik as story editor. Shubik later moved to the BBC where she produced a similar series *Out of the Unknown* (BBC2, 1965–71), again to much acclaim.

116 *The Great War* was a 26-part documentary series transmitted on BBC2 between 30 May–22 November 1964.

117 *Beat the Clock* was a popular game show segment of *Sunday Night at the London Palladium* (ATV, 1955–65). Contestants on the show had to carry out various comic tasks before the time elapsed on a large countdown clock.

118 The Speight plays were *The Compartment* (BBC-TV, 22 August 1961) and *The Playmates* (BBC-TV, 16 July 1962). Both starred Michael Caine, and they were later remade for *The Wednesday Play* under the group title *Double Bill* (BBC1, 26 November 1969) with Marty Feldman taking the lead.

119 Sydney Newman was an influential figure in the development of television drama. Born in Canada, he worked in both Canadian and American television before moving to London in 1958 to work for ABC Television. At ABC, he took on the series *Armchair Theatre* (1956–74) and made it a critical and popular, though controversial, success. He also devised *The Avengers* (1961–69) before moving to the BBC on 15 January 1963 as Head of Drama. There he was responsible for some ground-breaking shows such as *Doctor Who* (1963–89,1996,2005–) and *The Wednesday Play*. He left the BBC in 1967.

120 PC Sweet (played by Terence Edmond) was a character from the popular police series *Z Cars* (1962–78). On 4 March 1964, Sweet was killed off in the episode "A Man…Like Yourself." The event shocked the nation.

121 The Alberts were an anarchic music and comedy act, consisting of two brothers – Anthony and Douglas Gray – and Bruce Lacey. They were friendly with Spike Milligan and Michael Bentine – Lacey worked for a time on *The Goon Show* (BBC Radio, 1951–60) and met the Grays on *Son of Fred* (Associated-Rediffusion, 17 September–5 November 1956) – and were an influence on the Bonzo Dog Doo Dah Band. – Julian Cowley, "Quirk, strangeness and charm", *Wire*, n.368, October 2014, p.33.

The Alberts regularly performed live, and as well as appearing at The Establishment, they also featured at a restaurant/cabaret venue called The Poor Millionaire. The latter was one of a number of restaurants owned by ex-journalist Stephen Kennedy, and on 28 October 1963 he staged 'a twice-nightly, one-hour "Cityrical" revue…combined with a meal…Price 42s for show and dinner.' – Anthony Shields and Robert Gaddes, "Night life", *What's On In London*, 25 October 1963, pp.58-59.

This first show *Dear Sir, Stroke Madam* had a number of *TW3* writers on its roster including Dennis Potter and David Nathan. The director was Joe McGrath. Potter and Nathan worked on two subsequent shows at the club, *Is it True What they Say About…?* (9 December 1963–8 March 1964) and *Excuse Fingers* (9 March–5 June 1964), before calling it a day. The Alberts made their appearance shortly after this, performing their show *60 Minutes of British Rubbish*, a cut-down version of *An Evening of British Rubbish* which had recently finished a year-long run in the West End.

122 On 7 May 1962, *Panorama* featured a debate on boxing which included a clip of Benny Paret's final fight. Baroness Summerskill and Jack Solomons were the participants in the debate, which was refereed by Richard Dimbleby.

123 This line, much beloved by music-hall comics, came from a stage version of Ellen Wood's melodramatic 1861 novel *East Lynne*.

124 On 21 October 1966, a pile of coal waste slid on to the village of Aberfan in South Wales. 144 people died, of whom 116 were children. Pantglas Junior School took the brunt of the landslide, which happened just after the children had returned from their morning assembly.

125 This article had the following title in the Scottish edition: "It takes courage to watch your play on TV".

126 It's probable that Potter is referring to *Shaggy Dog*, which was eventually transmitted on 23 November 1968.

127 The idea of people gathering in the street to be sacramentally sick was one of Potter's favourite conceits, to which he returned on many occasions.

128 "If I Only Had Time" by New Zealand pop singer John Rowles had reached number three in the hit parade in late April.

129 Thomas Jonathan Wooler was a Radical publisher in the early nineteenth century. He published the *Black Dwarf* as a response to various government Gagging Acts, and was frequently imprisoned for sedition and libel.

130 The Tratoo was a Soho-based Mario & Franco restaurant. Lexicographer Jonathon Green described it as 'the "little brother" of La Trattoria Terrazza, which reigned as super-chic.'

131 Kenneth Tynan (1927–80) was a renowned theatre critic and writer, who was also Literary Manager of the National Theatre from 1963–74. In this guise, he had commissioned a play from Potter in 1967, which was apparently completed but remained undelivered. On 16 July 1968, Tynan wrote a memo to Laurence Olivier which included a reference to 'The Dennis Potter – which, as I told you, he finished last November. However, he refuses to show it to us in its present form because "it isn't a play, it's a scream of pain." He promises that by October 31 he'll show us either (i) a revised version or (ii) the original scream.' – Kathleen Tynan (ed.), *Kenneth Tynan: Letters* (London: Weidenfeld and Nicolson, 1994), p.421.

The play was never produced. Some have speculated that it later became *Son of Man* but this does not fit with the dates of the BBC commission. Carpenter suggests it was 'autobiographical' (p.205), quoting letters from both Clive Goodwin and Potter himself. By Tynan's description, it is likely to have been a stage version of *The Rivers of Babylon*, rejected by the BBC in 1967 and rewritten for London Weekend Television as *Moonlight on the Highway* in 1969. For a detailed account of *The Rivers of Babylon*, see Carpenter, pp.195-203.

132 In May 1968, the streets of Paris were filled with a series of demonstrations by striking workers and students that briefly threatened to bring France to a standstill. Student leaders Daniel Cohn-Bendit and Alain Krivine became radical icons, and British political groups such as the Workers' Revolutionary Party became briefly fashionable in the light of the May events.

133 Potter's literary agent at this time was Clive Goodwin (1932–77). As well as being an agent, he was a well-known figure in radical politics, although often considered to be

something of a political poseur. He died in tragic circumstances in Los Angeles while representing his client Trevor Griffiths during the pre-production work on Warren Beatty's film *Reds* (1981). Goodwin fell ill in the lobby of his hotel, but was mistakenly arrested and put in a police cell overnight, where he died of a brain haemorrhage.

During his lifetime, Potter's agents were, sequentially, Roger Hancock, Clive Goodwin, and Judy Daish.

134 The disruptive figure in Potter's first play *The Confidence Course* (1965) is called William Hazlitt, posing as the essayist despite the contemporary setting.

135 Potter was first hospitalised by psoriatic arthropathy in June 1962, and this seems the likely date that he came across this volume of Hazlitt.

136 When presenting his selection of literary pieces for *With Great Pleasure* (BBC Radio 4, 5 September 1976), Potter commented that 'Hazlitt could quite properly claim that he never wrote a single line which betrayed a principle or disguised a feeling. To read him is to *know* him.' His ongoing enthusiasm for Hazlitt was such that when he later appeared on *Desert Island Discs* (1977), he selected 'the best possible collection of Hazlitt's essays' as his book of choice.

137 This idea came closest to fruition in December 1974, when Mike Wooler (Acting Head of Arts, Television) commissioned Potter to write a 50-60 minute script on William Hazlitt for the *Omnibus* strand on BBC1. Although a contract was issued on 17 December, the project died later that month because a fee could not be agreed. (RCONT20, Solicitors and Copyright Registry, Dennis Potter 1970–74, BBC Written Archives Centre.)

138 Hartlepool is a town in the North-east of England. During the nineteenth century two towns grew from the development of the Hartlepool Dock and Railway Company, and later the West Hartlepool Harbour and Dock. When Potter visited, the two towns were thus referred to as Hartlepools. In 1967 they were formally unified as Hartlepool.

139 From the poem "Leisure" by W.H. Davies.

140 Although Potter hoped and expected to return, this was his final piece for the *Sun*.

INTRODUCTION TO PART TWO: TELLING STORIES

141 Potter, "Acid drops", *Plays and Players*, 19:2, November 1971, p.58, and on p.123 of this volume.

142 Potter, "Lightning over a dark field", *Times*, 7 December 1968, p.20, and on p.106 of this volume. On being 'sustained' through six years of pain by 'the conviction that one day I will write a masterpiece,' see "I really must tell you I'm so very happy", *Sun*, 13 May 1968, p.3, and on p.87 of this volume.

143 *Saturday Night Theatre: Lay Down Your Arms*, London Weekend Television, 23 May 1970. It was directed by Christopher Morahan and produced by Kenith Trodd. The second of Potter's two plays made by Kestrel Productions, it was recorded in October 1969 and released on DVD by Network as part of *Dennis Potter at London Weekend Television, Volume 2* on 24 September 2007.

144 *Play for Today: Angels are so Few*, BBC1, 5 November 1970. It was produced by Graeme McDonald and directed by Gareth Davies. Delivered to the BBC on 15 December 1969, it was recorded on 11 April 1970.

145 Anonymous, "A spy in the War Ops room", *Sunday Times*, 17 May 1970, pp.44-45.

146 "Let's sell the army on laughs", *Daily Herald*, 9 September 1961, p.6. Potter's byline was 'Pte. Dennis Potter (retd.).' In 1980, Potter retold this story but qualified his description of his experiences as a Russian language clerk at the War Office with the more positive comment that 'I enjoyed it. Very much. It gave me a play!' (*Guardian Lecture* interview with Philip Purser, National Film Theatre, 30 October 1980). Potter discussed his reasons for refusing the chance to become an Officer in "I am proud of my home and family... no obsession", p.7, and on pp.24-26 of this volume.

147 Potter, "Britain's natural break army", *Times*, 25 April 1970, p.V. This review of Correlli Barnett's *Britain and Her Army 1509–1970* (London: Allen Lane, 1970) attracted complaints from *Times* readers.

148 A letter to the *Times* connected *Lay Down Your Arms* with 'a recent television play about Sandhurst' (presumably *The Wednesday Play: Sovereign's Company*, BBC1, 22 April 1970) in order to 'protest at the stream of distorting and lying propaganda about the Army poured out by television.' – Gabrielle Evelegh, "Knocking the army", *Times*, 30 May 1970, p.9.

149 Potter, "Kafka and Brasso", *Times*, 14 May 1973, p.11, and on p.135 of this volume.

150 Nancy Banks-Smith, "*Lay Down Your Arms* and *Burma Star Gala* on television", *Guardian*, 25 May 1970, p.6.

151 Potter, quoted by Graham Fuller, "Dennis Potter", *American Film*, March 1989, p.33.

152 *The Hart Interview*, and on p.145 of this volume.

153 Bishopbriggs Town Council agreed their Provost's request to complain about *Angels are so Few*, the play having left him 'shattered at the filth and disgusting expressions that were popping out.' A Councillor described the programme as 'vulgar and pornographic.' – Anonymous, "Council to protest about 'filth' on television", *Glasgow Herald*, 10 November 1970, p.21.

154 T.C. Worsley, "Potter and Bergmann" (sic), *Financial Times*, 11 November 1970, p.3. Worsley felt that *Play for Today* showed dramas that would not be taken seriously at the National Film Theatre or Royal Court but, by being shown on television, would be seen as '"controversial" and therefore interesting and therefore good.'

155 Potter, "The only meat was in the cookery class", *Sun*, 15 February 1968, p.14.

156 "Boy in a landscape", *New Statesman*, 29 March 1974, p.459, and on p.149 of this volume.

157 *Sunday Night Theatre: Paper Roses*, Granada, 13 June 1971. It was directed by Barry Davis and produced by Kenith Trodd, who had joined Granada after the break-up of Kestrel in 1970. Rehearsed in November 1970, it was being filmed in the 'now defunct Cross Street offices of the *Guardian* in Manchester' when the *Guardian* went behind the scenes (Anonymous, "Tele verité", *Guardian*, 4 December 1970, p.12). A radio version

of *Paper Roses*, adapted by Derek Hoddinott, was first transmitted on the BBC World Service on 18 May 1980.

158 Peter Fiddick, "*Paper Roses* on television", *Guardian*, 14 June 1971, p.8.

159 Potter, "Various kinds of scavenger", p.38, and on p.202 of this volume.

160 *The Hart Interview*, and on p.144 of this volume.

161 See Philip Purser, "Dennis's other hat" in Vernon W. Gras and John R. Cook (eds.), *The Passion of Dennis Potter: International Collected Essays* (Basingstoke: Macmillan, 2000), pp.179-193.

162 Julian Critchley, "Out of his system", *Times*, 25 May 1970, p.5.

163 Maurice Wiggin, "Private faces, public spaces", *Sunday Times*, 4 November 1973, p.40. When asked about criticism, Potter stated that 'I take it personally' but not necessarily 'seriously.' – Cordell Marks, "The way a writer beat arthritis", *TV Times*, 23–29 May 1970, p.6.

164 For Potter's response to Philip Purser's negative review of *The Bone-grinder*, see "Dennis Potter exposed", p.12, and on pp.88-90 of the volume.

165 Qualifying his praise, Fiddick observed that the 'only thing he got wrong' was the portrayal of the television critic: 'I, for one, was watching it in a professional viewing room, at 2pm on a Friday afternoon' ("*Paper Roses* on television", p.8). In an era of regular press viewings, Potter's enforced but also preferred domestic conditions of viewing made his reviewing consistently personal.

166 Potter, "Switch on, switch over, switch off", *Times*, 15 March 1973, p.10, and on p.131 of this volume. For a sample of Potter's long-running sparring with fellow critic Clive James, see "Glop", *New Statesman*, 22 April 1977, p.535, and on pp.190-192 of this volume. See also p.360 endnote 274 of this volume for further discussion.

167 *Play for Today: Traitor*, BBC1, 14 October 1971. It was directed by Alan Bridges and produced by Graeme McDonald. Potter discussed *Traitor* on the night of transmission on BBC2's *Late Night Line-Up*; part of the interview was transcribed in "Red cheeks", *Listener*, 4 November 1971, p.616. A radio adaptation written by Derek Hoddinott and starring Denholm Elliott was transmitted on the BBC World Service on 25 May 1980 and BBC Radio 4, as part of *Afternoon Theatre*, on 20 May 1981.

168 Potter would also mention Philby in *Blade on the Feather* (1980).

169 Fuller (ed.), p.45.

170 Carpenter, p.266.

171 Nancy Banks-Smith, "*Traitor* on television", *Guardian*, 15 October 1971, p.10. Potter muddied the waters in a characteristic overlapping of themes across his fiction and non-fiction: *Traitor*'s depiction of an adult's obsession with Camelot as part of Adrian Harris's childhood problems partly echoed Potter's review of Geoffrey Ashe's book *Camelot and the Vision of Albion* (London: Heinemann, 1971), which alluded to different traumatic events in his own childhood ("King Arthur and a vision of childhood country lost", *Times*, 18 January 1971, p.8). *Traitor* had already been written – commissioned as *Treason*

on 23 January 1970, it was delivered as *Traitor* on 24 March 1970 – and was recorded between 9-11 April 1971.

172 Raymond Williams, "Against adjustment", *Listener*, 4 June 1970, p.770.

173 *Casanova*, BBC2, 16 November–21 December 1971. The serial was produced by Mark Shivas and directed by John Glenister (three episodes) and Mark Cullingham (three episodes). This piece was as complex logistically as it was conceptually: commissioned in February 1970, the six scripts were delivered in instalments between August 1970 and February 1971 and recorded out of sequence between June–October 1971. The six episodes, averaging 52 minutes each, were reworked into two omnibus editions of approximately 100 minutes each, that were transmitted on BBC2 on 9–10 September 1974. The six-part serial received a Region 2 DVD release by 2Entertain on 31 May 2004.

174 Interviewed by Michael Billington on *Scan*, BBC Radio 4, 25 November 1971.

175 *Scan*.

176 Potter later recalled that, while reviewing books for the *Times*, he received a new translation of Casanova's memoirs and thought 'That's something one might write about,' but 'had to stop reading them, and I never reviewed them because, as a writer, I didn't want to know too much' (Fuller (ed.), p.68). Biographers have noted that Potter would have been referring to Willard R. Trask's six-volume *The History of My Life* that began publication in 1966. However, in 1969 Potter reviewed John Masters' book *Casanova*, which he compared with 'the unity of style and attitude of the original' – Potter, "The art of trespass", *Times*, 29 November 1969, Saturday Review, pp.I,V.

177 Fuller (ed.), p.70.

178 Potter, "The art of trespass", p.I.

179 Potter, "The art of trespass", p.I.

180 Anonymous, "TV play 'lewd' complaint", *Times*, 2 December 1971, p.5.

181 "TV play 'lewd' complaint". In response, Whitehouse argued that the implication was that 'individuals and organizations have no right publicly to express their concern about the policy of the BBC whose personnel are public servants.' For Whitehouse, 'those who subscribe to, and act upon, this view' were the ones who should be 'labelled "dangerous"' (Mary Whitehouse, "Casanova", *Times*, 14 December 1971, p.13). For further reading see Ben Thompson (ed.), *Ban This Filth! Letters from the Mary Whitehouse Archive* (London: Faber and Faber, 2012), pp.172-180.

182 Philip Oakes, "Potter's path", *Sunday Times*, 7 November 1971, p.38. For Potter on Whitehouse as leader of the 'populist wing of the anxious puritans', see "Switch on, switch over, switch off", p.10, and on p.131 of this volume.

183 *The Hart Interview*, and on p.136 of this volume.

184 *The Hart Interview*, and on pp.136-137 of this volume; and Potter, "One man's week", *Sunday Times*, 18 April 1976, p.32, and on p.173 of this volume.

185 John R. Cook, *Dennis Potter: A Life on Screen* Second edition (Manchester: Manchester University Press, 1998), p.160. Indeed, Potter withdrew from the 30 October 1970 edition

of radio programme *Any Questions?* on 26 October owing to illness (WE/13/977/1, Bristol contributors, Dennis Potter 1966–1980, BBC Written Archives Centre). When he appeared on the 26 November 1971 edition, he defended the nudity in the first two episodes of *Casanova* as a legitimate device given the context of depicting 'a man in a sense imprisoned by his desires.' As a comparison, he argued that '*Miss World* is an obscenity.'

186 Carpenter, p.278.

187 For further details, see Carpenter, p.297.

188 In particular: *The Hart Interview*, and on pp.143-144 of this volume; "Boy in a landscape", p.459, and on p.149 of this volume; and "One man's week", p.32, and on p.173 of this volume.

189 Potter, "A Frosty night", *Sunday Times*, 8 May 1977, p.38, and on p.194 of this volume. Other examples include Potter's description of a dream involving 'some indistinct trees,' from which he awoke to find 'only the neat row of beds on the other side of the hospital ward'; reading *The Dynamics of Creation* in hospital, Potter drew his common observation that 'Psychiatrists and biographers have differing levels of access to two kinds of evidence: the life and the work' – both from "The artist on the doctor's couch", *Times*, 4 September 1972, p.15.

190 Potter quoted in Cook, "Dennis Potter: A Personal Interview (10 May 1990)", in Gras and Cook (eds.), p.242.

191 Potter, "Telling stories", *New Society*, 15 May 1975, pp.419-420, and on pp.164-168 of this volume.

192 *The Sextet*: *Follow the Yellow Brick Road*, BBC2, 4 July 1972. Directed by Alan Bridges and produced by Roderick Graham, the play was recorded on 4 April 1972. The script was published in Robert Muller (ed.), *The Television Dramatist* (London: Elek, 1973). *The Sextet* (BBC2, 13 June–1 August 1972) was a series of eight plays by different writers featuring a repertory cast including Denholm Elliott and Billie Whitelaw. Potter was originally commissioned in February 1971 to write a play with the working title *Mustang Has Already Been Used*, in which a poet was hired by a car firm.

193 *Play for Today*: *Only Make Believe*, BBC1, 12 February 1973. It was directed by Robert Knights and produced by Graeme McDonald. The play was delivered on 6 January 1970, just three weeks after *Angels are so Few*. The play was accepted in March 1970 after requested rewrites, but the play had still not entered production in July 1972, when rights were sought for another year. Studio recording took place on 10 September 1972. A theatre version directed by Richard Wilson was previewed at the Playhouse, Marlow from 26–30 November 1974 and opened at Oxford Playhouse on 10 December.

194 Reviewing *Paper Roses*, Mary Holland hoped that Potter 'will turn his eye to the next branch of the media he knows well – television itself' ("A journalist in decline", *Observer*, 20 June 1971, p.27), while Maurice Wiggin stated more specifically that 'I await, keenly, Mr Potter's low-down on the Television Centre.' – "Needling time", *Sunday Times*, 20 June 1971, p.27.

195 *Hide and Seek*, Andre Deutsch Limited/Quartet, 1973. The novel was commissioned in 1969 by Gollancz, who had previously published *The Glittering Coffin*. Potter submitted it in early 1972 with the title *The Mountains of Tasgi*. Editorial director Giles Gordon expressed satisfaction with it in March 1972 but its brief sexual explicitness concerned owner Livia Gollancz and a dispute broke out in April 1972. Gordon moved on and Potter's book attracted the interest of other publishers. – Anonymous, "Exit Gordon from Gollancz", *Guardian*, 3 May 1972, p.13.

196 'He realized that he had to watch every word, that he had to edit with great caution, crossing out, interpolating, amending. Nothing had to get through which could be used by his enemies' (*Hide and Seek*, p.119). Peter Stead argued that *Hide and Seek* 'is absolutely essential to any understanding' of how Potter 'wants to be seen as The Author, a character or rather an agent in our culture who exists alongside his works and comments on them.' – Peter Stead, *Dennis Potter* (Bridgend: Seren, 1993), p.14.

197 The sequence that includes 'Mouth upon mouth, tongue against tongue, limb upon limb, skin rubbing at skin. Faces contort and organs spurt out a smelly stain, a sticky betrayal' – *Hide and Seek*, p.118.

198 'No cartographer can trace on any known map the place where we were born and bred. Unlocatable is that lost land where we first hear someone calling our name. Gone is the place where we learn to speak and read and laugh and cry (or, worse, not cry), gone like trees walking' (*Hide and Seek*, p.20). See also "King Arthur and a vision of childhood country lost", p.8: 'The place where we are born and bred, where we learn to speak and read and laugh and cry (or, more painfully, not to cry) must often take on for us a weird cast as unknown to the cartographer as the ache in our souls is to the physician or even the psychiatrist.'

199 Potter, quoted in Lesley Thornton, "Innocence and experience", *Radio Times*, 27 January–2 February 1979, p.8. As in *The Singing Detective*, 'the whole dynamic of *Hide and Seek* is the possibility of using fiction in order to discover the truth about oneself' (Cook, p.127). Memory and storytelling are connected: here, as in Anthony Hilfer's description of *The Singing Detective*, 'the distinction between *replaying* and *revising* becomes crucial, as story-revision becomes self-revision" – "Run over by one's own story: genre and ethos in Dennis Potter's *The Singing Detective*", in Jonathan Bignell, Stephen Lacey and Madeleine Macmurraugh-Kavanagh (eds.), *British Television Drama: Past, Present and Future* (Basingstoke: Palgrave, 2000), pp.133-134 (italics in original).

200 The similarity between these elements of *Stand Up, Nigel Barton* and *The Singing Detective* was aided by the casting of Janet Henfrey as the schoolteacher in both. Potter acknowledged the seeming 'impossibility of referring to something 20 years ago in television terms,' but wanted 'to say, yes, there is, this medium does, after all have some continuity' and a writer can construct a body of work that coheres over decades. – Cook, in Gras and Cook (eds.), p.246.

201 Potter, introduction to *Brimstone & Treacle* (London: Eyre Methuen, 1978), p.3.

202 Interviewed by Ludovic Kennedy on *Tonight*, BBC1, 7 November 1977, and on p.236 of this volume.

203 Interviewed by Colin Morris on *The Anno Domini Interview*, BBC1, 13 February 1977.

204 *Tonight*, and on pp.235-236 of this volume.

205 Potter argued that '*Casanova* was more religious than [*Son of*] *Man*' and *Follow the Yellow Brick Road* 'was essentially and passionately a religious play' (*The Anno Domini Interview*). Potter stated that he did not understand Mary Whitehouse's objections to *Only Make Believe* 'which, if anything, is a religious play' – Stanley Reynolds, "Potter loves the idea of Mrs Whitehouse. He sees her as standing up for all those people with ducks on their wall who have been laughed at", *Guardian*, 16 February 1973, p.10.

206 *Play for Today: Joe's Ark*, BBC1, 14 February 1974. It was directed by Alan Bridges and produced by Graeme McDonald. Its delays and rewrites are discussed on p.373 endnote 386 of this volume. The play was later adapted for radio by Derek Hoddinott and transmitted on the BBC World Service on 1 June 1980. The script was published as part of *Dennis Potter on Television: Waiting for the Boat* (London: Faber and Faber, 1984; reprinted as *Blue Remembered Hills and other plays*, Faber and Faber, 1996).

207 Potter, "The celluloid messiahs", *Sunday Times*, 10 April 1977, p.33. See p.367 endnote 344 of this volume.

208 Potter, "And with no language but a cry", BBC Radio 3, 27 December 1976, and on p.188 of this volume.

209 *Where Adam Stood*, BBC2, 21 April 1976. Adapted from a small passage of *Father and Son*, a memoir by Edmund Gosse published in 1907, it was directed by Brian Gibson and produced by Kenith Trodd. It was commissioned on 17 August 1973 for the *Playhouse* strand, but would ultimately be transmitted as a standalone. Delivered on 14 May 1975 under its working title *Father and Son*, the play was filmed between 8 September–10 October 1975. Mary Whitehouse enjoyed the play so much that she sent praise to the BBC and to Potter – Thompson (ed.), pp.174-176.

210 *Wessex Tales: A Tragedy of Two Ambitions*, BBC2, 21 November 1973. It was directed by Michael Tuchner and produced by Irene Shubik. Adapted from the short story by Thomas Hardy first published in *Life's Little Ironies* (London: Osgood, McIlvaine & Co., 1894), the script was commissioned on 12 October 1972 and delivered on 1 February 1973. Filmed between 21 May–14 June 1973, the play was transmitted as part of *Wessex Tales* (7 November–12 December 1973), a strand of Hardy adaptations.

211 *Late Call*, BBC2, 1 March–22 March 1975. It was directed by Philip Dudley and produced by Ken Riddington. Adapted from the 1964 novel by Angus Wilson, the scripts were commissioned on 21 August 1973 and delivered in December 1973. Studio recording of the first episode took place on 28 May 1974, intended for transmission on 14 September, but the serial was disrupted by industrial action for many weeks due to an ongoing strike at Television Centre by production assistants in the Drama Group. Studio recordings were rescheduled for dates in January and February 1975 and the transmission dates moved to March.

212 *Play for Today: Schmoedipus*, BBC1, 20 June 1974. It was directed by Barry Davis and produced by Kenith Trodd. The script was delivered on 13 June 1973 and the play was

recorded on 17–18 December 1973. *Track 29*, a film version of *Schmoedipus* written by Potter, was released in 1988: see p.364 endnote 308 of this volume.

213 *Brimstone & Treacle*, originally scheduled for BBC1 on 6 April 1976 as a *Play for Today*, but not transmitted until 25 August 1987. It was directed by Barry Davis and produced by Kenith Trodd. The production was released on Region 2 DVD by 2Entertain on 31 May 2004 in its most complete form but with music substitutions for rights reasons.

214 "A note from Mr Milne", *New Statesman*, 23 April 1976, pp.548-549, and on pp.175-179 of this volume.

215 *Play for Today: Double Dare*, BBC1, 6 April 1976. It was directed by John Mackenzie and produced by Kenith Trodd. Commissioned as an untitled idea on 6 July 1973, the script was delivered on 12 July 1974 and filmed at Ealing, with half a day on location, from 5–23 January 1976. Its transmission date of 6 April had been intended for *Brimstone & Treacle*. Kika Markham played two roles: actress Helen, questioned by writer Martin Ellis (Alan Dobie) about how far she will go sexually in a role, and an escort with a client at the same hotel. The exploration of sexual politics and 'the border-lines between reality and fantasy' (Cook, p.90), as Martin's script ideas seem to leak into the world around him, was heightened by the resemblance to a meeting that Potter had with Markham to discuss an unwritten play during his own writer's block. Director John Mackenzie took Potter's recommendation that he 'do it your way' and developed a formal thriller style with resonances that exploited the echoes of Alfred Hitchcock's *Vertigo* (1958) in its concern with doubles, transferred guilt and redressing women (Gilbert, pp.210-211). Helen criticises Martin's questions as the product of the way in which society views women, but is powerless to change that gaze – Potter would return to these issues in *Blackeyes*.

216 Potter (1978), p.2.

217 "Family Announcements", *Dean Forest Guardian*, 28 November 1975, p.8.

218 "One man's week", p.32, and on p.173 of this volume.

219 In a particularly jolly tirade on *A Plus* (Thames/ITV, 2 February 1984), Potter grinned and encouraged interviewer Mavis Nicholson to agree with him as he said: 'Some of those shits walking around the corridors of the television companies, you've only got to look at them to know that they're treacherous even as soon as they open their mouths. I mean, you can see it on their faces, can't you? Well say yes!'

220 Mary Holland, "Coming back to class", *Observer*, 17 October 1971, p.2.

221 Banks-Smith, "*Traitor* on television", p.10.

222 "Acid drops", p.58, and on p.122 of this volume.

223 Potter, "Tsar's army", *New Statesman*, 13 October 1972, p.526, and on p.128 of this volume.

224 "Switch on, switch over, switch off", p.10, and on pp.131-133 of this volume.

225 *The Hart Interview*, and on pp.135-145 of this volume; and Potter, "In a rut", 22 November 1974, pp.752-753, and on pp.156-158 of this volume.

226 "Realism and non-naturalism", p.37, and on p.212 of this volume.

227 Cook, p.144.

PART TWO: TELLING STORIES

228 Elsewhere, Potter less discreetly attributed this request to a memo by Humphrey Burton about *Lay Down Your Arms*, during the latter's time as Head of Drama, Arts and Music at LWT. – Joan Bakewell and Nicholas Garnham, *The New Priesthood: British Television Today* (London: Allen Lane, 1970), p.84.

229 *Casanova* was commissioned the day after the broadcast of the final episode of *The Six Wives of Henry VIII* (BBC2, 11 January–5 February 1970), and broadcast in the same year as *Elizabeth R* (BBC2, 17 February–24 March 1971). Potter 'self-generated' *Casanova* and critiqued both the costume drama trend and claims of 'historical accuracy,' but 'the Plays department spied a suitable follow-up to its last big costume success' (Cook, p.151). Publicity stressed the fact that crew from the earlier serial were working on *Casanova* – see Martin Jackson, "*Casanova* gets 'royal' treatment", *Daily Express*, 26 March 1971, p.17; Yvonne Thomas, "Frank Finlay, about to lose his anonymity in *Casanova*", *Radio Times*, 13-19 November 1971, pp.15,17.

230 Potter's comments echo those of television writer Nigel Kneale in 1959 recalling canteen 'arguments about the missing mystique, the TV Philosopher's Stone that would confer legitimacy on a bastard medium' – "Not quite so intimate", *Sight and Sound*, 28:2, Spring 1959, p.86.

231 Potter was writing a play of this description: *Joe's Ark* was delivered on 9 December 1971 with the summary 'Joe owns a pet shop in Wales. Above the shop his much-loved daughter is dying.' In his introduction to *Waiting for the Boat* (1984), Potter wrote that the plot 'sounds like a winning entry in a *New Statesman* Competition parodying gloomy pretension' that would give the rival channel ITV 'a warm glow of instant gratitude' (p.20).

232 Potter's reworking of John of Gaunt's 'this blessed plot, this earth, this realm, this England' speech from Shakespeare's *Richard II* Act 2 Scene 1 is particularly playful given that, though it was subsequently used as a shorthand for patriotism, the source speech ends with a critique of leadership: this England 'is now leased out' and 'Hath made a shameful conquest of itself.' Potter often mentioned toothpaste when arguing that television and the wider culture reduce all aspirations to the same type of experience as mass consumption and advertising. Nigel Barton condemned himself for selling his ideals like the latest brand of toothpaste in *Stand Up, Nigel Barton*, while Potter's reviews included such statements as 'the best tele-cowboys are not interrupted by the claims of striped toothpaste and detergents,' and 'surely the responsibilities of drama executives are slightly different from those needed by toothpaste salesmen?' – *Daily Herald*, respectively "Too tough for a sheriff", 7 May 1962, p.7; "100 helpings of soporific sugar", 7 December 1963, p.6.

233 The phrase 'the sweetest music this side of heaven' was associated with the style of the Guy Lombardo Orchestra. – Albert McCarthy, *The Dance Band Era: The dancing decades from ragtime to swing, 1910–1950* (London: Studio Vista, 1971), p.64.

234 In *Moonlight on the Highway* (1969), Peters plays Al Bowlly and the Lew Stone Band's "Just Let Me Look At You" to Marie, a television researcher working on a programme about the singer, and tries to force himself on her. He later confesses, at a Bowlly fan meeting, to having paid for sex with 136 prostitutes.

235 Potter stressed the distinction between mere nostalgia and his deeper interrogation of memory in *Waiting for the Boat* (p.34). As Peter Stead notes, overcoming that second-order emotion formed part of Potter's attempt 'to find his own literary voice' – *Dennis Potter*, p.11.

236 This resembles a passage from *Hide and Seek* in which Daniel Miller recalls hearing in childhood the lyrics 'When the deep purple falls/Over sleepy garden walls/And the stars begin to flicker in the sky/Through the mists of memory/You wander back to me…' Asking himself such questions as 'How could a colour fall over a wall?' he realises that these mixed-up words 'meant more than they said' and associates the song with 'the thing grown-ups whispered about together' (see pp.30-34). The lyrics come from Mitchell Parish's lyrics for "Deep Purple" of which there were several versions including one by Adelaide Hall released in Britain in 1939. Potter's phrasing recalls *Moonlight on the Highway*, in which psychiatrist Dr Chilton describes Peters as longing for a lost Eden: 'They're the songs he might have heard on the radio downstairs while drifting off to sleep in childhood.' Potter's appearance on *Serendipity* (BBC Radio 4, 2 January 1978) was structured around extracts from 1940s radio drifting upstairs, according to producer Anthony Wall, though no recording or transcript is currently known to exist.

237 *Dad's Army* (BBC1, 1968–77), the much-loved sitcom about the largely elderly Home Guard defending Britain during the Second World War, starred John Le Mesurier, who appeared in Potter's *Traitor*.

238 English film actor Stewart Granger joined the cast of the Western *The Virginian* (NBC, 1962–71) in its ninth series (1970–71), by which stage it was retitled *The Men from Shiloh*. Granger played Colonel Alan MacKenzie, the new English owner of Shiloh Ranch. – Alvin H. Marill, *Television Westerns: Six Decades of Sagebrush Sheriffs, Scalawags, and Sidewinders* (Lanham MA: Scarecrow Press, 2011), p.71.

239 Count Rostov was played in this 1972–73 BBC version of *War and Peace* by Rupert Davies, who was best known to television viewers as Chief Inspector Maigret in *Maigret* (BBC-TV, 1960–63).

240 Elwyn Jones was a writer, producer, former Head of Drama Series (1963–66) and prolific contributor to *Z Cars* and its spin-offs such as *Softly, Softly* (BBC1, 1966–76). Potter clashed with Jones on discussion programme *Talkback* (BBC1, 4 February 1968) over the similarities between Jones's *Softly, Softly* episode "Major Incident" (BBC1, 1 February 1968) and the Aberfan disaster, and over whether such topics should be addressed in plays rather than popular drama series.

241 See "This was a glorious wallop", p.8, and on pp.49-50 of this volume; and see p.343 endnote 110 of this volume.

242 *Country Matters* (20 August 1972–11 March 1973) was a series of adaptations of short stories by A.E. Coppard and H.E. Bates. Writers included James Saunders and Jeremy Paul and directors included Donald McWhinnie and Silvio Narizzano.

243 Media and academic concerns that audiences identified with Alf Garnett's provocative statements about immigration and race, despite writer Johnny Speight's satirical intent, motivated BBC audience research discussed in *"Till Death Us Do Part* as Anti-Prejudice Propaganda" in *Annual Review of BBC Research Findings no. 1, 1973/74*. Referring to an earlier internal version and archive documents, Brett Bebber observed that, despite some findings to the contrary, Director of Programmes Alasdair Milne welcomed the research's support for the BBC's view that the programme was anti-racist – *"Till Death Us Do Part*: Political satire and social realism in the 1960s and 1970s", *Historical Journal of Film, Radio and Television*, 34:2, 2014, pp.253-274.

244 Philip Jenkinson was a presenter specialising in programmes about film, in series such as *Late Night Line-Up* and *Film Night*. He was also familiar to readers as film critic for *Radio Times* during the 1970s.

245 Philip Purser reviewed several Potter plays for the *Sunday Telegraph*, such as *Stand Up, Nigel Barton* (12 December 1965), *Where the Buffalo Roam* (6 November 1966) and *The Bone-grinder* (19 May 1968; for Potter's response see "Dennis Potter exposed", p.12, and on pp.88-90 of this volume) and appeared on the discussion programme *Son of Man Reviewed* (BBC1, 20 April 1969). Potter's praise here contrasts with his earlier use of Purser as an example of how critics abandon 'meaningful criticism': 'Philip Purser noticed that Isobel Black in Thomas Clarke's play on BBC1 last week "unshipped her brassiere for the third time in a Wednesday play." It's about time he and [Maurice] Wiggin and [Maurice] Richardson packed it in and grew roses or something' ("Glowing bubbles", *New Statesman*, 28 April 1967, p.594). Purser later interviewed Potter at the National Film Theatre on 30 October 1980 and wrote a pioneering essay on Potter for George W. Brandt (ed.), *British Television Drama* (Cambridge: Cambridge University Press, 1981), pp.168-193. Purser discussed Potter's television criticism in Gras and Cook (eds.). Their former enmity was acknowledged in Purser's memoir *Done Viewing* (London: Quartet, 1992), pp.188-196.

246 Recorded in Bristol on 4 April 1973.

247 One of three documentaries made by photographer David Bailey for ITV, *Warhol* was due to be transmitted on 16 January 1973 but was withheld by an Appeal Court injunction following a writ issued in response to adverse press coverage of a preview screening. *Warhol* was eventually broadcast on 27 March 1973, eight days prior to the recording of this interview. Potter and Hart echo Bailey's view that 'it's going to be a terrible anti-climax' for viewers mistakenly expecting shocking sexual and drug-fuelled content. 73 per cent of people polled by the Opinion Research Centre for the IBA felt that 'all the fuss was about nothing.' – Steve Rogers, "Fun with David and Andy", *Bailey On Andy Warhol* booklet accompanying *Warhol* DVD release, Network, 2010.

248 Derek Hart interviewed Potter for *Tonight* (BBC-TV, 8 February 1960).

249 3 May–3 August 1972.

250 Potter uses the phrase 'tit and thigh' as a condemnation of newspaper trends in *Paper Roses* and *Traitor*. The topless centre-spread in the *Sun* on 18 November 1969, the second issue from new owner Rupert Murdoch, soon led to the first 'birthday suit girl' in the 17 November 1970 first anniversary issue and the regular feature of a topless 'Page 3 girl' (Adrian Bingham, "Pin-Up Culture and Page 3 in the Popular Press", in Maggie Andrews and Sallie McNamara (eds.), *Women and the Media: Feminism and Femininity in Britain, 1900 to the Present* (London: Routledge, 2014), p.189). Page 3 still exists in 2015. However, in a foreshadowing of later controversies, critics started to see in Potter's work the same trends he was critiquing: Mary Holland's review of the first episode of *Casanova* bemoaned 'an unparalleled amount of tit and thigh' – "Breaking down the barriers", *Observer*, 21 November 1971, p.30.

251 Jack Black mentions 'monosodium glutamate' in *Follow the Yellow Brick Road*. In his later discussion of that play, Potter wrote that 'Even in a future land of muzak, monosodium glutamate and melamined encounters, the old resilient dreams will insist on making metaphors and finding illumination in the midst of the surrounding dross. There is, then, no place where "God" cannot reach.' – Potter (1978), p.3.

252 The result of the February General Election, the first of two elections in 1974, was a hung parliament and the resignation of Conservative Prime Minister Edward Heath. Labour, under Harold Wilson, took office in a minority government. Between 1 January–17 March 1974 Britain observed the three-day week, in which many companies were limited to opening on three days per week in order to reduce the consumption of electricity during industrial action by coal miners. Television was similarly affected, having to end at the early time of 10.30pm, as happened on BBC1 after *Joe's Ark* on 14 February 1974. Several Potter columns for the *New Statesman* addressed coverage of the February election. In "Moderates all" (22 February 1974, pp.268-269), he attacked the 'gloomy smog of platitude, pretence, technical challenge, anxious counterchallenge and careful deceit' of politicians and 'the professional anaesthetists employed as interviewers.' Potter watched 'every election programme except one,' finding the campaign 'reduced to the soporific proportions of a studio panel game.' In Potter's sketches Wilson seemed befuddled by his recent dental work and Heath was 'as expressive as a tub of lard.' These reviews enabled Potter to return to themes from his 1950s and 1960s polemics about the Labour Party, which needed 'to address its own supporters in a language that breaks the mould of "moderation".' Labour's failure to communicate was restricted in part by 'television itself,' which with its talk of 'common ground' and 'reasonable men' genuflected 'before all those smug value-judgments which the media elevate into solid, objective fact.' In "Something called fear" (1 March 1974, p.302), Potter connected political coverage with his wider theories about television: unlike writers, politicians had not grasped that television 'has a perpetual tendency to emasculate all passion and narrow the scale of the human voice down to a range safe enough to dribble out onto a nylon carpet in a distant living room.' Potter yearned for 'some new and more alert way' to cover the topic 'which bypasses the embalmed corpse of "balance."'

253 In the October General Election, Labour won with a majority government; the Conservative Party replaced Heath with Margaret Thatcher in February 1975. In his *New Statesman* coverage of this election, Potter expressed dread at the imminent blanket coverage ("Well, basically", 20 September 1974, pp.390-391) and anticipated presenter Alastair Burnet's 'big night of bumbling among the collapsible tables, portable swingometers, red-eyed explanations, surprising gains and unsuspected losses' ("Helter-skelter on the tightrope", 11 October 1974, p.514). Potter put his continued disdain for the dominance of 'balance' in 'lickspittle' coverage in the context of political practice, as 'paranoid officials measuring comment by the tenth of a second' observed coverage with stopwatches. Potter gratefully skipped over the aftermath to review a gardening programme with Percy Thrower – "Back to nature", 18 October 1974, pp.549-550.

254 Amis's episode of *Softly, Softly: Task Force* was "See What You've Done" (BBC1, 13 November 1974).

255 This was Potter's first *New Statesman* column since 10 January 1975. *Churchill's People* was a critically-mauled 26-part drama series based on Winston Churchill's *A History of the English-Speaking Peoples*, transmitted on BBC1, 30 December 1974–23 June 1975. It was produced by Gerald Savory.

256 This is an interesting objection given that *Funny Farm* had already been shortened, under protest, from 105-minutes to 90-minutes, though this still exceeded its commissioned length of 75-minutes.

257 When Potter told the daffodil story on the 25 September 1987 edition of BBC1 chat show *Wogan*, he gave the boy's name as 'Abraham'. Host Terry Wogan observed similarities between scenes of classroom betrayal in *The Singing Detective* and *Stand Up, Nigel Barton*, and contended that, despite Potter's claim not to write autobiography, some elements of his life must appear in his work. In reply, Potter said that 'the whole root of that [scene] was actually the case' and re-telling it 'made me go dry-throated even now.'

258 In "A Christmas Forest" (BBC Radio 4, 26 December 1977), Potter recalled that because of rivalry between Salem chapel and the Methodist Zion chapel, 'the most unpopular hymn for the boys at Salem – one which we could never understand being asked to sing – was "We're marching to Zion, Beautiful, beautiful Zion" "Oy," as one hissed, "to knock the stuffin' out on 'um."'' This anecdote revisits Potter's column "New shoes don't only come at Whitsun", *Sun*, 3 June 1968, p.12. The song is sung by Sunday school children in Potter's unproduced *The Rivers of Babylon* (Carpenter, p.196) and by seeming angel Tom Biddle in *Angels are so Few*.

259 Potter often returned to *Sankey's Songs and Solos*. His non-fiction included a piece in which he fantasised about strangling Sankey ("Ira D. Sankey", *Independent Magazine*, 17 March 1990, p.46). In his final interview, Potter recalled more warmly that 'I can think of the number before I can think of the chorus, I can see it as clear as though it were written in front of me on the slat – 787, hymn number 787: "Will there be any stars, any stars in my crown, when the evening sun goes down, when I wake with the blessed in the mansions of rest, will there be any stars in my crown?"' (Potter (1994), pp.7-8). The song is sung by Forest children at the end of Potter's final drama, *Cold Lazarus* (1996).

260 *Critics' Forum* (10 April 1976) was chaired by Anthony Quinton with a panel consisting of John Weightman, Edward Lucie-Smith and Gillian Tindall. Reviewing *Double Dare*, Lucie-Smith stated: 'It has a certain rancid puritanism, the play, which is a disagreeable element I found.' (Transcript, BBC Written Archives Centre.)

261 The banning of *Brimstone & Treacle* will be discussed in "A note from Mr Milne" (pp.175-179). Potter's comment about a campaign 'within the BBC' seems a little disingenuous. On 29 March, Morahan explained that the 'Drama producer' and 'BBC worker' quoted in news stories were probably 'invented ones, to fit the briefing the journalists have undoubtedly had from Potter.' (T62/244/1, *Brimstone & Treacle*, BBC Written Archives Centre.)

262 Potter's most recent piece for the *New Statesman*, "Heavenly news", was published on 12 March 1976. He returned with "A note from Mr Milne" on 23 April.

263 A dramatisation of Quentin Crisp's autobiography, *The Naked Civil Servant* was broadcast to much acclaim on ITV on 17 December 1975, having been made by Thames after the BBC pulled out.

264 Milne's phrase reads as 'I am afraid that I believe in this case' in the copy of his letter to Potter (19 March 1976) in the BBC's files. (T62/244/1, *Brimstone & Treacle*, BBC Written Archives Centre.) This omission of two words arguably helps the expression and is not significant, although the phrase 'I am afraid that I believe' might have drawn comment given the themes of the play. Their correspondence makes clear that Potter was ill with flu during these events.

265 Meeting members of the public was a regular feature on singer and presenter Cilla Black's Saturday night entertainment series *Cilla* (BBC1, 1968–76).

266 On 30 March, Milne wrote to Morahan accepting that people disagreed with his decision but questioned their judgment in not allowing people with final responsibility to be involved much earlier. He stressed that difficult work should be referred upwards, 'not to be "censored" but because it is just possible that colleagues who have toiled in the business as long as you or your producers might have something to offer in confirmation of your judgment; or, very occasionally, in rejection of it.' (T62/244/1, *Brimstone & Treacle*, BBC Written Archives Centre.)

267 *Brimstone & Treacle* was formally commissioned on 7 September 1973, and delivered on 22 November 1974. It was accepted on 15 January 1975. In a memo on 31 March 1976 during the controversy surrounding the ban, Christopher Morahan (Head of Plays) told Milne that his lateness in referring the play upwards 'was solely due to a delay in production because the director Ken and I wanted wasn't available earlier.' (T62/244/1, *Brimstone & Treacle*, BBC Written Archives Centre.)

268 According to Milne, an instant decision was needed because the next issue of *Radio Times* was due to go to press a few days later, on 24 March, with a feature on Potter that singled out *Brimstone & Treacle* as the most interesting of his three new plays. – Cook, p.54; Robert Cushman, "The values of a television playwright", *Radio Times*, 3–9 April 1976, pp.61-65.

269 The *Star Trek* episode "That Which Survives" was discussed in "Warp factor 1", *New Statesman*, 21 May 1976, p.693.

270 The 2 December 1976 edition of *Tomorrow's World* included an item in which 'Judith Hann and Raymond Baxter reported on a new electronic sorting machine for potatoes.' (BBC1 Programme-as-Broadcast log, BBC Written Archives Centre.)

271 Recorded on 13 December 1976. It had been previewed in the *Listener* on 4 November 1976 as part of BBC Radio 3's *Meditation at Christmas* strand.

272 In *Where Adam Stood*, Philip Gosse (Alan Badel), as a naturalist and Christian preacher in the age of Darwin, faced difficulties in, as Potter put it, 'being able to maintain what was thought to be important literal belief in Genesis, but which he knew as a scientist to be disproved by incontrovertible evidence'. Potter claimed that this was 'what interests me about faith – that it can try and join up those two things.' – Fuller (ed.), p.54.

273 '*Mission Impossible* is glop from the schlock-hopper. *Columbo* (Anglia) tries harder – which in my view makes it less interesting, since although I would rather have art than schlock, I would rather have schlock than kitsch' (Clive James, "This is impossible", *Observer*, 12 January 1975, p.26), anthologised as "Mission unspeakable" in Clive James, *Visions Before Midnight: Television criticism from the Observer 1972–76* (London: Jonathan Cape, 1977), p.115.

274 Fellow critic and author Clive James once pointed out that Potter 'frequently evinces a loathing for yours truly which it would be pusillanimous not to reciprocate' (Clive James, "Wishing you welcome", *Observer*, 30 March 1975, p.22). James still gave a positive review to Potter's *Late Call*, so Potter found himself, during a repeat of *Schmoedipus*, 'idly wondering if I could again trap Clive James into giving me a Good Review by the simple expedient of abusing him in this column' (Potter, "Seething trouble", *New Statesman*, 18 April 1975, p.522). Potter could indeed be vitriolic, but there was also respect, as when James appeared on *The Book Programme* (BBC2) to discuss Raymond Chandler's Philip Marlowe: '"His tone of voice got into the English language," James said, summoning up Chandler's snap-crackle prose. I held my breath. The minutes passed on tiptoe. I hate to admit it, but Clive James is not on anybody's sucker list. He works up his enthusiasm into a nice racket. I stared at him, jiggling my cigarette. Something was bothering me. Why are you so entertaining? I thought. There's an answer to that, but I held my tongue. I don't want him to know how good he is. Not yet.' – "Down those mean streets once more", *Sunday Times*, 27 November 1977, p.36.

275 Harold Francis Davidson (1875–1937) was defrocked by the Church of England after being convicted of immorality.

276 Paradine Productions, one of the earliest independent television production companies in the UK.

277 'They sailed away, for a year and a day,/To the land where the Bong-tree grows' – Edward Lear, "The Owl and the Pussy-Cat", *Nonsense Songs, Stories, Botany and Alphabets* (London: Robert John Bush, 1872), p.3.

278 Potter delivered this paper at BBC Queen Street as part of the Edinburgh International Television Festival, in whose programme the piece was published. Potter was on a panel

chaired by Melvyn Bragg and which also featured David Hare, James Cellan Jones and John McGrath. The paper was followed by a debate with industry practitioners and academics. McGrath had similarly criticised fellow programme makers for not debating form, and not taking up the challenge of Troy Kennedy Martin's "nats go home", in his 1976 James MacTaggart Memorial Lecture – see "TV Drama: The Case Against Naturalism", *Sight and Sound*, 46:2, 1977, pp.100-105.

279 An alumnus of the BBC's *Monitor*, Burton was a prominent arts broadcaster and programme maker who set up LWT's *Aquarius* (LWT/ITV, 1970–77). At the time of Potter's lecture he was the Head of Arts at the BBC.

280 Potter had often written about 'the choices between "naturalism" and its alternatives' but this paper was a timely intervention in a period when programme makers and academics were debating the possibility of a 'progressive form' that broke up the naturalistic style of most film and television to reveal the ideological workings of television and, partly as a result, of wider society. For an introduction to these debates, see Lez Cooke, *British Television Drama: A History* (London: British Film Institute, 2003), pp.90-127.

281 *The British Experience in Television* (BBC1, 26 February 1976).

282 'Garnett-Loach-Allen' referred to writer Jim Allen, producer Tony Garnett and director Ken Loach and was used as shorthand for dramas about working-class experience and political organisation that were shot in a realist style stressing their authenticity. Potter's praise here is significant given that the film journal *Screen* had critiqued Garnett, Loach and Allen's *Days of Hope* (BBC1, 11 September–2 October 1975) to test whether the radicalism of its content, such as its argument that the 1926 General Strike was betrayed by the collusion of the left, was cancelled out by a naturalistic style that did not generate wider questions. However, Potter still favoured internal drama over external observation as a way of exploring 'a more comprehensive reality.' For further reading putting Potter in the context of these debates, see Cook, pp.142-148.

INTRODUCTION TO PART THREE: TICKET TO RIDE

283 *Third Ear*, BBC Radio 3, 20 November 1989. Interview by Chris Cook.

284 Purser, in Gras and Cook (eds.), pp.179-193.

285 *Desert Island Discs* (1977).

286 *Pennies from Heaven*, BBC1, 7 March–11 April 1978. The serial was produced by Kenith Trodd and directed by Piers Haggard. The scripts were published by Faber and Faber in 1996 and the complete production released on Region 2 DVD by 2Entertain on 31 May 2004 and on Region 1 DVD by BBC Warner on 27 July 2004.

287 *Severn Sound*, Gloucestershire Broadcasting Company Limited, 1979, p.30. The period of application was 1 February–6 April 1979 and the four selected bidders were interviewed over the coming months, with Potter attending meetings on 9 May and 6 June. GBC's licence was confirmed on the weekend of 16–17 June. (Independent Broadcasting Authority archive, University of Bournemouth.)

288 For a useful primer see Ian Potter, *The Rise and Rise of the Independents: A Television History* (London: Guerilla, 2008), pp.76-77.

289 On 16 October 1978, James Cellan Jones commissioned Potter to adapt Anthony Powell's novels as 12 x 90-minute plays for BBC2's *Play of the Week* strand. The initial plan was for the scripts to be completed between February 1979–April 1980 and produced between August 1980–September 1981, with fortnightly transmission between December 1981–May 1982. This was reduced to six 75-minute plays only, and by May 1979 this was down even further, to five 50-minute plays with less provision for the use of film. The project was formally abandoned in August 1979. (RCONT21, Dennis Potter 1975–79, BBC Written Archives Centre.)

290 Potter, "How I'm shaking up the mush machine", *Daily Mail*, 25 May 1979, p.6.

291 Anonymous, "What Dennis Potter said about it", *Stage and Television Today*, 24 May 1979, p.18. The press conference was held on 17 May 1979, the panel comprising Kenith Trodd, Dennis Potter, Michael Grade and LWT's Head of Drama, Tony Wharmby.

292 Cook, p.195.

293 *Blade on the Feather*, London Weekend Television, 19 October 1980. It was directed by Richard Loncraine, produced by Kenith Trodd and the executive producer was Tony Wharmby. The first of the PfH/LWT trilogy to be transmitted, *Blade* was the third to be shot. Filmed on the Isle of Wight in May–June 1980 the shoot was beset by bad weather, leading to a £150,000 overspend. The production gained US distribution on VHS in 1990 as *Deep Cover*. It was released on Region 2 DVD by Network as part of *Dennis Potter at London Weekend Television* on 12 September 2005, and on Region 1 DVD by Koch Vision as part of *Dennis Potter: 3 to Remember* on 10 February 2009.

294 *Rain on the Roof*, London Weekend Television, 26 October 1980. It was directed by Alan Bridges, produced by Kenith Trodd and the executive producer was Tony Wharmby. Filmed in February 1980, the production was released on Region 2 DVD by Network as part of *Dennis Potter at London Weekend Television* on 12 September 2005, and on Region 1 DVD by Koch Vision as part of *Dennis Potter: 3 to Remember* on 10 February 2009.

295 *Cream in My Coffee*, London Weekend Television, 2 November 1980. It was directed by Gavin Millar, produced by Kenith Trodd and the executive producer was Tony Wharmby. Inspired by a holiday in Eastbourne in August 1979 (see "Anteroom to purgatory" on pp.278-282 of this volume), the play was filmed in March 1980 and premiered at the National Film Theatre on 30 October 1980 as part of a comprehensive Potter season. The script was published as part of *Dennis Potter on Television: Waiting for the Boat* (London: Faber and Faber, 1984; reprinted as *Blue Remembered Hills and other plays*, London: Faber and Faber, 1996). The production was released on Region 2 DVD by Network as part of *Dennis Potter at London Weekend Television* on 12 September 2005, and on Region 1 DVD by Koch Vision as part of *Dennis Potter: 3 to Remember* on 10 February 2009.

296 Potter, "Why British TV is going to the dogs – and I'm going to California", *Daily Mail*, 30 July 1980, p.6.

297 On its launch Channel 4 established *Film on Four* as a means to commission and fund new British films. All projects were designed for both cinema release and television transmission. For further reading, see John Pym, *Film on Four: A Survey 1982/1991* (London: BFI Publishing, 1992).

298 *Guardian Lecture*.

299 Potter, "Potter rights", *Broadcast*, 6 October 1980, p.9, and on p.286 of this volume.

300 The $19m film adaptation of *Pennies from Heaven* was directed by Herbert Ross and was a Hera Production for MGM. The box office returns totalled just $7m. The US release was in December 1981 and the UK release in May 1982, and a novelisation by Potter was published by Quartet.

301 *Omnibus*, BBC1, 16 May 1982. In this interview alone Potter refers to four active film projects.

302 The film version of *Brimstone & Treacle* was directed by Richard Loncraine and produced by Kenith Trodd. It was a PfH film presented by Namara Films and Alan E. Salke in association with Herbert Solow. The film opened in the UK on 9 September 1982 and an accompanying novelisation of the film was written by Sarah Potter and published by Quartet.

303 The first stage production of *Brimstone & Treacle*, in its revised form, opened at the Crucible Theatre in Sheffield on 11 October 1977 and was directed by David Leland. The play's London debut was at the Open Space Theatre on 7 February 1979, in a new production directed by Robert Chetwyn. Sequences were shot for *The South Bank Show* (LWT/ITV, 11 February 1979). The script was published by Eyre Methuen in 1978 and by Samuel French in 1979.

304 *Sufficient Carbohydrate*, directed by Nancy Meckler, opened at the Hampstead Theatre on 7 December 1983 where it continued in an extended run until 28 January 1984. It then transferred to the Albery Theatre, running from 31 January–28 April 1984, where sequences were shot for *A Plus* (1984). Publication of the playscript in 1983 marked the beginning of a 15-year relationship between the writer and Faber and Faber.

305 *Play for Today: Blue Remembered Hills*, BBC1, 30 January 1979. Produced by Kenith Trodd and directed by Brian Gibson, it had originally been commissioned as *The Merchant's House* – an entirely different play – on 19 April 1978. The script was delivered on 12 June 1978 and the production shot on location between 6 August–6 September 1978. The script was published as part of *Dennis Potter on Television: Waiting for the Boat* (London: Faber and Faber, 1984; reprinted as *Blue Remembered Hills and other plays*, London: Faber and Faber, 1996) and as a standalone Samuel French edition in 1984. The original television production gained a limited BBC Education release on VHS as well as a wider release as a Region 2 DVD edition from 2Entertain on 26 September 2005. It also formed part of *The Helen Mirren Collection*, released on Region 1 DVD by BBC Home Entertainment on 19 February 2008 and on Region 2 DVD by 2Entertain on 25 February 2008.

306 *Mesmer* was written in 1983 (Fuller (ed.), p.113) and revised for production on 5 April 1993 (Cook, p.370). The film was made in Vienna during autumn 1993. *Mesmer*

was a Lance W. Reynolds and Wieland/Schulz-Keil production, directed by Roger Spottiswood, which premiered at the Montreal World Film Festival on 25 August 1994. However, a dispute ensued over revisions to the script, made during production, and this halted distribution (Maureen Paton, *Alan Rickman: The Unauthorised Biography* Second revised edition (London: Virgin, 2003), pp.195-212.) *Mesmer* received its UK television premiere on Bravo on 11 October 1997. A Region 1 DVD release appeared via Image Entertainment on 23 May 2000, with a Region 2 DVD edition released by 2Entertain on 29 January 2007.

307 *Dreamchild* was a Thorn EMI Screen Entertainment production of a Pennies from Heaven film, directed by Gavin Millar, produced by Rick McCallum and Kenith Trodd, and executive produced by Verity Lambert and Dennis Potter. The script was completed on 26 April 1983 and the film shot in the summer of 1984. Its distribution faltered due to the resignation in July 1985 of Lambert from Thorn EMI, the organisation then ceasing all in-house production. There was a limited US release of *Dreamchild* in October 1985 and the London opening followed on 24 January 1986. It received a Region 1 DVD release by MGM on 15 January 2011 and a Region 2 DVD edition was issued by 101 Films on 26 January 2015.

308 *Track 29* was a Handmade Films production directed by Nicolas Roeg and produced by Rick McCallum. The script was completed in 1982 and went through the working titles *Tears Before Bedtime* and *Track 39*. The film was originally set to be directed for the BBC by Joseph Losey with a planned start of 5 August 1983, but production was abandoned on 23 July (David Caute, *Joseph Losey: A Revenge on Life* (London: Faber and Faber, 1994), pp.458-459). Filming of the Roeg remount commenced in April 1987. The UK cinema release was on 5 August 1988 and in the US the following month. Region 2 DVD editions appeared via Anchor Bay on 26 March 2007 and Optimum on 8 March 2010. A Region 1 DVD edition was released by Image Entertainment on 21 February 2012.

309 *Tender is the Night*, BBC2, 23 September–28 October 1985. Adapted from the F. Scott Fitzgerald novel, this was a BBC co-production with Showtime Entertainment and The Seven Network in Australia. It was directed by Robert Knights and produced by Betty Willingale. Potter signed the contract to adapt the novel on 14 October 1983 and had delivered all six scripts by 17 February 1984, which were then shot from 6 August 1984–2 February 1985. After transmission of the final episode, an on-screen advert appeared for both the BBC Records soundtrack LP and a VHS release promised for 'early December.' The latter never materialised.

310 Potter, introduction to Thomas Hardy, *The Mayor of Casterbridge* (London: Pan, 1978), p.viii.

311 Potter, introduction to F. Scott Fitzgerald, *Tender is the Night* (London: The Folio Society, 1987), pp.5-12.

312 *The Singing Detective*, BBC1, 16 November–21 December 1986. This co-production with the Australian Broadcasting Corporation was directed by Jon Amiel, produced by Kenith Trodd and John Harris, and executive produced by Rick McCallum. It was originally commissioned as *Smoke Rings* on 23 February 1984 and its first draft

completed in the spring of 1985. Following conversations between Amiel and Potter, the scripts underwent significant revision between October–December 1985. Shooting was from 14 January–29 July 1986. The scripts were first published (with a variant Episode Five) by Faber and Faber in the UK in 1986 and by Vintage in the US in 1988. The production received a Region 1 DVD release by BBC Warner on 15 April 2003 and a Region 2 DVD release by 2Entertain on 5 July 2004.

313 *Ticket to Ride* (London: Faber and Faber, 1986). US edition published 1987. The novel was written during 1985, between drafts of *The Singing Detective*.

314 *Blackeyes* appeared first as a novel but was initially conceived as a serial for television. The first draft of Episode One was completed in October 1986 and revised by Potter in November 1986. Starting over on 26 December 1986, he swiftly abandoned the script format and moved towards prose. This, his second novel, was completed on 14 February 1987. On 28 September 1987 the novel was published by Faber and Faber and, with revisions to the final page, a second edition appeared on 7 November 1988.

Blackeyes was commissioned as a six-part serial for the BBC on 17 November 1986. By 26 October 1987, the scripts for *Blackeyes* – now a four-parter – had been accepted. The serial was shot between 6 February–21 July 1989 and material previewed at the Telluride film festival in Colorado in September. The serial was transmitted on BBC2, 29 November–20 December 1989.

315 Brian Turner to Judy Daish, 26 June 1984. (RCONT22/1,180, Copyright Registry Dennis Potter 1980–84).

316 Charles Langley, "BBC braces itself for sex outrage", *Sunday Today*, 30 November 1986, pp.1-2.

317 Kenith Trodd, speaking on Sky News, 7 June 1994: 'It can now be revealed that when a Sunday tabloid featured very provocative pictures on the morning of the third episode of *The Singing Detective*, the "sneak" who had supplied that story to that tabloid was one D. Potter...and the audience doubled as a result of that gesture.'

318 Vincent Canby, "Is the year's best film on TV?", *New York Times*, 10 July 1988, Arts & Leisure, pp.1,8. Despite our reservations about the enduring critical tendency to praise television only when it resembles film, this piece is a useful indication of Potter's increasing profile.

319 *Christabel*, BBC2, 16 November–7 December 1988. The producer was Kenith Trodd and the director Adrian Shergold, with Potter acting as executive producer. Potter had optioned the rights upon reading a review of Bielenberg's memoir (Anonymous, "Not guilty", *Economist*, 13 November 1982, p.116). The serial was shot in January–June 1988. The scripts were published by Faber and Faber in 1988, and the original soundtrack LP by BBC Records in 1988. A 147-minute movie version was released in the US on VHS in 1993, its sole home video release.

320 *Third Ear*.

321 Fuller (ed.), p.124.

322 *Screen Two: Visitors*, BBC2, 22 February 1987. Produced by Kenith Trodd and directed by Piers Haggard, it was filmed in Italy between 1 September–4 October 1986. The working title of the abandoned 1985 production was *All of You*.

323 Anonymous, "Potter and Bleasdale series head Channel 4's winter season", *Guardian*, 15 December 1988, p.4.

324 For the full disputed story, see Cook, pp.256-258 and Carpenter, pp.477-478.

325 Kenith Trodd, "Don't leave town", *Listener*, 8 June 1989, p.20.

326 *The John Dunn Show*, BBC Radio 2, 13 December 1989, and on pp.303-312 of this volume.

327 In response to a question from a *Scotland on Sunday* journalist. – Deborah Orr, "Potter's wheel", *City Limits*, 30 November–7 December 1989, p.76.

328 *Third Ear*.

329 Cook, pp.270-271.

330 *Third Ear*.

331 Simon Hattenstone, "The shooting party", *Guardian*, 1 October 1991, p.34.

332 *Secret Friends*, initially mooted as a BBC project in 1989, was a Whistling Gypsy production for Channel 4 and Robert Michael Geisler & John Roberdeau in 1991. The producer was Rosemarie Whitman and the director Dennis Potter. The US release was in February 1992 and in the UK in September 1992. It was later screened on television as a *Film on Four* (Channel 4, 13 December 1994). The film was also released on VHS.

333 Richard Brooks, "Return of politically incorrect Den", *Observer*, 14 February 1993, p.63.

334 *Lipstick on Your Collar*, Channel 4, 21 February–28 March 1993. The serial was a Whistling Gypsy production with Potter as executive producer, Rosemarie Whitman as producer and Alison Barnett as co-producer. The director was Renny Rye. The scripts were published by Faber and Faber in 1993, and the complete production released on Region 2 DVD by Acorn Media on 4 October 2010.

335 *Without Walls Special: An Interview with Dennis Potter*, Channel 4, 5 April 1994. The complete transcript was published as part of *Seeing the Blossom: Two Interviews and a Lecture* (1994). It was released on VHS in the UK as a double bill with the MacTaggart Lecture, *Dennis Potter in Person* (1994). The US release on VHS, by New Video Group on 26 September 1995, went under the title *The Last Interview*. The interview's sole digital release was as an extra on *Dennis Potter: 3 to Remember*, a Region 1 DVD from Koch Vision on 10 February 2009.

336 *Karaoke*, BBC1, 28 April–19 May 1996, with repeats on Channel 4, 29 April–20 May 1996. The serial was a Whistling Gypsy production for BBC and Channel 4, produced by Kenith Trodd and Rosemarie Whitman, and directed by Renny Rye. The executive producers were Michael Wearing for the BBC and Peter Ansorge for Channel 4. The scripts were published as part of *Karaoke and Cold Lazarus* (London: Faber and Faber, 1996), and the complete production released on Region 2 DVD by Acorn Media on 6 September 2010.

337 *Cold Lazarus*, Channel 4, 26 May–16 June 1996, with repeats on BBC1, 27 May–17 June 1996. The serial was a Whistling Gypsy production for BBC and Channel 4, produced by Kenith Trodd and Rosemarie Whitman, and directed by Renny Rye. The executive producers were Michael Wearing for the BBC and Peter Ansorge for Channel 4. The scripts were published as part of *Karaoke and Cold Lazarus* (London: Faber and Faber, 1996), and the complete production released on Region 2 DVD by Acorn Media on 6 September 2010.

338 "Putting television to the test", *Guardian*, 12 April 1994, p.21. The letter was signed by Alan Plater (President, Writers' Guild), Alan Ayckbourn, Maureen Duffy, Eva Figes, Debbie Horsfield, David Nobbs and Jack Rosenthal.

339 Angela Levin, "I thought Dad was invincible…", *Daily Mail*, 22 October 1994, Weekend, p.6.

340 Potter on William Hazlitt. See "The face at the window", *Times*, 3 August 1968, p.15, and on p.97 of this volume.

PART THREE: HIDE AND SEEK

341 See "Realism and non-naturalism", on pp.203-213 of this volume.

342 Keeffe's play, he argued, 'managed to make every character hateful, every other speech bilious and any possible conclusion even more sickening.' – "Black magic and chalk dust", *Sunday Times*, 17 April 1977, p.38.

343 'These New Reactionaries cannot see change unless everything changes. They glimpse fascism round the corner because they refuse to look at what is capable of repair in the road directly in front of them. Violence and corruption take the centre of the stage, and there is nothing else in the wings.' – "The spectre at the harvest feast", *Sunday Times*, 19 June 1977, p.39, and on pp.198-200 of this volume.

344 When discussing screen depictions of Christ, Potter said of Powell's portrayal in *Jesus of Nazareth* (ITC/RAI/ITV, 3–10 April 1977), 'A Christ nourished on the disinfectant bottle, carrying out his mission under salmon pink skies and Holman Hunt filters, a man or God so conscious of divinity that he stares into the middle-distance when he speaks and is made to look as though he has a bad case of piles when he walks.' – "The celluloid messiahs", p.33.

345 American feminist Shere Hite's book *The Hite Report on Female Sexuality* was published in the UK in September 1977 and serialised in the *Sun*. It was based on the frank responses of 3,000 anonymous women to a questionnaire about their sex lives. – Katharine Whitehorn, "What not enough men know", *Observer*, 25 September 1977, p.23.

346 Sir Richard Dobson had been Chairman of British Leyland for just over eighteen months when he was secretly taped delivering a speech to an exclusive group of businessmen at the Dorchester Hotel in London on 27 September 1977. Responding to stories that his company held a slush fund for overseas payments, he told those gathered that it was a 'perfectly respectable fact that [British Leyland] was bribing wogs.' The

recording was made by Peter Cooper, son of one of the businessmen present, and the full transcript published in *Socialist Challenge*, 19 October 1977. The paper's editor, Tariq Ali, also made a formal complaint to the Commission for Racial Equality. Sir Richard Dobson resigned on 21 October 1977. – Keith Adams, "Forgotten chairmen – Sir Richard Dobson", *AROnline*, 20 March 2013: www.aronline.co.uk/blogs/facts-and-figures/people/forgotten-chairmen-sir-richard-dobson/, accessed on 9 December 2014.

347 Recording date not known, but likely the day of transmission.

348 Potter, "Where comedy is king", *Sunday Times*, 16 October 1977, p.37.

349 Potter, "Facing the future with Piglet and Pooh", *Sunday Times*, 10 October 1976, p.35.

350 Bakewell, "Wrestling with a vision", p.66.

351 When asked 'Can the team explain why the art of the comedian is so largely a male preserve?' Potter responded, 'I'm not sure the question is entirely correct. I mean, I find Angela Rippon extremely funny.' – *Any Questions?*, BBC Radio 4, 21 October 1977 (Transcript, BBC Written Archives Centre).

352 "The celluloid messiahs", p.33.

353 Interviewed by Colin Morris, Potter asserted: 'I am sure of this one thing, that there is no access to God without pain. I don't necessarily mean physical pain, but there is no access without some sense of horror, or shock or nausea or guilt or rejection of what this world does to this flame of life.' – *The Anno Domini Interview*. A partial transcript appeared as "Godslot", *Listener*, 17 February 1977, p.207.

354 Information on this is somewhat hazy and contradictory. The *Guardian* reported on 8 October 1977 that Potter was writing a new play for the Belgrade Theatre, Coventry (Anonymous, "Potter's weal", p.10) and in an earlier interview with Margaret Potter for the *Daily Mail*, it was stated that Potter was 'planning to adapt his banned play *Brimstone & Treacle* for the National Theatre and he's preparing a play for the Oxford Playhouse' (Anne Batt, "The man over the moon", 5 April 1977, p.7), yet no Potter play reached those three venues in the late-Seventies. *Brimstone & Treacle* in fact opened at the Sheffield Crucible on 11 October 1977. Following its run, Potter himself made further reference to National Theatre and Oxford Playhouse commissions during his first appearance on *Desert Island Discs*, recorded 22 November 1977. A National Theatre contract was signed on 19 January 1978 but did not specify title or subject matter (Carpenter, p.367).

355 This alludes to incidents of sexual interference by Potter's uncle when they lived together in Hammersmith in 1945. There are a number of references to this in his non-fiction writing, most prominently in the introduction to *Dennis Potter on Television: Waiting for the Boat* (1984): 'caught by an adult's appetite and abused out of innocence' (p.33). The earliest reference was in "King Arthur and a vision of childhood country lost", *Times*, 18 January 1971, p.8, and the theme appeared in his fiction too, most conspicuously *Moonlight on the Highway* (1969), but he was quick to challenge its significance during a 1990 interview with John R. Cook: 'A lot of things can be traced to that, but to trace *everything* to that is absolute nonsense. People endure what they endure and they deal with it. It may corrupt them. It may lead them into all sorts of compensatory excesses

in order to escape the nightmare and the memory of that but it is a footnote – or a sidenote, not a footnote. It's important but it's not *that* important. Because still, you're left with your basic human strivings and dignity and talent.' – Cook, in Gras and Cook (eds.), pp.249-250.

356 The Potters travelled to New York on 9 September 1977, holidaying there for a fortnight.

357 In his October 1977 talk at the Cheltenham Literary Festival, "Tell it not in Gath", Potter noted that MOMA in New York was 'one of the few havens in that archipelago of vulgarity, fear and insanity. The Museum is a place to make your eyes pop and your mind blaze.' – "The philistine stigma", *Guardian*, 15 October 1977, p.7. Potter selected a painting on display at MOMA, *Gas* by Edward Hopper, as his luxury item on *Desert Island Discs* (1977). Hopper's work later influenced scenes in MGM's *Pennies from Heaven* (1981) and *Dreamchild* (1985).

358 William Pfaff, "Reflections: The special relationship", *New Yorker*, 19 September 1977, pp.113-118,121-123.

359 Nine days after publication of this column, Potter recorded an interview for his own *South Bank Show* profile, titled "Dennis Potter: Man of Television" (LWT/ITV, 11 February 1978). – Duncan Wu, *Six Contemporary Dramatists* Second edition (London: Macmillan Press, 1996), p.157.

360 George Fox (1624–91) was a founding Quaker.

361 *The Mayor of Casterbridge*, BBC2, 22 January–5 March 1978. Potter was commissioned to write the serial, an adaptation of the 1886 novel by Thomas Hardy, on 29 December 1975. The seven scripts were delivered by 6 September 1976 and shot entirely on location from 5 September–18 November 1977, simultaneous to production of *Pennies from Heaven*. A Pan paperback of the novel, released to coincide with transmission, featured an introduction by Potter. The serial was the first of Potter's works to be shown in the US, as part of PBS's *Masterpiece Theatre* in 1978. *The Mayor of Casterbridge* was issued on Region 1 DVD by Acorn Media on 27 May 2003 and on Region 2 DVD by 2Entertain on 26 September 2005.

362 David Coward filled in on 5 March and 12 March, reviewing in his first piece Potter's adaptation of *Casterbridge*. Peter Dunn took over the television column on 19 March, but a dispute between Times Newspapers Ltd and engineers belonging to the NATSOPA union stopped publication on 26 March. A further dispute with machine assistants stopped the 2 April edition. Both the *Sunday Times* and Potter returned on 9 April.

363 Potter's *Sunday Times* column had not appeared since 15 October 1978.

364 Jean Rook (1931–91), a *Daily Express* columnist for two decades, was on the *Sun*'s staff alongside Potter at the time of its 1964 launch. Her long stint as the forthright and frequently outrageous 'First Lady of Fleet Street' gave inspiration to the *Private Eye* character Glenda Slagg.

365 The subject of *Panorama* had been Times Newspapers Ltd's intention to suspend publication of newspaper titles after 30 November if the print unions refused to sign

up to new working agreements. Potter informed the *Guardian* on 25 November that the next day's column would be his last if management pressed ahead with their plans for 'a good old fashioned lockout.' Paul Foot and Paul Johnson had already contributed pieces for the 26 November edition of the *Sunday Times* addressing the *Panorama* report, and it was therefore anticipated that a third article on the subject, written by Potter, would not be included (Philip Jordan, "Potter's Hard Times starts row", *Guardian*, 25 November 1978, p.1). *Sunday Times* editor Harold Evans wrote in response, clarifying that when asked to limit references to *Panorama*, 'Mr Potter insisted on writing not a review of the programme, but simple abuse unadorned with any of his customary perception and wit.' Evans added that the *Sunday Times*' lawyers deemed some of it libellous, and so two sentences were cut with Potter's consent ("The *Sunday Times*: insight into Dennis Potter's television review", *Guardian*, 27 November 1978, p.12). Evans also wrote privately to Potter on 25 November to say that he found the manner of the leak to the *Guardian* 'discourteous and unprofessional' (Carpenter, p.375). The management lockout ran uninterrupted from 1 December 1978–12 November 1979.

366 Marmaduke Hussey, Chief Executive of Times Newspapers Ltd., would later become Chairman of the Board of Governors at the BBC. In Potter's 1993 lecture "Occupying Powers", he linked Hussey with John Birt as all that was presently wrong with the Corporation: 'You cannot make a pair of croak-voiced Daleks appear benevolent even if you dress one of them in an Armani suit and call the other Marmaduke' (Potter (1994), p.38). Some measure of this remark's impact can be found in the pages of *Private Eye*, where cartoonists have for decades since depicted Birt as a Dalek.

367 Recorded 8 February 1979.

368 The Grand Hotel, Eastbourne, was the setting for Potter's play *Cream in My Coffee*. Speaking on the day of its premiere, Potter recalled another element of this four-day trip which directly inspired the play: 'There was a group playing electronically in what was once obviously a superb ballroom. The mixture of irritation and emotion that it triggered off in me made me want to use that hotel, that setting.' – *Guardian Lecture*.

369 Friday 26 August 1977, at the start of rehearsals for the serial.

370 Amami, a setting lotion for women's hair, reached a peak of popularity in the 1950s with an advertising campaign which declared Friday night 'Amami night.' – Alastair Jamieson, "Lotion that set hair curls for generations of women is discontinued", *Telegraph Online*, 31 March 2010: www.telegraph.co.uk/finance/newsbysector/retailandconsumer/7540250/Lotion-that-set-hair-curls-for-generations-of-women-is-discontinued.html, accessed on 9 December 2014.

371 According to Campbell it was at this lunch when Potter indicated he might be in a position to cast her as Eileen in the forthcoming MGM film version of *Pennies from Heaven*. 'And without any hesitation, I said no,' she recalled during a BFI Southbank panel discussion on 19 July 2014. 'It would not be fair to Bob [Hoskins] or Gemma [Craven].'

372 This report had highlighted omissions from the forthcoming Potter retrospective at the National Film Theatre (13–30 October 1980), including plays that were missing

from the archives as well as 'another, later and acclaimed work which may prove more difficult for anyone to see, and this time for reasons *within* Potter's control: *Pennies from Heaven*' (Christopher Griffin-Beale, "What price Pennies from Hollywood", *Broadcast*, 15 September 1980, p.7).

The scheduled two-part screenings on 22 and 27 October and 23 and 28 October were in fact shelved for the reasons cited by Potter. Repeat screenings of the following plays served as substitutes: *Son of Man* and *Brimstone & Treacle* (22 October); *Blue Remembered Hills* and the Barton plays (23 October); *Casanova* (27–28 October); *Traitor* and *Joe's Ark* (28 October) (*Time Out*, 17–23 October 1980 and 24–30 October 1980). A complete one-day screening of *Pennies from Heaven* belatedly followed on 12 August 1984.

373 The screen adaptation of Martin Cruz Smith's popular thriller, the first in the Arkady Renko series of novels, was an Orion Associates production directed by Michael Apted and distributed by Orion. The first draft of Potter's script was delivered in October 1981, according to Potter's interview with Barry Norman for *Omnibus* (1982). Filming took place in Helsinki, during the early weeks of 1983 and the film saw its US premiere on 15 December 1983 and in the UK on 6 January 1984. *Gorky Park* has been released and repackaged on home video many times, most recently appearing on Region 1 DVD and Region A Blu-Ray via Kino Lorber on 21 October 2014, and on Region 2 DVD courtesy of UCA on 8 May 2006.

374 Charles Wesley (1707–88) was a member of the Methodist movement who authored several thousand hymns.

375 The *Observer* had invited Potter and 26 other writers to reflect on their voting preference ahead of the June General Election. Potter wrote: 'The election campaign has too often seemed to be nothing more than a raucous marketing exercise in which we are cajoled into choosing between three shoddy advertising agencies. The most appropriate response would be to hawk up a contemptuous gobbet of spittle onto the ballot paper. But this is no time for fastidiousness. Mrs Thatcher is the most obviously repellent manifestation of the most obviously arrogant, dishonest, divisive and dangerous British government since the war. All that really counts is to get these yobs and louts away from the swill bucket. I shall of course be voting for the patriotic party: Labour. But not with a song in my heart, or a plastic rose in my lapel.' – "How I shall vote", *Observer*, 7 June 1987, p.19.

376 Having dismissed Potter's words on Margaret Thatcher as 'hysterical vitriol,' Stephen Glover professed to have no interest in writers' political views. 'What matters is their moral judgment. Above all, we expect great writers to demonstrate a knowledge of (which implies a recognition of) good and evil. A writer who says that Mrs Thatcher is an evil woman is not simply evincing a want of political judgment; he is suggesting a distinctive moral judgment, a twisted view of the world.' Glover concluded by hoping that writers 'will either keep quiet until the next election or base their criticisms upon a proper moral sense.' – Stephen Glover, "Writers who tell a twisted tale about Margaret Thatcher", *Independent*, 12 June 1987, p.20.

377 Edward Pearce of the *Sunday Times* attacked the same *Observer* piece by questioning Potter's authenticity. 'There is the voice of 1960s man, trying to shock 25 years late, a

dedicated sham-proletarian,' Pearce wrote. 'Few people are as genuinely unpleasant as Potter but others share his inability to be corrupted by the gentle pattering of royalties falling like spring rain upon the incremental aesthete' ("Big namehunting for starry-eyed opinions", *Sunday Times*, 14 June 1987, p.29). Potter responded, 'In no way I can think of am I proletarian, sham or otherwise – not in my income, habits, interests, comforts or behaviour. It does not follow, though, that my political opinions are entirely based upon my self-interest, and this clearly troubles [Pearce].' – "I don't pretend to be proletarian", *Sunday Times*, 21 June 1987, p.31.

378 This interview took place between transmissions of Episodes Two and Three of *Blackeyes*. The critical reaction to the series, particularly in the tabloids, had been fiercely negative.

379 Although viewing figures began well at 7.15 million, the remaining episodes saw a drop to 5.73m, 5.32m and 3.87m respectively (Cook, p.276). The sharp drop for the final episode could be viewed as a reflection of the serial's growing complexity or the fact that it was up against a repeat of the popular drama *Boon* (Central/ITV, 1986–92).

380 Richard Wallace, "Potter launches new TV sex bomb", *Sun*, 23 November 1989, p.7: 'The first programme opens with the sound of a couple bonking.' See also Garry Bushell, "Garry's Choice", *Sun*, 29 November 1989, p.14: 'From bonking to sleazy strip shows, all human lust is here.'

381 Maria Lexton, "Sex, lies and misogyny", *Time Out*, 22–29 November 1989, p.29: 'Potter is, as we are constantly hearing, a sick man. He suffers from psoriatic arthropathy, a rare disease he transmitted to his hero in *The Singing Detective*. It's not a disease that invites a lot of sexual activity and I dare say this may have contributed to the writer's twisted attitude to women and fucking, much as he might try to refute that idea. I know Potter dislikes his physical illness being mentioned almost as much as he hates being criticised, but one thing you can't hide is when you're crippled inside.'

382 Orr, "Potter's wheel", p.76: 'His unpleasant subject matter (perversity, sexual manipulation, disease, death, loneliness, repression and so on) combined with his equally unpleasant personality, make him an obvious target for tabloids and qualities alike.'

383 This was a nickname shared with Den Watts, a character played by Leslie Grantham in the BBC1 soap opera *EastEnders* (1985–). Its repurposing for Potter probably originated in Ramsay Smith, "All clever stuff or just dirty, Den?", *Daily Mirror*, 29 November 1989, p.9. See also Madeleine Pallay, "Pain that drives Potter potty", *Sun*, 30 November 1989, pp.12-13: 'The real life of telly's rudest writer – "Dirty" Dennis Potter – is as tragic and bizarre as any of the characters he invents for his shocking TV dramas.'

384 Potter's 'deep depression' over the critical reaction to *Blackeyes* continued into the New Year, according to a report in the *Daily Mail* (Anonymous, "Dennis Potter: I'm too upset by criticism to write", 30 January 1990, p.3). A BBC adaptation of his 1987 novel *Ticket to Ride* was due to shoot in April 1990 but was now postponed. It eventually resurfaced at Channel 4 as a film commission, *Secret Friends*, in 1991, and gained distribution in 1992.

385 An extensive Potter retrospective was held at the Museum of Television and Radio in New York from 23 January–31 May 1992. The season was preceded by three seminars, all of which featured Potter. For further reading on these fraught encounters, see: Carpenter, pp.517-520; James Wolcott, "Untrue grit", *New Yorker*, 4 October 1993, p.217; David Bianculli, "Dossier: Dennis Potter in America", *Critical Studies in Television*, 8.1, Spring 2013, pp.91-107.

386 Significant rewrites in Potter's television past go back as far as *Vote, Vote, Vote for Nigel Barton*, but here he is most likely referring to *Joe's Ark*, commissioned on 22 January 1971 but not transmitted until 14 February 1974. The script arrived at the BBC on 9 December 1971 and was accepted on 23 February 1972, with 'substantial' revisions delivered on 13 September 1973. (RCONT20, Solicitors and Copyright Registry Dennis Potter 1970–4, BBC Written Archives Centre.)

387 In an anonymous, untitled *Guardian* report of Potter's illness (p.2), it was stated, 'Doctors recently told Mr Potter, who is 58, and is a heavy smoker, that he has a terminal form of the disease after a lifetime of ill-health."

388 This text first appeared as "Writing for dear life", *Observer*, 31 March 1996, Review, pp.1-2, and was later published as the introduction to the script collection *Karaoke and Cold Lazarus*.

389 *Midnight Movie* was a BBC Films production in association with Whistling Gypsy, which received its premiere at the 38th London Film Festival in the early afternoon of Sunday 6 November 1994 at the Odeon West End, Leicester Square. Dennis Potter produced and the director was Renny Rye. Executive producers were Ruth Caleb and Mark Shivas and the co-producer was Rosemarie Whitman. The film was inspired by *Moths*, a 1976 novel by Rosalind Ashe. It was televised as a *Screen Two* presentation on BBC2, 26 December 1994. The production was released on VHS by BBC Video on 1 February 1999.

Bibliography

The following is not intended as an exhaustive list of sources by or about Dennis Potter (DP). Instead, it brings together all the published and broadcast sources that are either reproduced in this volume or discussed in each section's introductions and explanatory endnotes. The list of broadcast sources does not cover Potter's screen fiction – see the Chronology and Index – but includes the non-fiction pieces to which Potter contributed. For more information about the fiction and non-fiction broadcast sources, see the Notes and Index. For detailed lists of Potter's works and further reading, see Carpenter's *Dennis Potter: An Authorised Biography*, Cook's *Dennis Potter: A Life on Screen* and Gilbert's *Fight and Kick and Bite: The Life and Works of Dennis Potter*.

Published sources

Adams, Keith, "Forgotten chairmen – Sir Richard Dobson", *AROnline*, 20 March 2013, www.aronline.co.uk/blogs/facts-and-figures/people/forgotten-chairmen-sir-richard-dobson, accessed on 9 December 2014.

Allsop, Kenneth, "The Angriest Young Man of all...", *Daily Mail*, 8 February 1960, p.6.

Amis, Martin, "In the fast lane", *Observer*, 12 March 1978, p.35.

Anonymous, "Progress of Operation Britain", *Times*, 29 October 1957, p.12.

– "Tribunal report: Text of Union Society findings", *Cherwell*, 18 January 1958, p.10.

– (ed.), *Isis*, 18 June 1958.

– "Class", *Dean Forest Guardian*, 29 August 1958, p.7.

– "Mr Dennis Potter Married", *Dean Forest Guardian*, 16 January 1959, p.1.

– "Forest protest to BBC *Panorama*", *Dean Forest Guardian*, 11 December 1959, p.3.

– "Verdict of the voters", *Sun*, 17 October 1964, pp.4-6.

– "Dud and Pete win Best Comedy Series award", *Daily Express*, 11 March 1966, p.10.

– "A spy in the War Ops room", *Sunday Times*, 17 May 1970, pp.44-45.

– "Council to protest about 'filth' on television", *Glasgow Herald*, 10 November 1970, p.21.

– "Tele verité", *Guardian*, 4 December 1970, p.12.

- "Red cheeks", *Listener*, 4 November 1971, p.616. (Short transcript of DP interview from *Late Night Line-Up*, BBC2, 14 October 1971.)

- "TV play 'lewd' complaint", *Times*, 2 December 1971, p.5.

- "Exit Gordon from Gollancz", *Guardian*, 3 May 1972, p.13.

- "Family Announcements", *Dean Forest Guardian*, 28 November 1975, p.8.

- "Godslot", *Listener*, 17 February 1977, p.207. (Transcript of *The Anno Domini Interview*, BBC1, 14 February 1971.)

- "Potter's weal", *Guardian*, 8 October 1977, p.10. (Section compiled by Tom Sutcliffe, Robin Thornber and George Armstrong.)

- "What Dennis Potter said about it", *Stage and Television Today*, 24 May 1979, p.18.

- "Not guilty", *Economist*, 13 November 1982, p.116.

- "Potter and Bleasdale series head Channel 4's winter season", *Guardian*, 15 December 1988, p.4.

- "Dennis Potter: I'm too upset by criticism to write", *Daily Mail*, 30 January 1990, p.3.

- untitled, *Guardian*, 25 March 1994, p.2.

Ashe, Geoffrey, *Camelot and the Vision of Albion* (London: Heinemann, 1971).

Ashe, Rosalind, *Moths* (London: Hutchinson, 1976).

Bakewell, Joan, "Wrestling with a vision", *Sunday Times Magazine*, 14 November 1976, pp.64-70.

Bakewell, Joan and Nicholas Garnham, *The New Priesthood: British Television Today* (London: Allen Lane, 1970).

Banks-Smith, Nancy, "*Lay Down Your Arms* and *Burma Star Gala* on television", *Guardian*, 25 May 1970, p.6.

- "*Traitor* on television", *Guardian*, 15 October 1971, p.10.

Barnett, Correlli, *Britain and Her Army 1509–1970* (London: Allen Lane, 1970).

Batt, Anne, "The man over the moon", *Daily Mail*, 5 April 1977, p.7.

Bebber, Brett, "*Till Death Us Do Part*: Political satire and social realism in the 1960s and 1970s", *Historical Journal of Film, Radio and Television*, 34:2, 2014, pp.253-274.

Bianculli, David, "Dossier: Dennis Potter in America", *Critical Studies in Television*, 8:1, Spring 2013, pp.91-107.

Bielenberg, Christabel, *The Past is Myself* (London: Chatto and Windus, 1968).

Bingham, Adrian, "Pin-Up Culture and Page 3 in the Popular Press", in Maggie Andrews and Sallie McNamara (eds.), *Women and the Media: Feminism and Femininity in Britain, 1900 to the Present* (London: Routledge, 2014), pp. 184-198.

Brooks, Richard, "Return of politically incorrect Den", *Observer*, 14 February 1993, p.63.

Bushell, Garry, "Garry's Choice", *Sun*, 29 November 1989, p.14.

Canby, Vincent, "Is the year's best film on TV?", *New York Times*, 10 July 1988, Arts & Leisure, pp.1,8.

Carpenter, Humphrey, *Dennis Potter: A Biography* (London: Faber and Faber, 1998).

Casanova, Giovanni Giacomo, *History of My Life*, Willard R. Trask (trans.), 6 vols (New York: Harcourt, Brace and World, 1966–72).

Caute, David, *Joseph Losey: A Revenge on Life* (London: Faber and Faber, 1994).

Clark, Leonard, *Green Wood: A Gloucestershire Childhood* (London: Max Parrish, 1962).

Cook, John R., *Dennis Potter: A Life on Screen* Second edition (Manchester: Manchester University Press, 1998).

   – "Dennis Potter: A Personal Interview (10 May 1990)", in Vernon W. Gras and John R. Cook (eds.), *The Passion of Dennis Potter: International Collected Essays* (Basingstoke: Macmillan, 2000), pp.239-251.

Cooke, Fred, "Miner's son at Oxford felt ashamed of home: The boy who kept his father secret", *Reynolds News*, 3 August 1958, p.7.

Cooke, Lez, *British Television Drama: A History* (London: British Film Institute, 2003).

Coward, David, "The infinite variety of human folly", *Sunday Times*, 5 March 1978, p.37.

Cowley, Julian, "Quirk, strangeness and charm", *Wire*, n.368, October 2014, pp.28-35.

Crisp, Quentin, *The Naked Civil Servant* (London: Jonathan Cape, 1968).

Critchley, Julian, "Out of his system", *Times*, 25 May 1970, p.5.

Cruz Smith, Martin, *Gorky Park* (New York: Random House, 1981).

Cushman, Robert, "The values of a television playwright", *Radio Times*, 3–9 April 1976, pp.61-65.

Davies, Hunter, "Atticus: Trial of a TV Man", *Sunday Times*, 30 October 1966, p.13.

Davies, W.H., *Collected Poems* (London: A.C. Fiefeld, 1916).

Evans, Harold, "The *Sunday Times*: insight into Dennis Potter's television review", *Guardian*, 27 November 1978, p.12.

Evelegh, Gabrielle, "Knocking the army", *Times*, 30 May 1970, p.9.

Fiddick, Peter, "*Paper Roses* on television", *Guardian*, 14 June 1971, p.8.

Fitzgerald, F. Scott, *Tender is the Night* (London: The Folio Society, [1934] 1987).

Foot, Paul, *The Vote* (London: Viking, 2005).

Frost, David and Ned Sherrin (eds.), *That Was the Week That Was* (London: W.H. Allen, 1963).

Fuller, Graham, "Dennis Potter", *American Film*, March 1989, p.31-33,51-55.

   – (ed.), *Potter on Potter* (London: Faber and Faber, 1993).

Gilbert, W. Stephen, *Fight and Kick and Bite: The Life and Works of Dennis Potter* (London: Hodder and Stoughton, 1995).

Glover, Stephen, "Writers who tell a twisted tale about Margaret Thatcher", *Independent*, 12 June 1987, p.20.

Gosse, Edmund, *Father and Son: a Study of Two Temperaments* (London: Heinemann, 1907).

Griffin-Beale, Christopher, "What price Pennies from Hollywood", *Broadcast*, 15 September 1980, p.7.

Hardy, Thomas, *Life's Little Ironies* (London: Osgood, McIlvaine & Co., 1894).

Hattenstone, Simon, "The shooting party", *Guardian*, 1 October 1991, p.34.

Hayman, Ronald, *Nietszsche: A Critical Life* (London: Quartet, [1980] 1981).

Hilfer, Anthony, "Run over by one's own story: genre and ethos in Dennis Potter's *The Singing Detective*", in Jonathan Bignell, Stephen Lacey and Madeleine Macmurraugh-Kavanagh (eds.), *British Television Drama: Past, Present and Future* (Basingstoke: Palgrave, 2000), pp.133-139.

Hite, Shere, *The Hite Report on Female Sexuality* (London: Summit, [1976] 1977).

Hoggart, Richard, *The Uses of Literacy* (London: Chatto and Windus, 1957).

Holland, Mary, "A journalist in decline", *Observer*, 20 June 1971, p.27.

– "Coming back to class", *Observer*, 17 October 1971, p.2.

– "Breaking down the barriers", *Observer*, 21 November 1971, p.30.

Housman, A.E., "XL", *A Shropshire Lad* (London: Kegan Paul, Trench, Trübner & Co Ltd., 1896), p.57.

Ialdabaoth, "The Forest decides that Dennis is a menace", *Cherwell*, 11 October 1958, p.4.

Jackson, Martin, "*Casanova* gets 'royal' treatment", *Daily Express*, 26 March 1971, p.17.

James, Clive, "This is impossible", *Observer*, 12 January 1975, p.26.

– "Wishing you welcome", *Observer*, 30 March 1975, p.22.

– *Visions Before Midnight: Television criticism from the Observer* (London: Jonathan Cape, 1977).

Jamieson, Alastair, "Lotion that set hair curls for generation of women is discontinued", *Telegraph Online*, 31 March 2010, www.telegraph.co.uk/finance/newsbysector/retailandconsumer/7540250/Lotion-that-set-hair-curls-for-generations-of-women-is-discontinued.html, accessed on 9 December 2014.

Johnson, B.S. (ed.), *All Bull: the National Servicemen* (London: Allison & Busby/Quartet, 1973).

Jordan, Philip, "Potter's Hard Times starts row", *Guardian*, 25 November 1978, p.1.

Kennedy Martin, Troy, "nats go home: First statement of a new drama for television", *Encore*, 11:2, March-April 1964, pp.21-33. (Reproduced with further responses from practitioners in "Television drama – Is this the way ahead?", *Screenwriter*, n.15, Spring 1964, pp.18-35.)

Kneale, Nigel, "Not quite so intimate", *Sight and Sound*, 28:2, Spring 1959, pp.86-88.

Langley, Charles, "BBC braces itself for sex outrage", *Sunday Today*, 30 November 1986, pp.1-2.

Lawrence, D.H., *The Complete Plays of D.H. Lawrence* (London: Heinemann, 1965).

Lear, Edward, "The Owl and the Pussy-Cat", *Nonsense Songs, Stories, Botany and Alphabets* (London: Robert John Bush, 1872), pp.2-4.

Levin, Angela, "I thought Dad was invincible...", *Daily Mail*, 22 October 1994, Weekend, p.6.

Lexton, Maria, "Sex, lies and misogyny", *Time Out*, 22–29 November 1989, p.29.

Madden, Paul, *Complete Programme Notes for a Season of British Television Drama 1959-73, Held at the National Film Theatre, 11–24 October 1976* (London: British Film Institute, 1976.)

Marill, Alvin H., *Television Westerns: Six Decades of Sagebrush Sheriffs, Scalawags, and Sidewinders* (Lanham MA: Scarecrow Press, 2011).

Marks, Cordell, "The way a writer beat arthritis", *TV Times*, 23–29 May 1970, p.6.

Masters, John, *Casanova* (London: Michael Joseph, 1969).

McCarthy, Albert, *The Dance Band Era: The dancing decades from ragtime to swing, 1910–1950* (London: Studio Vista, 1971).

McGrath, John, "TV drama: The case against naturalism", *Sight and Sound*, 46:2, 1977, pp.100-105.

Meyer, Michael, *Henrik Ibsen Volume 1: The Making of a Dramatist 1828–1864* (London: Hart-Davis, 1967).

Mitchell, Julian, John Fuller, William Donaldson and Robin McLaren (eds.), *Light Blue Dark Blue: An anthology of recent writing from Oxford and Cambridge Universities* (London: Macdonald, 1960).

Moran, Lord, *Churchill: The Struggle for Survival* (London: Constable, 1966).

Muller, Robert (ed.), *The Television Dramatist* (London: Elek, 1973).

Niblett, D.M. and Robina I. Brown, Ron Nelson, "Readers' Views: Dennis Potter gets a rough handling for his TV piece", *Dean Forest Guardian*, 10 June 1960, p.7.

Nuttall, Jeff, *Bomb Culture* (London: MacGibbon and Kee, 1968).

Oakes, Philip, "Potter's Path", *Sunday Times*, 7 November 1971, p.38.

Orr, Deborah, "Potter's wheel", *City Limits*, 30 November–7 December 1989, p.76.

Osborne, John, *A Better Class of Person: An Autobiography 1929–1956* (London: Faber and Faber, 1981).

Pallay, Madeleine, "Pain that drives Potter potty", *Sun*, 30 November 1989, pp.12-13.

Paton, Maureen, *Alan Rickman: The Unauthorised Biography* Second revised edition (London: Virgin, 2003).

Pearce, Edward, "Big namehunting for starry-eyed opinions", *Sunday Times*, 14 June 1987, p.29.

Pfaff, William, "Reflections: The special relationship", *New Yorker*, 19 September 1977, pp.113-118,121-123.

Plater, Alan and Alan Ayckbourn, Maureen Duffy, Eva Figes, Debbie Horsfield, David Nobbs, Jack Rosenthal, "Putting television to the test", *Guardian*, 12 April 1994, p.21.

Potter, Dennis, "Ashridge, 1952", *The Dane*, 35:11, July 1952, p.352.

– (ed.), *Verse and Prose* supplement, *The Dane*, 35:13, July 1953, pp.432-441.

– "The Artist", *The Dane*, 35:13, July 1953, p.441.

– "Changes at the top", *Isis*, 22 May 1957, pp.18-19.

– "Stubbornyuddedness", *Dean Forest Guardian*, 4 October 1957, p.4.

– "Base ingratitude", *New Statesman*, 3 May 1958, pp.560-562. (Also reproduced in Mitchell *et al.*, pp.88-93.)

– "Just gimmicks", *Isis*, 4 June 1958, p.5.

– "I am proud of my home and family...no obsession", *Dean Forest Guardian*, 5 September 1958, p.7.

– (ed.), *Clarion*, October 1958.

– (ed.), *Clarion*, November 1958.

– "Potter: 1", *Isis*, 21 January 1959, p.10.

– "It's time to get out of the rut", *Daily Mirror*, 3 October 1959, p.6.

– *The Glittering Coffin* (London: Gollancz, 1960).

– "Paradise Gained: Dennis Potter on Television", *Isis*, 27 January 1960, pp.14-15.

– "What's eating Dennis Potter?", *Daily Sketch*, 16 February 1960, p.7. (Serialisation of *The Glittering Coffin*.)

– "A land divided – by humbug", *Daily Sketch*, 17 February 1960, p.7. (Serialisation of *The Glittering Coffin*.)

– "Pay and Dennis Potter", *Daily Sketch*, 18 February 1960, p.15. (Serialisation of *The Glittering Coffin*.)

– "Dennis Potter replies", *Dean Forest Guardian*, 17 June 1960, p.7.

– "Unknown territory", *New Left Review*, January/February 1961, pp.63-65.

– "Let's sell the army on laughs", *Daily Herald*, 9 September 1961, p.6.

– "Flyover in my eyes", *Daily Herald*, 18 November 1961, p.6.

- *The Changing Forest* (London: Secker and Warburg, 1962).
- "Too tough for a sheriff", *Daily Herald*, 7 May 1962, p.7.
- "Pre-packed childhood", *Sunday Times*, 20 May 1962, p.34.
- "At last – free speech is creeping into TV", *Daily Herald*, 29 September 1962, p.6.
- "Greed in the corn", *Daily Herald*, 6 October 1962, p.6.
- "TV *can* make religion dynamic", *Daily Herald*, 17 November 1962, p.7.
- "This TV newcomer smiles as she bites", *Daily Herald*, 26 November 1962, p.3.
- "Secret of *Coronation Street*", *Daily Herald*, 12 January 1963, p.4.
- "Stop nagging at us!", *Daily Herald*, 9 February 1963, p.4.
- "Culture leaps out of its cage", *Daily Herald*, 9 March 1963, p.6.
- "This was a glorious wallop", *Daily Herald*, 30 March 1963, p.8.
- "Don't be so T-Victorian", *Daily Herald*, 3 August 1963, p.6.
- "And everyone seemed slightly ashamed", *Daily Herald*, 26 August 1963, p.3.
- "The sweet screams of success", *Daily Herald*, 14 October 1963, p.7.
- "I won't say no to *Doctor Who*", *Daily Herald*, 30 November 1963, p.7.
- "100 helpings of soporific sugar", *Daily Herald*, 7 December 1963, p.6.
- "Treasures of the past", *Daily Herald*, 14 December 1963, p.6.
- "Steptoe pushes out the television junk", *Daily Herald*, 18 January 1964, p.6.
- "Writers are kings without riches", *Daily Herald*, 25 January 1964, p.6.
- "Did I hear the poodle growl?", *Daily Herald*, 15 February 1964, p.6.
- "*Z Cars* comes to the end of the alley", *Daily Herald*, 14 March 1964, p.6.
- "Out goes pomposity", *Daily Herald*, 22 April 1964, p.7.
- Contribution to "Reaction", *Encore*, 11:3, May–June 1964, pp.39-48.
- "Sport is too good to leave with the experts", *Daily Herald*, 25 July 1964, p.6.
- "Letter to the *Stage*", 29 July 1965, p.11.
- "Drama with no safety curtain", *New Society*, 30 December 1965, p.27.
- "The art of true invective", *New Society*, 27 January 1966, p.33.
- *Vote, Vote, Vote for Nigel Barton* script, *Views*, n.10, Spring 1966, pp.40-71.
- "A Boswell in the bicarbonate", *New Society*, 26 May 1966, p.26.
- "Aberfan", *New Society*, 27 October 1966, pp.638-639.
- *The Nigel Barton Plays: Two Television Plays* (Harmondsworth: Penguin, 1967).
- "Glowing bubbles", *New Statesman*, 28 April 1967, p.594.
- "Young Ibsen: towards the southbound steamer", *Times*, 9 December 1967, p.18.
- "George Orwell", *New Society*, 1 February 1968, p.157-158.
- "The only meat was in the cookery class", *Sun*, 15 February 1968, p.14.
- "I really must tell you I'm so very happy", *Sun*, 13 May 1968, p.3.
- "Dennis Potter exposed", *Sun*, 20 May 1968, p.12.
- "New shoes don't only come at Whitsun", *Sun*, 3 June 1968, p.12.
- "Armchair revolution", *New Society*, 20 June 1968, p.916.
- "The face at the window", *Times*, 3 August 1968, pp.15,18.
- "Back – to weave dreams out of my own wallpaper", *Sun*, 21 October 1968, p.4.
- "Lightning over a dark field", *Times*, 7 December 1968, p.20.

– "The art of trespass", *Times*, 29 November 1969, Saturday Review, pp.I,V.

– *Son of Man* (London: Andre Deutsch/Samuel French, 1970; London: Penguin, 1971).

– "Britain's natural break army", *Times*, 25 April 1970, Review, p.V.

– "King Arthur and a vision of childhood country lost", *Times*, 18 January 1971, p.8.

– "Acid drops", *Plays and Players*, 19:2, November 1971, pp.58,60.

– "The sweetest music this side of heaven", *Times*, 2 December 1971, p.15.

– "The artist on the doctor's couch", *Times*, 4 September 1972, p.15.

– "Tsar's army", *New Statesman*, 13 October 1972, pp.525-526.

– "Alf takes over", *New Statesman*, 20 October 1972, pp.572-573.

– *Hide and Seek* (London: Andre Deutsch/Quartet, 1973).

– "Switch on, switch over, switch off", *Times*, 15 March 1973, p.10.

– "Kafka and Brasso", *Times*, 14 May 1973, p.11.

– "Moderates all", *New Statesman*, 22 February 1974, pp.268-269.

– "Something called fear", *New Statesman*, 1 March 1974, p.302.

– "Receding dreams", *New Statesman*, 15 March 1974, p.374.

– "Boy in a landscape", *New Statesman*, 29 March 1974, p.459.

– "Mimic men", *New Statesman*, 13 September 1974, p.357.

– "Well, basically", *New Statesman*, 20 September 1974, pp.390-391.

– "Second time round", *New Statesman*, 27 September 1974, p.438.

– "Helter-skelter on the tightrope", *New Statesman*, 11 October 1974, p.514.

– "Back to nature", *New Statesman*, 18 October 1974, pp.549-550.

– "In a rut", *New Statesman*, 22 November 1974, pp.752-753.

– "Violence out of a box", *New Statesman*, 29 November 1974, p.796.

– "Switch back", *New Statesman*, 7 March 1975, pp.319-320.

– "Seething trouble", *New Statesman*, 18 April 1975, pp.522-523.

– "Telling stories", *New Society*, 15 May 1975, pp.419-420.

– "Marching to Zion", *New Society*, 19 June 1975, pp.723-724.

– "Heavenly news", *New Statesman*, 12 March 1976, pp.338-339.

– "One man's week", *Sunday Times*, 18 April 1976, p.32.

– "A note from Mr Milne", *New Statesman*, 23 April 1976, pp.548-549.

– "Warp factor 1", *New Statesman*, 21 May 1976, p.693.

– "Poisonous gas", *New Statesman*, 28 May 1976, pp.724-725.

– "Facing the future with Piglet and Pooh", *Sunday Times*, 10 October 1976, p.35.

– "Puppets on a string", *Sunday Times*, 5 December 1976, p.40.

– "The celluloid messiahs", *Sunday Times*, 10 April 1977, p.33.

– "Black magic and chalk dust", *Sunday Times*, 17 April 1977, p.38.

– "Glop", *Sunday Times*, 22 April 1977, p.535.

– "A Frosty night", *Sunday Times*, 8 May 1977, p.38.

– "Whistling in the dark", *Sunday Times*, 12 June 1977, p.39.

– "The spectre at the harvest feast", *Sunday Times*, 19 June 1977, p.39.

– "Various kinds of scavenger", *Sunday Times*, 24 July 1977, p.38.

– "Realism and non-naturalism", *The Official Programme of the Edinburgh International Television Festival 1977*, pp. 34-37.

– "The philistine stigma", *Guardian*, 15 October 1977, p.7. (Section from Potter's talk "Tell it not in Gath".)

– "Where comedy is king", *Sunday Times*, 16 October 1977, p.37.

– "Trampling the mud from wall to wall", *Sunday Times*, 6 November 1977, p.35.

– "Down those mean streets once more", *Sunday Times*, 27 November 1977, p.36.

– "I accuse the inquisitors", *Sunday Times*, 4 December 1977, p.37.

– introduction to *Brimstone & Treacle* (London: Eyre Methuen, 1978).

– introduction to Thomas Hardy, *The Mayor of Casterbridge* (London: Pan, [1886] 1978), pp.vii-ix.

– "An innocent abroad", *Sunday Times Magazine*, 8 January 1978, pp.27-34.

– "Let the cry of rage be heard", *Sunday Times*, 29 January 1978, p.35.

– "A play astonishing in its excellence", *Sunday Times*, 5 February 1978, p.35.

– "Why not say it with music?", *Sunday Times*, 9 April 1978, p.37.

– "Bank holiday blues", *Sunday Times*, 3 September 1978, p.38.

– "The lascivious leer of the senses", *Sunday Times*, 19 November 1978, p.37.

– "Goodbye to all that", *Sunday Times*, 26 November 1978, p.38.

– *Brimstone & Treacle* (London: Samuel French, 1979).

– "How I'm shaking up the mush machine", *Daily Mail*, 25 May 1979, p.6.

– "Anteroom to purgatory", *Tatler*, November 1979, pp.58-60.

– "Cheryl Campbell – An appreciation by Dennis Potter", *Over 21*, March 1980, p.29.

– "Why British TV is going to the dogs – and I'm going to California", *Daily Mail*, 30 July 1980, p.6.

– "Potter rights", *Broadcast*, 6 October 1980, p.9.

– *Guardian Lecture* interview with Philip Purser, National Film Theatre, 30 October 1980. (Private transcript.)

– *Pennies from Heaven* novelisation (London: Quartet, 1981).

– "Writers' reading in 1981", *Guardian*, 10 December 1981, p.14.

– "Pruning dead wood in *Gorky Park*", *Sunday Times Magazine*, 18 December 1983, pp.40-42,44,47.

– *Sufficient Carbohydrate* (London: Faber and Faber, 1983).

– *Dennis Potter on Television: Waiting for the Boat* (London: Faber and Faber, 1984).

– *The Singing Detective* (London: Faber and Faber, 1986).

– *Ticket to Ride* (London: Faber and Faber, 1986).

– introduction to F. Scott Fitzgerald, *Tender is the Night* (London: The Folio Society, 1987), pp.5-12.

– *Blackeyes* (London: Faber and Faber, 1987). (Revised second issue in 1988 was Potter's preferred version.)

– Contribution to "How I shall vote", *Observer*, 7 June 1987, p.19.

– "Writers' attitudes to wealth creation", *Independent*, 17 June 1987, p.17.

– "I don't pretend to be proletarian", *Sunday Times*, 21 June 1987, p.31.

– *Christabel* (London: Faber and Faber, 1988).

– "Ira D. Sankey", *Independent Magazine*, 17 March 1990, p.46.

– "Sincerely theirs: letters as literature", *New York Times*, 27 May 1990, Book Review, pp.1,25-26.

– "Pride", introduction to John Belcher, *'Breathe on 'um Berry!': 100 Years of Achievement by Berry Hill Rugby Football Club* (self-published, 1992), pp.5-6.

– "Downloading", *New York Festival Programme*, January 1992, pp.55-58.

– *Lipstick on Your Collar* (London: Faber and Faber, 1993).

– "Occupying Powers", The James MacTaggart Memorial Lecture, Edinburgh International Television Festival, reproduced in *Seeing the Blossom* (London: Faber and Faber, 1994), pp. 33-56.

– *Seeing the Blossom: Two Interviews and a Lecture* First edition (London: Faber and Faber, 1994).

– "Smoke screen", *Guardian*, 28 March 1994, p.19.

– *Blue Remembered Hills and other plays* (London: Faber and Faber, 1996). (Reprint of *Waiting for the Boat*.)

– introduction to *Karaoke and Cold Lazarus* (London: Faber and Faber, 1996).

– *Karaoke and Cold Lazarus* (London: Faber and Faber, 1996).

– *Pennies from Heaven* script (London: Faber and Faber, 1996).

– "Writing for dear life", *Observer*, 31 March 1996, Review, pp.1-2.

Potter, Dennis and Natasha Edelman (eds.), *Oxford Clarion*, Michaelmas term, 1957.

Potter, Ian, *The Rise and Rise of the Independents: A Television History* (London: Guerrilla, 2008).

Potter, Sarah, *Brimstone & Treacle* (London: Quartet, 1982).

Priestley, J.B. and Jacquetta Hawkes, *Journey Down a Rainbow* (London: Heinemann-Cresset, 1955).

Price, W.G. and Cyril Baglin, "Readers' Views: What of the next 20 years in the Forest", *Dean Forest Guardian*, 18 December 1959, p.6.

Purser, Philip, "Studies from life", *Sunday Telegraph*, 12 December 1965, p.13.

– "Only the choir is missing", *Sunday Telegraph*, 6 November 1966, p.13.

– "Man's eye view", *Sunday Telegraph*, 19 May 1968, p.15.

– "Dennis Potter", in George W. Brandt (ed.), *British Television Drama* (Cambridge: Cambridge University Press, 1981), pp.168-193.

– *Done Viewing* (London: Quartet, 1992).

– "Dennis's other hat", in Vernon W. Gras and John R. Cook (eds.), *The Passion of Dennis Potter: International Collected Essays* (Basingstoke: Macmillan, 2000), pp.179-193.

Pym, John, *Film on Four: A Survey 1982/1991* (London: BFI Publishing, 1992).

Reynolds, Stanley, "Potter loves the idea of Mrs Whitehouse. He sees her as standing up for all those people with ducks on their wall who have been laughed at", *Guardian*, 16 February 1973, p.10.

Richards, Huw, *The Bloody Circus: The Daily Herald and the Left* (London: Pluto Press, 1997).

Rogers, Steve, "Fun with David and Andy", *Bailey On Andy Warhol* booklet accompanying *Warhol* DVD release (London: Network, 2010).

Rudd, Lewis (ed.), *Isis*, 26 February 1958.

Sankey, Ira D., *Sacred Songs and Solos: Revised and Enlarged, with Standard Hymns* (London & Edinburgh: Marshall, Morgan & Scott, Ltd., 1948).

Shakespeare, William, *The Life and Death of King Richard the Second*, in *William Shakespeare Complete Works*, eds. Jonathan Bate and Eric Rasmussen (Basingstoke: Macmillan, 2007), pp.833-891.

Shields, Anthony and Robert Gaddes, "Night life", *What's On In London*, 25 October 1963, pp.58-60.

Shulman, Milton, *The Least Worst Television in the World* (London: Barrie and Jenkins, 1972).

Silvey, Robert, *Who's Listening? The Story of BBC Audience Research* (London: George Allen & Unwin, 1974).

Smith, Ramsay, "All clever stuff or just dirty, Den?", *Daily Mirror*, 29 November 1989, p.9.

Stead, Peter, *Dennis Potter* (Bridgend: Seren, 1993).

Storr, Anthony, *The Dynamics of Creation* (London: Secker and Warburg, 1972).

Thomas, Yvonne, "Frank Finlay, about to lose his anonymity in *Casanova*", *Radio Times*, 13–19 November 1971, pp. 15,17.

Thompson, Ben (ed.), *Ban This Filth! Letters from the Mary Whitehouse Archive* (London: Faber and Faber, 2012).

Thornton, Lesley, "Innocence and experience", *Radio Times*, 27 January–February 1979, pp.7-8.

Trodd, Kenith, "Don't leave town", *Listener*, 8 June 1989, p.20.

Truffaut, François, *François Truffaut: Correspondence 1945–1984* ed. by Gilles Jacob and Claude de Givray, translated by Gilbert Adair (New York: The Noonday Press/ Farrar, Straus and Giroux, 1989).

Tynan, Kathleen (ed.), *Kenneth Tynan: Letters* (London: Weidenfeld and Nicolson, 1994).

Wagar, W. Warren (ed.), *H.G. Wells: Journalism and Prophecy 1893–1946: An Anthology* (London: Bodley Head, [1964] 1966).

Wallace, Richard, "Potter launches new TV sex bomb", *Sun*, 23 November 1989, p.7.

Whitehorn, Katharine, "What not enough men know", *Observer*, 25 September 1977, p.23.

Whitehouse, Mary, "Casanova", *Times*, 14 December 1971, p.13.

Wiggin, Maurice, "Choppy across the Channel", *Sunday Times*, 24 November 1968, p.59.

– "Needling time", *Sunday Times*, 20 June 1971, p.27.

– "Private faces, public places", *Sunday Times*, 4 November 1973, p.40.

Williams, Raymond, *Culture and Society 1780–1950* (London: Chatto and Windus, 1958).

– *Border Country* (London: Chatto and Windus, 1960).

– "Against adjustment", *Listener*, 4 June 1970, p.770.

– *Television: Technology and Cultural Form* (London: Fontana, 1974).

Wilson, Angus, *Late Call* (London: Secker and Warburg, 1964).

Wolcott, James, "Untrue grit", *New Yorker*, 4 October 1993, pp.217-219.

Wood, Ellen, *East Lynne*, 3 vols. (London: Richard Bentley, 1861).

Worsley, T.C., "Potter and Bergmann", *Financial Times*, 11 November 1970, p.3.

Wu, Duncan, *Six Contemporary Dramatists* Second edition (London: Macmillan Press, 1996).

Broadcast sources listed in chronological order

Does Class Matter? Episode Two, "Class in Private Life", BBC-TV, 25 August 1958. DP interviewed by Christopher Mayhew.

Panorama, n.180, BBC-TV, 30 November 1959. Feature "Closing of Pits in the Forest of Dean".

Tonight, BBC-TV, 8 February 1960. DP interviewed by Derek Hart.

The Wind of Change Episode Three, "Between Two Worlds", BBC-TV, 12 April 1960. DP production trainee.

Between Two Rivers, BBC-TV, 3 June 1960. DP writer and presenter.

Bookstand Series One, 16 October 1960–25 June 1961. DP script associate and occasional contributor.

Ten O'Clock, BBC Home Service, 6 October 1961. DP talk "The Establishment". (Script, BBC Written Archives Centre.)

That Was the Week That Was Series One Episode 15, BBC-TV, 2 March 1963. DP and David Nathan wrote "Entitled to Know: Nationalization Pamphlet". (Rehearsal script, privately held.)

Not So Much a Programme More a Way of Life, n.23, BBC1, 9 January 1965. DP and David Nathan wrote "School Sketch". (Script, BBC Written Archives Centre.)

Woman's Hour, BBC Light Programme, 23 June 1965. DP interviewed for "Ideas in the Air" feature.

Talkback, BBC1, 4 February 1968. DP on panel.

One Pair of Eyes: Border Country, BBC2, 1 August 1970. DP interviewed by Raymond Williams.

Scan, BBC Radio 4, 25 November 1971. DP interviewed by Michael Billington.

Any Questions?, BBC Radio 4, 26 November 1971. DP on panel.

The Hart Interview, BBC1 (West region), 14 August 1973. DP interviewed by Derek Hart.

Critics' Forum, BBC Radio 4, 10 April 1976. Discussed DP's *Double Dare*. (Transcript, BBC Written Archives Centre.)

With Great Pleasure, BBC Radio 4, 5 September 1976. DP writer and presenter.

"And with no language but a cry", BBC Radio 3, 27 December 1976. DP writer and presenter.

The Anno Domini Interview, BBC1, 14 February 1977. DP interviewed by Colin Morris.

Festival 77: Late Night Line-Up, BBC2, 1 August 1977. DP and Christopher Morahan interviewed by Michael Dean.

Any Questions?, BBC Radio 4, 21 October 1977. DP on panel.

Tonight, BBC1, 7 November 1977. DP interviewed by Ludovic Kennedy.

Desert Island Discs, BBC Radio 4, 17 December 1977. DP interviewed by Roy Plomley.

"A Christmas Forest", BBC Radio 4, 26 December 1977. DP writer and presenter.

The South Bank Show, "Dennis Potter: Man of Television", LWT/ITV, 11 February 1978. DP interviewed by Melvyn Bragg.

Serendipity, BBC Radio 4, 2 January 1978. DP writer and presenter.

All in the Waiting: "The other side of the dark", BBC Radio 4, 23 February 1978. DP writer and presenter. (Script, BBC Written Archives Centre.)

Start the Week with Richard Baker, BBC Radio 4, 13 March 1978. DP interviewed by Joan Bakewell.

Theatre Call, BBC World Service, 9 February 1979. DP interviewed by Michael Billington.

The South Bank Show, "Brimstone & Treacle" feature, LWT/ITV, 11 February 1979. Stage footage and DP interviewed by Melvyn Bragg.

Omnibus, BBC1, 16 May 1982. DP interviewed by Barry Norman.

A Plus, Thames/ITV, 2 February 1984. Stage footage and DP interviewed by Mavis Nicholson.

The John Dunn Show, BBC Radio 3, 2 February 1984. DP interviewed by John Dunn.

Wogan, BBC1, 25 September 1987. DP interviewed by Terry Wogan.

Third Ear, BBC Radio 3, 20 November 1989. DP interviewed by Chris Cook.

The Late Show, BBC2, 29 November 1989. Discussion of *Blackeyes*.

Start the Week, BBC Radio 4, 4 December 1989. DP guest.

The John Dunn Show, BBC Radio 2, 13 December 1989. DP interviewed by John Dunn.

Opinions: "Britain 1993: What's Wrong? What's Right? What's Next?", Channel 4, 31 March 1993. DP writer and presenter.

Without Walls Special: An Interview with Dennis Potter, Channel 4/LWT, 5 April 1994. DP interviewed by Melvyn Bragg.

Sky News, 7 June 1994. DP obituary package, broadcast throughout the day.

Unpublished broadcast archive sources

BBC WRITTEN ARCHIVES CENTRE

The following production, contributor and copyright files were consulted in the preparation of introductions and endnotes to this collection:

RCONT1 David Nathan Copyright File 1 1962

RCONT1 Dennis Potter Copyright 1961–1962 File 1

RCONT18 David Nathan Copyright File 2 1963–1967

RCONT18 Dennis Potter Copyright File 2: 1963–69

RCONT20 David Nathan Copyright Registry

RCONT20 Solicitors and Copyright Registry Dennis Potter 1970–4

RCONT21 Dennis Potter 75–79 Copyright

RCONT22/1,180 Copyright Registry Dennis Potter 1980–84

R134/115/1 Gramophone Records Agreements: Miming – *The Singing Detective*

T5/691/1 *Vote, Vote, Vote for Nigel Barton*

T5/698/1 *Where the Buffalo Roam*

T5/834/1 *Alice*

T5/882/1 *A Beast with Two Backs*

T5/994/1 *Cinderella*

T5/1,026/1 *The Confidence Course*

T5/1,307/1 *Emergency – Ward 9*

T5/1,665/1 *Message for Posterity*

T5/1,966/1 *Son of Man*

T5/1,982/1 *Stand Up, Nigel Barton*

T5/2,590/1 *The Mayor of Casterbridge*

T24/125/1 *Son of Man Reviewed*

T32/446/1 *Between Two Rivers*

T32/448/1 *Bookstand* 30 October 1960

T32/449/1 *Bookstand* 5 March 1961

T32/450/1 *Bookstand* 19 March 1961

T32/451/1 *Bookstand* 2 April 1961

T32/452/1 *Bookstand* 16 April 1961

T32/455/1 *Bookstand* 17 October 1961

T32/533/1 *Does Class Matter?* General

T32/533/2 *Does Class Matter?* General

T32/533/3 *Does Class Matter?* General

T32/533/4 *Does Class Matter?* General

T32/562/1 *Ernest Hemingway* 23 July 1961 [part of *Bookstand*]

T32/1,191/5 *Panorama* General 1957–59

T32/1,200/2 *Panorama* 1959–60

T32/1,246/1 *Panorama* November 1959

T32/1,246/2 *Panorama* November 1959 File II

T32/1,247/2 *Panorama* December 1959

T32/1,579/1 *Bookstand* General

T32/1,579/2 *Bookstand* General

T32/1,594/3 *Not So Much a Programme More a Way of Life* 13 November 1964–31 January 1965

T32/1,594/4 *Not So Much a Programme More a Way of Life* General File 1964–1965

T32/1,594/5 *Not So Much a Programme More a Way of Life* Pilots

T32/1,652/1 *That Was the Week That Was* 1–8 December 1962

T32/1,657/1 *That Was the Week That Was* 2–16 March 1963

T32/1,659/1 *That Was the Week That Was* 6–13 April 1963

T32/1,663/1 *That Was the Week That Was* 19–26 October 1963

T32/1,664/1 *That Was the Week That Was* 2–16 November 1963

T32/1,665/1 *That Was the Week That Was* 23–30 November 1963

T32/1,689/1 *Tonight* February 1960

T32/1,696/1 *Tonight* September–October 1960

T32/1,699/1 *Tonight* March–April 1961

T48/476/1 TV Scriptwriter Potter, Dennis 1964–1987

T48/476/2 Drama Writer's File Potter, Dennis

T55/15/1 *Late Night Line-Up* File II 1 August–31 December 1965

T55/17/1 *Late Night Line-Up* File II May–July 1966

T56/220/1 *One Pair of Eyes: Border Country*

T58/473/1 *Talkback* 7 January–4 February 1968

T62/244/1 *Brimstone & Treacle*

T62/297/1 *The Singing Detective*
T62/303/1 *Tender is the Night*
T65/49/1 *Brimstone & Treacle*
T65/55/1 *Pennies from Heaven* General File 1
T65/55/2 *Pennies from Heaven* General File 2
T65/56/1 *Pennies from Heaven* File 1
T65/56/2 *Pennies from Heaven* File 2
WE13/977/1 Bristol contributors Dennis Potter 1966–80

In order to collate recording, filming, transmission and other details, the editors also accessed scripts, script covers, transcripts, Programme-as-Broadcast and Programme-as-Completed forms for many television and radio programmes.

The endnotes refer to the BBC report "*Till Death Us Do Part* as Anti-Prejudice Propaganda", *Annual Review of BBC Research Findings no. 1, 1973/74*, but this is attributed to Bebber's quotation of it and the editors did not access this source at the BBC Written Archives Centre.

THIS WEEK ARCHIVE, UNIVERSITY OF BOURNEMOUTH:

TW-1, *This Week*: "Censorship and the mass media", 3 July 1969. Post-production script.

INDEPENDENT BROADCASTING AUTHORITY ARCHIVE, UNIVERSITY OF BOURNEMOUTH:

RK/3/148, RK/3/149
Reports, correspondence and other paperwork relating to the *Severn Sound* bid.

3995429

Severn Sound, ILR Franchise Application (Gloucester: Gloucestershire Broadcasting Company Limited, 1979).

INDEX

WWW.OBERONBOOKS.COM

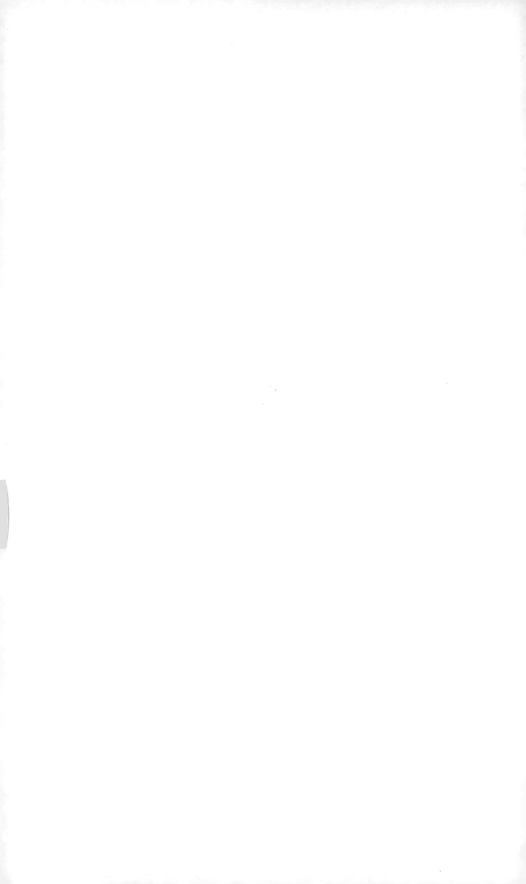

www.ingramcontent.com/pod-product-compliance
Ingram Content Group UK Ltd.
Pitfield, Milton Keynes, MK11 3LW, UK
UKHW031248020325
455689UK00003B/34